The Inner History: Tony Blair's Cabinet Papers, 1997 Volume Two

Devolution of Power to Scotland,
Wales and Northern Ireland

# The Inner History: Tony Blair's Cabinet Papers, 1997 Volume Two

# The Representative Government in Northern Ireland

## Peter Raina

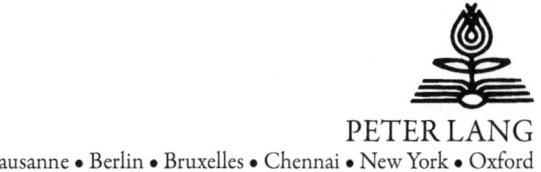

PETER LANG
Lausanne • Berlin • Bruxelles • Chennai • New York • Oxford

Bibliographic information published by the Deutsche Nationalbibliothek. The German National Library lists this publication in the German National Bibliography; detailed bibliographic data is available on the Internet at http://dnb.d-nb.de.

A catalogue record for this book is available at the British Library.
Library of Congress Cataloging-in-Publication Data

Names: Blair, Tony, 1953- author. | Raina, Peter, 1935- editor. | Great
    Britain. Cabinet Office.
Title: Devolution of power to Scotland, Wales and Northern Ireland : the
    inner history : Tony Blair's cabinet papers, 1997 / Peter Raina.
Description: Oxford ; New York : Peter Lang, 2023. | Includes
    bibliographical references and index. | Contents: Volume one. Devolution
    in Scotland and Wales -- Volume two. The representative government in
    Northern Ireland.
Identifiers: LCCN 2023020430 (print) | LCCN 2023020431 (ebook) |
    ISBN 9781803742502 (v. 1 ; hardback) | ISBN 9781803742533 (v. 2 ; hardback) |
    ISBN 9781803742519 (v. 1 ; ebook) | ISBN 9781803742526 (v. 1 ; epub) |
    ISBN 9781803742540 (v. 2 ; ebook) | ISBN 9781803742557 (v. 2 ; epub)
Subjects: LCSH: Blair, Tony, 1953- | Labour Party (Great Britain) |
    Decentralization in government--Great Britain--History--20th century. |
    Great Britain--Politics and government--1997-
Classification: LCC JN329.D43 D48 2023 (print) | LCC JN329.D43 (ebook) |
    DDC 941.085/9--dc23/eng/20230608
LC record available at https://lccn.loc.gov/2023020430
LC ebook record available at https://lccn.loc.gov/2023020431

Cover design by Brian Melville[†] for Peter Lang Group AG

ISBN 978-1-80374-253-3 (print)
ISBN 978-1-80374-254-0 (ePDF)
ISBN 978-1-80374-255-7 (ePub)
DOI 10.3726/b20975

© 2023 Peter Lang Group AG, Lausanne
Published by Peter Lang Ltd, Oxford, United Kingdom
info@peterlang.com - www.peterlang.com

Peter Raina has asserted his right under the Copyright, Designs and Patents Act, 1988, to be identified as Author of this Work.

This publication has been peer reviewed.

# CONTENTS

# LIST OF ILLUSTRATIONS

The permission is for one time / single use in the planned publication.

The images are provided free of charge.

Acknowledgement:

© CAIN (cain.ulster.ac.uk)

© Neil Jarman

# MAIN PARTIES THAT HAD TO BE RECONCILED

| Unionist Parties<br>wanting Ulster to stay with the UK | Nationalist Parties<br>wanting a united Ireland free from the UK |
|---|---|
| *Ulster Unionist Party* (UUP), founded 1905. The "official" ruling party till 1972 and still important. Split over negotiation with Sinn Fein. Leader: David Trimble. | *Social Democratic and Labour Party* (SDLP), founded 1970. The largest Nationalist Party. Leader: John Hume. |
| *Democratic Unionist Party* (DUP), founded 1997. Conservative, with hard line tendencies. Leader, the voluble Presbyterian Minister Ian Paisley. | Sinn Fein, founded 1905 to fight for an independent Ireland. Has close links with the IRA and mistrusted by Unionists. Leader: Gerry Adams. |
| *United Kingdome Unionist Party* (UKUP), founded 1995. Wanting direct rule from Westminster. Leader: Robert McCartney. | |
| *Ulster Democratic Party* (UDP), founded 1981. Associated with the UDA. Leader: Gary McMichael. | |
| *Popular Unionist Party* (PUP), founded 1980. Associated with the UVF. Leader David Ervine. | |

| Loyalist Paramilitary Groups | Nationalist Paramilitary Groups |
|---|---|
| *Ulster Volunteer Force* (UVF), formed 1965. Responsible for over 500 killings, nearly all Catholics. | *Irish Republican Army* (IRA), created 1919, in its various wings. Responsible for about 1,700 killings. |
| *Ulster Defence Association* (UDA), formed 1971 to defend Loyalist areas from the IRA. Responsible for over 400 killings, nearly all Catholics. | |

| Middle-of-the-Road Parties |
|---|
| *Alliance Party*, founded 1970. Liberal and centrist. Leader: Lord John Alderdice. |
| The Labour Grouping, founded 1996. Trying to revive the Northern Irish left. Leader: Malachai Curran. |
| The *Northern Ireland Women's Coalition* (NIWC). Wanting a Civic Forum. Leader: Monica McWilliams (Catholic) with Pearl Sagar (Protestant). |

# KEY NEGOTIATORS

**INTERNATIONAL**

**George Mitchell, US Special Envoy**

Bill Clinton, US President
General de Chastelaine (Canada)
Hari Holkeri (Finland)

*Transnational*

**BELFAST**

Leaders of:
    Unionist Parties
    Moderates
    Nationalist Parties

*East-West*

**WESTMINSTER**

**Tony Blair, Prime Minister**
**Mo Mowlam, Secretary of State for NI**

**Civil Service**, including:
- **John Holmes**
- Ken Lindsay
- Quentin Thomas
- William Ehrman
- Sean O'hUiginn

**Sinn Fein**

**Gerry Adams, Leader**
Siobhan O'Hanlon, Secretary

North-South

**DUBLIN**

**Veronica Sutherland, UK Ambassador**

**John Bruton, Taoiseach**
Dick Spring, Tanaiste
Paddy Teahon General Secretary

# ACRONYMS AND SPECIAL TERMS USED IN THE DOCUMENTS

## Acronyms

| | | |
|---|---|---|
| AIA | - | Anglo-Irish Agreement |
| BIC | - | British-Irish Council |
| BIGC | - | British-Irish Intergovernmental Conference |
| BSE | - | Bovine Spongiform Encepholopathy ("mad cow disease") |
| CAP | - | Common Agricultural Policy (EU) |
| CBM | - | Confidence Building Measure |
| CLMC | - | Combined Loyalist Military Command |
| COREPER | - | Committee of Permanent Representatives (EU) |
| DENI | - | Department of Education Northern Ireland |
| DFA | - | Department of Foreign Affairs |
| DHSS | - | Department of Health & Social Security |
| DSD | - | Downing Street Declaration |
| DUP | - | Democratic Unionist Party |
| EC | - | European Community |
| ECHR | - | European Convention on Human Rights |
| EMU | - | European Monetary Union |
| EPA | - | Emergency Provisions Act (counter-terrorism) |
| FCO | - | Foreign and Commonwealth Office |
| GB | - | Great Britain |
| GNP | - | Gross National Product |
| GOC | - | General Officer Commanding |
| HMG | - | Her Majesty's Government |
| IFI | - | International Financial Institutions |
| IGC | - | Inter-Governmental Conference |
| IPCP | - | Independent Commission for Police Complaints |
| IRA | - | Irish Republican Army |
| JFD | - | Joint Framework Document |
| L&B | - | Labour & Benefits |
| LEG | - | Legal (Committee) |
| MAFF | - | Ministry of Agriculture, Fishing and Food |

| mecu | - | Million European Currency Units |
| MOD | - | Ministry of Defence |
| NI | - | Northern Ireland |
| NICRA | - | Northern Ireland Civil Rights Association |
| NIO | - | Northern Ireland Office |
| NIWC | - | Northern Ireland Women's Coalition |
| NSMC | - | North-South Ministerial Council |
| OECD | - | Organisation for Economic Co-operation and Development (EU) |
| PAFT | - | Policy Appraisal and Fair Treatment |
| PD | - | Political Directorate |
| PES | - | Public Expenditure Survey |
| PIRA | - | Provisional Irish Republican Army ("Provos") |
| PS | - | Parliamentary Secretary |
| PTA | - | Prevention of Terrorism Act |
| PUP | - | Popular Unionist Party |
| PUS | - | Parliamentary Under-Secretary |
| QFL | - | Queen's Speeches and Future Legislation |
| QMV | - | Qualified Majority Voting |
| RPI | - | Retail Price Index |
| RUC | - | Royal Ulster Constabulary |
| SACHR | - | Standing Advisory Committee on Human Rights |
| SDLP | - | Social Democratic and Labour Party |
| SF | - | Sinn Fein |
| TD | - | *Teachta Dala* (Deputy of the Dail, equivalent to MP) |
| UDA | - | Ulster Defence Association |
| UDP | - | Ulster Democratic Party |
| UKUP | - | United Kingdom Unionist Party |
| UUP | - | Ulster Unionist Party |
| UVF | - | Ulster Volunteer Force |

## Special Terms

*Adare Manor* = luxury meeting venue in County Limerick

*Anglo-Irish Agreement* = 1985 agreement between Margaret Thatcher and Garret FitzGerald, for Britain and the Republic of Ireland, giving the latter an advisory role in the government of Northern Ireland.

*Armalite* = typical kind of rifle carried by the paramilitaries.

*Bloody Sunday* = 30 January 1972. British soldiers opened fire on Catholics marching in the Bogside area of Derry. They killed 13 and injured at least 14.

*Cameron Commission* = 1969 enquiry into the causes of the disturbances in Northern Ireland in 1968–69.

*Decommissioning* = proposed handover or destruction of weapons held by paramilitary groups.

*D'Hondt system* = method of dividing the number of seats each party gaines in the Assembly by an averaging process of votes cast.

*Diplock Report* = 1972 report recommending "legal procedures" for dealing with terrorist activity in Northern Ireland. These procedures went contrary to human rights.

*Downing Street Declaration* = 1993 joint agreement between John Major and Albert Reynolds, for Britain and the Republic of Ireland, affirming the right of the Northern Irish people to self-determination and enshrining the "principle of consent".

*Drumcree* = shorthand term for the Marches, or Parades. On the Sunday next to 12 July each year, triumphalist Protestant loyalists marched to and from Drumcree Church in Portadown, their route passing through a Catholic area and causing conflict likened to that of a war zone.

*East-West* = Between government of the British mainland and the two governments on the island of Ireland.

*Erskine May* = the standard book of British Parliamentary practice.

*Garvaghy Road* = Stretch of the annual Marches which was a particular flashpoint and source of loyalist threats against residents who wanted a stop to the marchers coming through.

*Good Friday Agreement* = popular name for the 1998 Belfast Agreement reached on 10 April (Good Friday), incorporating a Multiparty Agreement between the parties in Northern Ireland (except the DUP) and a British-Irish Agreement. It effectively ended the Troubles. The achievement of the work described in this volume.

*Hayes Report* = 1995 review of the handling of complaints against the RUC.

*Irish Republican Army (IRA)* = descendants of the army active in the Irish War of Independence, 1919–21, which refused to recognise an independent Northern Ireland and was prepared to use violence during the time of the Troubles. It was split into several factions,

*Lloyd Report* = 1996 report recommending specific counter-terrorism legislation.

*The Maze Prison* = Notorious prison for convicted paramilitaries, about 9 miles west of Belfast. Buildings also known as "H Blocks".

*Mitchell Report* = 1996 report by US Senator George Mitchell laying down principles on which peace negotiations in Northern Ireland could be based.

*North Report* = a 1997 report making recommendations for the peaceful management of Parades.

*North-South* = Between Northern Ireland and the Irish Republic.

*Oireachtas* = Parliament of the Irish Republic, consisting of the President, the Dail and the Seanad.

*Operation Motorman* = British Army operation, started in 1972, to retake "no-go" areas in Belfast, Derry, etc.

*Orangeman* = Member of the Protestant Orange Order, but generally applied to Ulster's Unionist Protestants. (William of Orange – "King Billy" – defeated the Catholic supporters of James II at the Battle of the Boyne in 1690.)

*Royal Ulster Constabulary* (RUC) = Police force in Northern Ireland, which was overwhelmingly Protestant and often accused of brutality and bias. Because of the threat from the IRA, it was heavily armed and militarised.

*Schengen Accord* (1985, 1990) = agreement to relax border checks between 14 European countries. Ireland and Northern Ireland were not included.

*Stormont* = the Northern Ireland Parliament (from its building)

*Tanaiste* = Deputy Prime Minister of the Irish Republic.

*Taoiseach* = Prime Minister of the Irish Republic.

*Three Strands* = parts of the framework of institutions set up to ease relationships between the parties and governments concerned with the Northern Ireland Troubles: Strand One – between the Northern Ireland parties; Strand Two – between Northern Ireland and the Irish Republic; Strand Three – between the British mainland and Ireland.

*The Troubles* = the period of violence in Northern Ireland, starting in the late 1960s.

*Twelfth of July* = traditional date for the Marches.

*Widgery Tribunal* = body enquiring into Bloody Sunday, whose conclusions were widely regarded as a whitewash.

# ACKNOWLEDGEMENTS

National Archives, Kew:
Reference no: PREM 49/108; PREM 49/109

The Belfast Agreement, April 1998

Northern Ireland Act 1998

The documents are crown copyright and are reproduced here under Open
Government Licence for public sector information.

# FOREWORD

The 'Troubles' in Northern Ireland was itself only one phase in a centuries-long struggle between, at one level, Irish nationalism and British power and, at another intertwined level, between Catholic 'natives' and Protestant 'settlers' in Ulster. As early as 1971, the American scholar Richard Rose defined Northern Ireland as a problem without a solution, and as one attempted settlement or governance structure after another failed to end the violence, most observers reluctantly agreed. Northern Ireland was virtually the definition of an intractable and perhaps insoluble problem.

It is the very knottiness of the Northern Ireland problem that makes Peter Raina's selection and discussion of key government documentation of vital and enduring interest. Over the years of violence, the Ulster question had never been far from British policy makers' minds, but it was rarely at the centre of their attention. The New Labour government, elected in 1997, was an exception. Having promised to broadly follow the tax and spend plans of the outgoing administration for two years, and enjoying a generally buoyant economy, Tony Blair's team had an unusual amount of 'bandwidth' available for Northern Ireland. The cautious but accelerating engagement of Ulster unionism with the 'political process' from the late 1980s, and the IRA's hesitant adoption of a 'peace process', signalled by its ceasefires in 1992 and 1997, meant that a window of opportunity, one that might shut again very quickly, had opened up.

For all its faults and inadequacies, the Belfast/Good Friday Agreement of 1998 stands as a landmark in Irish history and a model of conflict reconciliation internationally. Raina's documentation provides invaluable insight into the high-powered and high-level political calculations that made it happen. It is perhaps the most signal achievement of the era and this expertly curated collection on its genesis and evolution is unquestionably of permanent value.

**Prof Marc Mulholland**
**Professor of Modern History**
**Senior Tutor, St Catherine's College, Oxford**

# INTRODUCTION

The problem of Northern Ireland has aroused the passions of a large number of historians. Thus we are blessed with a very rich and varied literature. It is outside our remit to dig deep into this voluminous source material, yet we must refer to the most important historical aspects of the problem under discussion. For our purpose, we have drawn on a volume that satisfies this need. It has intensity and is perfect. The author examines all the peculiarities of the situation: "the grain he has to work against and, in doing so, a grain he polishes until it shines" (Seamus Heaney). Professor Marc Mulholland has composed a classic study: *The Longest War: Northern Ireland's Troubled History*.[1] We shall refer to the requisite sections of his work.

Ulster was the grain. The northern Irish counties were "until the plantation of Ulster culturally if not politically at one with Gaelic Ireland". In 1542, in an act of imperialism, Henry VIII declared Ireland forever "knit to the imperial crown and realm of England". After the death of Queen Elizabeth I in 1603, Ulster was "brought to heel", and from 1608 onwards English and Scottish settlers were "granted the land on the condition that they acted as garrisons. They were to guard against native resistance and build a society based upon Protestantism." English law prevailed and English imperial rule was consolidated. In 1641, however, Catholic Ireland revolted against the Protestant English Parliament. This rebellion had the sympathy of Ulster Catholics as well. The Catholics were accused of committing atrocities against the Protestants, and in 1649 Cromwell had them slaughtered wholesale near Dublin. The English Civil War made the situation worse. In 1689 the Catholic James II "was chased from the throne

---

1    Marc Mulholland, *The Longest War: Northern Ireland's Troubled History* (Oxford: Oxford University Press, 2002).

by the Dutch William of Orange, with the support of England's gentry. As James retreated to Catholic Ireland to rally his forces, Ulster became a battlefield." James was defeated. In 1703 an Act to Prevent the Further Growth of Popery was passed to prevent the return of Catholics to power. The activity of the Catholic Church was stringently restricted, and many wealthy Catholics lost their political and social rights. Amid the resulting animosity between the Catholics and the Protestants, a struggle for the ownership of land followed.

Sectarian conflict flared up when in 1795 a militant group called the Orange Order began to terrorise Catholic "disloyalists". The Catholic peasantry "responded with their Defenders, whose ideology combined traditional Catholic themes with revolutionary rhetoric". In 1801 the Irish Parliament was dissolved, and a small number of its representatives were transferred to the Westminster Parliament. The Protestants of Ulster welcomed the move.

From 1829 Catholic MPs were permitted to attend Westminster. The Catholic leader Daniel O'Connell staged public demonstrations demanding Catholic emancipation. This led to serious confrontations between Orangemen and the supporters of O'Connell, especially in 1829. People died on both sides. Then came the Great Famine of 1845–50. This terrible scourge was indiscriminate in its victims: Catholics as well as Protestants died of hunger, but around "21 per cent of the one million famine dead came from Ulster".

Sectarian confrontation continued, regardless. In 1849 an Ulster Orangemen's procession was attacked by Catholics and, in this clash, "some thirty Catholics were killed". From 1867, on the "Twelfth of July" (the date of the Protestant King William's victory over the Catholic King James), Orangemen started to stage annual marches.

In 1870, seeking to appease the Irish nationalists on the one hand, but not provoke the Unionists on the other, the Protestant Isaac Butt, a lawyer by profession, founded the Home Government Association, which aimed originally to strengthen the Union between the UK and Ireland. Its plan was to elect a Dublin parliament responsible for domestic affairs, while Irish MPs would continue to sit at Westminster. In 1873 the association changed its name to the Home Rule League.

Under the leadership of Charles Parnell, a Protestant, the Irish Parliamentary Party grew in popularity. In the general election of 1880, it won 61 seats, the elected politicians committing themselves to Home Rule. A new Irish National League, also emphasising Home Rule as its main objective, rallied Catholics behind it. Ulster Protestants recoiled at the prospect of joining forces with Unionists. After the 1885 election Parnell's party was sending 86 members to Westminster – a signal to the Prime Minister, Gladstone, that "Ireland had spoken". Gladstone introduced his first Home Rule Bill in 1886. Belfast saw fierce anti-Home Rule riots. The Bill was defeated in the Westminster Parliament, with 93 Liberal MPs (from Gladstone's own party) voting against it. A second Bill was introduced in 1893. This time, it was defeated in the House of Lords: the Tories were unyielding.

A political confrontation was not far off. The Liberal-Irish nationalists planned to achieve "an unequivocal all-Ireland home rule act". To counter this, the Ulster Unionist Council (UUC) was set up in 1905 under Edward Carson. The UUC claimed to represent all Unionists in the north in a wish to resist Home Rule for Ireland. Carson meant business. On 23 September 1911 he outlined his strategy. In the event of a Home Rule Bill passing, "we must be prepared to take such measures as will enable us to carry on the government of those districts of which we have control". British Tories "committed themselves to support Irish unionism's resistance". In September 1912 the Solemn League and Covenant, signed by over two hundred thousand Unionists declared:

> Being convinced in our consciences that Home Rule would be disastrous to the material well-being of Ulster as well as the whole of Ireland, subversive of our civil and religious freedom, destructive of our citizenship, and perilous to the unity of the Empire [we] do hereby pledge ourselves ... to stand by one another in defending for ourselves and our children our cherished position of equal citizenship in the United Kingdom and in using all means which may be found necessary to defeat the present conspiracy to set up a Home Rule Parliament.

In January 1913 the paramilitary Ulster Volunteer Force came into being. The Catholics responded with their own Irish Nationalist Volunteers. To politicians in Westminster, it became slowly evident that a partition of Ireland might solve the problem. David Lloyd George and Winston Churchill "presented the issue of exclusion of the northern counties from the home rule bill to the cabinet in February 1912. Later that year, the principal advocate of home rule, John Redmond, finally acquiesced to the proposal that the Ulster counties should be permitted to opt out of home rule on an individual basis for a period of six years". The Unions rejected the proposal. Any further negotiations were halted at the outbreak of World War I. However, a dramatic and tragic event rekindled the issue in Easter 1916. Republicans attempted a coup d'etat in Dublin. It failed, but, amid great publicity, sixteen republican leaders were executed. They came to be "added to the succession of Irish martyrs at the hands British oppression".

In the post-war elections the Irish Nationalist party Sinn Fein (Ourselves Alone) won almost all the Irish seats in the Westminster Parliament, but they refused to come to London to take them. Instead, in early 1919, the Sinn Fein MPs convened their own parliament of the Irish Republic, the Dail Eireann. The government in London acted fast in the hope of avoiding civil war in Northern Ireland. It enacted the 1920 Government of Ireland Act enabling the six counties of Ulster to set up their own parliament in Belfast, independent of Dublin but administered directly by the the Westminster Parliament. The split was now complete.

There seemed to be some hope for Ireland to be united again. A clause had been introduced in the Ireland Act which stipulated that a Council of Ireland be established "to harmonize and ultimately unify the island under a parliament for the whole of Ireland". But this was an expression of mere wish. Instead of harmony, violent confrontation between the Irish Nationalists and Protestant Unionists followed. There were casualties on both sides. More Catholics than Protestants died, mostly in Belfast, in the bloody violence of 1922. A "substantial majority of the 232 victims were Catholic, and 11,000 were made jobless and 23,000 homeless. Over 4,500 Catholic-owned shops and businesses were burned, looted or wrecked. Property worth £3 million was destroyed." Lloyd George attempted to sell a deal to the Unionists suggesting autonomy for Northern Ireland under a Dublin parliament. That attempt failed.

Instead, the North Ireland Parliament was founded in Stormont, near Belfast, controlled totally by the Unionists. Throughout the Stormont era Catholics were consistently discriminated against. The course of this is well portrayed by the author of *The Longest War.*

A change seems to have occurred on 5 October 1968 when a civil rights anti-Unionist march took place in Derry, attracting worldwide attention. This march was followed by a larger one on 27 November in London's Grosvenor Square, the crowd estimated to be 20,000 people. Counter demonstrations followed and the marches soon took a violent turn. Armed conflicts broke out between the Provisional IRA and the British Army in Northern Ireland, with fatal consequences. This again is ably described in *The Longest War.* The British government now felt an earnest need to resolve the impending crisis. A solution had to be found. This could only be a political settlement, but how could such a settlement be reached?[2]

The learned Irish historian Paul Bew has made a thorough study of the problem in his valuable *Ireland: The Politics of Enmity, 1789–2006.*[3] He assures us that violence is not the solution. It only creates exaggerated emotion, and it "is only when a moment has been reached when the combatants know for sure that further violence is unlikely to vindicate their project, and may even lead to dreadful defeat and democratisation, that the negotiators can gain the upper hand over the militants".[4] The following pages make it clear how correct this assessment is.

As a nation, the Irish have been proudly conscious of their indigenous culture and have striven to preserve and cultivate it with great dedication. In this desire they have been constantly thwarted by imperial and

---

2   Helpful sources: Charles River Editors: *The Partition of Ireland and the Troubles: The History of Northern Ireland from the Irish Civil War to the Good Friday Agreement* (2018); Dvid Mckittrick, *Making Sense of the Troubles: The Story of the Conflict in Northern Ireland* (2018).

3   Paul Bew, *Ireland: The Politics of Enmity 1789–2006* (Oxford: Oxford University Press, 2007).

4   *Ibid.*, p. 411. See also review by Marc Mulholland: <https.//reviews.hist ory.ac.uk/review/663>. Very significant is the article by John McGarry and Brendan O'Leary: "Consocianal theory, Northern Ireland's conflict, and its Agreement: What critics of consociation can learn *from* Northern Ireland", *Government and Opposition*, vol. 41, no. 2, 2006, pp. 249–77.

conservative elements in the Westminster Houses of Parliament. The far-sighted Victorian Liberal leader William Gladstone was the first Prime Minister to detect this injustice. His various Home Rule Bills (the first in 1886) sought to restore to Ireland a representative government, but the Bills failed to get though the Westminster Parliament; and although there was a separate Irish administration in Dublin, it was headed by a Lord Lieutenant, representing the British Crown, and a Chief Secretary, who was a member of the Cabinet in London. These officials were all English. Ireland was thus a dependency.

Irish Nationalists took up the cause of independence. They were not prepared to put up with subjugation and aspired to form a separate republic, severed from the United Kingdom. Westminster, however, was adamant that this should not happen. To appease the dissidents, various proposals on devolution and federalism were put forward by British politicians up to the time of the First World War; but the Irish refused to accept partial autonomy dressed up as "Home Rule". Finally, the Westminster Parliament gave in and the Irish Free State was established in 1921. The creation of the Irish Free State was fiercely rejected in some quarters. The new nation was a predominantly Catholic republic, and six counties with a Protestant majority declined to accept the deal that brought it about. These were the counties in the northern part of the island, Ulster. The Westminster Parliament was then left with no choice but to divide Ireland. Northern Ireland got its own Parliament at Stormont (though it was firmly under Westminster sovereignty); the Irish Free State could rule itself.

One might have thought that this settlement would resolve the Irish problem. Far form it. The Northern Irish Protestants (or Orangemen), who called themselves Unionists, were strongly pro-English and wanted close union with Britain. In contrast, the minority Catholic community in Ulster, who called themselves Nationalists, were keen to join the Republic of Ireland, and were the cause of much suspicion among the Unionists. Growing mistrust between the two communities led to mutual hatred and damaging clashes. Vernon Bogdanor ably defines the nature of this conflict.[5]

5    For historical details, see chapters on "Irish Home Rule" and "Northern Ireland" in Vernon Bogdanor, *Devolution in the United Kingdom* (Oxford University Press: Oxford, 2001); pp. 19–109.

Ulster Unionism, he writes, was "not an assertion of a separate Ulster nationhood, but a reaction against the claim made by Irish Nationalists that Irish nationhood was separatist in nature".[6] The effect of this thinking among the Unionists was that they treated the Nationalists as traitors. And it was the Unionists who held the power. The Northern Ireland Parliament was not a parliament in the true sense of the word, but a one-party state entirely ruled by the Unionists, who were in permanent majority. The Catholic minority had very little say in policies affecting their homeland.

Moreover, the situation could not be altered because of the supervision exercised by Westminster. Section 75 of the Government of Ireland Act categorically specified that "Notwithstanding the establishment of the Parliament of Northern Ireland … the supreme authority of the Parliament of the United Kingdom shall remain unaffected and undiminished over all persons, matters and things in Northern Ireland and every part thereof." Hence the workings of the Parliament in Northern Ireland came totally under the control of politicians far away. These politicians totally ignored the undemocratic and biased character of the Northern Ireland administration. Ulster had turned into a virtual police state. Political expression by the nationalist people, writes the Sinn Fein leader Gerry Adams, "who had never accepted the partition of Ireland and the authority of the British imperial presence, was ruthlessly suppressed as it had been since the foundation of the northern statelet. The Special Powers Act, in force since its early days, provided the Minister for Home Affairs with extraordinary powers of arrest without warrant, the death penalty for some firearms offences, imprisonment and flogging; he could intern men without charge or trial, ban organisations, prohibit inquests, and evacuate and destroy houses … Lord Craigavon, First Minister of the statelet, had made it quite clear that *I am an Orangeman first and a politician and a member of the parliament afterwards ….. All I boast is that we have a Protestant parliament and a Protestant state".*[7]

Unrest spread among the Catholic minority. It revolted, used force. Northern Ireland faced total chaos. In panic, the Belfast government

6   *Ibid.*, p. 57.
7   Gerry Adams, *Before the Dawn. An Autobiography* (Brandon: London, 2001), p. 54.

appointed the Cameron Commission in 1969 to look into the causes of this disturbance. The Commission came up with the following conclusions:[8]

1. a rising sense of continuing injustice and grievance among large sections of the Catholic population;
2. unfair methods of allocation of houses;
3. misuse in certain cases of discretionary powers of allocation of houses in order to perpetuate Unionist control of the local authority;
4. well documented complaints of discrimination in the making of local government appointments, at all levels but especially in senior posts, to the prejudice of non-Unionists and especially Catholic members of the community;
5. well documented complaints in some cases of deliberate manipulation of local government electoral boundaries and in others a refusal to apply for their necessary extension, in order to achieve and maintain Unionist control of local authorities and to deny to Catholics influence in local government proportionate to their numbers.

Harold Wilson's Labour government in London immediately reacted to the report. It warned that if Stormont did not solve the problems in the province it supposedly governed, the English authorities might act over its head. It justified this threat with a reminder that the Belfast government had "reaffirmed their intention to take into account to the fullest at all times the views of Her Majesty's Government in the United Kingdom, especially in relation to matters affecting the status of citizens of that part of the United Kingdom and their equal rights and protection under the law".

Stormont ignored the call. Northern Ireland now collapsed into civil war: an armed conflict between the Irish Republican Army (IRA) that had fought for freedom after World War One and the Ulster armed units

8    Quoted in Vernon Bogdanor, *Devolution in the United Kingdom* (Oxford University Press: Oxford, 1999), p. 76.

protecting the status quo, the "loyalists". The Heath government prorogued the Northern Ireland Parliament in 1972, so Westminster now ruled the province directly. A Northern Ireland Office was created under the chairmanship of a Secretary of State for Northern Ireland, who was entitled to sit in the British Cabinet. It was expected that the rule of law would return.

This was an illusion, however. As the strife that became known as "The Troubles" intensified, more than 20,000 British troops were sent in to Belfast with Centurion tanks, helicopters and armoured cars. The British Army was to launch what was called Operation Motorman against the IRA. This meant mounting "a major offensive against nationalist areas, taking over parks, schools, community halls and other buildings, and constructing forts from which they could enforce their military occupation".[9] British troops followed the recommendations of the Diplock Report, approved by the Westminster Parliament in December 1972. The report "recommended the combination of extra-judicial measures ('executive detention') and jury-less courts. Crucially, it also recommended that all confessions be admissible in the jury-less courts, and replaced the standard of 'fairness' with the issue of whether 'torture, inhuman or degrading treatment' had been used. Bail was not to be permitted, and the onus of proof was to be shifted to the defendant in cases allegedly involving weapons. By thus suspending many of the cornerstones of the British judicial process, the state would now be able to secure convictions with some ease".[10]

British respect for the rule of law was further disgraced by the internment camps. At Long Kesh there were "over twenty cages, each with four or five huts, housing either internees or sentenced prisoners. The cages for sentenced prisoners were located at the top and bottom parts of the camp, separate from those of internees. All the cages were surrounded by wire and watchtowers. Two-and-a-half or three-and-a-half huts were for living and sleeping in; thirty men to a hut ...".[11] In the camps, bigotry "expressed itself in small ways". At Christmas, writes Adams, "we received hundreds of Christmas cards, and the screws scrawled 'Fuck the Pope' and the like on

9   Gerry Adams, *op. cit.*, p. 211.
10  *Ibid.*, p. 214.
11  *Ibid.*, p. 223.

the religious ones, especially those with pictures of the Virgin Mary."[12] The prisoners were beaten fiercely. Relating his own experience, Gerry Adams tells how: "All of the people who beat me were in plain clothes, and at one point there were three of them in the cell. After the first initial flurry and my first fright at the frenzy of the assault, the beatings settled into a dogged routine, in which I was forced into the search position, palms against the wall, body at an acute angle, legs widespread. They tried to make me put only my fingertips against the wall but I resisted that, and those doing the beating stood behind and concentrated mostly on the kidney area and the sides of my stomach while also landing various kicks between my legs. They beat me, I fell to the floor. They flung buckets of water over me to revive me, pulled me back up against the wall, beat me until I fell again. When I passed out, my clothes were pulled from me. At one point I made a half-hearted attempt to defend myself, and this provoked my torturers to a frenzy. All the time they asked me for information on my associates, my family and my neighbours. After, in the beginning, replying with a polite 'I'm sorry, I can't answer your questions', I gave up saying anything at all."[13]

Encountering this last passage, readers might think they were hearing about an episode somewhere in a KGB prison in some remote part of the former Soviet Union. Not so: this was in a *British* prison. By 1977 the British government had opened interrogation centres at Castlereagh and Gough barracks, and through "the systematic application of torture techniques, these supplied the statements required to secure convictions in the courts. Despite the availability of well-documented evidence of torture and ill-treatment, people continued to be brutalised in large numbers and locked away".[14]

The Irish prisoners refused to be treated as criminals. They were, they said, political prisoners and demanded to be treated as such. Their demands included:[15]

12   *Ibid.*, p. 234
13   *Ibid.*, pp. 218–19.
14   *Ibid.*, pp. 260–61.
15   *Ibid.*, p. 291.

1. the right to wear their own clothing at all times;
2. exemption from all forms of penal labour;
3. free association with each other at all hours;
4. the right to organise their own recreational and educational programmes;
5. full restoration of remission.

A group of veteran prisoners, including the activist Bobby Sands, decided to go on hunger strike, even to starve to death, if these demands were not fulfilled. They "were pitching themselves, with the only weapons at their command – their lives – against the imperial power".[16] Sands began his hunger strike on 1 March 1981, and had carried on with it for sixty-six days when he died on 5 May. Others followed: Francis Hughes died after fifty-nine days of hunger strike; Patsy O'Hara and Ray McCreesh died after sixty-one days. When the news broke of Sands' death, the whole civilised world protested and expressed horror; some countries declared a day of mourning.

These hunger strikes and the subsequent deaths occurred when Margaret Thatcher was Prime Minister of Britain. All along, she was inflexible towards the demands of the protestors; the evident evil of British conduct in Northern Ireland hardly bothered her. This attitude only inflamed the anger of the IRA, which declared war on the British Army. The IRA men proceeded to put all that was British to death in cold blood. Madness, writes Samuel Johnson, "frequently discovers itself merely by unnecessary deviation from the usual modes of the world." In Northern Ireland brutal deviation did not seem to be unusual.

And yet sanity began to return to the Irish world when Gerry Adams was elected President of Sinn Fein in 1983. Sinn Fein (meaning "We Ourselves") was the party that had been founded in 1905 to fight for Irish independence and a wing of it had been associated with the current IRA violence. Adams sought to "open up discussion and public debate about the achievement of peace through dialogue and a democratic settlement".[17] His call was answered by a gang of loyalists, who, using British military

16    *Ibid.*, p. 292.
17    Gerry Adams, *op. cit*, p. 319.

intelligence to locate him, tried to gun him down.[18] Gerry Adams preserved his character – virtuous and moral. As Dr Johnson remarked, the morality of an action "depends on the motive from which we act" and Adams' motives were pure. In 1986 Gerry Adams again argued "that the military stalemate between the British and republican forces could only be resolved by a political settlement; there was no military solution".[19]

In 1990 the British government agreed to start up a dialogue with Sinn Fein. It lasted until 1993. In May of that year, the IRA agreed to a two-week cease-fire. This resulted in a significant pact: the Downing Street Declaration, made between the British and Irish governments on 15 December. This was a joint statement issued in 10 Downing Street by the Prime Minister of the UK, John Major, and the Prime Minister of the Republic of Ireland, Albert Reynolds. It affirmed the right of the people of Ireland to self-determination and pledged that Northern Ireland would be transferred to the Republic of Ireland from the UK only if a majority of its people so desired. It also underlined the principle of consent: the people of Ireland had the exclusive right to solve issues between North and South by mutual agreement.

At the end of August 1994 the IRA announced a complete cessation of military operations, suggesting that "its intention was to enhance the search for a negotiated peace settlement".[20] Both the British government and the Belfast Unionists "responded in a very negative way to the IRA cessation". John Major, the British Prime Minister, for example, "placed obstacle after obstacle along the path towards peace".[21] The momentum of the peace process was slowed down considerably. Adding to this the British government took several provocative actions. When British paratrooper Lee Clegg was released from prison in the summer of 1995, having served only two years for the murder of a 17–year-old Belfast girl, he was promoted in the Army. In Belfast the Army renewed its repressive measures, and the British appeared to side with the unpopular Royal Ulster Constabulary (RUC), which was armed and overwhelmingly Protestant.

18   *Ibid.*, p. 319.
19   Gerry Adams, *op. cit.*, p. 319.
20   Gerry Adams, *op. cit.*, p. 322.
21   *Ibid.*, p. 323.

A "number of provocative Orange parades were forced through Catholic areas by the RUC. Conditions for Irish political prisoners in Britain seriously deteriorated."[22]

Gerry Adams is right when he asserts that John Major was not keen on reaching an agreement with Sinn Fein. Thus "an unprecedented opportunity for peace foundered on the refusal of the British government and the unionist leaders to enter into honest dialogue and substantive negotiations".[23] Historical events are the product of human actions. The motives of Tony Blair, John Major's Labour successor, were, we believe, decidedly virtuous when he declared that he wanted peace through negotiation in Northern Ireland.[24] The 1997 election manifesto of the Labour Party showed a great willingness to engage:[25]

> Labour's approach to the peace process has been bipartisan. We have supported the recent agreements between the two governments – the Anglo-Irish Agreement, the Downing Street Declaration and the Framework Document. The government has tabled proposals which include a new devolved legislative body, as well cross-border co-operation and continued dialogue between the two governments.
>
> There will be as great a priority attached to seeing that process through with Labour as under the Conservatives, in co-operation with the Irish government and the Northern Ireland parties. We will expect the same bipartisan approach from a Conservative opposition.
>
> We will take effective measures to combat the terrorist threat.
>
> There is now general acceptance that the future of Northern Ireland must be determined by the consent of the people as set out in the Downing Street Declaration. Labour recognises that the option of a united Ireland does not command the consent of the Unionist tradition, nor does the existing state of Northern Ireland command the consent of the Nationalist tradition. We are therefore committed to reconciliation between the two traditions and to a new political settlement which can command the support of both. Labour will help build trust and confidence among the

---

22   Gerry Adams, *op. cit., p. 323.*
23   *Ibid., p. 325.*
24   See "The Northern Ireland peace process" in Tony Blair, *New Britain: My Vision of a Young Country* (London: Fourth Estate Ltd., 1996), pp. 276–7.
25   See section "Northern Ireland" in *1997 Labour Party Manifesto: "New Labour because Britain deserves better"*. Archives of Labour Party Manifestos.

Nationalist and Unionist traditions in Northern Ireland by acting to guarantee human
rights, strengthen confidence in policing, combat discrimination at work and reduce
tensions over parades. Labour will foster economic progress and competitiveness in
Northern Ireland, so as to reduce unemployment.

After a landslide victory in the elections, Tony Blair took office as Prime
Minister on 1 May 1997. On 2 May Gerry Adams sent him a letter congratulating him on his "outstanding electoral success". Adams assured
Blair that Sinn Fein was "totally committed to democratic and peaceful
methods of struggle and to a negotiated settlement to the conflict in our
country", and requested that the Prime Minister "authorise officials" of
his government to "meet with Sinn Fein as soon as possible so that we can
explore with urgency how this can be accomplished".

Blair shared this feeling of urgency. Already on 2 May he had on his
desk a lengthy report: *Governing Northern Ireland: An Integrated Approach*.
The report, prepared by the Political Directorate of the Northern Ireland
Office, defined Labour's strategy. The British government was to continue the peace process in cooperation with the Irish government and
the Northern Ireland political parties. In addition it aimed: to enhance
the principle that the future of Northern Ireland must be determined by the
consent of the people of Northern Ireland; to work for reconciliation between the two traditions and a political settlement which commanded the
support of both; and to build trust and confidence among both Nationalists
and Unionists. The government was resolved to explore the scope for an
unequivocal restoration of the IRA's ceasefire, which could enable the admission of Sinn Fein to the negotiations. All in all, the fundamental task
of the government was to reach "the goal of a peaceful, stable, prosperous
community in which each section of the community feels it has a fair share
and is offered equal respect for its rights, traditions and aspirations".

Tony Blair employed a group of excellent and efficient ministers and
civil servants, both men and women, to achieve this aim. A list of the
main ones is given at the beginning of this volume, but three deserve to
be singled out:

– *John Holmes*, the Prime Minister's Private Secretary, supplied him
   with "short snapshots and a few thoughts" on how to talk with

the leaders of the various parties. These proved extremely useful in sobering down conflicting, and at times volatile, talks.

- *Mo Mowlam* was the Secretary of State for Northern Ireland. She was perhaps the most dominant force in getting Sinn Fein to join the talks and in convincing the Unionists how important this was for reaching a peaceful agreement. In a private message to the Prime Minister on 6 May 1997, five days after the election victory, she proposed how she intended to "tackle the key peace/talks issue". She was going to write to Gerry Adams to "get our fundamental principles on the record with him". Her message was: "the need for a settlement on which both Unionists and Nationalists agree, ultimately endorsed in a referendum". She insisted on "our determination to pursue the current talks process", promising that "a way is open for Sinn Fein to join that process, on proper terms"; "but we shall carry it forward with or without Sinn Fein."

- *Veronica Sutherland* was Her Majesty's Ambassador in Dublin. She thought it highly important that the British government should work closely with the Irish government on all aspects of the problems in Northern Ireland. Close bilateral cooperation, she informed those at Westminster, was "critical to the achievement of a peaceful settlement in Northern Ireland". Mistrust and misapprehension were "still the defining characteristics on the Irish side, while to them the British approach frequently smacks of arrogance and insensitivity".

The documents we attach below tell us a great deal that we did not know before. They are the key to the peace agreement in Northern Ireland. Included are: minutes of the meetings with party leaders; Labour strategy on how to conduct negotiations; talks on how to resolve the decommissioning impasse; contacts with Sinn Fein; meetings of the liaison groups; cooperation between the British and Irish governments; meetings with George Mitchell, the US Special Envoy to Northern Ireland, sent by Bill Clinton; and various press statements. The last document is a statement by President Bill Clinton made on 30 May 1997.

Referring to all the different, opinions, stances, parties and actions, the documents employ many acronyms and specialist terms. A guide to these is supplied at the start of this volume.

# GOVERNMENT DISCUSSIONS ON DEVOLUTION IN NORTHERN IRELAND

## Government papers and correspondence

Document 1   Governing Northern Ireland: An Integrated
            Approach

Political Directorate
Northern Ireland Office
May 1997

### *1. Labour's strategy*

1.1 Labour's manifesto repeats its bipartisan approach to the peace and talks process, including its support for the Anglo-Irish Agreement, and Downing Street Declaration and the Framework Documents.

1.2 The manifesto commits the new Government to:

- *continuing the peace and talks process*, in co-operation with the Irish Government and the Northern Ireland parties;
- taking effective measures to combat the terrorist threat;
- accepting that the future of Northern Ireland must be determined by the consent of the people as set out in the Downing Street Declaration;
- working for the reconciliation between the two traditions and a new political settlement which can command the support of both;

- helping to build trust and confidence among both nationalist and unionist traditions by:
  - acting to guarantee human rights;
  - strengthening confidence in policing;
  - combating discrimination at work;
  - fostering economic progress and competitiveness, so as to reduce unemployment.

1.3 An early discussion with Ministers of the priorities within this programme would be helpful. But action in the early months seems likely to include:

- an early and balanced confidence-building package, such as:
- reassurance on fundamental principles (consent, needed for unionist and nationalist agreement, three-stranded analysis, talks open to Sin Fein but continue without them if necessary);
- rights and equity measures, such as incorporation of the ECHR, a positive response to the Employment Equality Review, emphasis on PAFT;
- demonstration of a robust response to the terrorist threat;
- renewal of the Emergency Provisions Act, but with amendments – such as repeal of internment powers – to improve confidence;
- implementation of the North Report with first session legislation (but perhaps full implementation on the ground delayed beyond this summer giving a possible opportunity to see if and how unionist concerns can be met?);
- policing reform, with possible first session legislation;
- renewal of the Forum;
- continuation of Westminster Grand Committee reforms;
- consideration of greater transparency in the Anglo-Irish Agreement;
- pressure on the Irish Government for a more forward position on amendment of Articles 2 and 3 of the Irish Constitution.
- prepare for the start of talks on 3 June, almost certainly without Sinn Fein: early preparatory discussions with the Northern Ireland parties and the Irish Government to seek to resolve the issue of

decommissioning to allow the three strands to be launched before the end of the summer;

- explore the scope for peace: early moves to see if an unequivocal restoration of the IRA's ceasefire can be established leading to Sinn Fein's admission to negotiations (but, realistically, not by 3 June);
- help to manage the marching session, in conjunction with the RUC, the Parades Commission and others, to reduce tension, uphold the rule of law and minimise the threat to public order;
- communicate a coherent and balanced approach to all areas of Government.

1.4 The rest of this paper offers an overview of how to implement the Government's broad strategy as part of an integrated approach to all areas of policy. It examines:

- the nature of Northern Ireland's divided community (pages 5–8);[1]
- the need for an integrated approach (pages 9–13): its overall goal; the key elements; how to deliver such an approach.
- security policy (pages 14–17);
- political development (pages 18–34): the overall project of a new political settlement; the current talks process; the peace process; alternative strategies, in case of failure.
- economic and social policy (pages 35–37);
- presentation and communication of an integrated approach (pages 38–39).

1.5 The second volume offers a series of assessment and analytical papers which examine the individual issues in greater depth.

---

1  These page numbers and the following refer to page of the original Government paper.

## 2. *Northern Ireland's divided community*

2.1 The fundamental divisions in Northern Ireland's community reach into every area of life. Success in overcoming these divisions and implementing the Government's strategy depends on a concerted and co-ordinated approach by Government in every area of policy which consistently tackles the causes of these divisions.

2.2 The factors which divide the community are well-known: religion; identity; allegations; politics; culture. The divisions are reflected in where people live, where they go to school, where they look for employment, their chances of remaining unemployed, their views of the past and their hopes (and fears) for the future.

2.3 But there is not a single fault line cutting simply through society there are Catholics who want to remain part of the UK; Protestants who are comfortable with a broad Irish identity. The division between those in and out of work affects both communities. Although, as a whole, Catholics still suffer disproportionately from social deprivation, there are significant areas of deprivation and high unemployment in Protestant communities as well.

2.4 The picture is not static. In some areas divisions appear to be deepening:

- 25 years of terrorism has reinforced divisions;
- physically, local communities are more polarised;
- the ending of the IRA ceasefire has deepened existing prejudices among Catholics, that the British Government is out to defeat republicans and politically too dependent on unionists; and among Protestants, that the IRA will never change its spots and that constitutional nationalists put more effort into dialogue with Sinn Fein than reaching out to unionism;
- Drumcree, after several years when marches seemed to be diminishing as a source of conflict, has turned marches once more into the battlefront between the two communities, with the RUC's legitimacy questioned on both sides;
- sectarianism, after years of improving community relations, is on the rise with an ugly rash of church and hall burnings.

2.5 But there are positive signs as well:

- the consensus among all parties bar Sinn Fein in support of the principle of consent, namely that any change in Northern Ireland's constitutional status as part of the UK should only come about with the consent of a majority of its people;
- a well-established security policy and framework. What are now highly sophisticated security forces understand the political context in which they operate and the need to rescue the confidence of the whole community;
- a political talks process that embraces more of the community than ever before albeit not, as had been hoped, Sinn Fein;
- some convergence of expectations as to any political settlement. In terms of a realistic outcome from any current negotiations, unionists no longer expect a return to Stormont and nationalists do not expect a united Ireland, although it remains to be seen whether there can be agreement on a compromise;
- long-term co-operation with the Irish Government which has also seen a convergence of interest and analysis with the British Government, expressed in the Anglo-Irish Agreement, Downing Street Declaration and Joint Framework Document;
- the elimination of many of the original grievances underpinning unrest, including real progress in combating discrimination and in delivering increasingly equality of opportunity in employment against the background of economic growth and falling unemployment which benefit both sides of the community.

2.6 Although Protestants remain the clear majority in Northern Ireland, both sides of the community – Catholic and Protestant – can see themselves as communities under siege, with their fundamental identity under threat from oppressive forces:

- Protestants see a powerful pan-nationalist alliance – the IRA, SDLP, Irish Government and Irish-America – ranged against them, determined to bring about a united Ireland, whether openly or by stealth. They feel betrayed by the British Government – weak on terrorism, neutral on the constitutional issue, consorting with a foreign (Irish) government and making endless concessions to Sinn Fein. Protestants fear – unless they take a firm stand against these threats – they will continue to slide down a slippery slope to a united Ireland and they view all developments, including otherwise sensible reforms, through this distorting prism;

- Catholics see 800 years' of British oppression in Ireland, ending in a forced partition imposed to preserve a unionist state in Northern Ireland. They believe Protestants have never accepted them as equal citizens in Northern Ireland and will not seriously negotiate with them unless pressured to do so. They mistrust the British Government – unreliable, insensitive and in unionists' pockets – and see the security forces as unionist-dominated. Most believe the IRA is wrong and has damaged nationalism, but most also believe the 1994 ceasefire was a genuine opportunity for peace. They blame HMG for squandering it – either deliberately or through ignorance and incompetence.

2.7 Both sides can therefore see themselves as threatened minorities. But the position is not entirely symmetrical. The Catholic community believe the tide of history is with them. As well as their fears and grievances, never far beneath the surface, they share in a positive self-image with the wider Irish people – the modern Ireland: youthful, democratic, pluralist, sovereign, European, drawing on a misty but appealing Celtic past and putting the theocracy of the Catholic church behind them.

2.8 But the Protestant community feel the tide of history is against them. They know what they are against – a united Ireland dominated by Catholicism – but are uncertain what they are for. The rest of the UK no longer believes in Protestantism; it seems to have little sympathy with unionist tradition and belief; even the monarchy seems discredited. They fear that if they make a reasonable compromise, they will simply be asked for more.

## 3. An integrated approach

### (i) The goal

3.1 It is the task of the Government to combat these divisions in Northern Ireland's community which lead to conflict, instability, lack of confidence in the institutions and legitimacy of the state and, ultimately, to political violence. Fundamental to this is the goal of a peaceful, stable, prosperous community in which each section of the community feels it has a fair share and is offered equal respect for its rights, traditions and aspirations.

3.2 This goal requires a broad programme which is:

- concerned: just as Northern Ireland's divisions are seen in virtually all areas of life, the Government's response needs to be similarly wide-ranging;
- co-ordinated: the Government's policy across all departments and agencies, should be directed to a shared and common goal rather than being a collection of ad hoc policies with possibly inconsistent priorities and objectives;
- consistent: events will dictate tactical adjustments but, above all, the Government needs to be seen to pursue a consistent analysis and approach which has anticipated – and so is not knocked off course by – events, setbacks and the responses of others;
- coherent: the Government must communicate this broad programme and persuade all sections of the community that it addresses their needs and interests.

3.3 In short, Northern Ireland's problems require an integrated policy approach in all areas of the Government.

### (ii) The key elements

3.4 These are likely to remain:

- the principle of consent. A majority of people in Northern Ireland want it to remain part of the UK. It would be wrong to change its

constitutional status as part of the UK without the consent of a
majority of its people. A united Ireland will come about if – but
only if – a majority wish it. This is reflected in UK law, the 1985
Anglo-Irish Agreement, the 1993 Downing Street Declaration and
1995 Framework Documents;

- a security policy which is seen to be firm but fair and governed by
  the rule of law. It must secure the confidence of the community
  that political violence will not overturn the democratic process,
  while also actively working to secure the confidence of all in the
  forces of law and order (and the criminal justice system generally)
  by showing that the security response is both proportionate and
  consistent with human rights;
- an approach to political development which offers the prospect
  of stable and workable political institutions in Northern Ireland
  which command democratic legitimacy and allegiance across the
  community and which recognise the wider relationships involved.
  It needs to demonstrate also that there is a political route open to
  all, so denying legitimacy to those on both sides who claim violence is necessary to achieve political objectives.
- a partnership with the Irish Government across a broad agenda reflecting the relationship established in the Anglo-Irish Agreement
  and which seeks to co-opt the Irish Government to HMG's analysis and approach;
- the principles of parity of esteem between both main traditions,
  equality of opportunity and fair treatment, underpinned by a
  commitment to protect and enhance the rights of all;
- social and economic policies which reflect these principles and address the needs of all parts of Northern Ireland's society and consciously demonstrate that Northern Ireland can be governed in
  the interests of all. These policies need to buttress HMG's security
  and political policies by demonstrating that the democratic process can identify and respond to genuine grievances which alienate
  sections of the community;
- an effective communications strategy which gets across to the many
  different audiences the Government's approach and key messages

in a coherent and consistent manner, as well as responding rapidly to events and developments as they happen.

3.5 This is not to suggest that there is a pre-programmed approach to which any Government is inevitably committed. Far from it: it is possible to take radical initiatives in all these areas. But the fundamental lesson is that, whatever the direction in which the Government chooses to go, it should work to bring all areas of policy to bear on its common goal in an integrated approach. The negative lesson is that a perceived failing on even a trivial issue can impact on the Government's policies across the board.

3.6 By contrast to an integrated approach, one which is limited to one area of policy is unlikely to succeed. It is, for example, the view of the security forces and intelligence agencies that security measures alone – however vigorously pursued – do not offer a lasting solution. Nor is a political approach likely to succeed if either side of the community does not have the confidence that any violent or coercive challenge to it would be opposed. Nor can social and economic policies alone – however enlightened and targeted – be expected to overcome divisions which, at their heart, are about issues of politics, allegiance and identity.

3.7 Experience strongly suggests that Ministers must also anticipate setbacks in key areas of policy. Political progress, in particular, can only be achieved in co-operation with others – and such co-operation may not always be there. An integrated approach offers Ministers several strands of policy on which to fall back if thwarted in one area.

(iii) Delivery

3.8 Delivering an integrated approach requires:

- co-operation among NI Ministers, the NIO and NI departments which come under the Secretary of State;
- partnership with the other key agencies in Northern Ireland, particularly the RUC and Army while respecting their respective roles and, in the case of the RUC, their operational independence;

- co-ordination within the Cabinet with colleagues whose interests are engaged, particularly the Defence, Home and Foreign
Secretaries and the Prime Minister (and not forgetting the
Treasury which must pay the bills);
- the communication of a coherent and consistent message in public
by all these players.

3.9 Outside of the Government, success also depends on:

- securing confidence in both sides of the community in the
Government and its broad approach;
- maximising consensus across the community where possible;
- maintaining the support of public opinion in Great Britain which,
although understanding, can be brittle and should not be taken
for granted;
- recognising the international dimension and working to co-opt
the Irish (and, to a lesser extent US) Government to the merits of
HMG's broad approach.

3.10 The rest of this paper looks in more detail at the broad areas of security policy, political development, economic and social policy and the
presentation of the Government's overall approach.

## 4. Security policy

4.1 The aim of security policy is to contribute to the ending of terrorism
by ensuring that violence for political ends does not succeed and demonstrating to the public that it cannot succeed. Achieving this end requires
an effective combination of:

- physical resources – most obviously the RUC and Army (but not
forgetting the Prison Service), with the finance, equipment and
trained people they need);
- the criminal law, adapted where necessary to cope with the challenge of a concerted terrorist campaign, but in keeping with a

proportionate response and respect for human rights and civil liberties so that the legitimacy of the fight against terrorism is preserved;
- intelligence resources (not discussed here); and
- support from the community as a whole and effective security co-operation with the Irish Republic.

4.2 Since the 1970s there has been a well-established framework for developing and implementing security policy, reflecting the different roles, responsibilities and constitutional positions of those involved:

- the Secretary of State sets overall security policy, in consultation with the Chief Constable and GOC;
- in particular, the Government is responsible for ensuring that appropriate legislation and resources are in place;
- the RUC have primary responsibility for preventing and investigating all crime, including terrorism;
- The Chief Constable has operational independence, so that he alone is responsible for operational decisions and the implementation of the criminal law and cannot be given directions by the Government on operational matters;
- the Armed Forces act in support of the police in tasks allocated to them by the RUC;
- in all matters, members of the security forces remain subject to the law.

4.3 In Northern Ireland, community support cannot be taken for granted. In the events around Drumcree last year, the RUC was seen, almost simultaneously:

- by Protestants to be enforcing the deprivation of their traditional liberties at the diktat of a foreign (Irish) government, abetted by a supine British one;
- by Catholics to have caved in to the overturning of the rule of law by force of (Orange) numbers in part at the behest of an insensitive and partisan British Government.

4.4 Securing greater confidence in the security forces and the wider criminal justice system (e.g. the court, prison and life sentence review system from all sections of the community is vital to:

- challenging the legitimacy of political violence, where accepted in some areas of the community, and replacing it with the rule of law;
- obtaining practical information and co-operation from members of the public;
- maintaining the legitimacy of the RUC in their task of upholding public order, particularly over the marching season.

4.5 Any security response seeks to be proportionate to the likely threat. But the threat is unpredictable:

- the current IRA campaign could continue and, with the loyalist ceasefire already on – if not over – a knife-edge, violence could quickly spiral over the summer, bringing pressure to be seen to make a response (although if there was anything more which we thought would be effective, we would be doing it already);
- there could be a renewed IRA ceasefire, which would buttress the loyalist ceasefire. There would be pressure for a corresponding and confidence -building reduction in security measures, although both sets of paramilitaries would be intact and capable of returning to violence;
- the marching season could see public disorder from either side of the community, or both, which in turn could lead to a downward spiral of terrorist violence.

4.6 Ministers will want, as a priority, to ensure that the policy and mechanisms are in place to respond effectively to the range of possibilities – and in a manner which is consistent with the Government's overall approach.

4.7 The most pressing decisions will be on marches. Conflict over marches both reflects underlying political divisions and uncertainty and can itself destabilise further the political process.

4.8 The Government is committed to full implementation of the recommendation in the North Report. A bill has been prepared. But our assessment is that, even if passed through Parliament in time, it cannot be put into practical effect for this summer's marching season. Ministers will need to take early decisions on:

- when to legislate:
- what, if any, further measures should be put in place for this marching season;
- how best to use all the resources available this year to achieve a peaceful outcome;
- what steps can be taken to persuade unionists that the North Report does not represent the threat to the traditions they currently see.

4.9 A separate submission on the North Report will come forward in the first few days.

## 5. *Political Development*

5.1 The security forces and intelligence agencies agree that security measures alone will not solve the fundamental divisions m Northern Ireland which create instability. These divisions concern issues of politics, allegiance and identity: if they are to be overcome, they require a political approach.

5.2 The manifesto confirms Ministers' commitment to:

- the fundamental political project: the establishment of stable and durable political institutions in Northern Ireland which command acceptance across the community within an agreed framework of wider relationships;
- the current talks process, which seeks to achieve this by direct negotiation on a comprehensive agenda among the main parties in Northern Ireland and the British and Irish Governments;

- a peace process (or, perhaps more accurately, the potential for one). Its success is highly desirable – but in principle not essential to the overall political project or success in the current talks process.

5. 3 The Government may also need in its early months to construct:

- alternative strategies to ensure progress continues to be made towards the overall political project if the current talks and/or peace process fail.

(i) The political project

5.4 Ministers will be accused of secretly aiming to achieve many things:

- betraying unionists and making a united Ireland inevitable;
- bringing Sinn Fein in, whatever the cost;
- preserving the unionist veto;
- marginalising nationalists and defeating republicanism.

5.5 But successive Governments have pursued the goal of establishing workable and lasting political institutions in Northern Ireland which command acceptance on both sides of the community, within an agreed framework of wider relationships. This has been on the analysis that:

- direct rule leaves a democratic deficit which deprives local politicians and, through them, the local community of an opportunity to share in responsibility for governing Northern Ireland;
- Northern Ireland's history, particular circumstances and the nature of its divisions require local institutions which reflect its unique character;
- the fundamental issue of the legitimacy of Northern Ireland, itself a source of instability, will not be resolved until there are institutions in place acceptable to both sides of the community;
- Northern Ireland's problems cannot be solved in isolation, since each side of the community seeks to involve the wider British and Irish democracies;

- all three key relationships – within Northern Ireland, between North and South within the island of Ireland and between the two Governments within these islands – must therefore be addressed.

5.6 On this analysis, HMG's fundamental interest is not to promote a particular model for new institutions and relationships but to achieve agreement and consensus across the community – so that both sides feel they have a stake in the future government of Northern Ireland and their differing rights and aspirations are respected. This was explicitly set out in paragraph 4 of the Downing Street Declaration, in which the Government reiterated that it had "no selfish strategic or economic interest in Northern Ireland" and that its "primary interest is to see peace, stability and reconciliation established by agreement".

5.7 At its core, therefore, this political project requires agreement between unionists and nationalists in Northern Ireland. HMG can, and should, encourage, promote and seek to influence the achievement of that agreement: but it cannot dictate it or bring it about by coercion. So the process – allowing the parties and people of Northern Ireland to take ownership of the project and achieve agreement among themselves – despite the frustrations and slow progress, is as important, if not more so, than the outcome.

5.8 Nevertheless, [there are] some points of consent underpinning Northern Ireland's constitutional position. This is a position now endorsed by all parties in Northern Ireland except Sinn Fein and endorsed by both Governments in both the Downing Street Declaration and the Framework Documents (although the Irish Government have yet to reflect this by withdrawing their territorial claim in Articles 2 and 3 of the Irish Constitution). There is no doubt that a majority currently wish Northern Ireland to remain part of the United Kingdom and that such a majority will continue to exist well into the next century and, quite likely, beyond that. Convincing reassurance on this fundamental issue is central to unionist confidence so that they can participate in this overall political project without fearing that it can only end in Northern Ireland leaving the UK or that it is designed to bring that about quickly;

- but a purely internal solution will not be acceptable to nationalists, so any agreement on institutions internal to Northern Ireland
  will need to be set within a stable and agreed framework of wider
  relations covering both North/South relations within the island
  of Ireland (the Irish dimension) and wider relations between the
  British and Irish Governments and the two countries. This is the
  *three stranded framework*;
- it must be underpinned by a *recognition of the identity, traditions,
  rights and aspirations of both sides of the community*. All agree on
  the need for more protection of rights, but disagree on the rights
  to be protected.

5.9 All the parties currently participating in the talks process are signed
up – at least on paper – to these propositions.

5.10 So too is the Irish Government. Indeed, the fundamental project of
achieving agreement across the community in Northern Ireland is one
which the Irish Government shares and which it has worked, in partnership
with HMG, to pursue. The Irish Government (and this is true regardless of
its composition) accepts that a united Ireland, which remains an important
if misty aspiration, can and should only come about with the consent of
a majority of Northern Ireland's people. It also accepts that such consent
will not in practice be forthcoming in the foreseeable future, and in in
that sense nationalism, both North and South, has accepted partition as a
reality for now and the foreseeable future.

5.11 Consequently, the Irish Government shares our analysis that the project
is essentially about securing unionist and nationalist consent for new institutions in Northern Ireland within the United Kingdom. But the partnership
between the two Governments is an important and visible sign for nationalists that they can engage in this project, even though their aspiration to a
united Ireland will not be brought about by it, with confidence that their
interests will be protected and the wider Irish dimension acknowledged.

5.12 But the Irish Government is still seen as a threat by unionists because of the role given to it under the Anglo-Irish Agreement and because it retains in Articles 2 and 3 of the Constitution a formal claim

on Northern Ireland as part of the national territory. They also believe – with some justification – that the Irish Government tends to think that HMG could "persuade" unionists to be more reasonable if we really tried. But, in reality, such influence as the British Government had with the unionists has waned, as their lack of confidence in the Government has deepened over recent years.

5.13 The relationship with the Irish Government is central to the achievement of political progress – but it requires delicate management to assuage both unionist concerns at too visible a "joint" approach and Irish suspicions that any British Government is [willing to] abandon or distort the ultimate, shared project. Both these sides have an interest in exaggerating Irish influence. The relationship is reflected in formal agreements – the Anglo-Irish Agreement, the Downing Street Declaration, the Joint Framework Document – and in the mechanisms established under them – regular Ministerial Intergovernmental Conferences and the continuing Anglo-Irish Secretariat at Maryfield.

5.14 The relationship will require personal input from Ministers. They are likely to find that Irish Ministers will co-operate more readily in meeting unionist concerns if they are convinced in private of the British Government's firm commitment to the shared political project and its readiness to carry it forward in partnership with the Irish Government. Some mechanism for private dialogue – whatever transparency is introduced elsewhere – is vital to an effective partnership.

5.15 The fundamental political project is only worth pursuing if there is at least a prospect of a solution – a three stranded agreement to which both unionists and nationalists could assent. Some argue that the two positions are irreconcilable. But our assessment remains that in principle an agreement is available which, although it should require compromise on both sides, would not strain beyond breaking point fundamental principles for either side.

5.16 This sort of outcome was set out in the Framework Documents:

- a balanced constitutional approach based on the principle of consent and including withdrawal of the Irish territorial claim;

- agreed devolved institutions in Northern Ireland, with power dis-
  tributed proportionately;
- a North/South body with some executive role but operating solely
  on the basis of agreement, North and South;
- a new Anglo-Irish Agreement;
- enhanced protection for rights;
- endorsed by dual referendums, North and South.

5.17 Despite the negative reaction of unionists which owed much to the
premature and misleading leak, any agreed outcome is likely to be of that
character. But the issue which remains open is whether the parties have
the political will and confidence to make the necessary compromises – at
least in the current talks process.

5.18 Since there was a good measure of agreement on the nature of local
political institutions in Strand 1 in 1992, overall agreement now turns on:

- will unionists accept a North/South body which goes beyond the
  merely consultative? (This may well prove the key point on which
  negotiations succeed or founder);
- will the Irish Government offer sufficient assurance to satisfy
  unionists that the territorial claim will be removed?
- will nationalists be confident that unionists will not work only
  those elements of the outcome attractive to them and stymie
  the rest?
- will the UUP and SDLP, if they represent a majority in each community, have the confidence to make a compromise and sell it in
  teeth of extremist opposition?

5.19 Ministers will want to reach their own views at an early stage on these
questions and the prospect for progress.

(ii)  The current talks process

5.20 since 1991, the overall political project of achieving agreement between unionists and nationalists has been pursued through the talks process. It has gone through various permutations but essentially consists of:

- direct negotiation between the parties in Northern Ireland and the British and Irish Governments;
- on a comprehensive agenda under which any issue can be raised;
- in a three stranded format;
- with participation left open to Sinn Fein on proper terms.

5.21 When Ministers join its resumption on 3 June, the process will remain preoccupied and apparently deadlocked on the issue of decommissioning. Paradoxically, while there is no IRA ceasefire this is an almost entirely hypothetical issue despite the presence of loyalists. But it is a proxy for the highly charged issue for both communities of whether the process is to go forward inclusive of Sinn Fein or exclusive of them.

5.22 How to resolve this, and secure agreement on the issue of decommissioning on the basis of the Mitchell Report, will need early decisions from Ministers before the talks resume – and is likely to require preparatory discussions well before 3 June with the Irish Government and at least the main political parties. The key questions are:

- will unionists agree any scenario which still allows Sinn Fein to join the talks?
- if so, can unionists be given sufficient assurance that, if Sinn Fein does join the talks, there will be some actual decommissioning of arms during the negotiations as Mitchell suggested (and, if no arms are delivered, that unionists will not stand alone in insisting that they should be)?
- will nationalists and the Irish Government prefer to keep the threshold low for Sinn Fein even at the price of making agreement with unionists impossible?

5.23 Officials have already canvassed with the Irish Government some possible options to break the impasse. Ministers will want to review these at an early stage and decide whether, and how, to pursue them.

5.24 But for now, it is important to note:

- the current talks process pre-dates the 1994 ceasefire and was not designed solely or even principally to accommodate Sinn Fein;

- it is highly desirable for Sinn Fein to join any political process if they can do so on proper terms;
- progress towards the political project of agreement between unionists and nationalists does not in principle require Sinn Fein's participation and should not be hostage to its actions;
- nevertheless, for now, the talks process is inextricably linked with the peace process.

(iii)  The peace process

5.25 Much would be simpler if we had greater insight into what the republican movement – the IRA and Sinn Fein – were really about. Detailed assessment papers offer our best analysis, but the short answer is: We don't know for certain. (Nor possibly does the movement itself.)

5.26 But it can be said with some confidence:

- the possibility that Adams and McGuinness are genuine in their desire to bring the republican movement into the political process cannot be ruled out. On this view they set out over a decade or more to achieve a difficult, but benign, transition from terror to politics expressed in the message apparently sent by McGuinness in February 1993: "The conflict is over but we need your advice on how to bring it to a close". They will only accomplish the transition if they bring all, or most, of the IRA with them which therefore constrains their room for manoeuvre;
- but nor can a more malign interpretation be ruled out. Whether Adams and McGuinness – who are undoubtedly central to the leadership of both the IRA and Sinn Fein – are cynically seeking to interchange terror and politics, or whether they want to deliver a transition but are unable to carry the IRA with them, it is clearly possible that the IRA may never reach a definitive commitment to politics and will prove irredeemable;
- whatever HMG's view, nationalists generally – and the SDLP and the Irish Government in particular – have so far been prepared to give Adams the benefit of the doubt. Most nationalists have so far

taken the view that Sinn Fein should be taken at its word and admitted to any negotiations following a ceasefire.

5.27 The result since 1994 at least is that nationalists have not been prepared to participate in any political process which formally denies Sinn Fein the opportunity to participate. But unionists have not been prepared to negotiate with Sinn Fein, even after a ceasefire, unless there are clear and credible signs that violence has been abandoned for good.

5.28 The 1994 ceasefire, and its subsequent breakdown, has largely reinforced existing prejudices. On one view, it represented a serious and genuine – but contingent – commitment to giving politics a chance which, if Sinn Fein had joined genuine negotiations, could over time have been transformed into a lasting peace. On the other view, it was always a tactical manoeuvre which did not remove the ideology of violence – seen during the ceasefire in punishment beatings, surveillance, targeting and other preparations.

5.29 As far as the Government's approach is concerned:

- the achievement of peace is central to HMG's fundamental objectives in Northern Ireland. It would save lives, improve economic prospects, release public resources and create a positive climate for political agreement. Even a ceasefire which ultimately did not prove lasting would nonetheless deliver many of these benefits in the interim and could not lightly be spurned.
- in pursuit of its ultimate project of agreement between unionists and nationalists, HMG cannot afford to ignore or be seen to be unreasonable on the peace issue – because it will affect nationalists' readiness to reach agreement even without Sinn Fein.
- HMG can influence any debate among republicans – we can seek to draw them into policies to the point where a return to terrorism would be very costly;
- the loyalist ceasefire will not hold indefinitely without an IRA ceasefire. All the loyalist paramilitaries have already taken retaliatory action, including at least one murder and several bombs;

– even on a cynical view of the republican movement's intentions, it remains in HMG's interest to ensure that blame for failure rests squarely with them – and not, as most nationalists still attribute blame for the breakdown of the last ceasefire, with HMG's failure to respond positively.

5.30 The Government's approach needs therefore:

– to be robust for any eventuality: lasting peace, continued terrorism or a mix of politics and terror;
– consistent with the overall political project: in other words, giving nationalists confidence in HMG's good faith in approaching this issue but avoiding the impression, which undermines unionist confidence, that securing Sinn Fein's entry is the only issue that matters;
– consistently pursued and articulated whatever the circumstances. There may well be further atrocities; there is likely to be another ceasefire. The Government should be seen to be pursuing a consistent approach which should not be dictated by the politics of the last atrocity or the last Sinn Fein statement.

5.31 It is likely that events will bring the issues to the fore. Even without Sinn Fein's [being] there, the issues are central to the current talks process. The key strategic questions for Ministers to review are:

– do Ministers wish to isolate republicans, seeking to exclude them from the political process and building on constitutional nationalism? Or do Ministers wish to try to co-opt republicans into the political process, providing it can be achieved on proper terms?
– assuming Ministers wish to make the continuation of violence as difficult as possible, is that best served by erecting low or high barriers for entry by Sinn Fein into the political process?
– can HMG act as a neutral observer of the process, waiting to see whether peace or war is the outcome? Or are we, as Sinn Fein view us, a central player in that process whose actions and responses can help to determine in what direction republicans go?

- how best to send clear and consistent messages to Sinn Fein which discourage violence and encourage politics?
- how best to manage the process to ensure that wider confidence in HMG is maintained? In particular, how best to reassure unionists that they can engage in the central political process, whether Sinn Fein is there or not, with confidence that their fundamental interests will not be compromised?
- what should be the balance between pursuing peace and pursuing talks? To make progress in talks without Sinn Fein could bring helpful pressure on them to join the process, but both unionists and nationalists could be reluctant to go forward while Sinn Fein still hang around the door. A determined bid for peace might bring Sinn Fein in and encourage nationalists but would most likely lose unionists, at least for the time being.

5.32 These issues will be central to how HMG responds to any initiative from the republican movement. That is likely to focus on what we assess to be a narrow, but deep, gap between the two sides focused upon:

- the certainty with which a renewed ceasefire will lead to Sinn Fein's entry to negotiations. Having, as they see it, been betrayed by the Government over the last ceasefire, Sinn Fein will want to know with some assurance that the essential deal – a ceasefire in return for entry to genuine negotiations – is on offer and will be delivered;
- HMG's good faith. The republican view of the Government's actions during the last ceasefire is that we set out deliberately to stretch it out with the intention of destroying the IRA without conceding negotiations. The republican leadership will be looking for some sign that HMG is committed to a practical confidence-building agenda (including release of prisoners, reform of the RUC and progress on the equity agenda and will engage with them in the right circumstances in good faith – even quite small gestures could be significant;

- equally, the Government will want to know whether republicans are acting in good faith. The breakdown of the last ceasefire raises obvious questions and, whatever HMG's view, unionists will not engage with Sinn Fein unless they can point to some credible assurance that republicans are intent on making a definitive commitment to the political process;
- whether there are genuine negotiations on offer, for which republicans want some idea of the overall time frame and some indication that unionists cannot veto the negotiation process;
- the issue of decommissioning. As the first issue which Sinn Fein would have to confront if it joined any negotiations, both they and we want some assurance that there is a possible way through the issue into substantive political negotiations. The IRA is determined that there will be no decommissioning short of an overall agreement during negotiations.

5.33 While these issues remain unresolved, the reality is that the IRA will continue with war even while Sinn Fein is talking peace. But if these issues can be resolved satisfactorily then a renewed ceasefire could be delivered, although the IRA grass-roots are now extremely suspicious of any further ceasefire. A further ceasefire could again contain the potential, if cemented by genuine and inclusive negotiations which led to an exercise of self-determination by dual referendums, to become a lasting peace. But, at the outset, it would at best represent a contingent commitment to the political process which, as in 1996, could be rescinded.

5.34 Ministers do not have a free hand to decide whether or not Sinn Fein should join the negotiations. The issue of entry to the negotiations is governed by law – section 2(2) and 2(3) of the Northern Ireland (Entry to Negotiations, etc.) Act 1996, under which Sinn Fein must be invited to participate unless the Secretary of State considers that the conditions in paragraph 8 and 9 of command Paper 3232 (Ground Rules for the Negotiations) are not met – in which case Sinn Fein must not be invited. The conditions require:

- an unequivocal restoration of the IRA ceasefire of August 1994;
- Sinn Fein (like all the parties already in the talks) to establish a commitment to exclusively peaceful methods and have shown that they abide by the democratic process.

5. 35 The last Government set out the policy which it would follow in applying these requirements in its statement of 28 November 1996. while in Opposition. Ministers supported the principle that words, actions and all the circumstances must be consistent with an unequivocal restoration of the ceasefire. But some room for manoeuvre over the other elements of the 28 November statement may be helpful.

(iv) Alternative strategies

5.36 Ministers may need them – that is realism rather than defeatism.

5.37 The key point is that the overall political project does not stand or fall according to whether the current talks process succeeds or fails. There are alternative routes to progress on this ultimate objective – although experience suggests they take months (or even years) to develop and put in place.

5.38 Clearly the first priority is to achieve progress when the talks resume on 3 June so as to avoid the need for fallback strategies. We have been doing some thinking on these and can explore the alternatives with Ministers when they are ready. The Irish Government, who find the current talks process frustrating, may already be working on their fallback approach.

## 6. Economic & social policy

6.1 As overview paper of this sort cannot cover the individual issues in this vast field. Some are explored in the analytical papers attached and all will be covered in more detail in departmental briefing.

6.2 But the key point is that these areas also should be approached as part of an integrated programme of government:

- they offer opportunities to support the overall political project, e.g. by taking confidence building measures in these areas which

encourage either or both communities to engage more positively
and with greater confidence in the political process. Political progress and peace are more likely in a prosperous and fairer society;
– how the Government approaches these apparently "ordinary" decisions will also send important signals throughout the community
  about its fundamental political approach, e.g. is the Government's
  commitment to the principle of equality of opportunity, parity
  of esteem and fair treatment merely words or reflected through
  everyday decisions? The Government's response to SACHR's recommendations in relation to the Employment Equality Review –
  now due in June – will be an early test;
– more negatively, in Northern Ireland even seemingly trivial
  issues – such as whether the National Anthem is played at a gradu-
  ation ceremony – can suddenly become invested by both sides of
  the community with enormous symbolic importance and seen as a
  political test of strength which impacts the real political process;
– in these social and economic areas –particularly in promoting
  economic growth, jobs, investment and other "bread and butter"
  issues – there is the opportunity to engage the local politicians on
  an agenda where their interests converge rather than diverge and
  so show that politics can be "win/win" rather than only "win/lose".

6.3 That is not to say that every decision of the Government should be
taken on political grounds. There is an excellent case for taking decisions
on their objective merits and demonstrating the benefits of competent,
fair and impartial government. But that should be on the basis of an informed decision which recognises the possible political implications.

6.4 In handling these sorts of issues Ministers will find that:

– they have to deal with many issues which, elsewhere in the UK,
  would be left to local government but with Northern Ireland's
  democratic deficit are decided by central government;
– they must deal with these issues against the background of local
  politicians who have no share in responsibility, no interest in

sharing the burden of difficult choices and a political culture of opposition.

6.5 There is therefore a premium on taking decisions in as open a fashion as possible with a wide opportunity for consultation with the local community and local political leaders.

6.6 Unfortunately, decisions in this area will also have to be taken against the background of severe public expenditure constraint over the next few years.

## 7. Presentation

7.1 The integrated approach suggested by this paper needs also to be communicated positively, coherently and consistently. Success in the political project is only likely to be achieved if both sides of the community understand and have confidence in the British Government and its broad approach and believe we will stick consistently to it. The Government cannot hope to say what both sides want to hear – if it tried to send different messages to each side, that would only breed mistrust and suspicion.

7.2 This points to articulating a clear and positive message about the central political objective of the Government to both sides in a way which is consistent and gives confidence that the Government means what it says and will act accordingly. There need to be different emphases for different audiences – nationalists, republicans and unionists in Northern Ireland, the Irish Republic, the GB audience and the international audience – but these should be, and be seen to be, consistent with a core series of messages that apply across the board and remain the same over time. Such an information strategy needs not only to communicate the Government's policy proactively but also to respond effectively and rapidly to events which are inevitably unpredictable.

7.3 Ministers will want to satisfy themselves at an early stage that the mechanisms are in place to deliver an effective presentation of their policy along these lines. But there are some traps worth avoiding from the start:

- "pendulum" policy: swinging from a pro-unionist to a pro-nationalist presentation according to who shouted loudest and last. That only breeds suspicion and mistrust in both sides;
- the politics of the last atrocity: there is no easy or "right" way to respond to such events. Emotion can – and sometimes should – take over. But unfortunately, such events are to be expected in Northern Ireland – and consequently should be factored in to the Government's presentation form the start. The Government should obviously respond appropriately, but it should not be seen to be knocked off course by events which can be anticipated;
- rhetoric out of line with reality. Sometimes this may be unavoidable but if trust and confidence is to be created, the Government should endeavour to ensure that what it says in private it is prepared also in public.

*8. Conclusion*

8.1 This paper has argued for an integrated approach to overcoming the divisions in Northern Ireland which lead to conflict. It has sought to set out the key elements to be addressed in such an approach and to identify some of the strategic issues Ministers will need to consider.

8.2 To summarise, Ministers might like to consider:

- Do Ministers agree the need for the sort of integrated approach set out here?
- Do they agree with the overall goal identified?
- Are they satisfied with the mechanisms in place to ensure the co-ordination and presentation of a genuinely integrated approach?
- Do they agree with the key elements of the broad approach?
- Are there any major omissions?
- Do Ministers want at this stage to indicate their sense of strategic priorities, bearing in mind that events will always dictate their own imperatives?

Political Directorate
2 May 1997

## Document 2  Letter from Gerry Adams to Tony Blair

Gerry Adams
President of Sinn Fein
51/55 Bothar na bhFal
Beal Felrste BT12 4PD

*Private and Confidential*

2 May 1997

Tony Blair MP
Prime Minister
10 Downing Street
London-based

A Chara

Congratulations on your outstanding electoral success. Good luck to you in your new position, and in your efforts to implement the priorities you have set for yourself and your government.

I am certain that these will include the issue of a lasting peace in Ireland. Be assured that this is a priority for me also and that Sinn Fein is totally committed to democratic and peaceful methods of struggle and to a negotiated settlement to the conflict in our country.

The rebuilding of a credible peace process must be tackled without further delay. I would request, therefore, that you authorise officials of your government to meet with Sinn Fein as soon as possible so that we can explore with urgency how this can be accomplished.

While I am mindful of the difficulties for all concerned, I remain confident that the peace process can be established on a solid basis of equality and inclusive dialogue.

That certainly is my commitment.

Le gach dea mhein
Gerry Adams

## Document 3   Letter from Tony Blair to Gerry Adams

10 Downing Street
London SW1A 2AA

2 May 1997

From the Private Secretary

Ken Lindsay Esq.
Northern Ireland Office

*Sinn Fein*

Dear Ken,
I attach a letter to the Prime Minister from Gerry Adams, congratulating
him on his success in the Election. The key point is a request for officials
to meet Sinn Fein to explore the rebuilding of the peace process.

I would be grateful for rapid advice and a draft reply if appropriate,
either from the Prime Minister or me.

I am copying this letter to Jan Polley (Cabinet Office).

Yours ever,
John Holmes

*Draft*
Mr G Adams
President of Sinn Fein
5155 Falls Road
Belfast BT12 4PD

May 1997

Thank you for your letter of 3 May. The Prime Minister has asked me to
reply to your letter of 2 May. I was, in any event, on the point of writing
to you, because I am anxious that, while I am meeting the leaders of the
other parties in Northern Ireland, you and those you represent should
also be in no doubt as to the Government's fundamental approach in

seeking to promote reconciliation and overcoming the divisions which have contributed to conflict.

We endorse in full the principles, agreements and undertakings set out by the then British Government in conjunction with the Irish Government, including the Anglo-Irish Agreement, the Downing Street Declaration, the Framework Document and the 28 February 1996 communique. These set out the guiding principles of our approach.

We uphold the principle of consent, set out in the Downing Street Declaration and endorsed by the Irish Government and the overwhelming majority of parties and people throughout these islands. A united Ireland will never come about through violence or intimidation.

Our primary interest is to see peace, stability and reconciliation established by agreement. We will implement any such agreement reached on the basis of self-determination and consent as set out in the Downing Street Declaration. No outcome is excluded or predetermined: the only limitation is the need for agreement between unionists and nationalists.

We believe the talks process offers the opportunity for genuine negotiations, on an inclusive basis and on an open agenda. But it is fundamental that such negotiations can take place only among those committed to exclusively peaceful methods and who have shown that they abide by the democratic process. In Sinn Fein's case, this requires an unequivocal restoration of the IRA ceasefire of August 1994, reflected in words and deeds so that the statutory requirements under the Northern Ireland (Entry to Negotiation etc.) Act 1996 are met. This is the most pressing step needed to reinvigorate the peace process. Other than this, there are no preconditions to negotiations. But while Sinn Fein does not meet these fundamental requirements, agreed with the Irish Government, the talks must continue without Sinn Fein.

We recognise the overwhelming need to promote genuine confidence among both unionists and nationalists in Northern Ireland. We shall play our part. But the greatest gap in credibility and confidence is over whether republicans are prepared, genuinely and definitely, to commit themselves exclusively to the political process and to resolving all differences exclusively by peaceful means.

These are the principles which will underlie our approach in Northern Ireland, and to which we will hold. We shall not be diverted by violence or threat of violence. It is vital that there should be no misunderstanding about our approach and our commitment to follow through consistently.

In your letter (to the Prime Minister) you propose a meeting between Sinn Fein and officials to explore with urgency how, as you put it, the peace process can be rebuilt without further delay. As I have already said the unequivocal restoration of the ceasefire is the most pressing step needed.

We are ready in principle to envisage meetings between officials and Sinn Fein to carry that forward and, in particular, to ensure there are no avoidable misunderstandings about the need for such a ceasefire as soon as possible and how, following it, Sinn Fein would be brought to join the political process in accordance with the principles I have set out and the statutory requirements. Agreement to such a meeting will depend, of course, on events on the ground. Subject to that, and to your agreement that it will be for the purpose stated, I shall ready to consider authorising a meeting.

We are committed to a genuine peace process. We are prepared to play our part to build the trust and confidence necessary for it to succeed. But a genuine peace process can only be based upon a genuine commitment to lasting peace, exclusively peaceful methods and the democratic process.

I do not propose to release this letter to the press, but I will acknowledge publicly that I have written to you and for what purpose.

## Document 4  The Secretary of State Has Written to Sinn Fein

*Draft Press Release*

The Secretary of State has written to Sinn Fein explaining the Government's approach to the peace process and to Sinn Fein's possible involvement in the Talks.

She reaffirmed that an unequivocal restoration of the IRA ceasefire was the most pressing step needed.

She also made clear, as did the previous Government, her willingness in principle to envisage a meeting between officials and Sinn Fein to carry this forward and to establish that there are no avoidable misunderstandings about the basis for Sinn Fein's involvement in the political process.

Agreement to such a meeting will be subject to events on the ground.

## Document 5  Ulster Democratic Party

Ulster Democratic Party
Central Office
36 Castle Street
Lisburn
County Antrim
BT27 4XE
*Telephone: 01846 667056*
*Fax: 01846 605159*

Rt. Hon Tony Blair MP
Prime Minister
10 Downing Street
London

2nd May 1997

Dear Prime Minister,
First of all, can I congratulate you on a resounding victory. I hope the changes you bring for the United Kingdom shall benefit us all.

You face many challenges in the next five years, but I hope you shall give Northern Ireland the priority its people deserve and that your commitment to assist the search for a democratic resolution to our conflict shall not wane.

I would welcome the opportunity to meet with you at your earliest convenience so that we may discuss the peace process. The multi-party Talks resume on June 3rd and there shall be much to do in the first few weeks to bring stability to the process and I think it would be useful for us both if we could exchange views upon how that can be achieved.

I look forward to Hearing from you soon.

Yours sincerely,
Councillor Gary McMichael
Party Leader

## Document 6   The Taoiseach to Call on the Prime Minister

10 Downing Street
London SW1A 2AA

From the Private Secretary

5 May 1997

Dominick Chilcott Esq.
Foreign and Commonwealth Office

*Call by the Taoiseach, 8 May*

Dear Dominick,

Further to my letter of 29 April, I have now discussed this again with Paddy Teahon. We have agreed that the Taoiseach should call here for an hour at 1600 on Thursday, 8 May. We would plan to hold the meeting in the White Room here, to emphasise its informality, rather than in the Cabinet Room. The Taoiseach will be accompanied by the Tanaiste, and by one or two officials. I hope that on our side the Foreign Secretary and Northern Ireland Secretary can be present, probably without accompanying officials, again to emphasise the informal nature of the occasion.

The agenda, insofar as there is one, should cover not only Europe and Northern Ireland, but East/West issues. Teahon said that the Taoiseach was not at all happy about how Sinn Fein had been talking since the Election, and wanted to down play the Northern Ireland aspect of the meeting. Talking about cooperation between the Republic and Britain in areas such as education would contribute to this. I said that I saw no difficulty with this from our side.

We also discussed press handling. I said that I thought we would not announce the meeting, but simply confirm it as necessary, not least since there was a general expectation that it was happening anyway. Teahon agreed. I also said that I thought we would probably wish to avoid the Prime Minister and Taoiseach going out into the street to speak to the press afterwards, as they would after a normal Summit. They would otherwise face mostly awkward questions from the Irish press about the IRA and Sinn Fein, which both might prefer to avoid for the moment. Teahon was inclined to agree, but suggested that Shane Kenny and Alastair Campbell should discuss this further on the telephone in the next day or two.

I would be grateful if the FCO and NIO could prepare appropriate briefing for the meeting. It should be *extremely* short, covering only the main points the Prime Minister should seek to get across. The idea is to have a general exchange to get the feel of respective priorities, rather than any kind of detailed negotiating session.

I am copying this to Ken Lindsay (Northern Ireland Office), Jan Polley (Cabinet Office) and Veronica Sutherland (in Dublin).

Yours ever,
John Holmes

# Document 7   Statement by the Taoiseach, Mr John Bruton

10 Downing Street
London SW12AA

From the Private Secretary

5 May 1997

Dominick Chilcott Esq.
Foreign and Commonwealth Office

*Visit by the Taoiseach*

Dear Dominick,
My letter of 5 May referred to the Taoiseach's interest in highlighting East/West issues during his visit to London later this week. I now attach the statement he is making this evening about this. Clearly we will need to cover the points in our briefing.

I am copying this to Ken Lindsay (Northern Ireland Office), Jan Polley (Cabinet Office) and Veronica Sutherland (in Dublin).

Yours ever,
John Holmes

*Statement by the Taoiseach, Mr John Bruton, T. D., on Monday 5th May, 1997 on his Forthcoming Visit to Britain*

I am visiting Britain this week to meet the new Prime Minister, Tony Blair, to meet representatives of the Irish Community in Britain, to promote trade, and to address the Oxford Union.

My meeting with the Prime Minister is particularly important, as it is my first with Tony Blair as Prime Minister. I am very much looking forward to it, as I believe we can develop many new possibilities for cooperation in regard to Northern Ireland, bilaterally and within Europe. Work in each of these areas is mutually reinforcing. During my visit, I will focus particularly, as I will explain later, on the position of the Irish in Britain.

There are many positive areas where structured cooperation between the two Governments can meet vital needs, and where we can use existing East/West institutions more fully.

The most exciting area of all for potential cooperation is in Education. Educational improvement in Ireland is my own personal priority. This is one of the reasons why I launched the Information Society proposals, which commit the Government here to a major investment in training teachers in information technology, and in giving every child full familiarity with the potential of the information super highway for educational purposes, for work, and for life.

This investment can be made most-effective if there are elements of compatibility with what is being done in Britain and elsewhere. The new British Government, plans to "wire up schools, libraries, colleges and hospitals to the information super highway". They plan a National Grid for Learning, franchised as a public/private partnership, which will help teachers update their skills. They also plan a new University for Industry, collaborating with the Open University to bring new opportunities to adults seeking to develop their potential.

The Irish education's curriculum is, and will always remain, quite distinctive from that in Britain. But these new developments open up huge opportunities for savings on educational hardware and software investments, for cooperation on particular courses and subjects, and for enhancing mutual understanding through education both between Ireland and Britain, and within Ireland itself, North and South. I look forward to discussing these possibilities with Tony Blair. Specifically, I would like Ireland to have inputs to, and benefits from, both the proposed new National Grid for Learning, and the new University for Industry.

I welcome the new British Government's commitment to sign the E. U. Social Chapter, and agree with them that the Social Chapter allows European countries, working together, to promote employability and flexibility, not high social costs. Neither Ireland, or Britain, should attempt to compete as low wage economics, with countries paying a tenth or a hundredth of our wage levels.

Therefore we must each of us work to enhance the skill and added-value potential of our work forces. The Irish Government will be publishing very soon, a comprehensive White Paper on Human Resources. It will detail the measures we plan to encourage employees and employers to invest more of their money in training, and to ensure that training qualifications are mutually and internationally recognised. As Ireland and Britain are, in effect, part of the same labour market, investment in employee training in Britain benefits Ireland, and vice versa. The two Governments should consciously work together on an agreed plan to maximise these benefits.

Organised crime represents a threat to society in Ireland and Britain, and there is a common travel area between the two islands. On the continent of Europe a similar common travel area exists, under the Schengen Accord, and it is being accompanied by an immensely detailed system of cooperation on anti-crime measures. Neither Ireland nor Britain are part of this accord as yet, so we need to develop our own, equally effective measures against crime, in parallel and conjunction with what is happening on the continent.

One of the issues that the new British Government has committed itself to tackle is that of homelessness. Structures exist for East/West cooperation between the two Governments, and I would particularly like to develop joint initiatives between these structures to deal with the plight of Irish people who are homeless in Britain, and who represent a disproportionate share of all the homeless in Britain. Many of them are young Irish people, who have been living rough on the streets. The two Governments can work together, in a structured way, in both Ireland and Britain, to deal with the causes, and the symptoms, of the homelessness problem.

# Document 8   Meeting between the Taoiseach and the Prime Minister

*Press Statement*

On Northern Ireland, the Taoiseach and the Prime Minister reviewed developments since their meeting in London on 8 May.

They reviewed in particular the official level meetings which had been held, on both sides, with Sinn Fein. They expressed the hope that these would lead to an unequivocal IRA ceasefire, thereby facilitating the fully inclusive talks which they both want to see.

The Taoiseach and the Prime Minister also reviewed the preparations for the resumption of the multi-party talks on 3 June.

They reaffirmed their total commitment to seeing the talks through to a successful conclusion as quickly as possible.

The Taoiseach and the Prime Minister agreed separately on a joint statement of intent on Irish-British (East/West) co-operation (attached).

*Joint Statement of Intent on Cooperation between the Irish and British Governments*

At their meeting in London on 8 May 1997, the Taoiseach and the Prime Minister agreed to intensify cooperation between the two governments.

The Prime Minister and the Taoiseach noted that there was already a substantial degree of cooperation in many fields, including policies aimed at tackling long-term unemployment, consumer affairs, health and medical issues, education, culture, the environment, the fight against drugs and crime, civil law matters, processing of social security payments and measures to combat fraud, youth and school exchanges, and transport links.

They agreed that cooperation in the above areas should be maintained, and that the two governments should in particular consider options for cooperation in the following areas:

1. the search for ways to benefit from the potential of new information and communication technologies in education, having regard to progress towards the Information Superhighway and

proposals in the United Kingdom for a new National Grid for Learning and University for Industry;
2. the enhancement of the skill and added-value potential of the workforces;
3. having regard to the Common Travel Area in these islands, detailed cooperation in the fight against organised crime;
4. measures to deal with the issue of homelessness, with particular reference to those Irish people in Britain affected by it;
5. ensuring the highest possible food safety standards in these islands;
6. strengthened cooperation in environmental issues.

Meetings at official level have already taken place on a number of the issues identified and further such meetings are envisaged. The primary responsibilities for taking forward cooperation lies with the Ministers, Departments and Agencies most directly affected. Meetings at Ministerial level will be arranged when they can productively take place.

The Taoiseach and the Prime Minister welcomed the initiative of Encounter in organising, with Leargas and the Youth Exchange Centre, a Youth Conference in Dublin from 6–8 June. They hoped that the conference would contribute to an enhancement in cooperation in the youth sector between both countries.

# Document 9   Meeting with Trimble

FROM: QUENTIN THOMAS
Political Director
7 May 1997 ID/56
PS/SECRETARY OF STATE(L&B)

cc:
PS/Mr Paul Murphy(L&B)
PS/PUS(L&B)

PS/Sir David Fell
Mr Steele
Mr Stephens
Mr Watkins
Mr Maccabe
Mr Brooker
Mr Hill
Mr Warner
Mr Holmes No. 10

I think there is a little compression in the remark attributed to me in paragraph six of your note of this meeting.

The passage might read:

"Mr Thomas recalled that the UUP had shown some interest in ideas on decommissioning HMG had canvassed towards the end of the talks. He sensed that Mr Trimble needed some assurance that, if he moved, he would be met from the other side. Likewise, Mr Thomas felt that the Irish side might consider moving if they felt it would be reciprocated by the UUP. A bridge might be built from both sides. Mr Trimble did not dismiss this altogether but said he was not prepared …."

In other words I do not think I said that the Irish side had expressed an interest in UUP proposals; and if I had said that it would not have been true!

QUENTIN THOMAS
11 Millbank

FROM: CONFIDENTIAL PS/SECRETARY OF STATE 8 MAY 1997

Document 10  Meeting with Dr I R K Paisley, 7 May

From: PS/Secretary of State
8 May 1997

cc:
PS/Mr Murphy (L&B)

PS/Mr Ingram (L&B)
PS/Mr Worthington (L, DENI & DHSS)
PS/PUS (L&B)
PS/Sir David Fell
Mr Steele
Mr Thomas
Mr Stephens
Mr Bell
Mr Leach
Mr Watkins
Mr Brooker
Mr Maccabe
Mr Lavery
Mr Warner
Mr Holmes
Mr Hill

The <u>Secretary of State</u>, accompanied by Mr Murphy, Mr Ingram and Mr Thomas met Dr Paisley yesterday evening in the fourth of her meetings with Northern Ireland Party leaders. It was a friendly meeting with Dr Paisley taking a reasonably constructive tone throughout. He covered a range of Northern Ireland issues, including education, health, agriculture and policing. He offered a copy of his speaking notes as an aide memoir and these are attached for information. Covered below are additional comments which he made.

2. <u>Dr Paisley</u> had just come from what he described as a very good meeting on BSE with Mr Rooker in MAFF. Dr Paisley reported that he, John Hume and Jim Nicholson had a very good working relationship with Commissioner Bonino and hoped she would visit Northern Ireland at the end of June. He hoped that the Northern Ireland Office would treat her well on this visit. It was agreed that Dr Paisley would contact Lord Dubs to arrange a more detailed discussion on BSE and agriculture matters generally.

3. On confidence building measures and particularly policing, <u>Dr Paisley</u> said it was insensitive of the Secretary of State to talk about the <u>reform</u> of policing. Instead, she should speak of the need to fight terrorism. He was sure that there

was going to be a serious escalation of violence in Northern Ireland and was coming round to the view that a ceasefire was becoming less likely. The Secretary of State said that reform of the RUC was shorthand for the Police Bill, which had been sent to parties and had attracted no Opposition. She accepted that the shorthand was not helpful and that there was some misunderstanding in the RUC. It may be necessary for her to do something to clarify this.

4. Asked what confidence building measures Dr Paisley envisaged, he said that quangos were a case in point. He was not against quangos per se but the fact that they were filled with unelectable people who had lost elections – but this of course did not include DUP supporters. He also mentioned the Parades Commission, the membership of which he described as "most unfair". Until there was fair representation on the Committee they should not be given any further powers.

5. The Secretary of State said she was not sure what confidence building measures the DUP or Unionists generally would ask for – she guessed it would be for the status quo. Dr Paisley offered to prepare a paper on CBMs for Unionists. At present CBMs were seen as concessions to Republicans – perception in Northern Ireland was everything. He hoped that the new team in the Northern Ireland Office would keep in touch with elected representatives and let them know what was in their mind. The previous Secretary of State had favourites – he claimed that David Trimble was seen every Thursday after Cabinet.

6. On actual parades, Dr Paisley recounted the situation at Dunloy, how the agreement with local people had fallen through and had caused the protests at Harryville. He also said that there was a virtual agreement at Drumcree last year with Councillor Ignatius Fox, but then the "ecumenical clergy" came in, the Jesuits said they could get more and the whole thing fell apart with serious consequences. The Secretary of State said that, central to the government's policy was the right to march and it was quite conceivable that the Commission would, after consideration, take the view that a march should go ahead, just as it could take the opposite view. Clearly, the best way was to get local agreement.

7. Moving on to education, health and training cuts which he said were imposed to help security, Dr Paisley said that the Police Authority had told him they had got nothing extra. On education, he said he would get

Oliver Gibson to prepare a paper on how best to improve spending, particularly by the Boards. He suggested that the Boards needed direction on what the money was for – in his view it should be for more teachers, as a lot of experienced teachers were trying to get out of the profession. He also thought that there should be scrutiny of the Department of Education itself because they were often in the position of saying "physician heal thyself". The same applied to the Health Service.

8. The <u>Secretary of State</u> thanked Dr Paisley for coming, assured him that she looked forward to having regular meetings with him and other party leaders and hoped for a constructive time ahead.

W K LINDSAY
PS/SECRETARY OF STATE

## Document 11  Speaking Note: Dr Paisley, 7 May 1997

### INTRODUCTION

The cut of £120 million from the education, health and training budgets in order to pay for increased security following the resumption of IRA violence is opposed right across the Province. No other part of the UK has to face these cuts in order to pay for extra security. It means pupils and parents are being punished for IRA violence.

### EDUCATION

1. The number of teachers being made redundant is totally unacceptable. Morale is very low in the teaching profession and pupil/teacher ratios will increase.
2. The cuts in research for universities and third level institutions are causing alarm to industry as well as academics.
3. Plans for nursery education – we would like to see one year of nursery education for all children.

4. The current Boards set up should remain until a locally elected assembly can deliberate on administration of education for Northern Ireland.

## HEALTH

1. There is intense concern at what is seen as the dismantling of the Health Service with operations cancelled, waiting lists lengthened, wards closed, Services cut, residential and nursing homes cut, and staff not replaced.
2. Care in the community as a concept is good but it has not been properly implemented. The cuts to the Home Help Services have been outrageous. Elderly and disabled people have suffered as a result.
3. We oppose the process which means those needing residential or nursing care have to sell the family home or take out extra Insurance to pay for it.
4. There must be more nurses, doctors etc. and less bureaucrats in administration.

## CUTS IN ACE FUNDING

1. Ace schemes have made a very valuable contribution to improving employment prospects and community development particularly in deprived areas. Since inception it has put more than 40,000 people into jobs. It is aimed at the long term unemployed in Northern Ireland fall into that category.
2. Last year funding was £39.8 million. The plan is to reduce that by £11 million or 28% this year with the loss of more than 2,000 places and further cuts to follow.
3. A number of projects which fall below a threshold for core positions will have to close completely.
4. The cuts to ace schemes should be abandoned.

# Document 12  Dinner with the Tanaiste

From: Quentin Thomas
Political Director

7 May 1997
ID/58
*Immediate!*

PS/Secretary of State (L&B)

cc:
PS/Mr Murphy (L&B)
PS/Mr Ingram (L&B)
PS/Mr Worthington (L, DENI & DHSS)
PS/PUS (L&B)
PS/Sir David Fell
Mr Steele
Mr Bell
Mr Thomas
Mr Stephens
Mr Leach
Mr Watkins
Mr Brooker
Mr Maccabe
Mr Beeton
Mr Hill
Mr Lavery
Mr Lamont
HMA Dublin
Mr Budd
Mr Warner
Mr Holmes

Last night the Secretary of State, Mr Warner and I dined at Lancaster House with the Tanaiste, his private secretary and Mr Sean O hUiginn.

2. In summary. the evening was pleasant and cordial. Apart from general pleasantries, all the focus was on Sinn Fein, the prospects of securing a new IRA ceasefire and Sinn Fein's early entry into talks. The Irish side see this as the key issue for the meeting between the Prime Minister and the Taoiseach and attach importance at their doorstep (which, whatever may have been agreed, they still anticipate) to the two sides signalling, in common language, warmth towards the prospect of Sinn Fein's inclusion in the talks.

*Detail*

3. The Irish side clearly believe that, following Sinn Fein's relative success in the General Election, there is now an opportunity for a renewed ceasefire. They pick up signals, partly from the Americans, that the Provisionals are beginning to position themselves again for a ceasefire designed to secure their entry into talks on 3 June. On the one hand they anticipate the possibility of a unilateral ceasefire in mid-May for this purpose; on the other hand, they argue that it is virtually inconceivable that there will be a renewed IRA ceasefire unless there is some certainty about what would follow, and in particular some "precision" about, if not immediacy for, Sinn Fein's entry into the talks process.

4. We noted the heroic efforts by the Irish Government to characterise what they had said in advance would be a vote for terrorism as having been in retrospect a vote for peace. But it appears to be the case that the Irish side now believe that Sinn Fein and their IRA colleagues are poised to use the position of strength which their electoral performance has given them to bring the Movement as a whole into talks. The Irish side mentioned two areas of worry; certainty of entry for Sinn Fein and doubt about the nature of the outcome of the Talks process as a whole. They say they have consistently explained to Sinn Fein that they cannot give more assurance about what may come out of the process - beyond of course the general indication that the framework document provides the area in which the outcome will be found.

5. We emphasised in turn:

- that the Government would clearly wish to see inclusive talks on proper terms;
- that while both Governments should do all they could to advance the talks process without Sinn Fein that would be a "sub-optimal" option;
- the Government was settling in, local government elections on 21 May were a factor and accordingly it was unlikely that there would be a positive response to Sinn Fein overtures in the immediate future;
- on the other hand everything should be done to convey to Sinn Fein – and the Irish side indicated that they might find a way of doing this – that the Government might be on the verge of making some positive move, but that any further atrocities, or disruption through hoaxes, in Northern Ireland or Great Britain, would fatally damage the prospects for this;
- in any event a ceasefire in mid-May (one of the options the Irish side mentioned) was very unlikely to secure Sinn Fein's entry when the talks resume on 3 June.

6. In discussion, we noted the possible relevance of the forthcoming Irish General Election (June). While initially insisting that whatever was happening on that front, the Irish Government was determined that the talks should indeed take place on 3 June, the Irish side on reflection saw the possible case for using that election as a pretext for adjourning the talks – thereby prolonging the natural gap during which Sinn Fein might become qualified for entry.

7. We gave no indication that there was any prospect of early contact with Sinn Fein in response to Gerry Adams' letter. The Irish side in turn mentioned that their current Position was that meetings with Sinn Fein could only be resumed if there was some clear prospect that the IRA was on the verge of a renewed ceasefire. Nonetheless the Irish side seemed confident that they could find some way of conveying that there might be positive developments, but that any further terrorist action or disruption could prove fatal to it.

8. Although the British side registered their understanding that the meeting between the Prime Minister and the Taoiseach would essentially be an informal courtesy call, and that there would be no joint appearance before the press, the Irish side seemed confident of the need to co-ordinate a shared press line. After discussion it seemed that, leaving aside whatever was said about European union and East/West matters, the Irish side might agree to something conveying commitment to the talks, and warmth about the possibility of making them inclusive without adopting any new substantive position. This suggests that:

The two Prime Ministers reaffirmed their commitment to the talks process, to the prospect that they offer a mechanism for meaningful negotiations and their shared determination to carry them forward without Sinn Fein if necessary, but with Sinn Fein if possible. They emphasised their wish to make the talks inclusive but stressed that a genuine and unequivocal ceasefire was the necessary prerequisite for achieving this. They hoped there would be an IRA ceasefire so Sinn Fein could be brought in. They believed there should be no unnecessary delay in Sinn Fein's inclusion if there were a credible ceasefire. They emphasised the need for the two sides to co-ordinate language in advance of the meeting.

*Parades*

9. There was a lengthy discussion of the prospects for the marching season. Mr O hUiginn deployed his familiar argument that, while the British genius naturally reached for a compromise, this might not be the right thing. On analysis it seemed that he preferred a concession to Nationalist interests! However, when pressed, he suggested that the best outcome might be for marches to go through – most of the discussion focused on the Garvaghy Road expressly – with tight conditions (small numbers, no bands, furled banners) but following some engagement between the Residents' Association and the Orange Order. The fact of some exchanges - inevitably, in his view, involving Brendan McKenna – was the essential prerequisite to achieving acquiescence in the march going through.

10. The Irish side emphasised how any movement on "peace" – that is any moves towards a ceasefire and Sinn Fein's inclusion in the talks – was likely to have a benign effect on the parades' issue. To some extent Sinn Fein could call the shots, and could use the parades issue as a proxy for the armed struggle. If they felt that HMG was responding positively to any overtures, and that a path towards a ceasefire and the talks process was opening up, this was likely to have a very benign effect, on the Irish view, on the parades' issue,

11. The Secretary of State signalled clearly, but without commitment, that given other confidence building measures (police reforms; ECHR; parades legislation) she might well decide, in consultation with the RUC, that a march had to go down the Garvaghy Road. The Irish side listened intently and clearly appreciated being given an insight into the Secretary of State's current thinking. She also emphasised the Government's commitment to implementing North, while bringing out that it was unlikely to be achieved in time for this year's marching season.
QUENTIN THOMAS


Document 13  Address by the Taoiseach, Mr John Bruton, T.D. to the Oxford Union, Wednesday, 7 May 1997


Mr. President,

I am honoured by your Invitation to address the Oxford Union this evening.

I do so with a sense of history, a theme to which I will return shortly. I do so also with a sense of immediacy. On this, a visit during which I will meet, for the first tune as Prime Minister, Tony Blair and his colleagues, I come with a sense that an historic breakthrough is possible in Northern Ireland.

A detailed plan for peace is already in place. It consists of two elements:-

- a talks process open to all parties and involving the two Governments;
- an end to IRA violence.

The Irish Government has, with the British Government, delivered the first clement – the all-inclusive talks process. The talks [began] in Belfast on 10 June last year and resume, following national and local Northern Ireland elections, on 3 June less than four weeks from to-day.

I welcome Dr. Mowlam's Statement on Saturday, on her appointment as Secretary of State, that it is her aim, through these talks, to reach a fair, long-term political accommodation. At my meeting tomorrow afternoon with the Prime Minister, I will be offering the whole-hearted co-operation of the Irish Government in this project.

It is now time for the Republican Movement to deliver the second element of the peace plan – the long promised IRA ceasefire.

The Republican Movement should make up its mind, once and for all, unreservedly to enter the political process, and throw away for good die crutch of violence or threatened violence. Once it does that, the road to peace and prosperity is open to all.

This moment of opportunity was not easy to construct There have been difficult and patient negotiations along the way but the plan for peace now available includes the following elements. Many of these were put in place during the IRA ceasefire, giving the lie to the myth that "nothing happened" during the ceasefire. Let me list the elements of the plan for peace already in place:

- first, the Irish and British Governments have agreed the Joint Framework Document. This document, jointly launched by John Major and me in February, 1995, sets out our shared understanding of the political structures which might form a basis for a comprehensive political settlement. It commands the support of all the major political parties in Dublin and in London,
- second, to deal with decommissioning, an International Group, chaired by Senator George Mitchell, was set up and has reported to both Governments on how the issue might best be dealt with.

- third, the parties already in the talks have successfully negotiated Rules of Procedures. These were published on 29 July 1996 and are there for all to see;
- fourth, a role has been agreed for a group of independent, impartial, international chairmen. They have already shown their considerable skill, energy and patience;
- fifth, the Dublin Forum for Peace and Reconciliation has reported. For fifteen months, Sinn Fein had the opportunity to work with all the political parties represented in our parliament and with the SDLP, the Alliance Party and the Workers' Party front Northern Inland in this Forum. That Forum opportunity will be re-opened for them when the IRA declares a ceasefire;
- sixth, during the IRA ceasefire, the Irish Government joined with others in gaining top level access for Sinn Fein in the United States;
- seventh, during the ceasefire, the British Government rescinded Exclusion Orders (on prominent members of the Republican Movement) in March 1995;
- eighth, both Governments lifted broadcasting restrictions on [Sinn Fein] representatives;
- ninth, British military patrolling in support of the RUC in Northern Ireland was reduced by 75% during the ceasefire;
- tenth, the National Emergency was formally ended in my jurisdiction and. with the taking of that step, the Emergency Powers Act 1976 expired;
- eleventh, 36 IRA prisoners in my jurisdiction were allowed early release during the IRA ceasefire;
- twelfth, the Convention on the Transfer of Sentenced Persons was signed and brought into force, opening the way for Irish prisoners in British jails to be transferred to Irish jails;
- thirteenth, the British Government restored remission rates for prisoners in Northern Ireland to 50%. This led to the early release of a significant number of prisoners.
- fourteenth, and most importantly, we set up the all-inclusive talks process, open to Sinn Fein, to which I have already referred.

These are but some of the measures taken to facilitate reconciliation for the Republican Movement during the 16 months of the IRA ceasefire, and most of them were done since I became Taoiseach.

There is a phrase in French, "to reunite the circumstances". It means, I think, that a stage can be reached where everything is in place for something to happen. Everything is now in place to end the agony of Northern Ireland. If we fail to move forward towards a settlement, the excuses for inertia on one side or the other will gain credence.

Is it really our wish to allow hardliners in the paramilitary Organisations to argue that the only language other people understand is the language of murder?

Is IT REALY our wish to allow the high priests and reverend doctors of inertia to fall back once again on the delusion that violence is the only thing wrong with Northern Ireland and that the extirpation of certain other political groups is the one thing required for a solution?

Is it really our wish, as Seamus Heaney once said about a political killing, "to hug our little destiny again?"

Mr President – The republican movement is at a crossroads. They have said they will end violence if only they can be part of a meaningful negotiation on the future of Ireland. The British and Irish Governments have said that they can be part of such negotiation if only they end violence. If they make good their promise to take the political road, the two Governments will receive them at the gates of Stormont Buildings into inclusive talks where no topic is excluded and all the relevant players are present.

On the other hand, the republican movement may choose not to suspend their campaign of violence at all, or to half-suspend it, and as someone has put it well, to combine syntax and surtax [?]. Under those circumstances the Irish Government and the parties representing the majority of Nationalists in Northern Ireland will not postpone progress in the negotiations in Belfast. The Irish Government will not for their sake withhold the hand of friendship from our Unionist neighbours. The Irish and British democracies will not be the hostages of the republican movement. We want peace, but we will not compromise our democratic values.

Mr President – Allow me also to address myself directly to Unionists in Northern Ireland. You will remember the lines of the Northern Protestant poet John Hewitt about his own people:

> "this is our country also, nowhere else;
> and we shall not be outcast on the world".

The pressure under which Unionists have been placed by the provisional IRA, not least in border areas, makes these lines especially poignant I want to say without reservations that the Unionist and Nationalist traditions have equal validity. We recognise the right of the one million Unionists in Northern Ireland to be British – "to be what you are, where you are", as a party colleague of mine once said.

What my government is looking for today is a recognition by Unionists that Nationalists too must be allowed to be what they are, where they are – to have a System of Government to which they can give full-hearted allegiance.

Unionists have argued that a compromise with Nationalists will not be a compromise, but a first step that will lead inevitably to a united Ireland. There are fears here that must be genuinely addressed. I would not only expect but welcome a searching Investigation of these issues by Unionist negotiators at the Stormont talks. That is the best place, face to face across the table, where these fears can be addressed.

What I find more difficult to understand is that, after a whole year, the talks have failed to move to the consideration of substantive issues within the Three Strands, because Unionists want a tougher position on decommissioning – tougher even than either the Mitchell Report or the two Governments envisage.

Unionists have resisted violent terrorism for twenty-five years. If there was an end to violence, what, by comparison, is there to fear from sitting at a table with Sinn Fein? If republicans cannot bomb Unionists into a united Ireland, how likely is it that they could trick or talk them into it against their will? No Chance. Unionists have nothing to fear from talks, once the threat of violence is off the table.

My appeal to Unionists is this. Let us all raise our sights this summer and enter the substantive negotiations. Let us focus on the real issue, which is the content and quality of a comprehensive accommodation between the two communities, the two allegiances, which share the same lands and [illegible], and will always do so.

Let me now return to the sense of history of which no visitor to your Union can fail to be conscious. From the 1880s until the First World War, the issue of Home Rule for Ireland was as prominent an issue here in the Oxford Union as in the political life of these islands. Home Rule sought to accommodate Irish Nationalism by giving a united Ireland local autonomy within the United Kingdom. In this way, it was hoped to solve the two main problems at once: the relationship between the communities in Ireland and the relationship between the two Islands. It was an attempt at a new beginning.

The two Prime Ministers most closely Associated with this attempt, Gladstone and Asquith were ex-Presidents of the Oxford Union. I understand that the very first practising politicians to visit the Oxford Union for debates, T. P. O'Connor, Lord Randolph Churchill and John Morley, came here in the 1880s to speak on Home Rule. On 6th June 1907, almost ninety years ago, the leader of the Irish Parliamentary Party, John Redmond addressed the Union on the motion "That in the opinion of this House, Ireland should have the right to manage her own affairs". The motion was carried by 359 votes to 226.

But Home Rule was not to be. Although every family in Ireland, North and South, Catholic and Protestant, had relatives in the trenches of World War One, and although many of the 49,000 Irishmen who died in that war believed that they were fighting for Gladstone's vision of the future, by the time of the Armistice in 1918, history, as history does, had moved on.

The Irish Republic was declared in front of the General Post Office in Dublin at Easter 1916. From this action, in gestation for many years. flowed a more ambitious agenda for Irish Nationalists. In 1920, Lloyd George's Government brought in the Government of Ireland Act partitioning Ireland and offering what was in effect Home Rule to each part. But it was too late to halt the course of events. The Anglo-Irish Treaty was signed in December 1921. During the Treaty negotiations, Lloyd George looked forward to a common Irish future assisted by what he described as the "benevolent neutrality" of the British Government.

But the Unionist minority based in Northern Ireland had been determined long since to oppose a united Ireland, even under Home Rule. It was inevitable that they would be reluctant to become too closely involved with an Irish State emerging from the difficult circumstances of 1919 to 1921.

Let us pause here. The turmoil and suffering of the 19th century had brought forth Gladstone's vision of economic and political justice for an Ireland enjoying Home Rule within the United Kingdom. For some years, perhaps until the fall of Parnell in 1891, it seemed just possible that Gladstone had found the answer to the Irish Question. But in the following generation, up to the Treaty of 1921, events in Ireland evolved rapidly and unpredictably, as indeed could be said of European history as a whole over the same period. Anyone in the 1880s who spoke of new horizons in Irish-British relations was right, but would have found it hard to foretell the solution that came to pass between 1920 and 1922: an independent Irish State in twenty-six counties, deeply divided from the six counties of Northern Ireland, against the background of a political gulf between Ireland and Britain.

The Settlement of 1922 was in many respects a success. But we would be doing ourselves a disservice to deny that that settlement, emerging very rapidly in very contentious circumstances, fell short of accommodating satisfactorily the interests of everyone. The most troubling residue of difficulty was in Northern Ireland.

To speak in crude terms, the problem for London in the 19th Century, for Irish Nationalists at the beginning of the 20th Century, and for Unionists from the 1920s, has been the same problem: how to conciliate a disaffected minority so that it would not seek to break away but would settle instead for an accommodation within a larger unit. Westminster, perhaps inevitably, was unable to conciliate Ireland as a whole. A united Ireland. even under Home Rule, was prevented by the determined Opposition of the Unionist minority in Ireland. In the 1920s, the border made the Unionists in Northern Ireland the local majority. But the border also locked in with those Unionists a new and substantial Nationalist minority.

If majority-minority tension is the subject, and history a camera, then the lens that bad taken in first the whole of Britain and Ireland, and then the Island of Ireland was now zooming in on the narrow ground of Northern Ireland. The question was this: could the Unionist majority conciliate their own minority so that Northern Nationalists would accept what had been done and settle down within the new area?

It may be argued whether Nationalists would have ever settled down on the basis of a fair deal within Northern Ireland. They were conscious that a somewhat arbitrary line had been drawn on the map. The rest of Ireland was close by. They, the Nationalists, were themselves in a majority across much of the territory of Northern Ireland. Demography might work in their favour to undermine an unacceptable arrangement.

But whatever the prospects may have been for creating a unified society in Northern Ireland, the effort was not made. The Unionist Party, in government at Stormont for fifty years, did nothing to carry through an agenda of conciliation, or to co-opt the Nationalist minority to acceptance of the 1922 Settlement.

In talking of the residue of the 1920s, I believe that we in the South should recognise that another part of that residue was the narrowness of the society that we ourselves created. In the absence of the countervailing influence of Northern Protestants, our way of life took on some of the assumptions of the Roman Catholic Church of that time. It is important to preserve balance in our judgements. We resisted, let it be said, the forces which in other parts of Europe produced Mussolini's Concordat, and the constitutions of Franco and Salazar. But in the eyes of many Unionists, and of some of our own citizens, the Republic of Ireland was in the 1930s, 1940s and 1950s a place far from the mainstream of life.

In the 1970s, for the first time since the Settlement of 1922, a new and broader Vision for the future of these Islands became possible. The present era in Northern Ireland could be said to have begun in June 1968 when Austin Currie, formerly of the SDLP and now a minister in my own Government, engaged in the first direct action of the civil rights campaign, by staging a sit-in in a council house at Caledon, Co. Tyrone. Mr Currie was protesting against the allocation of this house to an unmarried

Protestant woman instead of to a Catholic family, by a Unionist-dominated local authority.

At another level, and as an annotation to my basic point, it could be said that the 1944 Act, which meant so much to the Catholic minority in Northern Ireland was in turn the trigger of the civil rights movement. The generation of Northern Irish Catholics which included Austin Currie, John Hume and Seamus Heaney, and so many other potential leaders in the political and cultural spheres got the education which ensured that they would never be corralled, as earlier generations had been, by the un-balanced winner-takes-all dispensation of Stormont.

Both the SDLP and the Alliance Party were founded in 1970 as par-ties committed to peaceful means and to an honourable accommodation between Nationalists and Unionists. Since then, it has been clear that un-qualified Unionist majority rule would never bring stability to Northern Inland. The challenge has been to find a new basis for stability.

As we look at the ideas and options that began to shape themselves at that time, I believe it is relevant to look also at the surrounding cir-cumstances. These were very different than in the era of Gladstone and Parnell. One obvious change was the end of the European empires. In the Eurocentric world of the generation before World War One, the standard Unionist argument was that Irish independence, or the abandonment of loyal Unionists, would be the beginning of the dissolution of the Empire with all that that was supposed to mean for civilisation itself. Nations like the Irish, on the other hand, struggling towards independence and the preservation and full expression of their cultural identity, may, perhaps. have over-accentuated their undoubted distinctiveness, and over-stressed what is expressed in the Irish words, Sinn Fein, meaning "ourselves alone". International affairs are seen very differently today than in 1914. The new approach creates a new menu of options for solving the age-old problem of division in Ulster.

A collective approach to security, of course a very fragile construct, began to crystallise after the First World War. After the Second World War, this collective approach was intensified with added urgency. It also came to be appreciated that nation states, if they avoid coming into con-flict, must deliberately develop and accentuate the interests they have in common. This was reflected in the Charter of the United Nations in the role given to the UN on economic and social questions. It is reflected most of all by Germany's attempt to subsume German nationalism in a new united European identity. For the sake of harmony in the 21st Century, this attempt must succeed and every European state has a responsibility to build unity in Europe.

One of the most impressive aspects of international politics at the end of the 20th Century is the recognition that to inhabit common ground, to live and move in the same space, requires that we share common values. A straight forward example is that respect for human rights is now a legitimate subject in international diplomacy. Among the religious traditions, it is increasingly understood that actions unite, abstractions divide. The Christian traditions, except in pockets here and there, have adopted dialogue as the way forward in relations among themselves and with those of other cultural backgrounds. The search for common values is in part a response to complexity. The volume of contacts across borders, the mixing of ethnic groups. the pace of scientific research, the trade in money, information, and financial instruments that has overtaken the trade in goods and services; the pressure on resources like oil, water, and air – all of this is likely to elude political authority if politics relies on national measures of control alone. To produce integrated and cohesive societies, governments need to encourage common values. In particular, we need to find the means of translating personal values which we all still recognise, such as responsibility in relationships and the readiness to share, into a way of life at the level of states, regions, business, and the international community.

The growing interest in the ethics of public affairs has been matched by another phenomenon of the late twentieth century, the constructive involvement of third parties in situation of conflict. Investigation and mediation have been accompanied by aid and investment. It is not surprising, therefore, that the United States, the European Union, and a number of other governments and organisations have in one way or another put their services at the disposal of the Northern Ireland parties. The technique of "working the common ground" as John Hume puts it, is fundamental and explicit in the European Community, or as we now call it, the European Union.

Europe bas always impacted on Irish affairs. At the turn of the 19th Century, the Napoleonic Wars brought about the Act of Union; at the turn of the 20th Century, the Great War in Europe created the conditions for its repeal in most of Ireland. The European element in the Irish equation is now very different. As the 21st Century approaches, the states of Europe have developed new modes of co-operation and mutual accountability – what might be called coalition politics on an international scale – for the simple reason that it promotes peace. This is an opportunity for peace in Ireland. One of the most famous things ever said about Northern Ireland was said by Winston Churchill after the end of the First World War in a Speech to the House of Commons: "The modes of thought of men, the whole outlook on affairs, the groupings of parties all have encountered violent and tremendous change in the deluge of the world. But as the deluge subsides and the waters fall short, we see the dreary steeples of Fermanagh and Tyrone emerging once more. The integrity of their quarrel is one of the few institutions that has been unaltered in the cataclysm which has swept the world." What Churchill was saying in 1921 about a lack of perspective in Northern Ireland was even more obviously true by the 1970s. In the modern era "the modes of thought of men, the whole outlook on affairs" point overwhelmingly to new ways of reconciling differences in Northern Ireland. Will the parties in Northern Ireland adapt themselves to these new perspectives?

The Americans have the concept of a zero sum game. In a zero sum game, the gains on one side of the ledger equal losses somewhere else. It is impossible for me to win unless you, to the same degree, lose out. In the middle years of this century, the politics of Northern Ireland seemed to many a zero sum game. By the 1970s, a more sophisticated approach became possible. It was understood that an honourable accommodation could benefit both Nationalists and Unionists. A Settlement could be devised under which neither side would claim victory and neither suffer a defeat.

Another very important change of circumstance as between past generations and the present is the change that has come over the Republic of Ireland. The country whose government I head can no longer be accused, as we have been in the past, of turning our backs on the world. We have just completed our fourth Presidency of the European Union. President

Robinson is a candidate for the position of UN High Commissioner for Human Rights. Seamus Heaney, U2, Riverdance are Irish-based but outward-looking. Through people of Irish background and through visitors to our own shores we have the closest of links to this country, to the United States, to Australia, to the European continent. As a percentage of GNP, our exports of goods and services are the highest in the OECD with the possible exception of Belgium. I am almost tempted to make the claim of an over-enthusiastic Speaker in Joyce' s *Ulysses*, that "our galleys furrow the waters of the known globe!"

Nor can it be said that we lag behind economically. In the period up to 1959, the Irish economy was relatively stagnant. But since the 1960s, and in particular in more recent years, our economy has been changing beyond recognition. Net disposable income per head is now close to the British level and to the European average. In a recent article, one of my Fine Gael predecessors as Taoiseach, Dr Garret FitzGerald, ventured that the catching up process in the Irish economy has no European parallel since the recoveries of the German, Italian and Greek economies in the aftermath of the last war. For a number of reasons, including the age structure of our population, our system of education, and a practice of social partnership, there is every prospect that our economy will continue to grow at rates well in excess of the European average. One of the most important consequences of social and economic change in Ireland has been an evolving attitude towards Northern Ireland. But that is a special subject to which I will return in a few moments.

An account of the improved circumstances for a new approach to Northern Ireland is incomplete without touching on British-Irish relations as a whole. History has left Britain and Ireland with more in common than any other two sovereign states in Europe or perhaps anywhere in the world. We share not one but two languages - English and Gaelic. We share the same religious and political traditions. Ireland, like Britain, is a common-law country, although with a written constitution. That we share the same genetic pool is a minor point compared to the number of Irish families with relatives in Britain, or English, Scottish, or Welsh families who have an Irish relative. We read the same authors, watch the same television programmes, and support many of the same football teams. In rugby. there is both a single all-lreland team and a joint British-Irish team.

It is obvious that Britain is, and will always remain, Ireland's most important trading partner. What is less widely known is that the volume of trade in the other direction is such that we, although one sixteenth of your population, are now Britain's fifth most important trading partner in the world.

If one considers the rights and obligations of citizenship, Irish citizens in Britain are on something very close to the same footing as British subjects themselves. The same applies to British people living in Ireland. We vote in one another's elections. We can travel and settle down freely in one another's countries. We can take employment in one another's public Services. These British-lrish exchanges are of particular importance for Northern Ireland but they are also important I believe, for the wider British-Irish relationship. I welcome that under the Ireland Act, 1949, the Republic of Ireland is not a "foreign country" for the purposes of any law enforced in any part of the United Kingdom.

In sum, one of the advantages we have enjoyed in recent decades in working out new approaches for Northern Ireland is the uniqueness of the Anglo-Irish relationship. The intimacy of relationships within these Islands makes Northern Ireland qualitatively different to any other divided society in Europe.

Mr President – I have argued that from the 1970s on, the circumstances have been propitious for a new approach to Northern Ireland. I have suggested that the emergence of new political leadership, in particular within the nationalist community, made change inevitable. I have tried to describe the favourable international background, some of the changes in the Republic of Ireland, and the quality of the wider British-lrish relationships, within which we jointly face the Northern Ireland issue. That picture, which I believe in its essentials to be true, has been clouded or complicated by the emergence of the provisional IRA. or should I say its re-emergence, at roughly the same time as the SDLP and in direct competition with that democratic political party. As long as there is a breakdown in trust between the authorities of the state and a section of its people, there is scope for a secret paramilitary organisation to present itself as a

line of defence. We have seen that this can happen on the either side of
the community in Northern Ireland. It would be a mistake, however, to
accept this as AN explanation of the IRA campaign. What the IRA has in
fact done is to exploit the uncertain situation in Northern Inland to pursue
what would be seen in modern European thinking, as a maximalist and
profoundly archaic objective for a society that is divided in its allegiances.
Normal feelings of insecurity have been harnessed to an out-of-date and
unrealistic ideology. The aggressive strategy of terrorism has no mandate
from the people of Ireland. Equally, Irish democracy repudiates the insidious
strategy of the Armalite and the ballot box, the combination of violence
and of electoral policy. An ideology of forced unity is rejected. It is out of
date It is inhuman. It is alien to the Irish nature.

Mr President – On the British side, it was an ex-President of the Oxford
Union, Sir Edward Heath, who, as Prime Minister in 1972, first recognised
the scope for a new approach to Northern Ireland. In the course of 1972.
the Heath Government prorogued the parliament at Stormont. It did so
mainly because it had come to accept that a Westminster type parliamentary
System, which in practice resulted in permanent one-party rule in Northern
Ireland, was no longer tolerable. Within a few months of taking this step,
the British Government produced a Green Paper and then a White Paper
outlining the concepts by which it proposed to be guided in its future policy
on Northern Ireland. The approach in those two papers has been progressively codified over the intervening twenty-five years. One thinks, for example, of the Sunningdale Agreement of 1973; the Joint Studies of 1980/
81; the Anglo-Irish Agreement of 1985; the Downing Street Declaration of
December 1993; the Framework Document of March 1955; and the launch
of political talks in Belfast [under] wider international chairmanship in
June 1996. When historians look back on this period, they will notice a
remarkable consistency of purpose in British and Irish Government policy
from 1972 onwards. Of course, there have been concrete developments
and changes in thinking between the Heath Government's Green Paper
of October 1972 and the Framework Document jointly published by my
own Government and the Government of Mr. Major in March 1995. But
the key elements in the approach of the two Governments have evolved in
a consistent, organic way over the entire period. The talks process which

began last year and resumes on 3 June is the crystallisation, or coming to fruition, of the efforts of a quarter Century.

The first of the guiding ideas shared by the British and Irish Governments is that London and Dublin should work together. This co-operative approach was given formal expression in the Anglo-Irish Agreement of 1985, a Treaty registered at the United Nations. But even before the Anglo-Irish Agreement, and outside the sphere of that agreement, the two Governments have learned to work together. Why should this be? I believe it has to do with the intimacy within these islands to which I have already referred. We have come to recognise that a Settlement in Northern Ireland must have an eye to history, and take into account all the relevant relationships: within Northern Ireland, within the island of Ireland, and between the two islands. In working together the two Governments seek to provide a moral centre of gravity, an anchor, in a situation where deep divisions produce deep emotions. London and Dublin have more "psychological space" than the parties in Northern Ireland. If between us we can agree on what is fair and feasible, we can restrain the flight from compromise and the multiplication of theories which are so often the consequence of conflict.

A second element of understanding concerns the stance of the British Government. Drawing on what the King, the then Prime Minister, and many others started at the time of the Anglo-Irish settlement of 1922, the British government has made it clear that its primary interest is to see peace, stability and reconciliation established by agreement among all the people who inhabit the Island of Ireland.

A third element of understanding is that the Irish Government, and Irish Nationalists in Northern Ireland, would be ready to work an accommodation falling short of a United Ireland. This key point is often poorly understood by Unionists. It is worth recalling some of the background. Membership of the European Union has placed our relationship with Britain in a fresh perspective. Violence in Northern Ireland has forced a reappraisal of the more simplistic assumptions of traditional nationalism. Essentially the conflict between the unionist and nationalist traditions on the island has come to be seen by many Irish people as a conflict, not between right and wrong, but between two parallel and potentially compatible sets of rights. A Conference of constitutional Nationalist parties of the island of Ireland held in Dublin in 1983 and 1984 under the title "The New Ireland Forum" gave expression to the flexibility that had been developing in Nationalist thinking for over a decade by tabulating a series of preferences. The first preference was indeed a United Ireland, the second a federal or confederal Ireland, the third, joint British-Irish sovereignty in Northern Ireland. But crucially the Forum also allowed that some other alternative to the three preferences might emerge from negotiation. The work of the Forum enabled Garret FitzGerald and Margaret Thatcher to go on to conclude the Anglo-Irish Agreement in which, among other things, the two Governments affirmed that "any change in the status of Northern Ireland would only come about with the consent of a majority of the people of Northern Ireland". That was a logical progression from earlier thinking.

A Conference modelled on the New Ireland Forum, entitled the Forum for Peace and Reconciliation, met in Dublin from 1994 to 1996 with a wider participation than the New Ireland Forum. This time, the participating parties included the Alliance Party and Sinn Fein. The Forum prepared a document entitled "Paths to a Political Settlement: Realities, Principles and Requirements". This document, which was largely but not fully agreed, states that a substantial consensus has developed around the acceptance by the Irish Government that the democratic right of self-determination by the people of Ireland as a whole must be exercised subject to the agreement and consent of a majority of the people of Northern Ireland. In this, it was simply reflecting an undoubted fact.

Seamus Heaney's career as poet has spanned the entire period since the Civil Rights campaign of 1968. When he received the Nobel Prize at the end of 1995, his Speech touched on his own response to Ireland's political difficulties and gave what I believe is a true reflection of much of the new thinking among those who come from the Nationalist tradition in Ireland:

"The crux of that problem involves an ongoing partition of the island between British and Irish jurisdictions, and an equally persistent partition of the affections in Northern Ireland between the British and Irish heritages, but surely every dweller in the country must hope that the Governments involved in its governance can devise institutions which will allow that partition to become a bit more like the net on a tennis court, a demarcation allowing for agile give-and-take, for encounter and contending, prefiguring a future where the vitality that flowed in the beginning from those bracing words "enemy" and 'allies' might finally derive from a less binary and altogether less binding vocabulary."

In an article in last week's *Irish Times*, Prime Minister Blair looked forward to replacing the direct rule of Northern Ireland by Westminster by a new three-stranded agreement. In the parlance of Northern Ireland politics, the three Strands refer respectively to political structures within Northern Ireland, the North-South relationship in Ireland, and the British-Irish or East-West relationship. As to Strand One, the 1972 Green Paper called for "power-sharing" between the representatives of the two main communities or traditions, Unionist and Nationalist. The 1972 Green Paper also recognised an "Irish dimension" to the governance of Northern Ireland. The Irish dimension, which is subject of Strand Two, was not of course a new idea. A fundamental part of the original 1920–1921 compromise was that the creation of a separate Northern Parliament and the continuing constitutional links between the North and Britain would be paralleled by strong North-South links. What was perhaps new in 1972 and what has survived in our thinking, is that a strong all-Ireland dimension is an important reassurance for Northern Nationalist that the new dispensation we envisage for Northern Ireland will take practical account of their identity. As well as a North-South dimension, there will be an East-West dimension to a lasting settlement. This will be negotiated in Strand Three. The two Governments look forward to developing an "Institutional recognition" of the special links that exist between the peoples of Britain and Ireland. We are ready to replace the Anglo-Irish Agreement by a new Agreement taking into account what has been agreed under the Three Strands.

The two Governments have also come to appreciate the importance of confidence-building measures, a term borrowed from the international diplomacy of the 1970s. Dr. Peter North, the outgoing Vice-Chancellor of this University, is the co-author of the Independent Review of Parades and Marches which has broken important new ground in helping us to understand the relationship between parades and marches and the underlying political problems of Northern Ireland. The North Report speaks of the "symbolic nature" of parades, "allowing them to mean different things to different people". One of the most important confidence-building measures

in Northern Ireland in the immediate future will be to ensure that the con-
sensual approach to parades recommended by Dr North and his colleagues
replaces confrontation on the streets. It will be helpful if those involved
in dialogue about parades, both Unionists and Nationalists, make more
sparing use of the term "rights", which often seems intended to end all discussion, and more generous use of terms such as "interests" and "concerns".

As Dr Marjorie Mowlam has pointed out, there are many other areas
in which confidence-building measures are desirable. The onus to undertake such measures is on political parties and paramilitary organisations
as well as on Governments. I will mention just one area of particular concern, prisons issues. If reconciliation and a new beginning are possible, a
sensitivity to the concerns of prisoners will be the proof. For example, it is
in keeping with policy throughout these Islands to transfer as many prisoners as possible to prisons close to their families.

Mr President – What I have been describing is a "fund of ideas" built
up in a coherent and consistent way by the British and Irish Governments
over twenty-five years. These ideas are still opposed in some quarters, by
politicians who want only a unitary Irish State and by harder-line Unionists
who adopt an inverse territorial agenda in United Kingdom terms. These
groups have more in common than they appreciate. Both rely on absolute notions of sovereignty devised at the Peace of Westphalia in the 17th
Century and by Blackstone in the 18th Century, in the service of long past
political interests of that time. Neither dogmatic unionists nor dogmatic
republicans are in touch with the more hopeful developments of the 20th
Century. In the politics of today, it is a safe rule of thumb that those who
advocate brusque and simple solutions place a discount on the convictions
of others. It is also a rule of thumb that the simpler the solution proposed,
the more ready is the proposer to rely ultimately on force. But the politics
of accommodation, and of learning to live with complexity, have become
the hallmark of maturity in public life. I have already spoken of the United
Nations and the European Union. I could as easily have mentioned the
imaginative and equitable constitutional models promoted by Britain in
Canada, Australia and South Africa, or the skills in coalition-building that
we have learned in Irish politics. The three-stranded approach in Northern

Ireland goes with the grain of history. Fundamentalism is an unsignposted road to disaster.

Mr President – The two Governments and the parties m Northern Ireland are, as I said at the outset, now face-to-face with an opportunity, unparalleled in our history, to put behind us the troubles of centuries. Gladstone's Vision of the 1880s, a courageous effort against the background of Empire to base relationships within these Islands on friendship and understanding, led to the settlement of 1922 with its residue of difficulty. From the 1970s onwards, against the background of common British and Irish membership of the European Union, a new spirit in [illegible] and in politics, and an economic renaissance in Ireland, we have developed a fund of shared ideas from which to negotiate a comprehensive settlement. The work of a whole generation is coming to its [illegible] now. The public mood is overwhelmingly for peace.

Mr President – Your invitation to me this evening, and the interest of the Oxford Union in Ireland through successive generations, speaks to me of something profound m British-Irish relations. and in politics as a whole. There is another dimension to politics. I am referring to the ability to forgive. In the course of a recent interview for the *Daily Telegraph*, the Secretary of State for Northern Ireland, Dr Mowlam, told about some of her personal experiences, "I have learnt to have a short memory when it comes to anger and shame." What hope is there in the Middle East, or among the formerly warring nation states of Europe, or for Africa, or for any one of us, if this insight is not brought to bear? If we fail to join Dr Mowlam in training that short memory?

In his speech to the House of Commons which I have already quoted, Churchill referred to "the power which Ireland has, both Nationalist and Orange, to lay its hands upon the vital strings of British life and politics." It is in the relationship with Ireland – and for those of us in politics in Dublin, in the relationship with the parties in Northern Ireland and with Britain – that we come unavoidably into contact with problems that can only be resolved in the light of unseen values, unseen values which are yet the most important values of all.

In 1825, the Oxford Union debated Ireland for the first time. The motion that the Act of Union was not beneficial to Ireland was carried by a narrow margin. Thus began an unbroken interest of this Union in Ireland over the best part of two centuries. As recently as January, the Oxford Union staged a Northern Ireland Forum bringing together among others, the then Secretary of State, Patrick Mayhew, John Hume, and David Trimble. By choosing a non-adversarial format, the Union reflected in its own way the seriousness of purpose which political parties have demonstrated by observing bipartisanship on Northern Ireland. The time has come to answer what so many speakers in this Chamber have known as the question of Ireland. In this generation, and in advance of the 21st Century, we can transform our differences into bonds of understanding within these islands and into a sign of hope for others all over the world whose lives are disrupted by an unwelcome legacy from the past.

## Document 14  Meeting between the Prime Minister and the Secretary of State for Northern Ireland

10 DOWNING STREET
LONDON SW1A 2AA

From the Private Secretary

7 May 1997

### NORTHERN IRELAND

The Prime Minister held a meeting with your Secretary of State today to have a first go over the ground, on the basis of Dr Mowlam's minute to him of 6 May.

NO FURTHER COPIES SHOULD BE MADE of this letter, and it should be made available ONLY to other Ministers and officials with a STRICT NEED to KNOW of its contents.

The Prime Minister said that he saw the Government's main aim in the present situation in relatively simple terms: to bring Sinn Fein into talks without losing the Unionists. The obvious way to get a ceasefire and Sinn Fein in was to offer a date for their entry into talks, but this would alienate the Unionists. It would therefore be necessary to combine this approach with reassurance to the Unionists about Government policy.

Dr Mowlam and your officials agreed this was the objective. But they argued that, with the best will in the world, it would be difficult if not impossible to bring in Sinn Fein without losing the Unionists, probably including the UUP, at least for a time. It was hard to identify specific moves to keep the Unionists on board in the short term. The current talks process might also be a casualty. But this should not be irretrievable and a "period of turbulence" would be worth it if a credible ceasefire could be achieved and Sinn Fein brought into the political process.

After a long discussion, the following approach was agreed:

- Sinn Fein should be told, through a low-level telephone call, that a reply to their approaches would come before too long. The message should also be got across that more violence could ruin everything for them;
- the Prime Minister should visit Northern Ireland on Friday, 16 May in order to give a speech about the new Government's approach. This would need to be balanced but its main purpose would be to assure the Unionists in person that there was no threat to the Union, since the consent principle and a referendum on any political settlement were essential parts of the Government's thinking;
- shortly thereafter a letter would be sent to Sinn Fein, on the lines of the draft attached to Dr Mowlam's minute, making clear that discussions with officials were possible.

A meeting between officials and Sinn Fein would follow thereafter, assuming no violence in the meantime. Officials would explore Sinn Fein's views and clarify those of the Government. No date for entry into talks would be offered immediately but this was a card which could be played at the right moment, if events on the ground continued to permit this.

I would be grateful for rapid advice on the shape of the proposed visit to Northern Ireland and for a very early outline of the proposed speech.

I am copying this to Jan Polley (Cabinet Office).

JOHN HOLMES

K. Lindsay, Esq., Northern Ireland Office.
From the Private Secretary
10 DOWNING STREET. LONDON SW1A 2AA7
May 1997

## Document 15   Call by the UUP, 7 May

10 DOWNING STREET
LONDON SW1A 2AA

From the Private Secretary

7 May 1997

Dear Ken,

The Prime Minister decided that, before he saw the Taoiseach, he would like to touch base in person with David Trimble. Trimble therefore called on the Prime Minister in the House of Commons for 10 minutes this afternoon, accompanied by Geoffrey Donaldson. Jonathan Powell and I were there on our side.

Trimble began by thanking the Prime Minister for seeing him. This would be an important signal to the Unionist community. The Prime Minister said that in the ideal world he would not have been seeing the Taoiseach so soon, but he was in town anyway and a meeting could hardly be avoided. Trimble accepted this. But the Irish were busy trying to make something of the meeting and giving the impression that things were being done behind the backs of others.

The Prime Minister said that his aim was to sort out the Northern Ireland problem. He had no predilection whatsoever for a united Ireland, and he would want to find the right way of making this clear in due course.

Trimble welcomed this. There was considerable nervousness on doorsteps in Belfast about the views of the new government. He hoped the Prime Minister would be able to spell his approach out before the summer got under way, because this would help Northern Ireland get through the summer without serious trouble. He hoped the Prime Minister would reassure the people of Northern Ireland of his objectives and set out his principles. It would be better to stick to the level of principles, while saying relatively little about day to day issues in Northern Ireland. Above all, hostages to fortune and sudden moves should be avoided. There was for example considerable concern about the idea of radical change to the RUC, which appeared to respond to an IRA agenda.

Returning to the talks, <u>Trimble</u> said that there was a desperate shortage of time before 3 June. A lot of thought needed to go into this, and he hoped to meet the Prime Minister again with more time available to go through the problems he saw, both about the talks process and the aim.

The <u>Prime Minister</u> asked where Trimble would want to see Northern Ireland in two or three years. <u>Trimble</u> said that he would want to see all the issues settled, with the claim in the Irish Constitution removed, satisfactory cross-border cooperation, and a reasonable administration in place in Northern Ireland itself. The latter would involve some changes to local government, and a devolved assembly. He was not overly prescriptive about the assembly, and was ready to look at the range of powers it should have. But he thought they should be similar to what was planned for Wales and Scotland. It would be good to arrive at a situation where Northern Ireland politicians could get on with the issues politicians normally concerned themselves with.

<u>Donaldson</u> said that the framework of the settlement needed to be looked at. Previous governments had talked about the totality of relationships in the two islands. But the new Government's policies towards Wales and Scotland created an opportunity to set a new framework across Britain. The <u>Prime Minister</u> asked Trimble's view on where the IRA were going.

<u>Trimble</u> said that they were in some difficulty. A return to full-scale violence was not really possible. At the same time they could not really make the plunge into politics because they were not ready to abandon violence and espouse exclusively peaceful methods. They could become political at some stage, but this would require a split because there were some hard cases in the movement (as there were on the Protestant side too). All in all, he thought that if the Government stayed steady on the fundamental, all would be well.

<u>Donaldson</u> added that the Prime Minister's emphasis on consent in the past, and the Interpretation he had given of it, had been absolutely right. It

would be important to repeat this in any speech. The <u>Prime Minister</u> said that the consent principle was fundamental. It was helpful in weakening the IRA that it was now accepted by everyone else. <u>Trimble</u> agreed but commented that the Sinn Fein vote was still going up.

The <u>Prime Minister</u> concluded that he would meet Trimble again before too long, when he hoped to be able to say more about his plans. He would certainly want to take an opportunity before the summer to demonstrate his complete commitment to the consent principle.
<u>Comment</u>

The atmosphere was very friendly, and Trimble and Donaldson clearly welcomed what the Prime Minister had to say. Their own approach was studiedly reasonable, although both made comments which confirmed that they wish to change the basis of the talks process.

I am copying this to Jan Polley (Cabinet Office).
JOHN HOLMES

Ken Lindsay Esq Northern Ireland Office

## Document 16   Northern Ireland: Implementing the North Report

PRIME MINISTER

From: John Holmes
Date: 7 May 1997

One unresolved issue for the legislative Programme, to be discussed at Cabinet, is whether the implementation of the North Report should be carried forward through primary or secondary legislation. At the moment, it is not being given priority for primary legislation, but there has been no decision to go for secondary legislation.

This is obviously a sensitive political issue for the Unionists. They oppose adjudicatory powers for the independent Parades Commission, and will do so whatever legislative route is taken. But they will feel much more aggrieved if they are denied the chance, as they see it, to attack and at least amend legislation if it is taken through by an Order in Council. The business managers have been thinking of an intermediate possibility, which is an Order in Council which would be amendable through a debate on the floor of the House. But it is not clear that this is do-able, and it would in any case be very much second best for the Unionists.

There is also another important argument. The obvious delay involved in primary legislation provides a perfect cover for delaying implementation of North beyond this summer's marching season. This is something of a confidence-building measure for the Unionists, and is what Mo has in mind anyway.

Mo is likely to raise this at Cabinet herself, but I wanted you to be aware of the arguments. I think you should support her.

JOHN HOLMES

## Document 17 Meeting with Bruton

From: John Holmes

Date: 7 May 1997
PRIME MINISTER
cc: Jonathan Powell
Alastair Campbell
Philip Barton

You will be seeing Bruton for an hour at 1600. We have fixed this in the White Room upstairs, over tea to emphasise its informal, get-to-know-you character. Bruton with be accompanied by Spring; Ted Barrington (Irish Ambassador here and a good thing); Paddy Teahon (my opposite number - cheerful but a bit vague;) and Sean O'hUiginn (the Northern Ireland expert from the Foreign Ministry) '

On our side, you will be accompanied by Robin Cook and Mo Mowlam. There will be no officials other than Jonathan and I – again to emphasise the informal nature of the occasion.

The form is that you should meet Bruton at the door of No. 10 (we will be warned when he is approaching). There is then a photocall in front of the fireplace in the hall, perhaps first with you and Bruton alone and then with accompanying Ministers. We will then all troop upstairs to the White Room.

You know Bruton and Spring already. Bruton is nice, straightforward and violently anti-IRA, but bound to follow a policy designed to bring Sinn Fein into the talks. Spring is greener, but not unreasonably so. Bruton is as good a Taoiseach as we are ever likely to get from a British point of view. He is about to declare elections in Ireland, probably on 6 June. The polls show that the position is extremely finely balanced between his coalition and the Opposition coalition of Ahern (Fianna Fail) and the Progressive Democrats. My guess is that Bruton will just make it, but it could easily be a hung Parliament, which would be bad news all round.

The meeting with you is important to Bruton, and he will want something positive out of it if he can. Ahern tends to accuse him of "losing" the ceasefire and not being tough enough on the British. I have damped down Irish expectations heavily but they are irrepressible.

The Irish economy is doing remarkably well, and the face of the country has been transformed in recent years. As you know, the Irish are very pro-Europe – not surprisingly given the amount of money they get from the EU. They are determined to go into a Single Currency even if Britain does not, but worry about the economic impact. The Irish pound has recently fallen sharply against sterling - this is not unwelcome to the Irish because it makes their exports more competitive, as long as it does not go too far and stoke up inflation. It should also help the punt to go into a Single Currency at a competitive rate in due course.

There are three areas to cover in the discussion: Europe, bilateral ("East West") relations and Northern Ireland.

Bruton is keen to make more of an issue than normal of *bilateral relations*. He made a statement on Monday calling for much greater cooperation in areas of common interest, citing the priorities of your Government as a starting point, notably education. We can happily go along with this and ask the Cabinet Office to liaise with the Irish Government to take this forward, including early meetings between British and Irish Ministers. It all helps to give the relationship substance, and prevent it being completely dominated by Northern Ireland (where things are bound to get scratchy from time to time).

On **Europe**, I suggest you do not need to go much further than the sort of general stuff set out in Doug Henderson's opening statement at the IGC the other day, and the broad approach agreed with Robin Cook. The area of most interest, because we have a common concern, is justice and home affairs (Third Pillar). Because of the Common Travel Area the Irish want to preserve their frontier Controls like us. But they are much more uncomfortable about it than we are and hanker after moving towards Schengen-style free movement across Europe. Nevertheless, we can work together to prevent wholesale communitisation of the Third Pillar. Spring and Robin Cook will no doubt be discussing this separately. In general, you will want to give this first European leader you are meeting the dual message: you are constructive but tough and determined to protect British interests and vetoes in the important areas.

On **Northern Ireland,** the aim must be to sound positive and ready to give fresh impetus to the peace process, without giving anything away on specifics. You can welcome close Cooperation and stress the importance of a new ceasefire (and make clear more violence will make any movement much harder). Bruton is bound to push on whether we are prepared to resume official level talks with Sinn Fein. The Irish are grappling with the same issue themselves. I suggest you say no more than that we are looking carefully at it, and are not necessarily against talking if the circumstances are right. You will want to be very cautious about a date for Sinn Fein's entry to the talks. But you could suggest that you are thinking about a speech on Northern Ireland before too long, in which you would set out your approach in a way designed to reassure all concerned.

A good line to reassure the Irish of your intentions, while keeping them at bay, is to say that pressure from them obviously makes it harder to move in ways which the Unionists will find difficult to accept.

The Irish will also be interested in implementation of North. Again you will want to be cautious for the time being about exactly how and when you will implement the recommendation to give the Independent Parades Commission adjudicatory powers. Meanwhile, you can say that you will be doing all you can to prevent trouble this summer.

Bruton may lobby for Mary Robinson's candidacy to be the new UN High Commissioner on Human Rights. She is an excellent candidate and you can say that we would be very happy if she finished up in the job. But I would be a bit cautious if he asks you to lobby directly for her.

At the end of the meeting, although you are not talking to the Press together, you will want to agree a broad line of what should be said to the Press. Alastair will have been talking to Bruton's spokesman separately but they could perhaps be brought in at the end of the meeting to agree the approach. There is plenty of obvious stuff about the need for a ceasefire, importance of the talks, need to work together, and positive mood music to keep the reptiles happy.

## Document 18 Letter from Gary McMichael, Leader of the Ulster Democratic Party, to the Prime Minister

10 Downing Street,
London SW1 2AA
From the Private Secretary

8 May 1997

I enclose a copy of a letter which the Prime Minister has received from Councillor Gary McMichael, Leader of the Ulster Democratic Party. I should be grateful if you would provide advice and a draft reply for the Prime Minister's signature, to reach this office by Thursday 22 May.

John Holmes

David Kyle, Esq.
Northern Ireland Office.

[Letter from Councillor Gary McMichael missing]

# Document 19   Call by the Taoiseach, 8 May

10 DOWNING STREET
LONDON SW1A2AA

From the Private Secretary

8 May 1997

Dear William,

The Taoiseach, accompanied by the Tanaiste, the Irish Ambassador, Paddy Teahon and Sean O'hUiginn, called on the Prime Minister this afternoon for an hour. The Foreign and Northern Ireland Secretaries, Quentin Thomas, Jonathan Powell and I were present on our side.

After some gossip about respective elections, during which Bruton indicated that he still favoured an early date, <u>Bruton</u> said that he was grateful for the opportunity to meet the Prime Minister so soon after the election. He wanted to cover Europe, Northern Ireland and bilateral Cooperation.

*European Union*

<u>Bruton</u> ran through his speaking note quickly. He welcomed the new Government's decisions to sign up to the Social Chapter and make the Bank of England independent. To a large extent, Britain and Ireland had a common view on Schengen. The Irish Government did not wish to opt out of too many aspects of the third pillar, but equally did not want to lose the Common Travel Agreement.

The <u>Foreign Secretary</u> said that he had been discussing this with the Tanaiste. We too would prefer to avoid wide opt outs in this area. We might need to have flexibility for ourselves over border controls, to which we wished to secure a legal right, but we did not wish to see this elsewhere. The <u>Tanaiste</u> agreed and suggested that the two sides should keep in very close touch about this in the run-up to Amsterdam.

<u>Bruton</u> continued that the Irish had worries about the idea of flexibility, as did the new British Government. Other Irish priorities were a

new employment chapter, where the new British Government's position was welcome, and drugs, which the Irish believed should be covered in the Treaty in their own right. On the institutional side, Ireland was very insistent that each member state should have the right to a Commissioner.

The <u>Prime Minister</u> said that he would be concerned to maintain the veto in areas like defence and foreign policy, and thought that here and in other areas there could be better cooperation without any question of new EU competence or a Commission role. He would be happy to see a new employment chapter, as long as Europe did not become too prescriptive in this area. He would not want to see too much interventionism. Other priorities were enlargement, including arrangements for it, and CAP reform (where he knew Irish views were different, but enlargement made it more important). On the institutional side, we would want to maintain a fair balance in any changes to the Commission and the voting system. More widely, he wanted Britain to play a clear and constructive role in Europe and begin to shape its future.

<u>Bruton</u> raised EMU. Ireland wanted to see Britain in the single currency and the sooner the better. Ireland would certainly be in the first wave. The <u>Prime Minster</u> said that Britain was unlikely to be in the first wave, but would keep her options open. It was nonetheless important that if it went ahead, it was successful. The changes to the Bank of England were incidentally not related to EMU, but sensible changes in their own right. One advantage his Government had over its predecessor was the absence of internal Party differences. The <u>Foreign Secretary</u> added on EMU that he had found genuine understanding of the British position in Paris and Bonn. He had made clear that Britain would not stand in the way of others, and would facilitate the project. But the British position would remain reserved.

The <u>Prime Minister</u> said that it would be important to work closely together on the key areas of the IGC agenda. Coming back from the IGC with a success would be crucial in turning round British attitudes to Europe. The Government had to demonstrate that a more constructive and engaged attitude could produce results. The IGC was a real test, and if there was a set back there, it would be difficult to repair the damage. Ireland could be a significant help.

<u>Bruton</u> said that the new British Government's plans for internal reform should be helpful in showing that sovereignty and power could be

shared. This would hold lessons for Europe. He was keen to see the extension of QMV in the IGC, to prevent the EU becoming bogged down after enlargement. He was also keen to see changes to the way the Commission worked. He agreed too large a Commission was not a good idea, but Santer had little real power at present.

The Foreign Secretary commented that the warm reception for the new Government from fellow Governments had not been matched by that from the Commission, who had already got in two kicks. Bruton sympathised. The Commission had also been effectively interfering in the Irish election campaign in a very sensitive area.

Bruton went on to talk about Kohl and his historic mission to integrate Germany into Europe in order to bury old German demons. This was a vital project, and he had worried that the previous British Government had not understood it. The Prime Minister agreed. His own view was that European Integration was acceptable in principle, as relationships developed naturally. But the problem was the pace and content of moves in this direction. If the pace was too rapid, and the people could not follow, they would worry about losing control of their affairs, and finish up blaming Europe. This could cause political turmoil in many countries. The issues needed to be fundamentally re-thought.

The Prime Minister continued that, in the IGC, it was important not to try to run before we could walk in areas like defence and foreign policy. There was a danger of a mismatch between maturity of European institutions, and the respect in which they were held, and the speed of European Integration. Changes which were necessary for enlargement should be made, but there should be no rush into Integration otherwise. The important thing was to have an agenda which made a difference to people's lives.

Bruton agreed with the last point. Crime was one area where Europe should be more visible, since it was clearly a cross-border issue. On integration more generally, the Commission had slowed down dramatically the rate at which they made new proposals. But it was true that they were still perceived as interfering in everything. It was also true that the European Parliament was not seen as relevant but just a source of lucrative jobs.

*Bilateral relations*

Bruton said that he was keen to build on the work done with the previous Government, including on a draft joint statement in this field. He had been struck in looking at the Labour Manifesto by the new possibilities for cooperation it opened up. He was particularly keen on cooperation in the education field, notably over plans for a National Grid for learning and a University for Industry. Ireland and the UK after all constituted a single educational market. Other areas of interest were digital TV, and its implications for public Service broadcasting; food safety, where both Governments had similar plans; homelessness, which involved many Irish people who would be better off in Ireland; and the environment, where the new Government's emphasis on international cooperation was welcome, despite the little local difficulty of Sellafield.

Bruton continued that he hoped officials in the various fields could meet soon, to prepare for meetings between appropriate Ministers. It would be good if this could be agreed today in principle. He was partly inspired by the idea that cooperation in these fields under a UK/Irish umbrella made North/South cooperation easier.

The Prime Minister welcomed these suggestions and agreed that they should be taken forward speedily, perhaps with the Cabinet Office acting as coordinator. He agreed particularly that education should be a fruitful field for cooperation. Bruton proposed that the draft joint Statement about this be revised and issued relatively soon, perhaps even in the margins of the informal European Council on 23 May or at Amsterdam.

*Northern Ireland*

Bruton said that a new IRA ceasefire was the most difficult issue, although by no means the only one. The question of a date for Sinn Fein's entry into talks after a ceasefire had been pursued unproductively with the previous Government. Their insistence that the IRA should call a ceasefire first had not produced results because the Republicans did not trust the British Government. The result was that the IRA had been allowed to opt out of their obligation to move away from violence. It was impossible to know whether the IRA would have declared a ceasefire if a date had been offered, because their intentions had never been tested. He did not want to press the new Government too soon on this, but it was an issue which had to be addressed rapidly.

Bruton continued that he had said in media interviews that Sinn Fein could possibly be in the talks on 3 June, but he had stressed the importance of the quality of any ceasefire. He had had to take this line, because it had been his earlier position and the media always asked the same question. In any case he was convinced that the sooner the IRA could be faced with the challenge of a firm date of entry into talks the better it would be. Meanwhile he welcomed what the new Secretary of State had said about parades and the importance of up-holding the rule of law. Obviously local agreements were best if they could be achieved. It was important to deal with the Sinn Fein issue before the marching season began in earnest, to keep down sectarian tension. He also strongly supported what Dr Mowlam had said about confidence-building measures. There were some prisoner cases which the Irish Government would be pursuing through the normal channels. They would also pursue separately the question of a new inquiry on Bloody Sunday. These were very important issues for nationalists. He recognised that confidence also needed to be built on the Unionist side. In some respects they were even more isolated than nationalists. He would be ready to take risks himself over this, if Britain was moving down a confidence-building road elsewhere.

The Prime Minister said that the new Government was less than a week old, and he was anxious not to block off options unnecessarily. He wanted to move forward, but in the right way. To be blunt, if he appeared to be under pressure to do certain things from the Irish side, it became harder to do them. Unlike his predecessor, he had no parliamentary constraints. But the basic constraint of moving both traditions together remained. So he was taking stock and looking for the best way of giving the peace process fresh impetus.

The Prime Minister continued that the Unionists were nervous about what his Government might do. They had nothing to worry about. Commitment to the consent principle was guaranteed. But any initiative could be misunderstood unless it was carefully undertaken. Meanwhile he would be interested in the Taoiseach's analysis of IRA intentions, and how strong the pressures were on them to bring about a new ceasefire.

Bruton said that the messages the Irish received were ambiguous. But there were strong signals that they did want a ceasefire soon. The same signals had been present last October when there had been discussion about the previous Prime Minister publishing a particular article. It had not been clear at the time what kind of ceasefire the IRA had in mind, a full-hearted one or a repetition of last time. Nevertheless, his fear was that if the IRA were not brought to make a move now, they might never do so. If Sinn Fein were not in the talks process, and the talks went on without them and made progress, they would lose their incentive to join because they would be faced with a fait accompli. Even if it was impossible to be sure that a genuine ceasefire was intended, now was the right time to play the card on an entry date.

The Prime Minister said that the issues were under close focus, and he was in no doubt about the importance of moving soon. But the British Government must be seen to move in its own time and in its own way. As he had already said, pressure from others only made it harder. We also had to try to find ways of moving forward which would not drive others out of the process. That was why he was taking some care.

The Prime Minister continued that the collapse of the previous ceasefire had appeared to justify the arguments of those who had said the IRA had never meant it, even if the reality was more complex than that. This meant that any new ceasefire needed to be genuine and permanent. But he was well aware that there was a window of opportunity now. It would be helpful if the men of violence could get the message that further violence made movement much harder.

Bruton said that there were channels to get this message across. Irish officials had not met Sinn Fein since the attack on Nigel Dodds, and the Irish position was that they would not resume contact unless it was clear that a new ceasefire was really on offer. But reopening channels was a way of testing the ground.

Bruton added that the whole talks process had been designed in its present cumbersome form precisely in order to bring Sinn Fein in. This illustrated the need to make a new effort to do so. A new Government could take a radical step and get it accepted where a Government several months down the line, tied down by commitments made to all sides, would be unable to move. Spring commented that he was not sure how long the present talks could be kept going. They would have collapsed already if the British election had not intervened.

The Prime Minister repeated that he wanted to keep his options open. He would be very guarded in what he said to the press about this meeting, and would not give interviews. But he was well aware of the time pressures. We were keen to bring in Sinn Fein, but equally did not want to blow apart the talks process. Bruton acknowledged that the Unionists could walk out of the talks but could not understand what they would have to lose by staying in. As far as the IRA was concerned he could not guarantee that they would come up with a satisfactory ceasefire. He did not understand how their minds worked. But his message was that if a new approach was to be tried, it should be tried soon. It was worth making this last effort to keep the talks train on the rails. Dr Mowlam commented that, if it did not prove possible to bring in Sinn Fein, the talks would have to go ahead without them. Bruton said that he fully accepted this.

The Prime Minister asked about security cooperation between the two countries. Spring said that this was now first class, particularly between the RUC and the Garda. There was a high level of personal trust, and no question marks on either side. The level of arms finds was a good illustration of this.

*UN High Commissioner for Human Rights*

Bruton said that he hoped we would be able to support Mary Robinson's candidacy. The Prime Minister said that we would.

*Comment*

This was a friendly meeting, but we had to fight off constant pressure from Bruton's office for the two men to meet the press together, and implicit pressure for us to make a move now and turn the meeting into a full-blown Summit. In the end, the presentation came out reasonably well with low expectations duly met.

I am copying this to Ken Lindsay (Northern Ireland Office), Jan Polley (Cabinet Office), and by fax to Sir John Kerr (Washington) and Veronica Sutherland (Dublin).

Yours ever,
John Holmes

William Ehrman, Esq.
Foreign and Commonwealth Office.

# Document 20 On Bruton Visit

From: John Holmes
Date: 8 May 1997

MR CAMPBELL
cc:
Jonathan Powell
Philip Barton

We spoke about presentation. When Mo Mowlam met Spring last night, the Irish pressed very hard for us to agree language which suggested Sinn Fein could enter talks immediately if they declared a ceasefire, or at least on 3 June. They were told firmly that this was not on, and that there was going to be no joint press conference. They (reluctantly) seemed to accept this.

But, as we discussed, Bruton has not exactly kept quiet, and presentation after the meeting will not be easy. We should avoid any joint Statement, but try to agree broad lines to take, even if this will not stop either side spinning things their way. As I said, there is plenty of positive stuff we <u>can</u> say:

- – Warmth of meeting. Determination to work closely together.
- – Common condemnation of violence from all quarters, including recent IRA attacks in Britain, and of recent appalling Sectarian attacks in Northern Ireland (burning churches etc).
- – Common determination to make speedy progress at the talks when they resume on 3 June.
- – Desire to see these talks become inclusive through Sinn Fein joining.
- – But absolutely clear they cannot do so until there is a credible ("unequivocal") ceasefire, adhered to in word and deed.
- – Determination to do everything possible to avert trouble in this summer's marching season. Support for Parades Commission.

The difficult question is the timetable for Sinn Fein after a ceasefire. The Government is bound by Statute to let Sinn Fein into the talks if they declare an unequivocal ceasefire, establish a commitment to exclusively peaceful methods and show they abide by the democratic process. In practice, there is obviously a significant degree of subjective judgement about this. But the law does mean we cannot say <u>absolutely and definitively</u> that Sinn Fein will <u>not</u> be invited to the talks on 3 June if they declare a ceasefire now. If the IRA all came out with their hands up, it presumably would be possible.

But we can make clear that, short of this, the Government would need time to verify that a ceasefire was indeed genuine in word and deed, so that entry on 3 June, even if a ceasefire were declared now (itself highly unlikely), is extremely unlikely. How much time? Can't say but we would not be looking for unnecessary delay. Are you prepared to fix a date in future? Hypothetical question. New government, just getting in touch with the parties. Priority is for IRA to declare a ceasefire.

You may like to talk this through further.

JOHN HOLMES

# Document 21  Visit of the Taoiseach, 8 May: East/West Issues

10 Downing Street
LONDON SW1A2AA

From the Private Secretary
9 May 1997

Dear Dominick,
One of the main themes discussed when the Taoiseach called on the Prime Minister on 8 May was East/West issues – i.e. matters of common interest between the government of the United Kingdom and the Republic of Ireland, outside the context of Northern Ireland. I attach a copy of the statement which the Taoiseach made earlier in the week.

The Prime Minister welcomed the strengthening of bilateral links, particularly between respective departmental officials and Ministers. Departments should look at opportunities for cooperation across the whole range of government activity, and not only those points highlighted in the Taoiseach's statement. Early meetings between British and Irish officials and Ministers, to establish personal contacts, would be helpful. The Cabinet Office will be calling an early meeting of members of the Official Committee on Anglo-Irish Relations to co-ordinate this exercise.

I am copying this letter to Private Secretaries of other members of the Cabinet, to the Private Secretary to the Minister without Portfolio, and to Sir Robin Butler.

JOHN HOLMES
Dominick Chilcott Esq
Foreign and Commonwealth Office

## Document 22  Contact with Sinn Fein

FROM: QUENTIN THOMAS
Political Director
9 May 1997

PS/Secretary of State (L6B)
cc.
PS/Mr Murphy(L&B)
PS/PUS(L&B)
PS/Sir D Fell
Mr Steele
Mr Stephens
Mr Wood(L&B)
Mr Ray
Mr Holmes No.10
Mr Budd Cab Office

As agreed, I spoke to Ms Siobhan O Hanlon, Mr Gerry Adams' secretary.

2. After a brief exchange of pleasantries I said, speaking slowly enough for her to take it down, that:

(i) Gerry Adams' letters to the Secretary of State and the Prime Minister had been received, were being studied and taken seriously.

(ii) It was helpful that they had not been publicised.

(iii) The new Government was finding its feet: obviously it was primarily focused on the Queen's Speech and other associated matters.

(iv) We would be replying before too long. I hoped something positive could be said.

(v) I had seen Gerry Adams' remarks about the value of confidence building measures. But confidence was clearly a two-way Street.

(vi) It was essential that events on the grounds made this possible. Any terrorist activity, real or hoaxes, in Great Britain or Northern Ireland could ruin the prospects of moving forward.

I then asked her to confirm that she had got what I had said. She said that she had and asked when a reply could be expected. I repeated that we hoped to reply "before too long" but that people were genuinely finding their feet. I said they should hang on to their hats: there was no Intention to string things out.

3. She thanked me and we said goodbye.
Press Line (Only if needed)
    I suggest that if needed the press line might be as follows:
    Are you in contact with Sinn Fein?
    Any serious approach from Sinn Fein would be given careful consideration. But everyone knows that any real advance requires an unequivocal restoration of the IRA ceasefire.
    Meetings with Sinn Fein?
    There will be no meetings between Ministers and Sinn Fein until an unequivocal ceasefire is in place. Like the last Government, we do not rule out in principle the possibility of meetings between Officials and Sinn Fein to ensure there are no misunderstandings about our position. In practice agreement to such a meeting would of course depend on events on the ground. There have been no such meetings since February 1996

QUENTIN THOMAS
11 Millbank
Ext.6447

## Document 23   Message from the Secretary of State for Northern Ireland to Sinn Fein

1800 HRS, FRIDAY 9 MAY 1997

"I want to assure you of our desire to make progress. We wanted to make an early and direct approach but we appreciate the need for sensitivity so let me reassure you that there is no intention on our part to make any of this public. Our desire is to help create conditions in which real progress can be made. The sooner this is done the better. We share your concern about events on the ground which are beyond our control. There are grave difficulties on our side also; not least among these is the treatment of the remand prisoner Roisin McAliskey, the delay in transferring sentenced prisoners in Britain back to Ireland and their conditions, the events surrounding the killing of Robert Hamill in Portadown, the actions of the RUC and the British Army and the ongoing loyalist attacks on our party and our community."

## Document 24 Northern Ireland: Meetings with Party Leaders

PRIME MINISTER

From: John Holmes

Date: 9 May 1997

cc: Mr. Powell, Mr Barton

We have arranged at short notice calls on you on Monday by Hume, Paisley and Trimble (again). We will try to fit in Alderdice later in the week. This is a somewhat grisly prospect but necessary. They are getting 30 minutes each. You have to see the party leaders from time to time. But they should not get into the habit of bypassing Mo, which they will be tempted to do, particularly the Unionists.

 I am not giving you detailed briefs for the calls. You will want essentially to be in listening mode with all of them. The main aim is to demonstrate your personal commitment to Northern Ireland progress and reassure all concerned of the balanced approach you will be taking. With all of them, you will want to reassert your rejection of violence but your desire to see Sinn Fein in if they give up violence; your commitment to the talks, despite the lack of progress so far; and your hope that the decommissioning issue can be resolved to allow real political discussion to start.

 Hume will press you about Sinn Fein's entry to the talks, on the same lines as the Irish Government. He will no doubt have talked to Adams in advance and is likely to tell you that a permanent ceasefire is within easy reach, with no need for you to compromise any principles to achieve it. We want to avoid getting in a Position where Hume is once again an intermediary. You will need to be careful not to give Hume messages to take back to Adams, and to avoid getting drawn into any text he may have in his pocket.

Apart from the peace process, Hume is likely to raise parades (where he has done noble work); BSE and the dependence of Northern Ireland on the beef export market; education cuts in Northern Ireland stemming from the last PES settlement; and the last Government's proposed reduction of the five Northern Ireland Education Boards to three (a pet hobby horse). He may also raise Bloody Sunday. Again, I suggest you should be in listening mode on all these.

It will not be difficult to be in listening mode with Paisley, although he is often the soul of joviality on these occasions. Robinson is much cleverer and more difficult to deal with. The DUP will not sit down with Sinn Fein until decommissioning is complete. They are also very strong on Loyalist violence and maintain that the Loyalists should be expelled from the talks because their ceasefire is a fiction (they have a point but we need to keep the Loyalists in). The DUP are pretty well a lost cause where a settlement is concerned. Paisley is also likely to raise BSE and education cuts.

The main point to watch with Trimble is to avoid encouraging him to think that he can change the basis of the talks process away from the current three Strands and towards an internal settlement without any formal North/South element. You could usefully urge him to drop any insistence on prior decommissioning, if there is a ceasefire and Sinn Fein's entry into talks becomes a possibility, and to stick instead to the Mitchell proposal of parallel decommissioning. You could also encourage him to work harder on links with the SDLP, with whom any deal will have to be done in the absence of Sinn Fein. Trimble is trying to see Bruton (which is much to be encouraged).

John Holmes

## Document 25  Northern Ireland Bills

10 May 1997

Prime Minister
I am writing to seek formal policy approval for the measures which I propose to introduce in the Bills to replace the Northern Ireland (Emergency Provisions) Act 1996 and to implement the broad recommendations of

the North report on parades. We agreed at Cabinet on 8 May that these two Bills would form part of the 1997/98 Legislative Programme.

The main policy proposals to be contained in the Bills are set out in the Annex to this letter.

I should be grateful for your agreement and that of other colleagues to what I propose. Since our intention to legislation will be announced in the Speech on 14 May, it is of course important to secure agreement before that date.

I am copying this letter to members of IN Committee, the Lord Chancellor, the Secretary of State for Scotland, the President of the Council and the Lord Privy Seal, the Attorney General, the Chief Whip, and to Sir Robin Butler.

M. M.


## Document 26  Call by UUP


12 May 1997

10 Downing Street
LONDON SW1A2AA

From the Private Secretary

Ken Lindsay Esq
Northern Ireland Office

David Trimble and John D Taylor called on the Prime Minister this afternoon for about 45 minutes. Dr. Mowlam, Jonathan Stephens, Jonathan Powell and I were present on our side. The Prime Minister began by asking for Trimble's assessment of the Situation.

Trimble said that he was particularly worried about the Loyalist ceasefire. The situation on the ground was worse than it had been for many years, with considerable tension in urban areas. Recent spontaneous attacks on individuals of one community or the other were the most obvious signs of this. The continuing IRA violence was a major factor, compounded by worry about what might happen in the marching season and, to a lesser degree, nervousness about a Labour government. Feelings in the Protestant community were not helped by public suggestions by Dr Mowlam that the RUC could be radically reformed.

Dr. Mowlam commented that she was proposing no more than what had been recommended by the Hayes Report. She would be taking an early opportunity to make this clear publicly. The Prime Minister asked how Unionists could best be reassured. Trimble said that Unionists feared a Labour government would favour Irish nationalism, both in terms of long term policy and day to day issues such as policing. Hume did not help by constant references to Labour as the sister party of the SDLP.

The Prime Minister said that he had no wish to favour republicanism. What he was looking for was a Settlement which would calm the Situation in Northern Ireland. Such a Settlement would obviously leave Northern Ireland inside the UK. Taylor said that he understood this, but people in Northern Ireland lived on fear, and the first message of the Government should be that there was no question of Northern Ireland leaving the UK. Trimble added that the importance of the consent principle should be repeated, and the Prime Minister should reiterate that he would not be a persuader for Irish unity. Those who had been involved in violence should also have to prove their commitment to peaceful means before they could join the political process.

The Prime Minister looked forward to the eventual solution. This would presumably involve a devolved assembly commanding confidence from both Unionists and Nationalists, and proper cross border arrangements. Both the UUP and SDLP appeared to envisage something like this. Taylor agreed but pointed out that there was a big difference between practical cross border cooperation e.g. the Foyle Fisheries Commission, and the kind of all-Ireland bodies with executive powers demanded by the Irish government. If discussion could move away from the latter proposal, the package could be sold to Unionists. Meanwhile the current talks process was stuck. If the governments continued to wait for the IRA to make up their mind, and the argument about decommissioning continued, there would never be progress.

The Prime Minister suggested that it would be better if Sinn Fein were in the talks. Taylor disagreed. It was better for them to be out. They were not in practice in a position to go back to full scale violence because people would not accept it. Trimble agreed. The republicans were in a difficult position. They were not ready to turn their backs on violence definitively and found the choice of going wholly political unpalatable. There was a lot to be said for keeping them in their present awkward position. In theory it would be good to get Sinn Fein in, but only if they had genuinely given up violence. Otherwise, the pressure on them should be maintained until the movement split. That would be inevitable because the Slab Murphys of this world would never give up violence.

Taylor drew attention to the problem for the UUP if violence got worse, and the Loyalists had to be thrown out of the talks. The UUP needed the Loyalists in Order to meet the rules of sufficient consensus. Otherwise they could be out-voted by Paisley and McCartney. So it was extremely important to keep the Loyalists in if possible. Trimble emphasised the same point.

The Prime Minister asked whether the UUP and SDLP could reach a settlement. Trimble said that he had tried to deal with Hume several times over the past 18 months, but it had never worked. Hume did not want to move without Sinn Fein. But there was a limit to how long it was possible to sit around waiting for Sinn Fein. In any case, he repeated, it was clear that the present talks process could go nowhere. The UUP would not bring it to an end, but that was the reality.

Taylor said that a way through could be found without Sinn Fein. 95 per cent of the population wanted peace, including many who voted for Sinn Fein. The key was agreement between Hume and Trimble. If this could be achieved and put to a referendum, it would attract massive support and the ground would be cut from under Sinn Fein's feet.

The Prime Minister commented that Hume would not go down this road until Sinn Fein had at least been given a last chance. Trimble said that he had heard talk of last chances before. Every time the supposed crunch came, discussion went back to how to bring Sinn Fein into the process.

The Prime Minister said that it should be clear that if Sinn Fein did not take an opportunity that was on offer, the process would have to go ahead without them. He believed deeply that Sinn Fein could not hold the process to ransom. If Sinn Fein had a chance and missed it, US and other opinion would be on our side. Extremists on either side might well not go along with a proposed settlement in the end. There was a chance of getting reasonable people to achieve agreement and of putting this to a referendum. But this would only be possible in practice if Sinn Fein had had their chance and put themselves out of the game. In other words, Sinn Fein had to be given a chance in order to get Hume to negotiate seriously. If they spurned it, that would at least be clear. If they entered the talks, Sinn Fein would probably never agree to the outcome. But there would still be a chance of getting together on the middle ground.

Trimble said that talk of a last chance and going on without Sinn Fein was easy. But in reality Hume would always pop up with some fresh information about republican intentions, or Sinn Fein would produce some messy initiative. Something more would be needed to bring in Hume, and this could not be in the context of the present talks process. Mitchell was for example a hopeless chairman. The only way forward was to get the key people together separately to talk turkey. The Prime Minister should get round the table with himself and Hume. Hume would find it difficult to stand aside from this. The Prime Minister said that he could see the logic of this, especially if there could be agreement on the end result. It might be easier to work backwards from that than trying to work forwards from where we were.

Discussion moved to Irish elections and the prospect of Ahern as Taoiseach. Taylor suggested that, judging from his most recent comments, Ahern would be happy to see Sinn Fein in talks even without a ceasefire. Trimble said that he did not think Ahern would adopt this policy. He was very ignorant about Northern Ireland. But he had just had a reasonably good private meeting with Ahern – which Ahern had kept secret, unlike Trimble's experience with Bruton. However, Ahern would be subject to the influence of Martin Mansergh and others.

Trimble went on to suggest that Clinton's visit here would be a good opportunity to get the Americans to weigh in helpfully. The Prime Minister agreed but suggested that Clinton would only really be helpful if we had managed to remove the last vestige of respectability from Sinn

Fein arguments. The Prime Minister concluded that there seemed to be a measure of agreement on the desired outcome of negotiations, but getting there remained very difficult. He would continue to reflect but time was not necessarily on our side.

Trimble mentioned that 29 May would be awkward for the Clinton visit because he and probably other Northern Ireland leaders would be in South Africa for a seminar. He was incidentally hoping to have a meeting with Mandela, which others would not have. This would help to undermine one of Sinn Fein's special relationships overseas.

Taylor raised one local problem, that of training centres in Northern Ireland. There were only ten, and the previous Government had proposed closing the one in East Belfast. He handed over a note, which the Prime Minister gave to Dr Mowlam.

Trimble raised BSE. The previous Agriculture Minister had assured him that, while the notification to the Commission about the certified herd scheme said that it would have a general UK application, he would accept a Commission proposal for Northern Ireland alone if they came back with this, as he expected. He wanted the Prime Minister to be clear that, whatever the official record said, they had been given these private assurances in the past. He added that Scottish and Welsh Opposition to Northern Ireland going ahead seemed to him short sighted. The Prime Minister said that the issue was being looked at urgently. He was well aware of all the sensitivities.

Comment

The atmosphere of the discussion was good, despite the obvious rivalry between Trimble and Taylor for the Prime Minister's ear. While the Prime Minister was sending reassuring signals about his commitment to the Union and the consent principle, Trimble and Taylor will no doubt have picked up that a move towards Sinn Fein of some kind is likely. For their part, the UUP agenda of changing the nature of the talks process was once again quite clear.

I am copying this letter to William Ehrman (Foreign and Commonwealth Office), Jan Polley (Cabinet Office) and Veronica Sutherland in Dublin by fax.

JOHN HOLMES

## Document 27   Northern Ireland: Meetings with Party Leaders

CC – FROM: THE PRIVATE SECRETARY
NORTHERN IRELAND OFFICE.
STORMONT CASTLE
BELFAST BT4 3ST
Tel. Belfast (01232) 520700

John Holmes Esq
Private Secretary to the
Prime Minister
10 Downing Street
LONDON
SW1A 2AA

12 May 1997

Dear John

You requested briefing for meetings which the Prime Minister hopes to have early next week with the leaders of the main Northern Ireland political parties. The Secretary of State or Mr Murphy hope to be present.

I set out below some general points for the Prime Minister to make and attach at Annex A particular points, directed at individual parties; Annex B contains background notes on those parties (we could provide personality notes when we know who is coming); and Annex C is an analytical paper on the search for a political settlement, which would usefully focus the Prime Minister's thoughts, if he had an opportunity to read it.

*Objectives*

These are introductory encounters and unlikely to be the occasion for detailed discussion. (The Secretary of State has so far had only brief meetings with the parties). The main objectives would be to:

- communicate the Government's and the Prime Minister's personal commitment to the search for a fair political accommodation and lasting peace in Northern Ireland;
- reassure the parties about the key bases of policy, summarised below;
- establish a basis of confidence and trust for future dealings.

*General Points to Make*

1. Determined to do all I can to bring about lasting peace and political stability in Northern Ireland. Full confidence in Mo Mowlam but will maintain a personal interest. Always ready to engage directly where that would be helpful.

2. Want to emphasise that our approach is based on firm principles and will therefore be consistent:

- completely committed to the principle of consent. Welcome near universal acceptance of it.
- equally committed to making Northern Ireland a place nationalists can feel comfortable to live in.
  - Parity of esteem. Equality of opportunity.
  - Appropriate expression of their Irish national identity (without prejudice to the constitutional guarantee).

3. Believe the Talks process offers the best chance of securing a comprehensive political settlement which could address and resolve the fundamental political concerns of all participants. No risk to anyone's fundamental interests. Any outcome must be agreed and widely supported before it can be implemented.

4. Determined to promote real progress in the Talks. Looking for ways to resolve the decommissioning issue on satisfactory terms and set an early date for substantive political negotiations.

5. Believe it is right to leave the door open for Sinn Fein to join the Talks, but ONLY if there is an unequivocal restoration of the IRA ceasefire. If they refuse the opportunity, quite ready to press on without them.

W K LINSDAY

**Annex A**
*Suggested points to cover: political issues*
*UUP*

- Assess Mr Trimble's/the UUP's Standing and confidence, especially vis à vis the DUP;
- express the Government's commitment to the principle of consent
  and to the three stranded talks process;
- respond cautiously to "Pathways to Peace within the Union",
  indicating a readiness to consider taking some elements forward
  within the talks process. Avoid any commitments on Northern
  Ireland Grand Committee, local government changes, structured
  relationship with parties etc;
- probe UUP commitment to the talks process;
- express determination to find an agreed way through the
  decommissioning issue, based on the Mitchell "compromise approach" (avoiding discussion of details), allowing an early date to
  be set for the launch of the three Strands;
- reaffirm criteria for Sinn Fein entry to negotiations, while refusing definitively to close the door. Assert readiness to proceed
  without them;
- Discuss the prospects for developing a constructive relationship
  between the UUP and SDLP, building confidence on both sides,
  to enable the talks to move forward constructively.

*SDLP*

- Confirm commitment to the search for a comprehensive and
  balanced political accommodation;
- express determination to find an agreed way through the
  decommissioning impasse, based on the Mitchell "compromise
  approach" (avoiding discussion of details), allowing an early date
  to be set for the launch of the three Strands;
- confirm desire to see Sinn Fein join the process on stated terms,
  but assert readiness to proceed without them. Note that progress

in the talks could add to pressure on the Republican Movement to make a definitive, commitment to politics;
- discuss the prospects for developing a constructive relationship between the UUP and SDLP, building confidence on both sides, to enable the talks process to move forward constructively;
- avoid discussion of alternatives to the talks process.

*DUP/UKUP*

- Emphasise Government's commitment to the principle of consent and to the three stranded talks process. Point to widespread acceptance of the principle of consent (by all except Sinn Fein) and the likelihood that any negotiated settlement would be predicated on that basis;
- point to the benefits of a widely acceptable political accommodation, acceptable to majorities on <u>both</u> sides of the community, which would enable significantly greater local political accountability and generate political stability;
- express determination to find an agreed way through the decommissioning issue, based on the Mitchell "compromise approach" (avoiding discussion of details), allowing an early date to be set for the launch of the three Strands;
- reaffirm criteria for Sinn Fein entry to negotiations, while refusing definitively to close the door. Assert readiness to proceed without them;
- dismiss criticism of Irish Government's role
- note any allegation that Loyalists have demonstrably dishonoured their commitment to the Mitchell principles; confirm that commitment to the principles remains a condition of participation in the talks; but point out that there will be opportunities to consider the Loyalist parties' entitlement to remain in the talks when they resume on 3 June.

*Alliance Party*

- Emphasise commitment to the three stranded talks process and belief that it remains viable;

- express determination to find an agreed way through the decommissioning issue, based on the Mitchell "compromise approach" (acknowledging the constructive role played by the Alliance Party in promoting what contingent agreement has so far emerged), allowing an early date to be set for the launch of the three Strands;
- reaffirm criteria for Sinn Fein entry to negotiations, while refusing definitively to close the door. Assert readiness to proceed without them;
- point to value of UUP/SDLP Cooperation, with Alliance Party support, in moving the talks process forward;
- seek Alliance Party assessment of the other parties' positions.

**Annex B**

**The Northern Ireland parties in the political talks**

*Unionist*

1. The *Ulster Unionist Party* has been led by David Trimble (Deputy John Taylor), a law lecturer, since the retirement of Sir James Molyneaux in 1995; has long been the largest Unionist party (though occasionally outpolled by Dr Paisley's DUP in European elections). It did fairly well in the general election, gaining a seat (now 10 in total) and reversing losses to the DUP sustained in the forum election last year. In the talks, its cautious position on decommissioning effectively blocked progress between last summer and their adjournment in March; though it was careful to avoid action which would bring the talks down (or at least which would result in its being blamed for a collapse). It often appeared directionless; there were important divisions and power- struggles within, and it was fearful of electoral advantage that the DUP and UKUP may take of apparent "weakness". The decommissioning position was a proxy for the question of Sinn Fein entry to talks: the UUP's willingness to accept that possibility, indeed its enthusiasm for a talks process at all, appeared to be waning.

It did fairly well in the election, however, gaining a seat (now 10 in total) and reversing losses suffered to the DUP in the entry to negotiations elections last May. Mr Trimble may therefore feel personally more secure; and, though he has remained difficult to read, he has appeared somewhat more upbeat about the talks recently. The UUP position is pivotal: they will need to be prevailed upon to compromise on their position on decommissioning if substantive discussions are to begin.

2. The *Democratic Unionist Party*, led by Dr Ian Paisley (Deputy, Peter Robinson) has traditionally been the hardline unionist party. In talks it was generally negative, though Mr Robinson, at least, privately sought to advance matters at times. Its election posture, portraying itself as struggling to save the endangered Union, failed: it lost a seat (Rev Wm McCrea) and its vote was down on last year. It is unlikely that Dr Paisley will be diverted into wholly constructive courses, and the talks arithmetic does not need him: but some softening of the DUP position would be useful, and will be worth working for.

3. The *United Kingdom Unionist Party* is little more than the vehicle of its leader Robert McCartney QC. He has portrayed himself at times as an "enlightened Unionist". In the talks, however, he aligned himself (not least for electoral reasons) with the DUP, and was thoroughly negative and obstructionist, portraying the process itself as corrupt, aimed at the appeasement of terrorism and the achievement by stealth of a united Ireland. He lost moderate support in the election, but got back with a reduced majority. His conviction of the corrupt nature of the process is probably genuine, but unlikely to be shakeable.

4. The *Popular Unionist Party*, led by David Ervine, is associated with the loyalist paramilitary Ulster Volunteer Force (UVF). Its leadership has worked hard to sustain the loyalist ceasefire since the collapse of the IRA's ceasefire.

5. The *Ulster Democratic Party*, led by Gary McMichael, is associated with the other principal loyalist paramilitary group, the Ulster Defence Association; it too has worked hard for loyalist restraint.

*Nationalists*

6. The *Social Democratic and Labour Party*, led by John Hume (Deputy, Seamus Mallon) has been since the early 1970s, the largest nationalist party, always entirely committed to constitutional methods. It was frustrated by

the lack of progress in the talks; it was also been concerned about pos-sible electoral consequences in view of Sinn Fein's strong showing in the talks elections last year. Mr Hume was eager to go on promoting dialogue with Sinn Fein – often with somewhat reckless optimism; many others in the party were uneasy about this after the end of the IRA ceasefire, and sought to put greater distance between the two parties. This tension is likely to continue in view of the election result, where the SDLP lost a seat to Sinn Fein, though increasing its share of the vote over last year. It is likely to be constructive in talks, it and the Irish Government taking similar positions. It will remain anxious to see the possibility of Sinn Fein entry kept open; it will press hard along the lines of the framework docu-ments, especially for measures to recognise the identity of nationalists.

7. *Sinn Fein*, led by Gerry Adams, is generally regarded as the political wing of the IRA and though it maintains it has a separate existence, the links are of the closest. It did well in the 1996 elections – though how far this was an endorsement of the apparently peace-seeking outlook of the leadership, or of the ending of the IRA ceasefire, has been disputed, and similar questions hang over its slightly further increased vote this year, when it gained two members. It is not clear yet how far this impacts on internal debates over the balance between politics and violence in the movement's activities.

### Other Parties

8. The *Alliance Party* led by Lord (John) Alderdice has consistently taken a middle of the road position, in favour of political compromise in Northern Ireland, upholding the Union so long as it is a majority wish. It has been constructive in the talks, though Lord Alderdice himself at times publicly and privately despairs that any progress is possible. It draws members from both parts of the community. It had a fairly good election, though not coming close to a seat. It is likely to go on being a wholly con-structive, though never pivotal, force.

9. The *Labour* grouping in the talks, led by Malachi Curran, derives from a coalition formed to contest last year's election – the latest in a long series of attempts to put together a viable Northern Ireland party of the left. It has split once, and is in the throes of doing so again. It has been constructive, but has limited influence.

10. The *Northern Ireland Women's Coalition* (leader Monica McWilliams) was also formed to contest last year's election, in reaction to the very limited representation of women in Northern Ireland political life. It too has been constructive, and gained in influence; its uncompromising attitude to obstruction has earned it abuse from the DUP and UKUP.

**Annex C**

*Achieving a Political Settlement*

1. The purpose of this paper is to recapitulate the case for seeking a comprehensive political Settlement in relation to Northern Ireland; set out the likely elements of such a Settlement; and identify the major obstacles to its achievement.

*The need for a political settlement*

2. The community in Northern Ireland is deeply divided: a series of fundamental divisions – political, religious, ethnic, cultural – largely coincide with and reinforce each other. Historical antagonisms, going back centuries, continue to be reinforced by differential experience of social and economic advances and ongoing disagreements on fundamental political questions. There is a long history of inter-communal tension and violence and extremists on both sides have a long tradition of functional (i.e. in their eyes, successful) terrorism.

3. The direct human and financial costs of terrorism and inter-communal violence in Northern Ireland since the late 1960s are huge and major terrorist atrocities have also taken place in the Republic and Great Britain and against British diplomatic and military personnel overseas. In addition there are vast indirect costs (chiefly in Northern Ireland, but also in Great Britain and the Republic) arising from magnified inter-communal suspicion, preventative security, investment and tourist revenue forgone and so on. The problems of Northern Ireland also damage the UK's international reputation.

4. In the absence of political consensus on how Northern Ireland should be governed there is no local political accountability for day to day decisions. This has given rise to the "democratic deficit" – the absence of any political decision-taking machinery between the UK Cabinet and the 26

Northern Ireland District Councils (with their relatively very low levels of responsibility). This produces serious practical disadvantages for the people of Northern Ireland. Meanwhile, without any responsibility for taking and implementing hard decisions, many in Northern Ireland politics enjoy the luxury of opposition, staking out extreme positions and criticising compromise.

*The genesis of the talks process*

5. Successive political initiatives in Northern Ireland since 1972 have been predicated on the twin assessment that

(a) *political stability in Northern Ireland will only emerge following a fundamental political accommodation between the two main parts of the community,* allowing Unionist and nationalist politicians to work together in new political institutions and address the many sources of division and tension within the community which would still remain. As such new and widely acceptable political institutions are intended to reflect and contribute to a deeper inter-communal reconciliation, and are bound to involve compromise, it follows that the politicians who will need to operate the institutions and respect the compromises must be involved in the negotiations which lead to their establishment. Equally, it is clear that a functioning political accommodation of the character which has been sought could not be imposed: without the positive support or at least acquiescence of the parties concerned and widespread support within the community no such accommodation could be claimed to exist;

(b) *any such political accommodation,* while respecting the views of the majority on the fundamental issue of Northern Ireland's constitutional Status, *must adequately acknowledge and recognise the Irish nationalist identity of the minority community.*

6. After the overthrow of the 1973/74 power sharing/Sunningdale initiative, a series of efforts were made to achieve these desiderata sequentially. But whether the focus was on the search for widely acceptable political institutions in Northern Ireland (as in the Constitutional Convention of 1975/76, the Constitutional Conference of 1980/81 or the Northern Ireland Assembly of 1982/86) or on the Irish dimension (as with the New Ireland

Forum of nationalist parties sponsored by the Irish Government in 1982/84 and the Anglo-Irish Agreement of 1985) it proved impossible to engage the positive support of one or other of the two main parts of the community.

7. The talks process which began in 1991, building on the ground covered in the "talks about talks" which began in 1987, has attempted to address all the relevant relationships at one and the same time. As such it offers the maximum opportunity to elected representatives of both main parts of the community to achieve their political objectives while being confident of their ability to protect their fundamental political interests. It maximises the scope for trade-offs and its potential to lead to a fully comprehensive settlement should avoid the danger of leaving any loose ends.

8. The elements of a possible settlement arising from the talks process are discussed in more detail below but it is important to note that the process as a whole relies on the assessment that a deal can be done – that there is a pattern of understandings, touching on all the relevant relationships, which would protect the essential political interests of all concerned and achieve enough of their political objectives to secure their support. Where the talks participants have discussed substantive issues this assessment has been borne out and in the view of officials remains valid.

*The link with the peace process*

9. The fundamental purpose of the talks process has always been to bring politically motivated violence in Northern Ireland to an end. Initially it was hoped that this could be achieved indirectly, that a fair political settlement endorsed by referendums in both parts of Ireland would undermine the whole rationale for Republican terrorism and lead to a reduction in support for the paramilitaries, thus putting pressure on them to give up their campaigns; and that the development of new broadly-based political institutions would lead to growing support for the RUC in their task of protecting such institutions and defeating terrorism. The 1991/92 talks had an observable effect on terrorist violence. The first CLMC ceasefire held throughout the 1992 talks (April-November 1992) and that period saw the lowest rate of terrorist incidents in Northern Ireland since 1971. The demonstrated potential of the talks process may have been decisive in persuading the Republican Movement to seek Sinn Fein participation.

10. The opportunity to engage Sinn Fein in the talks process has opened up the attractive possibility that the process could be used directly to achieve a total peace settlement in which all the various consequentials of bringing the IRA and Loyalist campaigns to a permanent end could be resolved in the context of the broader political settlement. Although there are divergent views within the SDLP and within the Irish political establishment, the SDLP and Irish Government have consistently promoted the project of seeking to bring the Republican Movement in from the cold in this way. Given the history of Irish Republicanism since the beginning of the 20th Century, they see the potential value of engineering a Situation in which at least the great majority of the Republican Movement is directly engaged in and committed to any political settlement.

11. In seeking to promote a political settlement, the engagement or potential engagement of Sinn Fein gives rise to enormous complications but a settlement which did involve them and secured the support of the Republican Movement more generally would undeniably be far more robust than one which did not.

*ELEMENTS OF A POLITICAL SETTLEMENT*

12. The Framework Documents published in February 1995 are widely acknowledged within the British and Irish political systems and among informed observers as embracing the key elements of any eventual political settlement in relation to Northern Ireland. They were published as an aid to discussion, not a blueprint – "a shared understanding on the parameters of a possible outcome to the talks process". However, the Framework Documents, especially the "New Framework for Agreement" published by the British and Irish Governments together, have been opposed by virtually the whole spectrum of Unionist opinion. Some of the reasons for this emerge from a consideration of the individual elements of the package. The key components are discussed below.

*(a)  Widely acceptable political institutions in Northern Ireland*

13. The first of the Framework Documents, "A Framework for Accountable Government", was published under the authority of HMG alone and builds largely on the provisional agreement between the four main

political parties engaged in the 1992 Talks. It envisages substantial legislative and administrative devolution with responsibility shared proportionately in a System of Committees with numerous safeguards for the minority community, including a directly-elected three-member Panel with consultative, monitoring, referral and representational functions. There is an argument that this is over-elaborate and could inhibit sensible decision-taking, but the conflicting desiderata which led to this model are likely to continue to exist unless particular parties achieve compensating gains elsewhere in the negotiations.

14. Besides the mechanisms necessary to cater for the implications of Northern Ireland's divided community, the proposals deal with more conventional difficult issues such as financing arrangements, securing a local input into the UK Government's handling of EU matters and other non-devolved issues (which would probably include security matters) and the enforcement of EU and human rights obligations. It seems very likely that in any resumption of substantive negotiations on this package the nationalist parties at least (and perhaps the Loyalists) will wish to place a considerable emphasis on the establishment of *new policing arrangements* with which the whole community can identify. The Government's own proposals in this area could have an important role to play.

*(b)  A new and constructive relationship between the two parts of Ireland*

15. This is the area which has so far been least canvassed in substantive inter-party discussions. It will have a major bearing on the overall outcome. The SDLP specifically linked their provisional acceptance of the outcome of the "strand one" discussions in 1992 to the achievement of a satisfactory outcome to "strand two". The "Framework for a new Agreement" postulated a new North/South body with a range of executive, harmonising and consultative functions and the Irish Government and the nationalist parties are likely to hold out for something pretty substantial in this area to help give practical and institutional expression to the Irish nationalist identity of the minority community in Northern Ireland. However, this is a highly neuralgic area for Unionists and *the limits of what might be feasible have not yet been tested in direct exchanges with the Unionist parties.* They all support the development of "good neighbourly" relations between the

two parts of Ireland but remain strongly opposed to the Framework proposals: they are suspicious that the establishment of any institutions with
all-Ireland executive authority would constitute a one-way ratchet to de
facto Irish unity. Although the joint Framework Document envisages that
the Northern Ireland interest in these bodies would be firmly under the
control of the Northern Ireland political institutions, with their Unionist
majority, Unionist fears arise from their (exaggerated) interpretation of
several aspects of the proposals. As nationalists have an equal, albeit opposite, interest in inflating the likely implications of establishing such
bodies it has proved difficult to tackle Unionist concerns (many of which
are beyond the bounds of rational argument anyway).

16. Quite apart from the fundamental underlying political question, the establishment of cross-border institutions would throw up a range of difficult
technical questions about accountability, financial controls and the necessary administrative infrastructure. The Framework for a new Agreement
suggests answers to most of these questions, and envisages a fairly radical
approach to the handling of EU matters on an all-Ireland basis.

*(c)  The relationship between the two Governments*

17. This is the formal focus of "strand three" of the talks but **it** *is central to
Unionist objectives in the talks process that it should lead to "an alternative
to and replacement for" the Anglo-Irish Agreement of 1985.* They oppose
this because its exclusive focus on Northern Ireland puts into question
Northern Ireland's constitutional status as an integral part of the United
Kingdom. They also resent the fact that the machinery of the Anglo-Irish
Conference and Secretariat appears to give the Irish Government more of
a "say" in how Northern Ireland is governed than local elected representatives. In fact, the Agreement – like the joint Framework Document –
explicitly envisages that the role of the Conference would contract in the
event of devolution and at the time the Agreement was being negotiated
the Northern Ireland Assembly provided a strong platform for exercising
local political influence – over 70% of its detailed recommendations on
policy and draft legislation were accepted by HMG - and it was only the
Unionist reaction to the Agreement which led to it being closed down.

18. There is of course a vibrant and robust relationship between the Republic and the UK generally and it is not immediately obvious that any particular inter-governmental machinery is needed to encourage it. Some formal broadening of the scope of the inter-governmental relationship could no doubt be achieved and in that context Unionists might be persuaded to take up their seats in the British/Irish Inter-Parliamentary Body. Unionist concerns in this area may be significantly reduced by any agreement on constitutional issues (see below); by any arrangement for formally associating devolved institutions with the work of the Conference (as envisaged in the joint Framework Document); and if the Irish Government's input to HMG's decision-making in relation to Northern Ireland were matched by an input for local elected representatives.

(d) *A shared understanding of constitutional issues*

19. The 1992 talks effectively stalled on the then Fianna Fail Government's refusal formally to accept the principle of consent or to agree, even contingently, to support the amendment of Articles 2 and 3 of the Irish Constitution. The rest of the Irish political System, led by John Hume and Dr Garret Fitzgerald, had long since accepted the concept of an "agreed" Ireland and the right of the people of Northern Ireland to determine their own constitutional future.

20. The most important feature of the dialogue between the SDLP and Sinn Fein from 1988 was the development of a new concept of Irish self-determination (a central Republican objective) in which it was argued that if the Irish people had a right to self-determination they also had the right to determine how that right should be exercised. This led ultimately to the formula in the Downing Street Declaration of December 1993 in which the Prime Minister acknowledged the right to Irish national self-determination on a basis consistent with the principle of consent and the (Fianna Fail) Taoiseach accepted that Irish national self-determination must be subject to the agreement and consent of a majority of the people of Northern Ireland. So far as the Republican Movement is concerned the significance of the Declaration is that it potentially enables the Republican leadership to argue that an act of Irish national self-determination on these

lines is an adequate substitute for the original Republican objective of a united, independent, socialist Ireland; but they have not yet felt able formally to adopt that position.

21. The approach to the constitutional issue which was set out in the Declaration, supported by the whole spectrum of political opinion in the Republic outside Sinn Fein, was enshrined and elaborated in the Framework for a new Agreement and in the main report of the Dublin Forum for Peace and Reconciliation (January 1996). There is also widespread political support for amending Articles 2 and 3 of the Irish Constitution in the context of an overall settlement. Although Unionists appear distrustful of these developments, they are hugely significant and provide good grounds for believing that this crucial component of any successful outcome from the talks process is indeed achievable.

*(e) Security/Human Rights/other matters*

22. There is a range of issues which cut across all the "Strands" of the negotiation and might need to be addressed in a "global" way. The objective would be to provide reassurance to all concerned that matters of importance to them would be properly dealt with under any conceivable future situation. The protection of *human rights* is an obvious example: the Framework for a new Agreement canvasses the idea that both Governments would encourage democratic representatives from both jurisdictions in Ireland to adopt a charter or covenant to reflect and endorse agreed measures for the protection of the fundamental rights of everyone living in Ireland.

*(f) Definitive commitment to non-violence*

23. The Downing Street Declaration of December 1993 set out the terms on which the two Governments would be prepared to see paramilitary-related political parties engaged in the talks process. The upshot is that if any paramilitary-related party is involved in the negotiations, machinery will need to be put in place to achieve the final and total elimination of that paramilitary group's terrorist capability.

## THE PROSPECTS FOR REACHING A SETTLEMENT

24. As indicated above there has been progress over recent years in relation to certain of the elements of any deal. The main focus in any new round of substantive negotiations is likely to be on "strand two" issues – the North/South relationship – and the outcome of that will be crucial to the project as a whole.

25. A number of other difficult issues remain to be addressed in detail – finance, EC issues, policing, human rights, the relationship between any new institutions in Northern Ireland and the Westminster Parliament, the scope of any new inter-governmental Agreement etc. Some of these will have echoes in the debates on Scottish and Welsh devolution, although they may be more highly charged in Northern Ireland. None of these issues will be easy to resolve and the cumulative strain may be too much to bear; but the problems are not intrinsically insuperable.

*The Unionist world view*

26. *The most significant obstacle to reaching a comprehensive political settlement on the lines sketched out above is the fear and insecurity of the Unionist community, and the apparent reluctance of its political representatives to engage wholeheartedly in substantive political negotiations.* (At various times the same might be said of nationalists!) There are a number of factors underlying this, with deep cultural and historical origins, although reinforced by recent experience of the real world, including the terrorist threat. It includes distrust of HMG and its long-term intentions; a fear, arguably exaggerated, of the demographic implications for Northern Ireland's future; and, in some cases, a hard headed calculation that negotiations are unlikely to lead to an unqualified improvement on Direct Rule, whatever its shortcomings. There is also a well justified understanding that negotiations involve compromise, which in Northern Ireland has proved politically and sometimes actually fatal. All of this can manifest itself as, and sometimes be misunderstood as, being no more than intransigence (e.g. by some nationalists, Irish Government and US observers).

27. Over the years constitutional nationalists have reconciled themselves to a settlement on broadly the lines sketched out above and there are occasional signs that the Republican leadership at least has recognised and accepted

that this is the best they can reasonably expect to achieve (although they have done virtually nothing to acclimatise their followers). The Unionist community in general, however, interprets virtually every word and action of the whole spectrum of nationalism/Republicanism as designed to lead to the achievement of the Unionists' worst fear – a united Ireland. The talks process is widely perceived within the Unionist community as a dangerous project, partly because of the leading role of the Irish Government but mainly because they fear the price they would be required to pay to achieve some of their objectives would be too high, because it would represent movement towards <u>de facto</u> Irish unity. The Joint Framework Document is widely quoted as illustrating that fear. Their hopes of achieving a definite renunciation of the Irish constitutional claim were dashed in 1992 and they demonstrate a grudging distrust in subsequent developments on this front.

28. The development of the "peace process" and the potential for involving Sinn Fein in the negotiations adds a new dimension of concern: that the Unionist negotiating position will be further undermined by the Republican Movement's ability to use the threat of renewed violence to toughen up the negotiating position of the Irish Government and SDLP and maximise the incentive on the British Government to enforce Unionist acquiescence in a pro- nationalist outcome.

29. *The ability of those Unionist politicians (principally in the UUP) who might be prepared to work constructively towards a settlement on the lines summarised above is adversely affected by the severe political tensions within Unionism.* Mr Trimble's own rise to power illustrates the advantages to any Unionist politician of maintaining an uncompromising position. Equally, his leadership is not secure and could be under threat if the UUP fails to recover the electoral ground lost to the DUP last May. Throughout the pre-election period and certainly since the beginning of 1997 the UUP's stance in the multi-party negotiations was dictated by the need to avoid exposing itself to simplistic criticisms (especially on political/constitutional issues and decommissioning) from the DUP and UKUP while at the same time differentiating itself from them by presenting itself as relatively moderate and willing to engage constructively with the other parties in the talks. The publication of "Pathways to Peace" on 4 March can be seen as an essentially "defensive" measure, designed to show that the UUP

was negotiating constructively in the talks right up to the last minute, but without standing out from the DUP/UKUP on any fundamental issue.

30. It is possible that with the elections out of the way, and if the party does well in relation to the DUP, the UUP could be persuaded to engage rather more constructively in the talks and participate in an agreement on how decommissioning should be handled. However, there are also grounds for fearing that "Pathways to Peace", which reflects Mr Trimble's long-held views on a range of subjects, represents an attempt to move decisively away from the inclusive three-stranded talks process (with all its perceived dangers for Unionism) and to pursue a more traditional Unionist agenda, including

- the development of the Northern Ireland Grand Committee;
- changes to Northern Ireland legislative procedures at Westminster, leading inevitably to greater Integration;
- local government reform, perhaps leading to greater powers for local councils;
- greater local political input, but without formal power sharing;
- good neighbourly relations with the Republic outside the Agreement;
- the deletion of Articles 2 and 3 of the Irish Constitution and replacement of the Anglo-Irish Agreement;
- commitment to the international principles of territorial integrity.

31. *A crucial question in the immediate aftermath of the election will be whether the UUP can be persuaded to accept that the talks process offers a means to secure Unionist objectives without prejudice to fundamental principles, and that any alternative course is unlikely to achieve anything.* The UUP leadership will also need to assess whether it can *sustain* contained and constructive participation in the talks while retaining the support of the party and of the wider Unionist Community when any compromise on the emotive issue of decommissioning is bound to attract virulent criticism from the DUP and UKUP and Sinn Fein's participation would almost certainly lead the two latter parties to walk out.

*The Decommissioning Issue*

32. The most immediate obstacle facing the talks process is the inability thus far to find an agreed way through the issue of decommissioning, which is itself a proxy for the concerns which many people (particularly Unionists) feel about engaging the political representatives of violent Republicanism (and indeed Loyalism) in a democratic talks process without knowing whether they have definitively renounced the physical force option. Officials have developed a set of propositions which we believe might be acceptable to the UUP as a basis for resolving the issue of decommissioning in a post electoral Situation. These propositions are consistent with the report of the International Body and therefore do not add to the terms the Republican Movement would have to fulfil in seeking to join the talks process. The Irish side is considering these suggestions: *if the two Governments can, shortly after 3 June, present firm proposals for resolving this issue and secure the launch of the three Strands of substantive political negotiations it would give considerable new impetus to the talks process and restore its credibility.* That in turn could have a positive, albeit probably minor, impact on communal tensions during the marching season and add to the pressure on the Republican Movement to make it possible for Sinn Fein to join the substantive negotiations when they begin.

Constitutional and Political Division
Northern Ireland Office

May 1997

Document 28   A Response from Sinn Fein

From: Political Director

12 May 1997

cc:
PS/Mr Murphy (L&B) - O PS/PUS (L&B) - O
PS/Sir David Fell - O

Mr Steele - O
Mr Stephens - O
Mr Wood (L&B) - O
Mr Ray - O
Mr Holmes, No 10
Mr Budd, Cabinet Office
PS/SECRETARY OF STATE (L&B) - O

As I reported at the time, Miss Siobhan O'Hanlon, Mr Gerry Adams' secretary, made contact on Friday evening.

2. I spoke to her at 8.00pm and she told me that she had a message for me, in response to mine of earlier in the day, from Gerry Adams. The message read as follows:

> "I want to assure you of our desire to make progress. We wanted to make an early and direct approach but we appreciate the need for sensitivity. So let me reassure you that there is no intention on our part to make any of this public.
>
> Our desire is to help create conditions in which real progress can be made. The sooner this is done the better.
>
> We share your concern about events on the ground which are beyond our control. There are grave difficulties on our side also: not least among these is the treatment of the remand prisoner Roisin McAliskey, the delay in transferring sentenced prisoners in Britain back to Ireland and their conditions, the events surrounding the killing of the young catholic man in Portadown Robert Hamill, the actions of the RUC and the British Army and ongoing Loyalist attacks on our party and our community"

Signed
QUENTIN THOMAS

12 MAY 1997

# Document 29  Call by the DUP, 12 May

10 Downing Street
London SW1A 2AA

From the Private Secretary
12 May 1997

Ken Lindsay, Esq.,
Northern Ireland Office.

Dear Ken

Dr Paisley called on the Prime Minister for 30 minutes this morning. He
was unaccompanied. Dr. Mowlam, Jonathan Stephens, Jonathan Powell
and I were there on our side.

Dr Paisley started by saying that he was off to Brussels this evening for
a meeting with Santer to secure further finance from the EU, both from
the Peace and Reconciliation Fund and under Objective 1 of the Structural
Funds. He was a fan of the Reconciliation Fund, although the Protestant
population had not been as quick off the mark as the Nationalists in getting their fair share. He added that previous Governments had never given
sufficient respect to the three Northern Ireland MEPs, who should be consulted on European matters.

The Prime Minister asked for Dr Paisley's assessment of the situation
in Northern Ireland. Dr Paisley was very worried about the paramilitaries.
His concern was less about the Loyalists, where he did not expect a major
upsurge in violence although the odd killing might continue, than about
the Republicans. He had just heard from his security men about an apparent PIRA plan to kill a prominent Loyalist in East Belfast. That would
really set the cat among the pigeons, and could by no means be ruled out.

Responding to the Prime Minister's mention of Sinn Fein's election
performance, Dr. Paisley said that there was a lot of anger in Mid-Ulster
about the way in which Hume had effectively given McGuinness his support. On the local elections, he hoped the DUP would gain a few seats,
but PR made the results very difficult to call. It was unclear whether the
Sinn Fein vote would stay up, or whether there might be a swing back to
the SDLP.

Paisley went on that the DUP was prepared to sit with Sinn Fein in
locally elected councils. He would also sit in the House of Commons with
them if they took their seats. But he was not prepared to negotiate Northern
Ireland's future with them. In any case, the Forum already provided a

democratically elected place where discussions could be held. Sinn Fein should be encouraged to take up their seats, and the SDLP to return there. The Prime Minister asked how the process could be moved forward. Dr Paisley said the key was to grasp the nettle of decommissioning. The previous Government and the Irish Government had said it would be dealt with first in the talks, but it was being avoided. A vote should be taken on it in the talks, as the DUP had already suggested. There was no point in waiting for consensus on the issue. It would never come. It was quite unacceptable for the prospects for decommissioning to depend on the two Army Councils, who had a common interest in "mutuality". If an attempt was made to move on to the three Strands in the talks without decommissioning, the Unionists would not be there, even Trimble. Decommissioning was the main confidence-building measure as far as the Unionists were concerned.

Dr Mowlam commented that one problem with decommissioning was that, even when weapons had been given up, more could easily be acquired. Dr Paisley said that this was not so clear these days, with a different US attitude.

This was followed by an argument about whether the proportion of votes won in the form of elections was taken into account in the voting system for the talks. Dr Paisley argued that it was not. Jonathan Stephens pointed out that it was taken into account in the rules of consensus.

The Prime Minister said that his priority was to make clear to the Unionists that he was absolutely attached to the principle of consent. His Government would not be acting as "persuaders" for Irish unity. He asked Dr Paisley the best way of reassuring the Unionists.

Dr Paisley repeated that the Forum should be exploited better. The SDLP should be persuaded to go back, and Sinn Fein told that this was the place to talk to the other democratic parties. Unfortunately. the impression had been given that the Labour Party did not like the Forum. But the reality was that the Forum was the place where parties were represented according to their voting strength. It could be the salvation of the peace process.

The Prime Minister pointed out that there were obvious difficulties with the forum as a basis for the future, given the attitude of the Nationalists. What else could Dr Paisley suggest? Dr Paisley said that the Framework Document was regarded by all the Unionists as a major Step on the inevitable road to a united Ireland. This was totally unacceptable. The Government should make clear that they would not force the Framework Document down people's throats.

The Prime Minister asked whether this meant no cross-border co-operation. Dr Paisley argued that the obstacles to this lay on the Irish side, particularly the Irish Constitution of 1937 and Articles 2 and 3. Good-neighbourly relations were impossible while they were there. The Government should press for the removal of Articles 2 and 3. It would help to overcome Unionist suspicions of Labour, which he did not share himself but were nevertheless real enough.

Dr Paisley concluded by handing over the attached paper about the closure of residential homes in David Trimble's constituency. He said that there were only two such homes left in Portadown, Hoophill and Edenderry. There was all-party cooperation on this and he had promised to give the Prime Minister the document.

Comment

This was a friendly enough meeting, but Dr Paisley had little new or constructive to offer. I assume the constituency point raised at the end is part of some game with Trimble.

I am copying this letter to William Ehrman (Foreign and Commonwealth Office), Jan Polley (Cabinet Office) and Veronica Sutherland in Dublin.

John Holmes


# Document 30   Sinn Fein in Westminster


PRIME MINISTER

From: John Holmes

13 May 1997

Prime Minister

cc:

Jonathan Powell

Alex Allan
Mark Adams
Alastair Campbell

I understand that the Speaker will make a Statement at 2.30 tomorrow in the House. She will say simply that anyone who has not taken his seat cannot speak in the House, take part in its activities, or have any access to its facilities. This means no office for Sinn Fein, but the Speaker will not spell this out, or go into detail about the reasons for her decision.

She has cleared this approach with the Attorney General. It is contrary to Erskine May, but Erskine May is only practice and tradition, not law.

The Speaker will expect support from the main parties for her decision, and will no doubt get it.

John Holmes

# Document 31 Northern Ireland Bills

Privy Council Office
Whitehall, London SW1A 2AA

13 May 1997

The Rt Hon Dr Marjorie Mowlam MP
Secretary of State for Northern Ireland

I have seen your letter of 10 May to the Prime Minister seeking policy clearance for measures proposed in two bills for the coming session of Parliament; the bill to replace the Northern Ireland (Emergency Provisions) Act 1996, and the bill to implement the broad recommendations of the North report on parades.

I have no problem with the policy considerations. However, I should take this opportunity to draw your attention to questions of Parliamentary handling. When we considered these bills at QFL, and indeed at Cabinet, the Emergency Provisions Bill was described as short and broadly uncontroversial; it is now being described as possibly controversial and long/substantial.

Similarly, the Parades and Marches Bill was described as fairly short; it is now considered to be medium-to-long. I have no wish to stand in the way of either bill, but I am concerned that with a packed Programme, it will be crucial that we are all aware well in advance what will be required, and that all options other than primary legislation are considered. If primary legislation is required, LEG Committee will need to consider carefully how the bills can be accommodated in the form required. In any case, it is important that bills are drafted in good time for introduction. This particularly applies to the Parades and Marches Bill if this is to be introduced in the Lords as suggested at Cabinet.

I am copying this to the Prime Minister, members of IN committee, the Lord Chancellor, the Secretary of State for Scotland, the President of the Council, the Attorney General, the Chief Whip, the Captain of the Gentlemen at Arms, and to Sir Robin Butler.

RICHARD


# Document 32   Northern Ireland Bills


13 May 1997

Prime Minister

Mo Mowlam copied to me her minute of 10 May seeking policy approval for Bills to replace the Northern Ireland (Emergency Provisions) Act 1996 and to implement the North recommendations on parades.

2. I am content with these proposals. So far as the longer-term position on new counter-terrorism legislation is concerned, I will discuss this further with Mo and ensure that interested colleagues are kept informed of how we wish to take this work forward.

3. I am copying this minute to members of IN Committee, the Lord Chancellor, the Secretary of State for Scotland, the President of the Council and the Lord Privy Seal, the Attorney General, the Chief Whip, and Sir Robin Butler.

J.S.

## Document 33 Emergency Provisions Bill

### A. BACKGROUND TO THE EMERGENCY LEGISLATION

Successive Northern Ireland (Emergency Provisions) Acts (EPA), along with the UK-wide Prevention of Terrorism Act 1989 (PTA), have provided a Supplement to the ordinary criminal law and afforded the police and the Armed Forces in Northern Ireland additional powers to enable them to be as effective as possible in dealing with terrorism.

2. Successive Governments have said that the emergency legislation will remain on the Statute book only for as long as necessary. Hence the EPA has a finite lifespan during which it is required to be renewed annually by both Houses of Parliament. The current EPA expires in August 1998 and the Government has said it will re-enact it, with amendments. (If this were not done and if there were no replacement legislation, a gap would be created, leaving the security forces with no means to counter terrorism, other than the ordinary criminal law.) In parallel, on foot of the Lloyd report of October 1996, the Government intends to establish a joint NIO/Home Office working party to produce a consultation paper which will form the basis for new and permanent UK-wide counter-terrorism legislation, to be brought forward at a later date.

### B. DESCRIPTION OF PROPOSALS

The current EPA comprises seven substantive and separate parts dealing with the process of law and the powers of the security forces. In summary it:

- creates the "scheduled" offences and provides special judicial processes for them;
- creates additional powers of arrest, entry, search and seizur
- creates special offences against public security and public order;
- provides for internment without trial;

- regulates the private security industry;
- lays down arrangements for suspected terrorists in police custody.

2. While it is not yet possible to say precisely to what extent the provisions will be re-enacted as they stand, or to what extent they will be amended, the Government has signalled its intention to remove the internment power; to change the present procedures whereby offences may be certified out of the list of scheduled offences and treated under the ordinary criminal law; and to introduce audio recording of police interviews with terrorist suspects.

## C. POLITICAL IMPACT

The Bill could be controversial, depending on the prevailing security situation in Northern Ireland and on the mainland, and the state of the political process at the time it is introduced. The Government will have to defend both its continued existence and any amendments which would render its provisions closer to the ordinary criminal law; however, the setting up of the working group and the promise of a consultation paper as a forerunner to future legislative change should help counter criticism.

## D. PRESENTATIONAL CONSIDERATIONS

No special handling arrangements are anticipated. The Bill could be substantial/long. Ministers have yet to decide on the precise form and length of the Bill; the existing EPA contains some 64 sections and seven schedules.

## E. PUBLIC EXPENDITURE/MANPOWER IMPLICATIONS

The Bill will continue, possibly with modification, the current arrangements for the payment of compensation to persons affected by the exercise of the emergency powers. PES Provision has been taken. There are no implications for the public service manpower level.

*F. VALUE FOR MONEY IMPLICATIONS*

Nil.

*G. RISK OF LEGAL CHALLENGE*

While the legislation continues to provide for any form of special treatment over and above the ordinary criminal law, we can expect it to remain open to challenge in the UK courts and under the European Convention on Human Rights. Aspects of the legislation have been so challenged in the past.

# Document 34 Public Order (Northern Ireland) Bill

*A. BACKGROUND TO BILL*

This Bill would replace the Public Order (Northern Ireland) Order, which is parallel to the 1986 Public Order Act in Great Britain, and would broadly implement the recommendations of the North Report.

Following serious public disorder surrounding contested parades at Drumcree and elsewhere last year, the Government established an independent review of parades and marches. Its report (the North Report) recommended substantial changes to existing legislation. The Secretary of State and Prime Minister committed themselves to implementing this Report and to their policy objective of upholding the rule of law, both in Opposition and since the Election. This legislation will be included in the first Queen's Speech of this Government, though the first marching season is already under way and it will not therefore be possible to implement it in advance of that, as the Government would have wished. Introduction in the Autumn would enable changes to be put in place before the start of next year's marching season.

## B. DESCRIPTION OF PROPOSALS

The North Report makes in total 43 recommendations. The most significant, however, are the establishment of an independent Parades Commission as a body corporate. This Commission would have a duty to facilitate education and mediation on the parades issue. It would also take over from the RUC the power to impose restrictions on contested parades, and would implement the Report's recommendation that a new criterion be created under which conditions can be imposed, enabling the Commission to take into account the "wider impact of the parade on the relationships within the community".

Finally, the Bill would re-enact, with some consequential amendments, much of the existing Order. The Bill would also empower the Secretary of State, on appeal by the Chief Constable, to review a determination made by the Parades Commission and to revoke, amend or confirm that determination.

## C. POLITICAL IMPACT

The Bill is likely to be controversial. Opposition can be expected from Unionists, and possibly also from the Opposition.

## D. PRESENTATIONAL CONSIDERATIONS

The Bill will be medium-to-long in length. It is yet to be decided whether the guidelines which are to define how the new criterion is to be interpreted in practice should be set out in regulations, or left to the Commission's discretion. The Delegated Powers Committee of the House may have views.

## E. PUBLIC EXPENDITURE/MANPOWER IMPLICATIONS

Apart from the cost of the Commission – around £1m per annum – there are no implications for public expenditure or manpower.

## F. VALUE FOR MONEY IMPLICATIONS

Nil.

## G. RISK OF LEGAL CHALLENGE

The Bill is likely to be challenged under ECHR. Our advice is that the European Court in Strasbourg would be reluctant to challenge a central plank of Government policy which is intended to serve the general good by resolving tension in this contentious area. It is not clear however how Northern Ireland and English courts would react were ECHR to be incorporated into domestic legislation, as planned.

# Document 35  Draft Letter for PS/Prime Minister

Don Mullan Esq
Bloody Sunday Justice Campaign
1 West End Park
Londonderry
Northern Ireland
BT48 9JF

Thank you for your letters of 15 and 23 May to the Prime Minister regarding the visit to Westminster ~~on 29 May~~ by the families of some of those killed on 30 January 1972 in Londonderry. As I am sure you can imagine, the pressures on the PM's time at the moment are enormous. He will not [illegible] be able to meet the families on June 2. The Prime

Minister has, however, asked Dr Mowlam, the Secretary of State for Northern Ireland, to meet the relatives on his behalf.

Please rest assured the Prime Minister is very aware of the continuing grief felt by the families of those killed, He is determined that the lessons of that day are not forgotten and to work with others to ensure that such a tragedy should never happen again.

## Document 36   The Bloody Sunday Justice Campaign

JUSTICE CAMPAIGN

The Rt Hon. Tony Blair, MP
c/o
Diary Secretary
10 Downing Street
London
15 May 1997

Dear Prime Minister,

On Thursday, 29 May 1997, a representative of all 14 families who lost a loved one on Bloody Sunday, together with two of the wounded, will visit Westminster. During their visit the delegation hopes to meet with many of the 65 MPs who signed the House of Commons Motion on 29th January 1997, calling for the repudiation of the findings of the Widgery Tribunal and the need for a re-examination of the events of the day.

I am writing on behalf of the families to request a meeting with you on May 29, 1997. The families would value the opportunity of expressing their hopes that your Government will ensure that an honest reappraisal of the Bloody Sunday events will contribute both to their own peace of mind and a lasting peace in Ireland.

The families will travel from Dublin following a briefing with the Irish Government concerning the Bloody Sunday dossier it is currently finalising for presentation to the British Government.

We look forward to your response.

Yours sincerely,

Don Mullan
Author, *Eyewitness Bloody Sunday*
1 West End Park, Derry, Ireland BT48 9JF
JOHN HOLMES

## Document 37  Northern Ireland Bills

14 May 1997

Prime Minister

Dear Tony,

We have seen Mo Mowlam's minute to you of 10 May, setting out her proposals for legislation in Northern Ireland to replace the current Emergency Provisions Act.

There is one part of the proposals with which we have considerable difficulty. This is the suggestion that the Government should "change the present procedures whereby offences may be certified out of the list of scheduled offences and treated under the ordinary criminal law".

Under the present law, the offences in which terrorists are most commonly engaged are contained in a schedule to the Emergency Provisions Act. Scheduled offences are subject to special procedural arrangements. Most significantly, trials are conducted by a judge sitting alone (a "Diplock court") rather than by a judge and jury.

For many of the offences in the schedule, including murder, manslaughter, kidnapping, threats to kill and robbery, the Act allows the Attorney to certify in any particular case that it is <u>not</u> to be treated as a scheduled offence. The effect of the certificate, therefore, is to confer on an accused person the right to be tried by jury in the normal way.

As we understand Mo's proposal, it is that the certification procedure should be reversed and that an offence should be tried before a jury unless the Attorney certifies otherwise.

We have two major concerns. First, the right to trial by jury is of such importance that it should be taken away only by Parliament. It would be invidious for a Minister to have the power to remove that right in individual cases. The Attorney's function, as it has been understood by successive Governments, is to reduce the severity of the law in favour of individuals, and not to increase it. The argument is particularly strong in this case, since the Attorney is ministerially responsible for the Director of Public Prosecutions in Northern Ireland. His main source of advice on whether a person should be deprived of jury trial would be the prosecutor. This would place both the Attorney and the Director in a very difficult Position. It would also have an adverse effect on public confidence in the integrity and fairness of the prosecution process.

Second, the proposal would place a considerable burden on the Attorney's Office. There were 356 Diplock trials in 1994, 278 in 1995 and 220 in 1996. The proposal would mean most of these cases, including the most serious of terrorist offences, coming to the Attorney for a decision on whether they should be treated as scheduled. At this very short notice, we are not in a position to agree to the burden and high profile which this would impose.

Clearly, the proposal would be a substantial change to the system of justice in Northern Ireland. Before receiving Mo's note on Monday, we had not been consulted on whether it is the right way to proceed in principle or whether it is workable in practice. We would add that the bid made to QFL Committee was simply for a short Bill renewing the life of the existing Emergency Provisions Act, pending a consideration of what should replace it in the longer term.

We are copying this to the members of IN committee, the Lord Chancellor, the Secretary of State for Scotland, the President of the Council, the Chief Whip, the Captain of the Gentlemen at Arms, and to Sir Robin Butler.

JOHN MORRIS QC MP
CHARLES FALCONER QC

## Document 38  Northern Ireland Bills

Secretary of State
Ministry of Defence
Whitehall
London SW1A 2HB

14 May 1997
David Kyle Esq.
PS/Secretary of State for Ireland

Dear David,

The Defence Secretary was grateful for the copy of the Northern Ireland Secretary's minute of 10 May to the Prime Minister. He agrees with the proposals.

We would be grateful, however, if the Northern Ireland Office would consult the MOD if, as the new legislation takes shape, there were any intention to charge the emergency powers currently exercised by the Army under the Northern Ireland (Emergency Provisions) Acts. These powers are of fundamental importance to the support that the Army is able to give to the RUC.

The Defence Secretary agrees with the analysis that the legislation on the EPA and on the North recommendations is likely to be controversial, and that it will require careful presentation, especially with the unionists.

I am sending a copy of this letter to the recipients of yours.

Yours ever,

M A Venables
Private Secretary

## Document 39   Further Contact with Sinn Fein

Rights & European Division

From Tony Beeton

15 May 1997

PS/SECRETARY OF STATE
IMMEDIATE
cc PS/Mr Murphy
PS/PUS
PS/Sir David Fell
Mr Thomas
Mr Steele
Mr Ray
Mr Stephens
Mr Wood
Mr Holmes, № 10
Mr Budd, Cabinet Office

At 1.30pm today I took a call from Siobhan O'Hanlon. She told me that she had a message for Quentin Thomas from Martin McGuinness which she wanted me to take down verbatim. I did so and read back the text to confirm that I had got down correctly.

The message reads:

> "There are some matters which I wish to bring to your attention. Some of these are issues of concern to us, others are for your Information.
>
> Gerry Adams and I intend to travel to Westminster early next week. Our intention is to pick up our passes and to spend a short time in the House of Commons. Notwithstanding the Speaker's speech yesterday we hope there will be no obstacles placed in our way.
>
> I am told that the British Embassy in Dublin has told some people that you have been in touch with us.
>
> We note in a recent statement by Secretary of State Mo Mowlam that the Tory party's Interpretation of the Mitchell Report's position on decommissioning has been

reiterated. You are aware of our party's position on this. The issue of decommissioning has been used as an obstacle to negotiations and in the some-party talks at Stormont which have made no progress whatsoever.

It is crucial that we work to resolve problematic issues and avoid taking up public positions which add to the difficulties even in this settling in period.

We wish to make the same point about the speech which we understand the Prime Minister Tony Blair will be making in the near future."

## Comment

It may be worth noting that Ms O'Hanlon's mood and tone during the conversation was relaxed and friendly (lighter than our telephone calls last week which had been the first for some months). She readily told me that she would be available on her usual numbers except during this afternoon when she would be visiting "the prison". I did not get the impression that she expected to be called back quickly, and she did not press me about a response to either of Gerry Adams' letters.

I would interpret the message as an attempt to show that while Sinn Fein want to remain engaged, they do worry about having their room for manoeuvre limited by events and that they hope to nudge us towards conciliatory or neutral positions if they can. It appears also to be designed to impress us with the breadth of their Information (and the depth of their political acumen?)

Tony Beeton

# Document 40   Call by Senator Mitchell

10 DOWNING STREET
LONDON SW1A 2AA

From the Private Secretary
Ken Lindsay Esq.
Northern Ireland Office

15 May 1997

Dear Ken,
We have arranged for Senator Mitchell to call on the Prime Minister from
1100 to1130 on Monday, 2 June. I understand that Mitchell will go directly from the call to Dublin for meetings with Bruton and Ahern, before
going on to the re-start of the peace talks.

Please could you let us have a short brief in due course.

I am copying this letter to Dominick Chilcott (Foreign and
Commonwealth Office), Jan Polley (Cabinet Office) and to Anthony
Cary in Washington (by fax).

PHILIP BARTON


## Document 41   Irish Contacts with Sinn Fein


From the Private Secretary
Ken Lindsay Esq Northern Ireland Office

15 May 1997

Dear Ken,
Paddy Teahon told me today that, in response to a message from Sinn Fein
asking for a meeting and saying that this was in the context of a ceasefire
being in sight, the Irish had agreed to meet them at official level. They
would be doing so this Saturday. Teahon said that the message from Sinn
Fein had fulfilled the essential Irish condition for such a meeting. But he
conceded that there might be an element of electoral politics in this, not
least in the wake of Bertie Ahern's meeting with Adams yesterday.

I told Teahon in confidence where we were. I gave him a rough outline
of the Speech, and hoped that the Irish Government would not over-react
to the Unionist reassurances it contained.

Teahon took note. He said that he would be in touch over the weekend
or on Monday to give me a read-out of their meeting.

I am copying this to William Ehrman (Foreign and Commonwealth
Office), Jan Polley (Cabinet Office) and Veronica Sutherland (Dublin)
by fax.

JOHN HOLMES

## Document 42  Sinn Fein: Meetings with Officials

FROM: DAVID BROOKER
IPL DIVISION

16 MAY 1997

DESK IMMEDIATE

cc:
PS/Mr Murphy (L&B)
PS/Mr Ingram (L&B)
PS/PUS (L&B)
PS/Sir D Fell
Mr Steele
Mr Stephens
Mr Leach
Mr Bell
Mr Watkins
Mr Hill
Mr Maccabe
Mr Beeton
Mr Priestly
Mr Budd, Cabinet Office
Mr Warner
MR THOMAS
PS/SECRETARY OF STATE (L&B)

Now that the Prime Minister has announced the Government's willingness to authorise meetings with Sinn Fein, and this has been confirmed by the Secretary of State in a letter to Gerry Adams, we can expect an early request for a meeting from Sinn Fein. They could telephone through, on the established link, very quickly. This minute invites Ministers to agree the parameters within which officials should operate.

What do WE want to get out of the meeting?

2. The Prime Minister's speech sets out the basis on which officials would approach the meetings. He said –

"I want to hear Sinn Fein's answer (to the choice between negotiations and violence). And to make sure there is no danger of misunderstanding, I am prepared to allow officials to meet Sinn Fein, provided events on the ground, here and elsewhere, do not make that impossible.

This is not about negotiating the terms of a ceasefire. We simply want to explain our Position and to assess whether the republican movement genuinely is ready to give up violence and to commit itself to politics alone. If they are, I will not be slow in my response. If they are not, they can expect no sympathy or understanding. I will be implacable in pursuit of terrorism."

3. Another part of the context is the Prime Minister's acceptance that, at the right point in these exchanges, a date for Sinn Fein's entry to the process could be given.

4. While the Prime Ministers speech gives officials their basic terms of reference there are other texts that are relevant –

The Entry to Negotiations Act 1996, which provides the statutory basis for parties' participation in talks. The Act States that the Secretary of State shall refrain from inviting parties to the talks unless they have met the requirements of paragraphs 8 and 9 of the Ground Rules (in Command 3232). Paragraphs 8 and 9 require the unequivocal restoration of the IRA ceasefire and a commitment to exclusively peaceful methods and the democratic process.

The communiqué issued by the two Governments on 28 February 1996. This confirmed the two Governments' agreement that the resumption of Ministerial dialogue with Sinn Fein, and their participation in negotiations, required a restoration of the ceasefire, and affirmed their joint determination to carry on working with the other parties if IRA violence was not brought to an end. It also made clear that all participants in the talks process would have to state their total and absolute commitment to the Mitchell principles at the beginning of the negotiations, and that they would also need to address the Mitchell proposals on decommissioning at that point.

5. In addition to these documents, the Government's other publicly stated positions are relevant. On "Inside Politics" on 29 March, for example, the Secretary of State said that if the republican movement "Show by word and deed their commitment to the democratic process …. we think they ought to swiftly move into the talks process, but we need a period where that can be seen."

6. The previous Prime Minister's statement of 28 November is also relevant. But the present Government is not – as we understand it – tied to every aspect of this.

7. Taking these various statements together, we might regard officials' <u>primary objective</u> as being *to explore the scope for securing a new IRA ceasefire on a basis compatible with the relevant statute, the communique of 28 February and the Government's other publicly stated commitments.*

8. Any such process of exploration may prove to be *wide-ranging* and, amongst other things, might cover –

- the republican movement's attitude to violence and whether it accepts, or can be persuaded to accept, that violence must now come to an end.
- how the movement would intend, through words and deeds, to persuade the community at large that any new ceasefire was for real, that is to say intended to be lasting, not tactical.
- the nature of the talks process and the opportunity it provides for a comprehensive agreement between the two Governments and the relevant parties.

9. Officials will want to probe the likely *terms of any ceasefire announcement* to see how far Sinn Fein are prepared to go towards a definitive statement on the ending of violence. In this context it is worth recalling that, in an article to the Irish Times on 22 February, Gerry Adams said that "Sinn Fein believes that any restoration by the IRA of its cessation of August 1994 will be genuinely unequivocal, containing a clear and unambiguous commitment to enhance a genuine peace process."

10. As to *deeds*, officials will need to convey the importance of the provisional movement, following a ceasefire, establishing by its actions as well as by words that it is for real. Relevant to that are issues such as targeting, surveillance and the movement of weapons.

11. Officials can also probe the scope for assurance that, if the direction of the negotiations or the outcome of talks were not to Sinn Fein's liking there would be no return to violence.

12. A further key objective for officials will be to *make sure that Sinn Fein [has]a full understanding of the Government's position.* Clearly Sinn Fein will want to know whether there are any changes of emphasis in the new Government's position from that of its predecessor. Officials will be able to use the Prime Minister's speech and the Secretary of State's letter to Adams as their authorised texts. Nevertheless, we can expect Sinn Fein to press specific issues with us.

13. The nature of these exchanges with Sinn Fein is, and is said to be, exploratory. The result we hope to achieve is clear: namely a formal and convincing declaration of a ceasefire, in persuasive terms, reflected in words and deeds. Officials will be ready to explain the Government's approach to this issue and to the talks process in general. It is in the nature of exchanges of this sort that tight instructions are neither needed nor likely to prove helpful. Officials will, of course, reserve their position on any substantive points, pending clearance with Ministers. Is the Secretary of State content for the official team to enter the exchanges on that basis?

14. Sinn Fein will no doubt come to the meetings wary that HMG will, as they would see it, attempt to string them along and prolong the exchanges artificially and unnecessarily. Officials will accordingly do what they can to convey a purposive approach and a workmanlike attitude.

What will Sinn Fein want?

15. It is likely that the first meeting, or conceivably meetings, will be devoted in effect to identifying the agenda. Accordingly, it is not necessary at this point to take up substantive positions on the issues that Sinn Fein are likely to raise. Some preliminary thinking would, however, be valuable.

16. It is more than likely that Sinn Fein will return to the four key points which remained unresolved during their exchanges with the Government, via John Holmes, between July 1996 and March this year. These points, which were referred to in the Analytical Paper *Giving Impetus to Peace,* which formed part of Ministers' initial briefing, are –

- Sinn Fein's demand for certainty about a date for entry into the political negotiations following a ceasefire;
- their demand for reassurance that there will be *no preconditions to* the negotiations, and specifically that there is no requirement for prior

decommissioning by the IRA before talks and that decommissioning will not be allowed to block progress in the negotiations;
- their *demand* for an *agreed timetable* for talks, so as to prevent the Unionists stalling or erecting obstacles to progress;
- their demand for the Government to take measures to boost *the confidence* of the nationalist community in areas such as prisoners, demilitarisation, and police reform.

17. Sinn Fein might also ask whether the new Government adheres to all aspects of the previous Prime Minister's Statement of 28 November, especially the section which envisages Sinn Fein having to pass through a sequence of stages after a ceasefire has been declared, during which time the genuineness or otherwise of the ceasefire would be evaluated. (The steps include meetings with Sinn Fein at various levels, the two Governments meeting Sinn Fein to receive a commitment to the Mitchell principles, and the two Governments proposing consultations with the other parties about bringing Sinn Fein into the process). These progressive steps may help both sides to fill the period between a ceasefire and Sinn Fein's entry into talks, but they are not necessary to fulfil any requirement of principle by HMG and may not be helpful to Sinn Fein as at one time was hoped.

18. It may be useful to consider the main points in order.

Date for entry to talks.

19. For a long time Sinn Fein demanded *immediate* entry to talks once the ceasefire was called. Over time, this has evolved to a situation where what they may really be after is *certainty* that they would gain admission to talks within a relatively short, defined period after a ceasefire. *This is the key issue for Sinn Fein;* if it can be resolved, the other outstanding differences should fall into place.

20. The outcome we seek, endorsed by the Prime Minister, is to resolve this by a formula along the lines of: "If an unequivocal restoration of the IRA ceasefire were declared now, and this was reflected in words and deeds so that the statutory requirements were met, then Sinn Fein would be invited to join the negotiations by X date." But given the crucial significance of this issue for both sides, we shall need to approach it carefully.

21. The line which officials would follow initially would be to take Sinn Fein carefully through the requirements of the Entry to Negotiations Act, the

Ground Rules and the Government's other stated positions on Sinn Fein's entry to talks, then seek to discover the terms in which the deployment of the date could be used to achieve maximum leverage with Sinn Fein.

No preconditions

22. Officials would adhere to the line in the previous Prime Minister's Statement of 28 November 1996 that "the British and Irish Governments agree that, beyond the unequivocal restoration of the IRA ceasefire, these negotiations are without preconditions". As mentioned above, however, Sinn Fein are likely to seek specific clarification about *decommissioning*. Officials will be ready to explain the Government's approach and to repeat the formula in the 28 November Statement that decommissioning should be carried forward without blocking the negotiations.

*Timeframe*

23. Sinn Fein will press for an agreed timeframe so that talks cannot be delayed or otherwise obstructed by the Unionists, whom they assess as standing to benefit the most from the status quo. In reality, any notion that the British Government or the two Governments together could impose a timetable, and expect participants to work it, is totally unrealistic. Nevertheless, there is nothing to prevent the two Governments *encouraging the adoption of an agreed indicative timeframe* if the other parties would find that helpful. This was the position of the previous Government, as set out in the 28 November Statement. Ultimately, we may find that what Sinn Fein really wants is not so much a detailed timetable for the talks process so much as a reassurance that the whole process will not last for more than, say, nine months to a year. For our part, officials will want to test what Sinn Fein's attitude would be if, by the indicative end point, agreement had not been secured.

Confidence building measures

24. Sinn Fein will look for assurances that the Government is committed to early positive action on prisoners, police reform, demilitarisation and other issues of importance to the nationalist community. These items are significant since Sinn Fein needs to be able to demonstrate to its supporters that dialogue with the Government produces results. The Prime Minister's speech and earlier articles by the Prime Minister and Secretary of State give a clear commitment to building confidence in both communities and explain what measures Ministers have in mind.

25. At the first meeting with Sinn Fein we can expect little more than a *generalised exchange about issues of interest to the two sides.* From the Government's side, officials will emphasise that confidence building is a *two-way street,* that the biggest single development that would build confidence would be a *restoration of the ceasefire,* and that there is just a much *onus on Sinn Fein* as on others to build confidence in the community through the early termination of activities like targeting, surveillance, etc. Officials will also want to convey the important message that if and when there is an unequivocal ceasefire, reflected in words and deeds, the *Government will be ready to respond* as the threat diminishes (by reducing the army presence on the streets, increasing unaccompanied patrolling by the RUC etc.)

Conclusion

26. I should be grateful to know if Ministers are content for officials to approach the meetings on the basis set out above.

27. The team on our side, as agreed with PUS, will be Mr Thomas, Mr Stephens and Mr Maccabe.

Press

28. Our approach will be that the meetings, though acknowledged, would be best left unadvertised in advance. We would look to Sinn Fein to respect this approach.

DAVID BROOKER


# Document 43   Letter to Ahern


10 DOWNING STREET
LONDON SW1A 2AA

From the Private Secretary

16 May 1997

Dominick Chilcott Esq
Foreign and Commonwealth Office

Dear Dominick,

I enclose a letter of congratulation to the Prime Minister from Bertie Ahern, leader of Fianna Fail, together with a draft reply for the Prime Minister's signature. Please could you and No10 let me have any comments you have on this, by *close of play on Monday 19 May*.

I am copying this letter to David Kyle (Northern Ireland Office).
PHILIP BARTON

**Draft Letter to Bertie Ahern**

Thank you for your letter of 2 May. I am very grateful for your congratulations and best wishes.

As you know, I attach the highest importance to Britain's relations with Ireland. I want the British and Irish Governments to work closely together on Europe, on the search for peace in Northern Ireland and more generally. I am determined to start a new and more constructive chapter in our relations with the rest of Europe. Strengthened co-operation with Ireland is a key part of this.

I am also determined to give new impetus to the search for peace in Northern Ireland. I paid my first visit there as Prime Minister last week. I am convinced that we must re-double our efforts to find a solution. I hope rapid progress can be made when the talks restart on 3 June.

I know you are just starting an election campaign in Ireland. Having just completed one here, you have my best wishes for the gruelling days ahead of you.

# Document 44  Northern Ireland

From: John Holmes

Date: 16 May 1997

Prime Minister
cc
Jonathan Powell
Alastair Campbell

On returning to London, the reactions to the speech still seem broadly okay, although the Sinn Fein talks element is now firmly in the lead. I attach interviews with Hume, Trimble and Paisley to give you a bit more of the flavour, if you want.

I spoke to Trimble to thank him for his reactions. He said he thought the balance of the speech was about right, but there was obviously concern about where the talks with Sinn Fein would lead. He would want to come and see you in a week or two to talk about this. I was non-committal.

I have also spoken to Hume. He said he was telling Sinn Fein not to get hung up on the Unionist reassurances but to look at the speech as a whole. Adams had told him they would be looking for a very early meeting and would want to know the Government's view in the 10 October Statement (the principles, not the words).

You are seeing Alderdice and McCartney on Monday for half an hour each. You are well enough steeped in the issues after today to need no briefing. You will know both of them. Alderdice has become very pessimistic about the prospects over the last year or so and was particularly frustrated by the lack of progress in the talks, for which he blamed Trimble above all. He is hesitant about getting Sinn Fein in. McCartney's agenda is hardline Unionism, with a clever face. His approach is entirely destructive in effect. He has nothing positive to offer. But he may ask some hard questions, not least about the Loyalist ceasefire.

As you may have heard today in Northern Ireland, it is now pretty clear that Adams and McGuinness will turn up in Westminster on Monday and seek access to the House of Commons. Under the Speaker's ruling, they are not denied the facilities of Parliament until the end of the Debate on the Queen's Speech, i.e. 10 pm on Tuesday. They could after all be coming to swear the oath, in theory. The likelihood is that they will be allowed in, at least to talk to House officials, and may be able to wander around the precincts. They could even go into the Chamber, although I do not think they could speak.

This is all very unsatisfactory, but trying to keep them out, and going back on what the Speaker said, is probably worse and more of a Propaganda gift to Sinn Fein. In any case, this is still a matter for the Speaker, not for the Government. I wondered about warning them off, saying we would be less ready to talk to them if they played silly games at Westminster. But I doubt we would get anywhere useful, and could end up looking silly ourselves.

John Holmes

## Document 45  Dunloy: Apprentice Boys of Derry

Ken Lindsay Esq
Northern Ireland Office

16 May 1997

Dear Ken,
As you know, I agreed to receive a letter from David Tweed earlier today in Northern Ireland. He duly handed it over while the Prime Minister was at the East Antrim Institute of Further and Higher Education. I undertook to ensure the Prime Minister was aware of it, and said that we would reply.

I now attach the letter, and would be grateful for rapid advice so that we can send a reply, presumably from me rather than the Prime Minister.

Yours ever,
JOHN HOLMES

Mr David Tweed
*on behalf of the Officers & Members of Dunloy Walker Club, Apprentice Boys of Derry*

16th May 1997

Dear Prime Minister,
It is with deep regret that I must bring to your attention a serious breach in the freedoms and civil and religious liberties of the historic Apprentice Boys of Derry Club.

For over forty years the members of this Club have met in their hall in the village of Dunloy and marched the short four-minute walk to worship in Dunloy Presbyterian Church.

That expression of religious belief is carried out to publicly demonstrate our thanksgiving to God for His deliverance of our forefathers. Today there is an attack on our liberty to walk and celebrate our past and give expression to our beliefs.

The leader of IRA/Sinn Fein, whom the Speaker has now banned from the Palace of Westminster, is free in Northern Ireland to, in his owns words, "Plan and prepare and exploit deliberately orchestrated tensions and disturbances" to prevent this expression of belief. He said: "Three years' work went into creating this Situation and fair play to those people who put the work in. These are the type of scene changes that we have to focus in on and develop and exploit."

You, Sir, have a duty to uphold and protect the rights of all the citizens of this United Kingdom. My Club planned to hold its annual parade and church Service on Sunday, 18th May. We have kept the law. We gave proper notice to the Royal Ulster Constabulary, yet we find that we are to be put off the street by a concocted counter-demonstration by republican sympathisers in the Dunloy village.

The police informed us of the counter-demonstration. We proposed to change the time of our service but that was not acceptable. We proposed to change the date of our parade and that was not acceptable. Every effort was made by my Club to reduce any area of dispute, including a restriction on members. All these efforts to find resolution were shunned. The Dunloy Residents Group Claim they wish to speak with the Apprentice Boys of Derry and want the Club to seek their permission and consent to walk in the village. The Dunloy Residents are not the guardians of who can enter and walk in the village. They are not interested in tolerance at all, and have in fact shunned a meeting with the local Member of Parliament. Last November in a similar situation the RUC found a crate filled with petrol bombs which were to be used on the Protestant worshippers. The agenda is to promote a republican demand that loyalists seek consent from republicans in order to carry out their traditions. That intolerance is not on. No self-respecting person will bow to that dictatorship.

My Club respects law and order. We are not law-breakers but neither will we allow our enemies to trample our rights into the ground.

This matter must be addressed urgently by your Government, otherwise it will fester and bring a summer of discontent and tension back to our streets. Please, sir, do your duty and ensure the rights of the Apprentice Boys and the loyal Orders.

Yours faithfully,
**David Tweed**

*Please reply to Dunloy Orange Hall, Dunloy, County Antrim*
RESTRICTED


## Document 46   Request for Meeting by Bloody Sunday Families


10 DOWNING STREET
LONDON SW1A2AA

From the Private Secretary
David Kyle, Esq.,
Northern Ireland Office.

16 May 1997

Dear David,
The Bloody Sunday Justice Campaign have requested a meeting with the Prime Minister on 29 May for a representative of the families of those killed on Bloody Sunday and two of those wounded (see enclosed fax). They will apparently come to London from Dublin, where they will have been briefed on the Irish Government's dossier of evidence.

I would be grateful for your rapid advice on how to handle this request. You should be aware of one complicating factor: President Clinton will be in London on 29 May. The Prime Minister will therefore have little or no free time that day, even if we wanted to offer a meeting (which I doubt). Nevertheless we will presumably want to avoid snubbing the families completely, not least in case they then try to involve the Americans. This points to our offering a meeting with your Secretary of State.

I am copying this letter to Dominick Chilcott in the Foreign Office.

PHILIP BARTON


# Document 47   Further Contact with Sinn Fein


From: Quentin Thomas
Political Director (L)

16 May 1997
cc: PS/Mr Murphy
PS/PUS (L&B)
PS/Sir D Fell
Mr Steele
Mr Ray
Mr Stephens
Mr Wood
Mr Beeton
Mr Holmes, No 10
Mr Budd, Cabinet Office
PS/SECRETARY OF STATE (L&B)

The message which Sinn Fein passed to us, through Mr Beeton, yesterday included the assertion that McGuinness had been told that the British Embassy in Dublin had told some people that I had been in touch with Sinn Fein.

2. This is just to record that I spoke to Mr Clarke at HM Embassy about this. He categorically denied this for the good and sufficient reasons that they were unaware that contact had taken place.

Quentin Thomas

# Document 48  Liaison Group with the Irish on 16 May

16 May 1997
MR HOLMES

cc Ms Polley
Mr Fittall

Mr Sanderson

I attended the pre-lunch talks ($2^1/_2$ hours), but not lunch itself. The Irish side was the usual mixture of DFA and Taoiseach's Office, led by Sean O hUiginn.

I gather from Quentin Thomas that the Irish let off a good deal of steam over lunch about the Prime Minister's speech, which they had been given at the end of the morning. They predictably disliked the emphasis on the Union being here to stay, and (especially) the challenge to them to amend their constitution before the end game. But Quentin's view overall was that their reaction could have been worse. HM Ambassador Dublin was due to call on Paddy Teahon this afternoon, and will be reporting in due course.

The morning talks went round and round in circles for a long time about decommissioning. Sean O hUiginn said many times that so long as the Unionists used the subject in order to prevent Sinn Fein getting into the talks, it would be impossible to make progress. Quentin Thomas interjected as necessary that we had to try to find a way forward consistent with Mitchell and capable of commanding consensus. At the very end O hUiginn threw out an idea which he could have more helpfully produced at the start: the Suggestion that the two governments might jointly say that they had registered the seriousness of the decommissioning question, and that they thereby gave an undertaking that this key agenda item would in due course be taken forward by the two governments on the basis of Mitchell, and would be resolved as part of the talks process. Quentin noted that to satisfy the Unionists there would of course also have to be a commitment to establish from time to time the extent of progress on that front.

After much hesitation the Irish finally committed themselves to produce a paper on decommissioning in response to ours, in time for discussion at a further liaison group on 27 May. There was talk of a possible meeting between Dr Mowlam and the Tanaiste on 30 May (which would fit well with the planned meeting of IN on 29 May).

COLIN BUDD

## Document 49 Northern Ireland Speech: Irish Reactions

10 DOWNING STREET
LONDON SW1A2AA

From the Private Secretary

18 May 1997
Ken Lindsay Esq
Northern Ireland Office

Dear Ken,
I discussed the speech at some length with Teahon on Sunday, having welcomed the Taoiseach's Statement.

Teahon was positive about the speech – it gave the impression of a Government really determined to move things on. Ninety per cent of it was acceptable to ninety per cent of the people in Dublin. However, on close reading, there were some passages to worry a "thinking nationalist" (by which I assume he meant O'hUiginn). Why was it necessary to make the reference to no one in the room living to see a united Ireland, even if it was only in one sense stating a fact? More specifically, did the passage about not negotiating cross-border arrangements which could be threatening to Unionists mean we were back-tracking from previous discussions, or giving the Unionists a new veto. I said that, while the sentence was admittedly ambiguous, in my view it should be taken as meaning that the kind of cross-border arrangements we had in mind, eg as set out in the Framework Document, would not in our assessment be really threatening to Unionists. Otherwise, we would not be prepared to negotiate them.

Teahon went on to make clear that, despite the official welcome for the speech, there was a sense of hurt in the Irish Government, both about the meeting on 8 May and because they had not been briefed about our thinking more in advance. Teahon distanced himself personally from this feeling – and confessed that he had not told Bruton and Spring what I had told him about the speech on Thursday afternoon (!) – but said it was no less real for that. He himself fully accepted that we could not clear our speeches with them in advance, any more than the reverse could be the case. Nevertheless, we needed to be aware of this Irish feeling. Spring seemed to feel it particularly because his was a sister party and he had thought he had a particularly close relationship with Dr Mowlam.

I explained again the background to the line we had taken on 8 May, and also said that our own thinking on the speech had only firmed up at a late stage. But I did not pursue the issue. Teahon seemed to be speaking more because he had been instructed to do so than because he believed we had behaved badly.

Veronica Sutherland told me that she had also picked this up from Teahon on Friday. Obviously we need to be conscious of Irish sensitivities, which are particularly raw at the moment. (Teahon freely acknowledged that elections inevitably played a large part in Irish reactions at the moment.) But I am not inclined to be defensive or apologetic. The Irish set themselves up for what happened on 8 May, and we behaved perfectly properly over the speech.

I am copying this letter to William Ehrman (Foreign and Commonwealth Office), Jan Polley (Cabinet Office) and Veronica Sutherland (Dublin).

JOHN HOLMES
10 Downing Street, London SW1A 2AA

## Document 50  Northern Ireland Speech

10 Downing Street
London SW1A 2AA

From The Private Secretary
18 May 1997

Ken Lindsay Esq
Northern Ireland Office

Dear Ken,

It may be useful, if only for the record, to report some of the conversations surrounding last Friday's Speech, and to set out some of the obvious questions which now arise.

The afternoon before the Speech, the Prime Minister spoke to his predecessor and gave him a broad outline of his plans and what he proposed to say. Mr Major thought an early visit was right and that the content of the speech also struck the right balance, although he warned against over-reassuring the Unionists.

Early on Friday morning, the Prime Minister also spoke to David Trimble and John Hume, giving both a rough outline of what he was going to say. To Trimble, he stressed that he was setting out to reassure Unionist opinion, as they had discussed but, as they had also touched on, wanted to give Sinn Fein one more opportunity to get themselves into the talks. Trimble reacted well, but did not say much at the time. To Hume the Prime Minister underlined the importance of the new opportunity being offered to Sinn Fein but made clear that, if they did not take it, he would be looking to Hume to move on without them.

Meanwhile, I had briefed both Paddy Teahon and Sandy Berger late on Thursday evening, and urged both to react constructively but without euphoria (just in case they felt any). Both were cautious, and clearly wanted to see the words first, but undertook to do their best.

After the speech, and the generally positive reactions it received, not least from Trimble and Hume, I rang both the latter to express the Prime Minister's thanks. Trimble said he thought the speech had been good and contained a reasonable balance. But he added that there was obvious concern about the planned meetings with Sinn Fein. He hoped this would not turn out to be a slippery slope, and would want to be in touch with the Prime Minister again before long.

Hume was very positive, as he had been in public. He said that he had already been in touch with Adams to tell him to focus on the overall

balance of the speech, and particularly the points about a political settlement. Adams had made clear that Sinn Fein would be taking up the invitation. They would want in particular to know where we stood on the
draft Statement of 10 October. I said that I hoped there would be no going
back to the idea of us having to make such a statement. Life had moved
on. Hume backtracked. What was important was not whether we made
the statement itself but whether the principles contained in it gave us any
difficulty. He did not see how they could.

I have recorded separately my exchanges with Teahon about the speech
on Sunday. I will speak today to Berger to thank him for the US reaction,
which struck me as just right. Meanwhile the meeting with Sinn Fein has
now been set up for Wednesday. I am recording separately what Teahon
told me about the Irish officials' meeting with them on Saturday. But it
may be helpful to set out some of the immediate questions we have to face,
with apologies for stating the obvious in some areas.

(i) How to play Sinn Fein: how many meetings do we envisage, and
at what stage would we play the date card, assuming they are giving us
enough to want to play it? What date would we set? Can we get away
from the sterile game of Sinn Fein demanding public statements from us,
and getting into negotiations about words?

What are we actually expecting from them – how far can we press them
on the language of a ceasefire declaration, especially if we want to avoid
negotiating about statements ourselves? How can we best use the Irish
and, especially, the Americans in all this (including Clinton's visit)?

(ii) How to manage Unionist and other opinion: how will we justify
giving a date if we do, especially if we have got nothing much specific out
of Sinn Fein, as is likely? How can we prevent the UUP saying in advance
that they won't be in the talks if Sinn Fein are? What are we going to say
about verification of the genuineness of any ceasefire?
(iii) The talks: do we resume on 3 June, or would it be better to use the
Irish elections as an excuse to delay (not popular with Unionists, presumably)? Could we for example delay the restart until end-June, thus giving

us only about a month to get through before August, and perhaps a latish Autumn restart when Sinn Fein might be there? Isn't this going to look very contrived and "waiting for Sinn Fein"-like?

(iv) Decommissioning (closely related to iii): Is there really a chance of a procedural way through, particularly if the Unionists begin to expect Sinn Fein to be there? Is there a chance of moving away from focus on decommissioning, eg transferring the onus onto consent, without creating a new precondition for Sinn Fein and causing the Unionists to shout betrayal?

I have no clear answers to these questions. Nor do I expect you to have all the answers. But we do need very rapid advice on (i), before the meeting with Sinn Fein. We must have a clear game plan before we start talking. They will certainly have one.

I am copying this to William Ehrman (Foreign and Commonwealth Office), Jan Polley (Cabinet Office), Sir John Kerr (Washington) and Veronica Sutherland (Dublin).

Yours ever,
JOHN HOLMES

## Document 51  Contacts with Sinn Fein

10 Downing Street
London SW1A 2AA
From The Private Secretary
18 May 1997

Ken Lindsay Esq
Northern Ireland Office

Dear Ken

Paddy Teahon rang me on Sunday to give me a read-out of the Irish officials' meeting with Sinn Fein the previous day. He, Sean O'hUiginn and

Tim Dalton had met Gerry Adams and Pat Doherty. (Teahon told me incidentally that the Irish were a bit fed up that some of their media were saying that they had just been copying us when, as we knew, their meeting had been arranged before the Prime Minister's Speech.)

The essential message from Adams had been that, if they got reasonable assurances from HMG on the four points below, there could be a ceasefire within 7–10 days. This was not the same line as Sinn Fein were taking in public, but it was very clear from both Adams and Doherty that a new ceasefire was on.

The four points were pretty familiar:

(i) Confidence-building: prisoners, policing, emergency legislation, equality, democratic rights, etc.

(ii) A timeframe for negotiations: Sinn Fein continue to have 6–9 months in mind. The Irish pointed out that the talks would in any case only have one more year to run under the UK legislation.

(iii) Decommissioning: Sinn Fein gave the impression that if we could find a way to move forward on the kind of basis discussed before the talks adjourned, and more recently at the Liaison Group, they might be able to live with this. Adams talked of being "pragmatic" on the issue.

(iv) Sinn Fein's entry into talks: the Sinn Fein position had hardened up. They insisted on equal treatment with the other parties and therefore on full participation in the talks as soon as a ceasefire was declared. Equality of treatment, on the basis of their electoral mandate, was a much-repeated mantra.

The Irish view after the meeting was that, if Sinn Fin were reasonably satisfied on the first three points, there should be some room for manoeuvre on the fourth, in terms of arranging the "choreography" to suit both sides. But it was clear that this would be the hardest area in which to agree, as it had been in the past.

I said that Sinn Fein still seemed to be in the mode of demanding concessions from us to make a ceasefire possible. This was bound to be difficult.

I hoped we were not going to go round the houses over a new statement we had to make. Teahon said that the 10 October statement had not been mentioned at all, and their impression was that assurances in the official talks would be enough for Sinn Fein, without the need for public statements.

Teahon added that Adams had appeared ready to do business and [was] relatively pragmatic. Sinn Fein had apparently expressed the hope that we would be ready to engage quickly, rather than repeating well-known positions at each other (as Adams had admitted had been the case during the last ceasefire). I said that we would certainly be serious, but I hoped Sinn Fein did not imagine all could be sorted out at one meeting.

Quentin Thomas will no doubt be in touch with Sean O'hUiginn to cross-check this account – Teahon is often prone to wishful thinking and is usually vague on details. On the face of it, the Sinn Fein approach sounds reasonably encouraging, but timing looks like being very difficult. I have asked separately for the earliest possible advice on the line we should take.

I am copying this letter to William Ehrman (Foreign and Commonwealth Office), Jan Polley (Cabinet Office), Sir John Kerr (Washington) and Veronica Sutherland (Dublin). .

JOHN HOLMES


# Document 52   Call by Lord Alderdice, 19 May


10 DOWNING STREET
LONDON SW1A2AA

19 May 1997

From the Private Secretary
John Alderdice called on the Prime Minister for 30 minutes this afternoon. He was alone. Dr. Mowlam and David Hill were present on our side.

Alderdice said that the positive feelings about the new government in Britain had been carried over into Northern Ireland as well. The Prime Minister's speech had been well received, not least for its honesty and the momentum it promised. But the situation on the ground was dangerous and polarised – people's expectations had been raised by the ceasefire, and anger and bitterness were the higher because of the subsequent disappointment. But this anger was matched by a fear of what would happen if Northern Ireland fell back into the abyss. This meant that the dangers were matched by possibilities for progress.

The Prime Minister said that, if the Government talked to Sinn Fein, people presumably thought that this ought to lead to a ceasefire and Sinn Fein's entry into the talks. Alderdice agreed. He thought that the Republican movement had nowhere else to go. But if Sinn Fein did not enter the talks, it was important that the settlement train really did leave without them. They could always catch up at a subsequent station. This would need real drive from the British Government, since virtually all the parties would find reasons for not moving on. It also meant that a timescale for the talks was vital. The legislation already set one, but the intention should be to sew up the political talks by Christmas – the summer should be used to tee up the process to tackle the three Strands seriously in the autumn. If the process got stuck (because Trimble was too terrified of Paisley and McCartney, or Hume could not break out of his candy floss language), the two governments would need to take it on themselves. It was best that this should be done relatively early in the life of the British Government.

Alderdice went on that the new Government's approach to devolution throughout the UK was helpful because it meant that Northern Ireland was no longer in an obviously different position. He was also happy that pressure was being applied to the Irish Government to move on articles 2 and 3 of the Constitution.

Discussion moved on to the marching season. The Prime Minister asked whether an IRA ceasefire would make the summer easier. Alderdice thought probably not. The parades issue was not a question of allegiance to tradition, but of marking out and defending territory. The Garvaghy Road had been a battleground for many years. If the Orange Order really were prepared to sit down and talk to the residents, a local accommodation could perhaps be found. But it might also be useful to say to the Orange Order privately that, if they sat down with the residents in a reasonable fashion, but met unreasonableness on the other side, the Government would let a suitably moderate march through. If they were not prepared to sit down and try at all, there would be no march. Another approach would be to treat the Parades Commission's recommendations as binding even before the legislation was through.

Dr, Mowlam said that the latter would just wind up the Unionists unnecessarily. In any case, Alastair Graham was not ready to take on such a role yet. But she was attracted by the idea of saying to march organisers that if there was any triumphalism or distasteful references to previous deaths during marches, there would be no march the following year. She went on to discuss the possible options for dealing with Drumcree. She expected that the RUC Chief Constable would want the Government to take the decision. In any case, she hoped that all those with any authority in Northern Ireland, especially those outside government, would stand up publicly for common sense solutions. The Prime Minister echoed this thought. He was struck by the role which businessmen might be able to play in exerting pressure on the politicians.

Alderdice suggested that the key was for local residents to feel that the Orange Order had some respect for them. Those on the Garvaghy Road did not want a war on their doorsteps, and would be prepared to be reasonable if they felt their rights were being respected. Meanwhile it was unhelpful that John Hume had chosen to go so public about the possibility of the leader of the Orange Order meeting the Garvaghy Road residents.

*Comment*
This was as friendly and rational a meeting as usual with Lord Alderdice. He struck me as less pessimistic than in most recent meetings.

I am copying this letter to William Ehrman (Foreign and Commonwealth Office), Jan Polley (Cabinet Office) and Veronica Sutherland in Dublin.

JOHN HOLMES
Ken Lindsay, Esq., Northern Ireland Office.

# Document 53   Reactions to Blair Speech

19 MAY 97

*SUMMARY*

1. Universally favourable reaction to Prime Minister's Belfast speech.

*DETAIL*

2. The Prime Minister's speech in Belfast on 16 May has received. a universally favourable reaction from political leaders and media commentators here. Reactions have concentrated on the offer of official-level talks with Sinn Fein, which is widely seen as opening the door to political progress, if only Sinn Fein will seize the opportunity.

3. The Taoiseach, Mr Bruton, in a press statement on 16 May, (by Fax to NIO/RID) welcomed the Prime Minister's emphasis on the principle of consent and his commitment to a settlement commanding the support of both nationalists and unionists. He agreed with the Prime Minister that, while it was desirable to have Sinn Fein on the "settlement train", the train would be leaving anyway. Mr Spring also welcomed the speech, urging the importance of grasping "the precious opportunity for political progress". Mr Ahern, while welcoming the speech, sought to make political capital by contrasting the Prime Minister's offer to Sinn Fein with the Irish Government's reluctance to meet them. The Government quickly countered by announcing that officials met Sinn Fein on 17 May, a meeting which they asserted had been authorised before the Prime Minister's speech.

4. Press comment has also been favourable with attention focussed predominantly on the offer to Sinn Fein. The *Irish Times*, in an editorial on 17 May, praised the Prime Minister's "determination and good judgement". He had made a "generous gesture" to Sinn Fein and it was now up to them to "seize the moment". The *Irish Independent* commended his "praiseworthy despatch" in fulfilling his pledge to put Northern Ireland at the top of his agenda. "Sinn Fein are dealing with a man who knows what he is doing and where he is going." They should "take his offer and get on the train." The *Sunday Independent* on 18 May said it was time to call Sinn Fein's bluff.

The only impediment to their inclusion in the talks was their own failure to persuade the IRA to abandon violence.

5. Most commentators note the pro-union sentiments in the speech and the view that Irish unity will not occur in the foreseeable future without adverse comment, many accepting that this is the logical outcome of the principle of consent. Neither is there criticism of the suggestion that the Irish Government should consider amending Articles 2 and 3 as a confidence-building measure in advance of a settlement.

*COMMENT*

6. Following the initial suspicious reaction by officials at the Anglo/ Irish Liaison Group on Friday, the mood outlined above is encouraging. Teahon (Taoiseach's Department) told me on Friday that the Taoiseach had been personally extremely enthusiastic when he heard the speech, and had overruled O'hUiginns's (DFA) advice to respond coolly. The Taoiseach clearly shares the general perception that a decisive step has been taken to try and move the peace process forwards.

7. ADVANCE COPIES TO: Holmes, No.10, Budd, Cabinet Office, Thomas, N10, Lamont, RID.

SUTHERLAND


# Document 54  Discussions with Paddy Teahon

British Embassy
Dublin

19 May 1997

To John Holmes, Esq.
PS/No. 10

Dear John,

1. I have read with interest your three faxes of 18 May. On the Prime Minister's speech you will have seen my telegram number 158 recording the favourable reaction here.

2. As I mentioned to you on the telephone on Saturday, I called on Paddy Teahon late on Friday afternoon. I had a further telephone conversation this morning, when he rehearsed the points in your letter on contacts with Sinn Fein.

3. In both conversations Paddy expounded at some length on our failure to engage substantively at the talks on 8 May, and to consult in advance about the speech. The Irish side were hurt, Paddy said. I responded by saying that to expect substantive engagement from a government which had been in office for under a week was unrealistic; and that prior consultation on the speech risked unwelcome leaks, of which there had been a number of unfortunate examples. I encouraged Paddy to follow the example of Dr Mowlam, who is reported as saying that she has learnt to have a short memory on issues of this nature. Paddy had the grace to laugh.

4. I am quite clear that we did, as you say, act properly over both the meeting and the speech. However, all this does underline the central message of my minute of 2 May, "Working with the Irish on Northern Ireland", which emphasised the crucial importance of close personal relationships between members of the two Governments.

Yours ever,
Veronica Sutherland
Ambassador


## Document 55  Letter to Ahern


Foreign & Commonwealth Office
London SW1A 2AH

John Holmes
10, Downing Street

19 May 1997

Dear John
Thank you for your letter of 16 May.

An additional point to bear in mind is that Ahern (like most of the Irish political establishment) will already have read the Prime Minister's speech last week in detail. You may therefore wish to recast your third paragraph to take account of this, perhaps on the following lines:

> "I am also determined to give new impetus to the search for peace in Northern Ireland. I hope that my visit there last week left no one in any doubt of my Government's commitment to finding a solution. I know that, whatever its complexion, the next Irish Government will share our desire for rapid progress when the talks restart on 3 June."

In official Communications, we use the term "Republic of Ireland" rather than "Ireland". To avoid giving offence it is usually possible to use neither. This could be done by omitting "in Ireland" in the first sentence of the last paragraph, or redrafting the paragraph to read:

> "Having just completed our own election campaign here, you have my best wishes for the gruelling days ahead of you."

I am copying this letter to David Kyle (Northern Ireland Office).

Yours ever,
Fiona Mylchreest
Private Secretary

# Document 56  International Fund for Ireland: Proposed EU Regulation

From the Secretary of State for Northern Ireland
The Rt Hon Robin Cook MP
Foreign and Commonwealth Affairs
Foreign and Commonwealth Office
King Charles Street
London
SW1A 2AH

19 May 1997

Dear Robin,
The International Fund for Ireland was established by the UK and Republic of Ireland Governments in 1986 following the Anglo-Irish Agreement and has played a valuable role in developing cross-community and cross-border co-operation in Northern Ireland and the six border counties of the Republic of Ireland. It has had two main donors – the United States and the European Union, but Canada, Australia and New Zealand have also made contributions.

The EU contributed at the level of 15 mecu from 1989 to 1994 and at the level of 20 mecu from 1995 to 1997. A draft regulation has now been prepared to extend EU assistance for the next two years (1988 and 1999) at an annual level of 15 mecu. While the annual contribution is somewhat reduced, the proposal to continue EU support for the International Fund is very welcome. There was the prospect that the funding might cease altogether given that the EU has supported the Peace and Reconciliation Programme, at much higher levels of funding. The renewed commitment of the EU to the IFI ties in very well with our approach to Europe generally and to the renewed efforts to move ahead with the political process in Northern Ireland. The financial implications have been agreed with the Treasury.

The Irish Government will be supporting the regulation. One of the benefits of the Fund has been the establishment of close working relationships between the two administrations in delivering IFI Programmes. The IFI plays a valuable role in demonstrating that joint working can deliver important benefits particularly to the more disadvantaged areas of Northern Ireland the border counties.

I therefore seek your agreement that the proposed Regulation should be supported by the UK in COREPER and in the Council of Ministers. Since COREPER are meeting on Wednesday and we understand that the Commission want to table the New Regulation for approval at that meeting, I would be grateful for an urgent reply no later than close of play on Tuesday 20 May 1997.

I am copying this letter to the Prime Minister, the President of the Board of Trade and the Chief Secretary and would be grateful for their approval also. My officials will be in touch with yours and with No 10 to agree a presentational line.

Marjorie Mowlam

## Document 57 Call by Robert McCartney MP, 19 May

10 Downing Street

London SW1A 2AA

From the Private Secretary

19 May 1997

Ken Lindsay, Esq.,
Northern Ireland Office.

Dear Ken,

Robert McCartney, accompanied by an adviser whose name I did not catch, called on the Prime Minister for about 40 minutes today. Dr. Mowlam and David Hill were present on our side.

After congratulations, McCartney said that he felt excluded from input into the Government's policy on Northern Ireland. Despite the fact that he had sat on the Labour Party benches and voted with them on every occasion, Trimble had been called to see the Prime Minister first. As far as the Prime Minister's speech was concerned, it had served its purpose in making most Unionists more comfortable, but it did not take actual policy further than the previous government. There were two concepts which did not run together: resolving the conflict between HMG and the IRA, and finding a political settlement. Efforts to find the IRA's bottom line in order to persuade them to stop terrorism had created serious obstacles to a political settlement. The peace process had paradoxically made the two communities hate each other more than ever. Unionists had been made paranoid by the lengths to which the British Government had gone in seeking to stop IRA violence, while Nationalist expectations had been raised too high.

McCartney continued that the consent principle was in fact nonsense. The IRA and Sinn Fein would never buy into it unless they had the glimmer of a promise of Irish unity. Adams' position remained as he had set it out in March 1993: the price of an IRA ceasefire was a declaration by the British Government that partition would be ended. Moreover, the consent principle was a double-edged sword, which Nationalists interpreted as consent to the transfer of sovereignty. That was why they insisted on

cross-border bodies with political significance. No one was against practical cooperation with the South, but why did this need to be encased in
political institutions?

The Prime Minister said that he came to the issues without prejudices.
He had said that Northern Ireland would be part of the UK for many years
to come, at least. He would be very happy with that. He wanted to see a
devolved government with a proper role for Nationalists, and sensible
North/South Cooperation. The latter did not need to undermine Northern
Ireland as part of the UK. Most people in Northern Ireland appeared ready
to support a settlement on these lines.

McCartney said that most people in Northern Ireland did not have a
clue. He was happy with devolution for Northern Ireland, along the same
lines as that for Scotland and Wales. But there was no precedent for dealing
with a minority problem by giving a foreign government a detailed say in a
country's affairs. The Anglo-Irish Agreement had driven a coach and horses
through normal principles of settling such issues in Europe.

The Prime Minister asked what McCartney actually wanted.
McCartney said he wished to see a settlement agreed between the constitutional parties (although he did not think this was likely), with the
two governments making clear that it would be backed even if Sinn
Fein did not agree, and that any violence would be severely dealt with.
However he had no faith that the Irish Government would ever agree
to this, following his meeting with Bruton over a year ago. His other
requirement was that Dublin's ability to influence Northern Ireland
should not be increased.

The Prime Minister said that one of the reasons why he believed
the prospects for progress were now better was that attitudes in the Irish
Republic had changed. The Irish were prosperous and focused on Europe,
and they did not really want Irish unity if any coercion were involved.
McCartney disagreed. The Irish liked Europe because of the money,
but no Irish government would agree to amend articles 2 and 3 of the
Constitution – at least not until they could swap the aspiration for the
reality of control, eg as set out in the Framework Document. The latter
could never be the basis for a settlement, although the NIO would no
doubt go on pushing it.

McCartney went on that events this July could turn Northern Ireland into a quagmire for the new Government. The idea of local negotiation settling disputes over parades was a recipe for disaster. The need for local approval would simply extend trouble to the vast majority of parades which were currently sorted out without difficulty. The basic principle should be simple: if a parade was inherently peaceful and well marshalled, it should be allowed to proceed without threat from third parties.

The Prime Minister commented that some parades could be provocative. McCartney was not inclined to agree, and went into the history of Drumcree to demonstrate how Unionists had been gradually cut back in what they could do. He also referred to recent suggestions that Sinn Fein had deliberately stirred up the parades issue. Dr Mowlam commented that some residents groups might be headed by Sinn Fein activists, but they were nevertheless broadly representative of residents' views. McCartney said that Drumcree was a classic symptom of the problems caused by constant attempts to stop IRA violence. Unionists' confidence had been fatally undermined, and protestations by successive Prime Ministers that they supported the Union were contradicted by their policy in practice.

McCartney finished by complaining about education cutbacks in North Down. The South East Education and Library Board had suffered more than others. Dr Mowlam pointed out that she had just authorised a further £4 million for education in Northern Ireland. The South East Board had been in particular difficulty because of a large overspend, but it had been agreed that this could be carried for a further two years. McCartney was unpacified.

*Comment*

McCartney was his usual provocative and negative self. I enclose some reading material he left for the Prime Minister.

I am copying this letter to William Ehrman (Foreign and Commonwealth Office), Jan Polley (Cabinet Office) and Veronica Sutherland in Dublin.

Yours ever,
John Holmes

## Document 58   Northern Ireland: Meetings with Mr Robert McCartney QC, MP and Lord Alderdice

From the Private Secretary
Northern Ireland Office
Millbank
London
SW1P 4QE

**Draft**

John Holmes Esq
PS/Prime Minister 10 Downing Street

We understand that the Prime Minister is to meet Mr Robert McCartney QC MP of the United Kingdom Unionist Party (UKUP) and Lord (John) Alderdice, Leader of the Alliance Party of Northern Ireland on Monday 19 May 1997 at 2 pm and 4.30 pm respectively. The Secretary of State and an NIO official will be present.

These are, like the earlier meetings, intended as introductory encounters. The objectives are the same as before:

- communicate Government's and PM's personal commitment to search for fair political accommodation and lasting peace in Northern Ireland
- provide reassurance to parties about key bases of policy – see below
- reiterate Government's desire to proceed with fullest cooperation, establish basis for trust and confidence and openness, for future.

Lord Alderdice is likely to be well-disposed, and may be constructive; though he has long been pessimistic about the talks process. Mr McCartney is firmly persuaded that the talks process is corrupt, indeed designed to appease Sinn Fein and ease Northern Ireland toward unification with the Republic. He may accept that these are not the Prime Minister's personal motivations; but he is unlikely to accept that the process is redeemable. He is, however, short on positive alternatives. It will be interesting to see how far their respective pessimism and suspicion have been countered by the Prime Minister's Speech.

At Annex A are some general points for the Prime Minister to make and attached at Annex B, particular points aimed at the individual parties. Annex C embodies background notes on the UKUP and Alliance, together with personality notes on Mr McCartney and Lord Alderdice.

W K LINDSAY

ANNEX A
**General points to make**

- Determined to do all in my power to secure lasting peace and political stability in Northern Ireland. Full confidence in Mo Mowlam; but I will maintain personal interest. Always ready to engage directly where that would be helpful.
- Want to emphasise that our approach is based on firm principles and will therefore be consistent; I outlined some in my Speech last week:
- completely committed to principle of consent; Northern Ireland's constitutional Status will not change unless majority of Northern Ireland wish it to do so. Welcome the fact that this has almost universal acceptance.
- Equally committed to making Northern Ireland a place in which nationalists can feel comfortable to live in. Parity of esteem. Equality of opportunity. Appropriate expression of their Irish national identity (without prejudice to the constitutional guarantee).
- Believe talks process offers best prospect of achieving a comprehensive political settlement, addressing and resolving the fundamental political concerns of all the participants. No risk to anyone's fundamental interests. Any outcome must be agreed and widely supported before it can be implemented.
- Determined to promote real progress in the Talks. Looking for ways to resolve the decommissioning issue on satisfactory terms and set an early date for substantive negotiations.

- No question of Sinn Fein coming in unless they meet the criteria: an unequivocal restoration of the IRA ceasefire – borne out by words and deeds.
- Believe it is right we leave the door open for them. If they meet the criteria, they come in. If they refuse the opportunity, we are quite ready to press on without them.

**ANNEX B**
**Specific points for parties**

*UKUP*

- Emphasise Government's commitment to the principle of consent and to the three Stranded talks process. Point to widespread acceptance of the principle of consent (by all except Sinn Fein) and the likelihood that any negotiated settlement would be predicated on that basis;
- Point to the benefits of a widely acceptable political accommodation, acceptable to majorities on both sides of the community, which would enable significantly greater local political accountability and general political stability;
- Express determination to find an agreed way through the decommissioning issue, based on the Mitchell "compromise approach" (some decommissioning during the negotiations), allowing an early date to be set for the launch of the three Strands;
- Reaffirm criteria for Sinn Fein entry to negotiations, while refusing definitively to close the door. Assert readiness to proceed without them;
- Dismiss criticism of Irish Government's role;
- Note any allegation that Loyalists have demonstrably dishonoured their commitment to the Mitchell principles; confirm that commitment to the principles remains a condition of participation in the talks; but point out that there will be opportunities to consider the Loyalist parties' entitlement to remain in the talks when they resume on 3 June.

*Alliance Party*

- Emphasise commitment to the three stranded talks process and belief that it remains viable;
- Express determination to find an agreed way through the decommissioning issue, based on the Mitchell "compromise approach" (acknowledging the constructive role played by the Alliance Party in promoting what contingent agreement has so far emerged), allowing an early date to be set for the launch of the three Strands;
- Reaffirm criteria for Sinn Fein entry to negotiations, while refusing definitively to close the door. Assert readiness to proceed without them;
- Point to value of UUP/SDLP cooperation, with Alliance Party support, in moving the talks forward;
- Seek Alliance Party assessment of the other parties' positions.

**ANNEX C**
UK UNIONIST PARTY (UKUP)

Prominent Members – Robert McCartney, QC MP
Cedric Wilson
Conor Cruise O'Brien

| ELECTORAL SUPPORT | |
| --- | --- |
| 1995 By-Election | 37.0% |
| Entry to Negotiations Election 1996 | 3.7% |
| General Election 1997 | 2.1% |

The UK Unionist Party represents the latest attempt by Robert McCartney to construct within Unionism his own individual power-base. McCartney was elected to Parliament in the North Down by-election of June 1995 (with DUP Support), but his challenging analysis of Unionism – that both traditional Unionist parties have condemned the cause they seek to uphold by failing to make Unionism a political philosophy which is capable of winning a wider spectrum of support – has proved to exercise a limited appeal, perhaps because his approach has so far been characterised by blustering negativism. In the Entry to Negotiations elections, his vote weakened in North Down, and (although respectable) he failed to make significant headway outside greater Belfast and its satellite constituencies.

On the constitution, the Party's position is unambiguous – maintenance of the position of Northern Ireland within the UK, and resistance to any expansion of the role of Dublin in the internal affairs of the province (a pronouncement which tacitly appears to recognise that a limited and controlled Irish dimension to the affairs of Northern Ireland does have a place in an overall settlement).

The core of the UK Unionists' analysis is that HMG policy towards Northern Ireland amounts to an unavowed strategy of securing the dissolution of the Union by consent. The development by the two Governments of a joint approach to the process of political development is interpreted as facilitating creeping Irish unity and a gradual disengagement of Northern Ireland from the life and politics of the UK.

With regard to negotiations, the Party has staked out an uncompromising position – the pro-Union parties should determine and maintain a common position, based on a shared assumption of a bottom line which cannot be breached; the absence of Sinn Fein or the Loyalist political representatives will not devalue negotiations; the resumption by the IRA of the August 1994 ceasefire is insufficient for SF to gain admittance to talks – only a total and permanent ceasefire will suffice; the agenda for negotiations should exclude the concept that the Union itself is negotiable; North-South institutions can be contemplated only insofar as they are of practical worth and mutual benefit – excluded are bodies driven by political considerations; Articles 2 and 3 of the ROI Constitution must be abandoned before any significant agreement can be reached; decommissioning must not be shunted off into a fourth Strand siding while political issues are progressed down the main track; and the Framework Documents are unacceptable as a conceptual framework for the negotiations.

In the Talks to date, McCartney and his supporters have concentrated their fire on the UUP, seeking to exert a restraining influence over what they see as Trimble's dangerous tendency to compromise on essential issues. When not instigating such attacks, they have supported the DUP efforts to the same end. Making political progress via the Talks process has not been an objective.

Given McCartney's long track record as a political loner, it remains a matter of speculation how long he will remain in partnership with Paisley, a politician for whom he is known to have a strong personal antipathy. The need for DUP support in the General Election, and the expediency of making common cause in the resumed Talks, will presumably maintain the nexus for the immediate future; but it is difficult to visualise a successful long-term relationship between two such strong and disparate personalities. By the same token, given McCartney's penchant for forming temporary groups to meet particular needs, it is possible to predict that the UKUP as a political party may have a limited life expectancy.

## Document 59   UKUP Leader and MP for North Down, Robert McCartney MP

*Background*

Born in 1936 in the Shankill area of Belfast: now one of Northern Ireland's leading barristers. First entered the political scene in late 1981, when he crossed swords with Dr Paisley following the assassination of the MP for South Belfast, the Rev Robert Bradford. Subsequently joined the UUP and unsuccessfully sought the UUP nomination in the South Belfast by-election, April 1982. About July 1982 founded a group within the UUP with the aim of encouraging the Party to broaden its liberal appeal. In August 1982 he visited the USA to put forward moderate Unionist views. Scraped into the 1982 NI Assembly (for North Down) on the eleventh count. Failing to make an impact in the UUP in 1986 he launched the Campaign for Equal Citizenship urging national parties to organise in Northern Ireland. He was expelled from the UUP in 1987.

Unsuccessfully contested North Down in 1983 and 1987, but won the seat in the by-election on 15 June 1995 when (once more leading a group of his own creation) he stood as a UK Unionist. In his maiden speech on 5 July he broke with tradition and mounted an attack on the Government, accusing it of offering Northern Ireland a policy of "covert institutional coercion into a united Ireland", and following a strategy "designed to buy off terrorists who still retain the means of damaging the British economy".

*Personality and Political Views*

McCartney is highly intelligent, ambitious and renowned for his inability to suffer fools gladly. Allegations of intellectual arrogance and of lacking the common touch have followed him throughout his career, and have contributed to his reputation for regarding politics as an extension of his legalistic pursuits. His experience in the courts leads him to an oratorical style which is structured and portentous in delivery. He is not known for his willingness to support a party line of which he disapproves, and his flirtation with various brands of Unionism probably made it inevitable that he should eventually create his own party for the promulgation of his views. His current allegiance with the DUP is, therefore, not only against his past history, but may be said to be in conflict with his penchant for regarding politics as a non-team sport.

McCartney is firm in his defence of the Union, but believes that an accommodation with nationalists would be possible provided the British Government gave Unionists the reassurance of their unconditional support. He has been highly critical, particularly in articles in the *Belfast Telegraph*, of the effect on the Unionist position of the 1993 Downing Street Declaration. He purports to believe that cross-community support can be generated for a concept of Unionism which eschews sectarian triumphalism and embraces instead a pluralistic approach to socio-economic politics. It has to be said that his performance in the current Talks process has been characterised more by blustering negativism than by any enlightened approach to a new vision of Unionism.

# Document 60　Alliance Party

Prominent Members – Lord Alderdice (Leader)
Seamus Close (Deputy Leader)
Mrs Eileen Bell (Chair)
Sean Neeson (Chief Whip)
Stephen McBride (Executive Committee Member)

| ELECTORAL SUPPORT | |
| --- | --- |
| General Election 1992 | 8.7% |
| Local Government Election 1993 | 7.7% |
| European Election 1994 | 4.1% |
| Entry to Negotiations Election 1996 | 6.5% |
| General Election 1997 | 8% |

The Alliance Party was formed in 1970 to appeal to moderate opinion in both Protestant and Catholic communities.

In October 1988 the Party produced a major policy document entitled "Governing With Consent", which set out to produce a summary of conclusions arrived at by a study group set up by senior party officials to review arrangements for the future government of Northern Ireland. The paper contained a good deal of helpful and balanced comment and realigned earlier proposals. It reaffirmed devolution of power to a Northern Ireland Assembly within the United Kingdom as the best way to achieve political progress in Northern Ireland. There was also a clear recognition of the importance of a guaranteed role for the minority in any future devolved administration, whilst accepting that the Irish Government should have a right of consultation on matters affecting Northern Ireland. This document remains the basis of Party policy.

The Alliance Party took an active role in the 1991/92 inter-party talks and participated in the Dublin Forum for Peace and Reconciliation. It was consistently measured in its approach to the Frameworks Documents and encouraged others to do likewise. As far as decommissioning is concerned, it believes that an International Body should be established to oversee the process.

Lord Alderdice was extremely disappointed by the performance of the Alliance Party in the 30 May 1996 Entry to Negotiations Election. The fall in its share of the vote was probably due to a reversion in some quarters to voting along traditional sectarian lines, and some votes would also have been lost to the plethora of smaller parties who stood in this election. In the Talks, the Alliance Party has been constructive in attempting to progress proceedings and reach some agreement.

## Document 61    Lord Alderdice of Knock, Alliance Party Leader and Member of Belfast City Council

*Background*

Lord Alderdice (then Dr John Alderdice) joined the Alliance Party in 1978, was elected to the Party council in 1979 and in 1984 he joined the Party Executive. In the 1987 Westminster Election he polled a significant 10,000 (32%) votes against Peter Robinson in East Belfast but failed to increase this substantially in 1992. Following the resignation of John Cushnahan (the then party leader) in October 1987 he defeated Seamus Close by 117 to 77 votes in the leadership election. He has been a member of Belfast City Council since May 1989, but is not standing for re-election in May 1997. Successful in Belfast East in the election on 30 May 1996 to select delegates to the Forum and Negotiations.

Born in 1955, the son of a Presbyterian Minister, he was educated at Ballymena Academy and Queen's University. He is married with two children and is a consultant psychiatrist. He was raised to the peerage in 1996 as Baron Alderdice of Knock.

*Personality and Political Views*

His performance in the 1992 Westminster Election in East Belfast was a disappointment as the Party had hoped for a better result, but Lord

Alderdice's profile is now much higher than previously - not least because of his exposure during the 1992 Talks. An articulate and ambitious man, though occasionally portrayed in public speaking terms as a deliverer of "sermons to the congregation", he is keen to attract new young blood to the party and increase its political depth should the pendulum swing in its favour at some future point. His style does not always endear him to some of his colleagues but this has not caused serious ripples in terms of relationships within the Party.

He is generally supportive of the direction being taken by Government in regard to political development, and has been helpful in undertaking visits to the USA to ensure that a corrective view is available to counter the wilder allegations of other visiting Northern Ireland politicians. Experience of the current talks to date has, however, left him pessimistic that the present crop of Northern Ireland politicians can ever reach a sensible compromise, especially given the pressures of Sinn Fein's potential involvement. He has recently been prone to argue that the attempt to bring Sinn Fein in should be abandoned and/or that the two Governments should begin to draw up their own proposals for a comprehensive political Settlement.

# Document 62  Meeting of Liaison Group

FROM: QUENTIN THOMAS
Political Director

19 May 1997

PS/Secretary of State (L&B)
PS/Sir David Fell
Mr Steele
Mr Bell
Mr Stephens
Mr Watkins
Mr Ray – MUFAX
Mr Beeton

Mr Brooker
Mr Hill
Mr Lavery
Mr Maccabe
Mr Lamont RID/FCO
Mr Budd Cab Office
HMA Dublin

A fuller note of last Friday's meeting of the Liaison Group will issue in due course.

In summary, the Irish side, having initially adopted their preferred position of making no further move on decommissioning unless they received a prior assurance that it would secure Unionist assent, were brought by a mixture of the carrot (an Adare meeting if sufficient progress were made) and stick (Ministers would be disappointed if their enthusiasm for the Anglo-Irish partnership were to be frustrated) to expose some ideas of their own, which on analysis seemed not a million miles from ours, and even to agree to draft the next paper which the Group will consider at a meeting on 27 May. All that, with various diversions, took up most of the meeting proper.

2. By the end of lunch, when the Irish side had managed to work their way through the text of the Prime Minister's speech which we gave them at the end of the meeting, there was a semi-fractious exchange occasioned by the allegedly pro-Unionist tone of the speech and the British effrontery in suggesting that amendment to their constitution might be a confidence building measure. (How sadly they must have discovered that John Hume had described the speech as the best since Demosthenes.)

3. If there is an Adare meeting – that is a Ministerial meeting confined to the political process with relatively small numbers – it might occur towards the end of the week beginning 26 May. In the light of our discussion, we identified two main issues:

(a). Decommissioning – in particular if officials have succeeded in drawing up a paper with a new proposition there will be important tactical questions about how this is played into due process. Beyond that there will be other issues about the handling of the talks when they are relaunched.

(b). What Mr O'hUiginn calls "Plan B" – that is how the two Governments would attempt to sustain the political process if, with a failure to resolve decommissioning, the present process implodes. We have ideas here, as the Secretary of State knows, and our dilemma will be how to encourage the Irish side that there is a good prospect that, in any event, the political process can be carried forward by a committed British Government, without rousing their enthusiasm to the point where they actually work to bring the present talks process to an early end. (We will separately provide briefing on Plan B.)

4. In the margins, and over lunch, I picked up a few more points from Mr O hUiginn:

He raised the issue of the possible need for an early adjournment, in the light of the Irish Government General Election, soon after the talks resume on 3 June. He clearly wanted to convey that, despite the Tanaiste's fairly dismissive posture on this at our meeting at Lancaster House, he himself could see that some adjournment might well be helpful or necessary depending on the outcome of the Irish General Election.

Mr O'hUiginn feared that we would not secure an IRA ceasefire immediately. This worried him because if it were not achieved by the end of the summer, he feared it might unravel.

Nonetheless if there were no ceasefire before then, though exchanges with Sinn Fein might be continuing at official level, he made clear that he saw merit in the scenario the British side had sketched in the meeting: namely that we might aim to secure agreement on the handling of decommissioning before the summer break; use July/August to recruit people to serve on the independent commission on decommissioning and to establish the other decommissioning architecture so that that could begin its work in September, at the same time that the three substantive Strands were launched.

Exchanging views about our dealings with Sinn Fein Mr O'hUiginn made some interesting observations. While their meetings could be friendly enough, he always found that at a certain point he ran into the brick wall of ideological absolutism. (We also exchanged nostalgic recollections of Mr McGuinness's Irish victimhood – Bloody Sunday Version – declamation,

which each of us had experienced more than once.) On the style of meetings with them, his own view [was] that there was little to be gained by
being other than relatively brisk and businesslike, though as far as possible
cordial and informal. That is how Sinn Fein would approach the meetings,
particularly with the British, and it was, in Mr O'hUiginn's view, best to
keep things on that level.

On the personalities, he explained his own strong preference for
dealing with Martin McGuinness. He talked directly and bluntly with a
clear view of the real issues and the bottom line. "In that, he is like me," said
Mr O'hUiginn. By contrast Gerry Adams, rather like De Valera, suggested
Mr O'hUiginn, was always using complex formulations and elaborate intellectual constructs, partly to bridge the various political strands in his
movement, so that it took a long time to pin him down and you had to
listen to hours of talk before you saw where he might be heading. I forbore
to point out that, despite Mr O'hUiginn's identification of himself with
the McGuinness (Michael Collins?) tendency, his description of Adams/
De Valera rather matched my own experience of him in the Liaison Group.

QUENTIN THOMAS
11 Millbank


## Document 63   Visit to Northern Ireland, 16 May


10 DOWNING STREET
LONDON SW1A 2AA

From the Private Secretary

19 May 1997
Ken Lindsay Esq
Northern Ireland Office

Dear Ken,
I should record that the Prime Minister had brief meetings in Armagh
with Archbishop Eames and Cardinal Brady, and with Seamus Mallon.

In both meetings, the Prime Minister set out his aims and what he would be saying in his speech.

The churchmen stressed the need for the new Government to avoid alienation of any group and to give people the feeling of ownership of the peace process. Both were very worried about Drumcree, although they thought few people wanted a repetition. They were working hard to prevent it. They also underlined the need for others to do more to bring about peace and a settlement, particularly the business community. People simply could not sit back and hope things would happen.

Mallon encouraged the Prime Minister to "go for it now". People should choose whether they were in or out of the process. If they were out, the caravan would have to move on without them. But he was worried about the resumption of the talks. A repetition of the wasted months up to the adjournment would be disastrous. He was content for the Prime Minister to reassure Unionists but asked him not to forget that Nationalists needed reassurance too – consent cut both ways.

I am copying this letter to Jan Polley (Cabinet Office).

JOHN HOLMES

## Document 64  Liam McCotter and Gilbert (Danny) McNamee

19 May 1997

Prime Minister
You will wish to be aware that I intend to give my consent to the temporary transfer to Northern Ireland of Gilbert (Danny) McNamee and Liam McCotter. McNamee and McCotter are serving 25 years and 17 years respectively for conspiracy to cause explosions. Details of the prisoners' offences are given at Annex A.

2. The transfer of prisoners between United Kingdom jurisdictions is governed by the Criminal Justice Act 1961 and criteria announced to Parliament in November 1992. The two prisoners meet the criteria for transfer and it is on this basis that I am giving my consent.

3. McCotter and McNamee are particularly high profile terrorist prisoners, not least because of their involvement in the attempted escape from Whitemoor prison in September 1994 and the subsequent collapse of two trials arising out of this incident due to prejudicial media coverage. McNamee is also the focus of a campaign to secure the referral of his conviction back to the Court of Appeal. It is likely therefore, that media and Parliamentary interest in the transfers will be significant.

4. Sensitivities also surround the location of the prisoners following transfer. Initially, and following past practice, the prisoners will be located at Maghaberry prison, but the Northern Ireland Prison Service has indicated that they are likely to move the prisoners to the Maze, which also houses other terrorist prisoners temporarily transferred. Given the recent difficulties at the Maze (the discovery of a tunnel under a Republican Block and the damage caused by a loyalist demonstration in response to increased security measures) and the history of these two prisoners in trying to escape, locating McNamee and McCotter there may attract criticism. However, this is an operational matter for the receiving Jurisdiction and I am content to leave it to them.

5. I have discussed the transfer of the two prisoners with Mo Mowlam who believes that there is considerable merit in an early decision. Subject to your views, therefore, I intend to have my decision communicated to the prisoners and their representatives on Wednesday 21 May. It is likely that the decision will be welcomed, particularly by moderate nationalist opinion in both Northern Ireland and the Republic. However, given the sensitivities surrounding the prisoners, notification of the decisions and subsequent media interest will need careful handling. We do not intend to make a formal announcement, but in the event of media interest, lines to take, which have been cleared with NIO, are attached at Annex B.

6. I am copying this minute to Mo Mowlam.

J.S.

## ANNEX A

## LIAM McCOTTER AND GILBERT (DANNY) McNAMEE: DETAILS OF OFFENCES

*Liam McCotter*

Mr McCotter was sentenced to 17 years imprisonment on 20 June 1988 for conspiracy to cause explosions and is due for release in on 21 June 1998.

McCotter together with his co-defendant Patrick Joseph McLaughlin (currently temporarily transferred to Northern Ireland) travelled from Belfast to the mainland in early 1987. From 15 February 1987 until their arrest on 19 February they were kept under surveillance.

They were seen to enter several DIY Stores in the Manchester area and purchase assorted items including plastic dustbins, Wellington boots. torch, insulation tape and waterproof tape. On 16 February they were seen to bury the dustbins in Delamere Forest and Macclesfield Forest. Later that day they purchased further items including dustbin liners.

On the night of the 17–18 February, both men drove to Camaes Bay, North Wales and on the Quay took possession of firearms. ammunition and explosives. They returned to the forest area where they buried the items. On 19 February both men were arrested. The property recovered included 150 lbs of explosives, 3 assault rifles (AK47), 2 pistols (9mm Tanaks) and detonators of various types.

*Gilbert McNamee*

Mr McNamee was sentenced to 25 years on 27 October 1987 for conspiracy to cause explosions.

McNamee's fingerprint had been found on bomb-making equipment discovered in Pangbourne (26 October 1983) and in Salcey Forest, near the M1 (26 January 1984). There were similarities between items found at these locations. There were also similarities between an amplifier board found at Salcey and one found after the Hyde Park explosion of 20 July 1982 when four men of the Blues and Royals Regiment were Killed. The Hyde Park board was of a type known to have been used by the IRA. McNamee's thumbprint was also found on part of a bomb which had been left in Phillimore Gardens, SW5 on 13 December 1983.

ANNEX B

TRANSFER OF PRISONERS TO NORTHERN IRELAND: LIAM
McCOTTER AND GILBERT (DANNY) McNAMEE
Lines to take

- The transfer of prisoners to Northern Ireland is in accordance
  with long standing statutory provisions. Requests are considered
  individually on their own merits under criteria announced to
  Parliament on 23 November 1992.
- The Home Secretary has approved the transfer of Danny McNamee
  and Liam McCotter to Northern Ireland;
- The prisoners have each been granted a temporary transfer for an
  initial period not exceeding 6 months.
- While temporarily transferred to Northern Ireland they remain
  under the jurisdiction of the Home Secretary. Their release dates
  will not be affected by the move.

If needed

- This is not a reward for terrorism. The requests of the two prisoners have been approved because they meet the criteria applicable to all prisoners seeking such a transfer.
- Both prisoners were involved in the attempted escape from
  Whitemoor prison. All legal and disciplinary proceedings arising
  out of this incident have been concluded.
- The location of prisoners temporarily transferred is an operational
  matter for the receiving jurisdiction.

## Document 65   Meeting between Officials and Sinn Fein

From The Private Secretary

NORTHERN IRELAND OFFICE
STORMONT CASTLE

BELFAST BT4 3ST
John Holmes Esq
Private Secretary to the Prime Minister
10 Downing Street
LONDON SW1A 2AA

20 May 1997

Dear John,

Thank you for your letter of 18 May.

You asked a number of questions about the next Steps, focusing in particular on the forthcoming meeting between officials and Sinn Fein. My Secretary of State agrees that not all of these questions are answerable or indeed need answering just yet.

On the meeting with Sinn Fein, the instructions which the Secretary of State has given have the effect that:

- After the necessary preliminaries establishing the purpose and context of the meeting, officials will seek to establish the agenda.
- Experience, press briefing by Sinn Fein, and their meeting with the Irish side, suggest that from Sinn Fein's perspective, this will focus on the four unresolved issues: timing and certainty of entry to the process;
- Decommissioning: time frame for the process; and confidence building measures.
- If that is the agenda, officials will seek to pin down Sinn Fein on the three issues other than the date. They will convey the impression that if these can be satisfactorily resolved then it would in principle be possible to contemplate movement on the date.
- On confidence building measures officials will rest on existing text, but take note of any additional concerns of Sinn Fein.
- On decommissioning officials will probe the extent of any gap. The solution is likely to turn on a form of words which will, of course, need to be consistent with the Mitchell Report.
- On time frame. officials might begin to signal that the Government does not expect the current talks process to be extended beyond

May 1998 - the date indicated by the Northern Ireland (Entry to Negotiations etc) Act.

- Officials will not deploy a formula on the date, at the first meeting. They will reaffirm that some period after a ceasefire declaration is needed in which *words and deeds* can be assessed. They may make clear that the judgement on this will be for the Secretary of State who will make "a political judgement of all the circumstances in the round". They may explain that the length of this period will be affected by whether, before the ceasefire declaration, there has been a period in which there has been an undeclared ceasefire and its duration.
- On the number of meetings, officials will be ready in principle to continue meeting, subject to events on the ground, while useful work is being done. They will be wary of being drawn in to an extended and purposeless series of meetings, or of conveying any impression that they for their part are seeking to drag things out.
- They will emphasise that the language of any ceasefire declaration. will be very significant and that any emphasis on adherence to and application of the six Mitchell principles would be helpful.

The Secretary of State believes it likely that Sinn Fein will seek to see any clarification which is established in this dialogue expressed in a text. If so, officials will be ready, without commitment, to begin work on the necessary textual formulations. (Sean O'hUiginn has told Quentin Thomas that Sinn Fein will be looking above all for signs of engagement from HMG.) She regards this as a benign outcome: a text will focus the discussions and avoid misunderstandings. A fresh text could help both sides avoid sterile questions as to whether Sinn Fein have compromised on their 10 October text or HMG on the 28 November text.

My Secretary of State emphasises that we shall be alert to the case for securing beneficial Irish and American pressure at the right moment. Her own forthcoming visit to Washington will provide a useful opportunity to influence American attitudes. Similarly, my Secretary of State is fully alive to the need to manage Unionist and other options. The form in which a date is given, if and when it is, will be such as to be consistent with the Government's principles and the statutory requirements. She has noted your concern that a date may be given without much specific being received from Sinn Fein. Her answer to this is that we hope in exchange to secure a ceasefire, which is an end in itself, or, failing that, to wrongfoot the Republican movement by demonstrating that every reasonable step has been taken to allow them to enter the political process. She shares the concern that we should do all we can to keep the UUP in the process but recalls that the current approach was embarked on in full knowledge that there might be a period of turbulence in which the UUP is only temporarily, lost to the process.

On the verification of the genuineness of any ceasefire, my Secretary of State believes we should emphasise that this will be a matter for her political judgement of all the circumstances in the round. She sees particular risks in emphasising, as has sometimes been done in the past, the role that security and Intelligence agencies may play in this.

*Talks*

My Secretary of State is clear that the talks should resume on 3 June as was agreed by all the participants.

It is likely, in her view, that HMG will not wish to take the initiative in seeking an adjournment. If it seems sensible, one approach will be, at the right time, invite Senator Mitchell to take soundings on the desirability of an adjournment. She believes that there are two circumstances which may produce a case for an adjournment: the first that following an Irish General Election there may be a period while a new Government is established, most obviously if it involves a different coalition of parties; the second is if there has been a recent ceasefire declaration or if otherwise continuing exchanges with Sinn Fein have the effect of so mesmerising the participants that no useful work can be done until the issue of Sinn Fein's possible entry in the process is resolved.

On decommissioning, my Secretary of State says that we are urgently seeking a procedural way through, initially with the Irish side through the Liaison Group (which met last Friday and is due to meet again on 27 May to consider a paper the Irish side has offered in response to one from the British side). If this work bears fruit, my Secretary of State will hope to meet Mr Spring to discuss this and related tactical issues before the resumption of the talks on 3 June.

Like you I am copying this letter to William Ehrman - FCO, Jan Polley - Cabinet Office, Sir John Kerr - Washington and Veronica Sutherland - Dublin.

Yours ever,
W K LINDSAY


# Document 66   Meeting with Sinn Fein


Rights & European Division

*From* Tony Beeton

20 May 1997

PS/SECRETARY OF STATE

*DESK IMMEDIATE*

cc
PS/Mr Ingram
PS/Mr Murphy
PS/PUS
PS/Sir David Fell
Mr Thomas
Mr Steele
Mr Ray
Mr Bell
Mr Leach
Mr Watkins
Mr Wood
Mr Brooker
Mr Hill
Mr Maccabe
Mr Lavery
Mr Perry-

Mr Holmes, No 10
Mr Budd, Cabinet Office

I have just completed negotiations with Siobhan O'Hanlon about tomorrow's meeting with Sinn Fein.

2. We agreed the meeting will be at noon tomorrow in Stormont Castle. Sinn Fein will field a delegation led by Martin McGuinness including Gerry Kelly, Caoimhghin o Caolain and Siobhan O'Hanlon herself. I confirmed that Quentin Thomas would lead for us with Jonathan Stephens and Chris Maccabe.

3. We agreed that since the media appeared to know already that a meeting was planned for tomorrow (and we both strenuously denied any responsibility for leaking that fact in advance of the final agreement today) it would be futile to attempt to keep the fact of the meeting confidential until after it had happened. Therefore both sides might confirm that a meeting was to take place at noon tomorrow. Sinn Fein's response to the point I had put to her at the weekend about the conditions set out in Dr Mowlam's letter to Gerry Adams came in the form of a reply to that letter which has been circulated earlier this afternoon.

4. Finally I confirmed that Robert Crawford would act as her contact for the details of arrangements on the ground and that he would telephone her shortly to discuss them. (Mr Crawford has just confirmed to me that he has spoken to O'Hanlon who will liaise with him tomorrow morning.)

Tony Beeton

# Document 67   Sinn Fein

10 DOWNING STREET
LONDON SW1A2AA
From the Private Secretary

20 May 1997
K. Lindsay, Esq.,
Northern Ireland Office

Dear Ken,

Thank you for your letter of 20 May about handling of the meeting with Sinn Fein on 21 May (which I now see is fixed for noon at Stormont). The Prime Minister is content for the broad approach you set out to be followed.

As we discussed, the prospect of being drawn into negotiation of a new Statement we are required to make is unattractive. It will no doubt tend to be a negotiation, however hard we try, where the pressure will come on to us to agree formulations we would rather avoid. The presentation of any Statement will also be tricky, particularly if it differs significantly from 28 November. However, getting into a new text may prove unavoidable – and worth it if the prize of a satisfactory ceasefire can be achieved without sacrifice of principle on our side.

I should add that, as I told Quentin Thomas separately, Irish officials are meeting Sinn Fein again this evening, apparently to bring up to speed McGuinness, who missed the last meeting.

Thank you also for letting us have your views on the initial handling of the talks and decommissioning. This is very helpful.

I am copying this to William Ehrman (Foreign and Commonwealth Office, Jan Polley (Cabinet Office), Sir John Kerr (Washington) and Veronica Sutherland (Dublin).

Yours ever,
John Holmes

## Document 68  Meeting with Sinn Fein

From: John Holmes

21 May 1997

PRIME MINISTER

cc:
Jonathan Powell
Philip Barton

The meeting today seemed to go about as well as we could have expected. It lasted some 3 hours, with half an hour break for a sandwich lunch. It was good-tempered, and the Sinn Fein side gave the impression of wanting to do serious business, despite some rhetoric at the outset. As expected, discussion focussed on four areas:

- confidence-building measures: no new problems emerged here;
- certainty of Sinn Fein entry into talks: Sinn Fein were given at least a hint that if everything else went right, the Government might be prepared to look seriously at this;
- decommissioning: nothing new;
- time frame: Sinn Fein were interested that the Government saw May 1998, when the legislative basis for talks expires, as a deadline.

There was also some discussion of parades, but nothing of great substance. It was agreed to meet again, possibly next week, but perhaps the week after given the absence of some of the Sinn Fein leadership at the proposed Conference in South Africa.

Both sides described the meeting afterwards as useful and constructive. Mo gave interviews on these lines, although she had not been at the meeting!

We should get a full record some time tomorrow, but so far so good, and reaction from the Unionists and others has not been too bad. We also seem to have got away reasonably lightly over the transfer of prisoners.

JOHN HOLMES

# Document 69   Meeting between Sinn Fein and No 10 Officials – Wednesday 21 May 1997

From C G MACCABE
POLITICAL AFFAIRS DIVISION
cc
PS/Mr Ingram (B&L)
PS/Mr Murphy (B&L)

PS/PUS (B&L)
PS/Sir David Fell
Mr Thomas
Mr Steele
Mr Ray
Mr Bell
Mr Leach
Mr Watkins
Mr Hill
Mr Brooker
Mr Perry
Mr Beeton
Mr Lavery
Mr Warner
Mr Holmes, No 10
Mr Budd, CO
Mr Lamont, RID
HMA, Dublin
HMA, Washington
PS/Secretary of State (B&L)

Today's meeting with Sinn Fein began at 12 noon and ended at 2.55 pm.
It was held in Stormont Castle. Sinn Fein were represented by Martin
McGuinness, Gerry Kelly, Caoimhghin o Caolain and Siobhan O'Hanlon
(notetaker). The Government team was led by Quentin Thomas and included Jonathan Stephens and myself.

*Summary*

2. This was a constructive exchange, with a degree of warmth and good
humour that was not present during Exploratory Dialogue in 1994 and
1995. We gained the impression that Sinn Fein see the arrival of the new
Government as providing a real opportunity to move things forward,
and may be prepared to reciprocate any flexibility they are shown. As expected, our discussion focused on four principal areas, namely:

- Confidence-building measures
- Decommissioning
- A timeframe for Talks
- Sinn Fein's entry into meaningful negotiations.

3. The meeting concluded with an agreement –in principle and subject to events on the ground – to meet again shortly.

*Detail*

4. We began by explaining the crucial importance of *events on the ground* in permitting this meeting and any further meetings. We then said we had already been struck by the determination of the new Government to see Sinn Fein enter the Talks process, provided they met the statutory criteria. But equally, they should be under no illusion that if they failed to comply, the process would go on without them. with this in mind we were keen to explore the areas they had identified, to see if there were ways through them.

5. Sinn Fein said they were pleased that the new Government seemed to be approaching the peace process with innovation and imagination. Our meeting, after such a long gap, was highly significant as dialogue represented the only path to a fair, just and permanent negotiated settlement for the people of the island of Ireland. There was, in the words of Mr McGuinness, a strong desire within Sinn Fein to "do the business".

6. After some ritual grumbling about the previous Government's failure to act imaginatively, leading to the breakdown of the IRA ceasefire, and about the failure of successive British (and Irish) Governments to recognise Sinn Fein's electoral mandate, the delegation turned to their four principal areas of concern. Under *confidence-building measures*, they included "political prisoners", the RUC, "repressive legislation" and the social and economic disadvantage of Nationalist areas. On *decommissioning*, they repeated that this must not be allowed to block progress. On a *timeframe for Talks*, they thought the two Governments should set a maximum period of six months for the parties to reach agreement, and if the parties failed to do so the

two Governments should act together to take things forward. As regards *Sinn Fein's entry into Talks*, their opening bid was for an early Statement by HMG that Sinn Fein would be able to join the Talks immediately after a restoration of PIRA's ceasefire of 31 August 1994. In relation to the last point, they believed they were not asking much, as "the popular feeling on the streets throughout Ireland and Great Britain", was that Sinn Fein's exclusion from the Talks was incredible. For too long, British Ministers had taken the bad advice of "militarists" within the British Establishment. Now was the time to strike out in a brave new direction, as ex-President De Klerk had done in South Africa in 1990.

7. Taking the most difficult of Sinn Fein's requirements first the notion of immediate entry into Talks following a ceasefire – Mr Thomas said this was simply not realistic, noting that even Mr Adams had acknowledged the [difficulty] of negotiating a "brief timeframe" for Sinn Fein's entry. He knew how anxious Sinn Fein were to have a date: frankly the Government would like to be able to give them one, for it was in the Government's interest to have them in the Talks. But although the Government would undoubtedly look at the matter rather differently than their predecessors, the Secretary of State would need some time following a ceasefire to determine if it met the terms of the Entry to Negotiations Act and the Talks Ground Rules. He added that if a ceasefire declaration came at the end of a sustained period of terrorist inactivity, this could have a significant bearing on the matter. The Secretary of State had a statutory duty to issue an invitation when the statutory criteria were met, and would reach her conclusion after making a "political judgement of all the circumstances in the round". Sinn Fein were obviously impressed by this, quickly seizing the point that the judgement would be primarily political (rather than intelligence-based). As an aside Mr McGuinness said he hoped we realised we were applying double stand-ards, for on a strict interpretation of the law the Loyalist parties should have been thrown out of the Talks long ago. He added, however, that Sinn Fein were not seeking this, for the continued presence of the PUP and UDP was another argument for Sinn Fein's immediate inclusion. After some discussion, led by Sinn Fein, about the need for trust on all sides, and a suggestion that they should be given an indication of how long we expected them to wait between any ceasefire and their entry to Talks, Mr McGuinness said it was best to leave it at that. But he asked us to see if we

could come up with ideas for an entry schedule, without prejudice to Sinn Fein's electoral mandate and their entitlement to be in Talks regardless of a ceasefire. Mr Thomas made no commitment but said that, if the other issues were resolved, then it should be possible to find a way of meeting the sensitivities on all sides on this issue as well.

8. Moving on to *confidence-building measures*, we pressed Sinn Fein to put more flesh on the bones of their concerns. Apart from rehearsing some of the matters above, and emphasising that the main problem for Irish "political prisoners" involved their treatment in the *English* prison system (including unreasonable use of Special Secure Units and delayed transfers from Great Britain to Northern Ireland), they had little to say. In sum this was that parity of esteem and fair treatment needed to be addressed in practical ways across a wide front to show Nationalists that their fundamental concerns were being dealt with. Mr Thomas drew attention to the emphasis the Government had already placed on confidence-building measures for both communities and the action it had embarked on in the Queen's Speech, for example.

9. As a parting shot under this heading, Sinn Fein were at pains to express the "total unacceptability" of the RUC to Nationalists as a result of their experience at the hands of the Force since 1921 right up to Drumcree. Taking the opportunity presented by the mention of Drumcree, Mr Thomas asked how Sinn Fein saw the prospects for this year's marching season. Mr McGuinness said that if *immediate* steps were taken, the situation could probably be defused. In this connection he welcomed the Secretary of State's visits to potential trouble spots earlier in the day. His greatest fear was that the Orange march down the Garvaghy Road in July would be put through by the RUC; if it was, there would be "big trouble". But whatever happened, he would be on the ground trying to help!

Mr Thomas pressed Sinn Fein to use their undoubted influence with residents' groups to avoid confrontation. Mr Kelly said that there was a tendency to overestimate Sinn Fein's influence on the ground, and to underestimate the genuine rejection by Nationalists of the concept of a Unionist "right to march".

10. Concluding this part of the discussion, Mr Thomas said Sinn Fein should remember that one item on the confidence-building menu was directly

related to the situation on the ground: "demilitarisation". On this, his sense was that the Government was ready to respond imaginatively to a ceasefire.

11. The meeting adjourned for lunch at 1.30 pm and resumed again at 2.00 pm. The good humour of the first session was maintained, with Mr McGuinness opening by asking us to wish the Secretary of State (whom he believed was now in the building) well and to tell her how glad he and his colleagues were that she had made a full recovery. He continued by asking how we were going to deal with *decommissioning*. Mr Thomas said it was a central issue. It had to be dealt with. The key to the door lay in the Mitchell Report, and we needed to use it so that the Talks could move into the three Strands. The Sinn Fein delegates showed a particular interest in the UUP's potential role in the matter, especially the attitude of David Trimble. We found ourselves sharing their hope that with two (successful) elections out of the way, the UUP would have the confidence to do meaningful business. The problem was that they – like most Unionists – did not trust the Republican movement, and were clinging to decommissioning as the one available way of establishing Sinn Fein's *bona fides*. We suggested that many Unionists might be convinced of Sinn Fein's sincerity by other means, by which we meant a combination of strong and unambiguous words and deeds (or more accurately the absence of deeds). We asked the Sinn Fein delegates to reflect seriously on this, reminding them that their predecessors had managed to convince a sceptical Unionist Population in 1961/2 that the IRA campaign was over, and that the Unionist Government of the day had responded with some remarkable confidence-building measures, especially in relation to prisoners. The Sinn Fein delegates seemed to take careful note of this.

12. As regards a timeframe, Mr Thomas said that the Government did not expect the process to extend beyond May 1998. Of course, if good progress was being made, this date could change, but Sinn Fein should take it that the process would end in a year. On the other hand, if the process got bogged down by, for example, Sinn Fein's entry to Talks after a ceasefire precipitating a Unionist walkout, the Government would not abandon the *project* of pursuing a solution acceptable to both Unionists and Nationalists. Against this background, there did not seem to be much between Sinn Fein's requirement of a six months time limit, and our own position. Mr Kelly, in

particular, seemed very interested in this proposition and asked if perhaps there might be provision for a review of progress, by both Governments after, say, three months. We explained that there was not but offered to discuss the matter with our Ministers and our Irish colleagues.

13. Moving on again, the Sinn Fein delegation asked what would happen immediately after 3 June if the Irish General Election resulted in several weeks of horse trading to form a new Government. We replied that the Signals were mixed. Mr McGuinness asked if an adjournment for say, two months, was possible and we replied that this was a matter for the Chairman, who was, however, bound to consult the other participants. Several scenarios were possible. They included the benign one where a new Irish Government took power swiftly and smoothly, decommissioning was resolved and the way was opened for substantive discussion in the three Strands. At this point, which could be the end of July, there could be an adjournment until the beginning of September. Another scenario, which could follow a IRA ceasefire, could see many of the Talks participants trans-fixed with the prospect of Sinn Fein's arrival in Castle Buildings. In these circumstances too, adjournment until September could be a useful tool.

14. At Mr McGuinness' request the meeting adjourned for ten minutes. When the Sinn Fein delegation returned, they said they were satisfied that their four main areas of concern had been exhaustively explored. They were also content with our assurance that we would consider the points they had raised, and *perhaps* come back on them. For his part, Mr McGuinness. said he would want to consult Gerry Adams urgently, *perhaps* coming back to us with a piece of text. He asked about another meeting. Mr Thomas, said that subject to events on the ground, we could agree to this in principle. Several dates were mentioned with Wednesday 28 May and Thursday 29 May, and Thursday 5 June and Friday 6 June as the most suitable, given that most of the Sinn Fein delegation will be absent at Padraig O'Malley's conference in South Africa from the end of next week. It was agreed that the details could be sorted out between our respective Offices. The meeting ended amicably at 2.55 pm with a brief exchange about the lines the Sinn Fein delegation and the Secretary of State would be taking with the press.

Chris Maccabe

## Document 70   International Fund for Ireland: Proposed EU Regulation

Ms Marjorie Mowlam
Secretary of State for Northern Ireland
Northern Ireland Office
Whitehall
London SW1 2AA

21 May 1997

Dear Mo,
I am replying on the Foreign Secretary's behalf to your letter of 19 May.

Like you, we have no objection to the proposed regulation, although we will need to put down a routine parliamentary scrutiny reserve. It is a welcome sign of the EU's continuing support for our efforts to achieve a Settlement in Northern Ireland. The small reduction (to 17 mecu) in the budget is to be expected in current financial circumstances and we have no difficulty in accepting it.

I am copying this letter to the Prime Minister, the President of the Board of Trade and the Chief Secretary.

I am yours,
Doug Henderson

## Document 71   International Fund for Ireland: Proposed EU Regulation

Treasury Chambers, Parliament Street, SW1P 3AG
The Rt Hon Dr Marjorie Mowlam MP
Secretary of State for Northern Ireland
Northern Ireland Office
11 Millbank

LONDON
SW1P4QE

21 May 1997

Dear Secretary of State

Thank you for copying to me your letter of 19 May to Robin Cook in which you sought colleagues' agreement to the proposed EU Regulation extending EU assistance to the International Fund for Ireland over 1998 and 1999.

2. I can confirm that I am content to see the proposed Regulation supported by the UK at today's meeting of COREPER and in the Council of Ministers. I agree that the European Union's continued support for the Fund is most welcome and it can only enhance our efforts to make progress with the political process in the Province.

3. I am copying this letter to the Prime Minister, Robin Cook and Margaret Beckett.

ALISTAIR DARLING

# Document 72  Request for Meeting by "Bloody Sunday" Families

NORTHERN IRELAND OFFICE
11 MILLBANK
LONDON
SW1P 4QE

From: The Private Secretary

Philip Barton Esq
Prime Minister's Office
10 Downing Street
London SW1A 2AA

22 May 1997

Dear Philip,

Thank you for your letter of 16 May in which you sought a response to the request for a meeting by the families of some of those killed on 30 January 1972.

My Secretary of State received a similar request and will be writing shortly to the Bloody Sunday Justice Campaign to offer a meeting with the families.

I attach a suitably sympathetic response for your consideration.

C D Kyle

## Document 73   Cooperation between the Irish and British Governments

MR HOLMES

22 May 1997

cc Ms Polley
Mr Sanderson
Mr Lamont (FCO)

We have now agreed with the Taoiseach's Office the attached joint Statement. Since you last saw the text:

(a)  the Irish have agreed to delete the second paragraph (but see also para 2 below);

(b)  we have deleted the last 6 words of the penultimate paragraph (because they were redundant)

(c)  we have corrected the date in the last paragraph.

2. Simon Hare, my interlocutor in Wally Kirwan's absence on holiday, added that Paddy Teahon still wants a Framework-type reference in the covering text which you and he are discussing, and will return to the charge with you on that. I attach your copy of the original Irish draft joint Statement: the language they want is in the passage you square bracketed

in paragraph 2. I have already tried on them the change you suggested in manuscript, which they consider inadequate. If Teahon goes on pressing, you will want to bear in mind the comments in the NiO's letter to me of 16 May (below): in particular, we should avoid a generalised reference to "Ireland".

COLIN BUDD

## Document 74 Great Irish Famine Event: Request for Prime Ministerial Video

Foreign & Commonwealth Office
London SW1A 2AH

22 May 1997

John Holmes Esq.
10 Downing Street

Dear John,

A televised open-air presentation, styled the "Great Irish Famine Event", will take place in Co Cork on 31 May-1 June to commemorate the 150th Anniversary of the Great Irish Famine. The organisers have asked the Embassy in Dublin if the Prime Minister would join other leaders in contributing a very short video-taped message for broadcasting at the occasion. The video-tape (of about one minute) would also include the lighting of a candle in commemoration of the victims.

The commemoration of the Irish Famine has been a difficult issue in presentational terms, with a vocal minority in the Republic and particularly the United States determined to vilify the actions of the British Government of the time and place the tragedy firmly in the context of continuing British crimes against Ireland. This is not a battle we can win; it is undeniable that different government policies at the time could have significantly reduced the impact of the disaster. Our approach has been to stress that in no way can the Famine be regarded as deliberate genocide, and to associate ourselves only with commemorative events which approach the issue in a spirit of reconciliation rather than recrimination.

This event is being organised by the Great Irish Famine Trust, a non-governmental body which has received some funding but not official endorsement from the Irish Government. The "Great Irish Famine Event" will consist of a "Gathering" on 31 May involving an open-air stage presentation of Irish history, the departure of a period famine ship and the lighting of a famine candle by President Robinson. Other Heads of state and Government are being invited to participate by similar pre-recorded video-tapes. The following day there will be a live concert ("the Awakening") with contemporary Irish musicians (and Bob Dylan).

The Irish end American Governments share our concern that the event could not turn into an opportunity for public recrimination. So far, however, it looks as if the tone will be reasonably positive. President Clinton has contributed a video-tape, subject to an understanding that the event will be non-political. Other European and old Commonwealth countries have also been approached and are considering their response.

Given the fact of television coverage and, more importantly, likely participation by Presidents Robinson and Clinton, British refusal to participate could easily be presented as continuing British reluctance to acknowledge the tragedy. President Robinson's involvement gives some reassurance, as she has consistently concentrated on the positive legacies of the Famine, such as the success of the Irish diaspora and Irish concern for the suffering in developing countries today. A message by the Prime Minister could avoid unnecessarily controversial ground by similarly focussing on the Irish diaspora and the importance of the Irish community in Britain. Against the background of his Belfast speech, the Prime Minister's participation would confirm to an Irish audience his commitment to a Settlement and his sensitivity towards events in our shared history.

We therefore recommend that the Prime Minister agree in principle to record such a video. Delivery would be shortly before the event and dependent on confirmed involvement by President Clinton and President Robinson. We would insist that the organisers did not edit it and that it would not be used in any other context. We would also reserve the right to withdraw use of the video-tape if we subsequently decided that the tenor of the event was unacceptable (for example change in format or participation).

If the Prime Minister is prepared to proceed on this basis, we will discuss details with the organisers (including delivery of the candle) and make arrangements for recording the video, including a draft text.

I am copying this to the Private Secretaries of the Secretary of State for Northern Ireland and the Minister without Portfolio, and to Jan Polley (Cabinet Office).

Dominick Chilcott
Private secretary

# Document 75  Meeting with the Taoiseach

10 Downing Street
London SW1A 2AA

23 May 1997

From the Private Secretary

*Northern Ireland: Meeting with the Taoiseach, 23 May*
The Prime Minister had a short bilateral meeting with the Taoiseach in the margins of the Informal European Council. The Taoiseach was accompanied by the Taniste, Paddy Teahon, Sean O'hUiginn and Shane Kenny. Teahon and O'hUiginn had presumably come specially for the meeting. Jonathan Powell and I were there on our side.

*Bruton* said that he was grateful for the initiatives the Prime Minister had taken since they last met. Things were moving. Irish meetings with Sinn Fein suggested they were serious, although he himself was always sceptical about Sinn Fein's intentions. There were four points of concern to Sinn Fein.

On *confidence-building measures*, they were looking for some practical reassurance. On decommissioning, the Irish side had promised to make some suggestions to us. They would base themselves on the Mitchell Report but try to present this in a new enough way for others to buy into it. On the *time-frame*, the British legislation already provided for the talks to finish in May. That could well be sufficient. The period of time Sinn Fein had to wait for *entry into talks* could be the most difficult issue. Clearly some time was needed between a ceasefire and entry, but Sinn Fein wanted at least an indicative period, perhaps four weeks or less. This would be subject to their meeting what was required of them under the ground rules.

*Bruton* repeated that he did not know how genuine Sinn Fein were, and how fully the leadership had the movement with them. It was clear that the grass roots had not been with the leadership for the last ceasefire. But it was worth testing Sinn Fein to find out where they really stood.

The *Prime Minister* said that he was sorry if his speech had taken the Irish a little by surprise, but at the last meeting he had still been thinking through how to move forward. He was keen to get Sinn Fein into the process to establish whether they were genuine or not. Being in the talks would put them to the test. He was telling the Unionists that this would not be easy for Sinn Fein. If they failed the test, we would know that we had to move on without them. He would be looking to the Irish and John Hume to help in those circumstances. His strategy was to leave Sinn Fein with no vestiges of an excuse for not giving up violence. If they were not prepared to negotiate, so be it. If they could be brought into the talks, he wanted to crack on with a detailed agreement.

The *Prime Minister* continued that there seemed to be agreement on the basic elements of the settlement: some form of devolution, and some form of cross-border cooperation. People were free to advocate a united Ireland, but he did not think this was realistic himself.

*Bruton* said that there was a need to achieve a break-through on the decommissioning issue. Meanwhile he was worried that the SDLP position was being eaten away by Sinn Fein. There was a danger that recent events were giving Sinn Fein a profile which would help them to become larger than the SDLP. The *Prime Minister* agreed that this was a danger. But their local election vote was roughly the same as that in the last General Election. He had felt the need to act quickly to stop the situation on the ground deteriorating. He wanted Sinn Fein to have no possible grievances, and to face them with the hard choices. If the talks could get underway in earnest, whoever wrecked them would have a heavy price to pay.

*Spring* asked how Trimble was reacting. The *Prime Minister* said that his position was not easy, with the constant danger of being out-flanked on the right. Trimble liked the idea of himself and Hume being engineers of progress in the talks. But the Unionists did need constant reassurance that they were not going to be pushed into arrangements they could not live with.

*Bruton* raised in conclusion the proposed statement on East/West links He suggested it be labelled the Noordvijk Declaration (!). It was agreed that it should be issued as drafted.

*Comment*

There was not much substance to these exchanges, but my impression is that our aim of smoothing ruffled Irish feathers was achieved, not least by the photograph of a smiling trio at the beginning. Paddy Teahon certainly seemed satisfied afterwards.

On the substance, Teahon told me afterwords that the "four weeks or less" idea was Bruton's, not Sinn Fein's. I said that it struck me in any case as a good deal too short. This seemed to shock him, and he launched into a frantic lecture [that] illegal activity by loyalist paramilitaries in Northern Ireland has never ceased entirely. There have always been punishment beatings (as on the Republican side). Since the end of last year, following the resumption of IRA activity in Northern Ireland, there have been a growing number of attacks of a more clearly political or sectarian motivation, several fatal – though some of the attacks involved paramilitaries from groups not associated with the parties, and it is often difficult to determine the degree of official sanction from the top of the groups concerned. The UDP and PUP have insisted that the CLMC ceasefire remains in place.

Both the Secretary of State and Mr Murphy have met the UDP since the change of Government. It appears from those discussions that loyalist paramilitaries, apart from their concerns over the IRA attacks that continued until recently, are now restive over Government contact with Sinn Fein, fearing a slackening of the requirements for a ceasefire entitling Sinn Fein to enter talks. Mr McMichael has publicly warned against the Secretary of State meeting Sinn Fein without an unequivocal IRA ceasefire in place, suggesting the consequence might be the end of the loyalist ceasefire. There were also complaints at the meetings here that loyalists prisoners had little advantage from the loyalist ceasefire (though this is an old refrain). Loyalists appear to have taken a measure of reassurance from the references to the Union in the Prime Minister's speech – but not a great deal.

The renewed loyalist violence clearly puts into doubt the loyalist parties' presence in the talks. Much to do with the future of the talks process hangs on this. It has always been made clear that talks are open only to parties that remain committed to democratic and non-violent methods. On entering, like other parties, the PUP and UDP formally adhered to the "Mitchell principles" of democracy and non-violence. The Ground Rules for the talks envisage expulsion of a party if the Governments conclude that it has "demonstrably dishonoured" its commitment to those principles. There is a mechanism by which one participant can make representations that another should be so expelled. It has already been invoked, unsuccessfully, against the loyalists.

If the tasks are to retain credibility, the procedure has to be applied with some care to the loyalist parties. The parties must to some degree be regarded as part of the same organisation as the paramilitary groups with which they are respectively associated, and if those groups have clearly returned to violence – whether or not their ceasefire are formally ended – dealt with accordingly. If the rules are seen to be a dead letter, unionists will conclude that Sinn Fein would be accorded similar indulgence, were it to be admitted and the IRA then returned to violence. Nationalists already with increasing intensity accuse us of double standards, tolerating loyalists in talks despite the violence, while excluding Sinn Fain.

But ejecting the loyalist parties from talks would have profound consequences. It might end the loyalist ceasefire completely; it would almost increase loyalist violence, and risk republican retaliation. It would transform the talks arithmetic, because the decision-making procedures, requiring agreement among parties representing a majority in both communities – a "sufficient consensus" – would thereafter require the assent of the DUP (or UKUP) to any agreement, making progress potentially much harder.

This is the context of the UDP request for a meeting. My Secretary of State believes the Prime Minister should agree to one. That might itself have a mild calming effect on the paramilitaries; and the Prime Minister would have the opportunity of emphasising the intolerable position that would be created by sustained loyalist violence. But the meeting might be at a date to be arranged in the future – perhaps several weeks – with an implicit message, which we should seek to reinforce, that it depended on good behaviour by the loyalist paramilitaries. There may be some criticism of such a meeting, from among nationalities, and the DUP and UKUP, inveterate opponents of the loyalist parties. But the Irish and the UUP are both on balance inclined, although like us uneasily, toward keeping the loyalists in the process for so long as it remains possible.

I attach a draft reply for your signature.

Yours sincerely,

R P Lemon
Private Secretary to Paul Murphy MP

# Document 76  Ulster Democratic Party

Northern Ireland Office
11 Millbank
London SW1 4QE

John Holmes Esq.
10 Downing Street

Dear John,

Your letter of 12 May asked for advice on the request by Gary McMichael, of the Ulster Democratic Party, for a meeting with the Prime Minister.

The UDP is closely associated with the loyalist paramilitary group, the Ulster Defence Association. The UDA is part of the "Combined Loyalist Military Command", which announced a ceasefire shortly after the IRA's in 1994, which remains formally intact – a surprising state of affairs in many ways, given that loyalist paramilitarism had often been the most vicious and sectarian motivated. The UDP leadership has exercised a clear influence with the paramilitaries against a return to violence, and been much praised for doing so.

It, together with the Progressive Unionist Party, which is associated with the Ulster Volunteer Force, forms part of the political talks in Northern Ireland. Both parties have on the whole been a constructive force, and exercised what influence they could for the talks to move on into substance. The last Prime Minister met them on several occasions, with a view both to advancing the talks, but also to sustaining the loyalist ceasefire. (…)

## Document 77  Draft Letter for Signature by PS/Prime Minister

Clir Gary McMichael
Leader, Ulster Democratic Party
36 Castle St
Lisburn
Co Antrim BT27 4XE

Thank you for your letter to the Prime Minister of 2 May.

The Prime Minister is ready to meet you and your party colleagues, so long as circumstance make that possible. We shall be in touch with you to arrange a date.

## Document 78  The Bloody Sunday Justice Campaign

The Rt. Hon. Tony Blair, MP
Prime Minister of Great Britain
c/o
Diary Secretary
10 Downing Street
London

23 May 1997

Dear Prime Minister,

I wrote to you on 15 May 1997, on behalf of the Bloody Sunday families, requesting a meeting on a planned visit to London, then scheduled for Thursday, 29 May 1997 (copy attached).

The families have asked me to inform you that their visit to London has, due to advice from several MPs, been postponed until Monday, 2 June 1997. The opportunity to meet with you on that date would again be sincerely valued by the families, for the same reason outlined in my previous letter.

The Taoiseach, John Bruton, TD, and Taniaiste, Dick Spring, TD, will meet with the families on next Wednesday, 28 May 1997, to brief them on the contents of the Irish Government's Bloody Sunday dossier which will be presented to the UK Government in the very near future. The families will be received by President Mary Robinson later that day.

Your consideration of this request is greatly appreciated.

Yours sincerely,

Don Mullan
Author, *Eyewitness Bloody Sunday*
1 West End Park, Derry, Ireland

# Document 79  Sinn Fein: A Possible Text

Northern Ireland Office

23 May 1997

John Holmes Esq
Private Secretary to the Prime Minister
10 Downing Street
London SW1

Thank you for your letter of 20 May. As you will have seen from the note of the meeting, officials followed the broad approach endorsed by the Prime Minister.

Although they could have been striking a deliberate pose, officials gained the impression that Sinn Fein were serious about wanting to be included in negotiations and understood the need to establish first a genuine and unequivocal ceasefire. Providing Sinn Fein thought the Government were also serious then, if reassurances could be offered on the four issues they raised, there seemed a possibility of a ceasefire. Although there was

little movement in substance on Sinn Fein's position on these issues, officials gained the impression that there was underlying flexibility and that
any gap could in principle be bridged.

If reassurances are to be given as a prelude to a renewed ceasefire, then
these will have to be written down. If they are written down, they will
have to be published. We agree with you that, despite the difficulties, this
is worth it if the prize of a satisfactory ceasefire can be achieved without
sacrifice of principle.

The attached first draft of a possible text sets out to achieve just this.
It has to strike a balance between:

- offering reasonable assurance on Sinn Fein's issues;
- remaining faithful to underlying principles of policy including
  those set out in agreements with the Irish Government;
- remaining consistent with the legal position which governs the requirements for Sinn Fein's entry to negotiations;
- exposing as little flank as possible for unionists and others to claim
  there has been a departure from previous policy.

It therefore deliberately uses a good deal of established language which it
is consequently harder for others to criticise.

It might seem attractive at first sight to have a simpler text with less
hallowed language. But my Secretary of State believes a text of this kind is
the right approach, partly because a number of the new positions involve
small but significant shifts which can only be conveyed in context. For example, the idea that there should be ministerial meetings with Sinn Fein
after a ceasefire declaration, but before they join the talks process, is not
new. But making it explicit that these would be in Castle Buildings is new.
Irish officials detected hints that this could be important to Sinn Fein.

Secondly, the agreement of the text with earlier ones, such as the previous Government's statement of 28 November, renders it much less open
to attack. We also have to take seriously the risk of judicial review if we
depart from the statutory requirements.

My Secretary of State believes that this is the sort of text we shall need
to think of deploying in public as a prelude to a further IRA ceasefire. If so,
it will need to form part of a common understanding as to events leading up

to and following a ceasefire and will consequently need to be shown to Sinn Fein in advance. We shall also want to gather the support of the Irish and US Governments by sharing this text with them in advance [text missing].

# Document 80  Meeting with Sinn Fein

*Possible Text (30 May 1997)*

1. In the meetings between officials and Sinn Fein, the Government has been asked to set out clearly its approach to four issues.

*Fundamental approach*

2. These issues should be seen in the context of the Government's fundamental approach to Northern Ireland, including:

- endorsement of the Anglo-Irish Agreement, Downing Street Declaration, Framework Documents and the 28 February 1996 communiqué;
- determination to uphold the principle of consent by respecting the democratic wish of a greater number of the people of Northern Ireland on the issue of whether they prefer to support the Union or a sovereign united Ireland;
- commitment to reconciliation and an overall political settlement which commands the support of both unionists and nationalists and is endorsed by the people of Northern Ireland in a referendum;
- rejection of violence, or the threat of violence, for political ends and determination to take effective measures to end paramilitary violence;
- undertaking to govern Northern Ireland with rigorous impartiality and with full respect for the rights of all citizens, reflecting the principles of parity of esteem and just and equal treatment for the identity, ethos and aspirations of both communities.

3. The Government believes the current talks process offers the best prospect for achieving an overall political settlement and a lasting peace. It will work to secure early substantive progress in political negotiations. It wants Sinn Fein to join the other participants in these negotiations. But that is only possible on the basis required by the Northern Ireland (Entry to Negotiations, Etc) Act 1996 and set out in paragraphs 8 and 9 of the "Ground Rules for Substantive All-Party Negotiations" (Cmnd 3232):

> Negotiations will involve the participation, in the appropriate strands, of representatives of both Governments and all those political parties operating in Northern Ireland (hereafter referred to as "the political parties") which achieve representation through an elective process and which, as set out in the Communiqué of 28 February 1996, establish a commitment to exclusively peaceful methods and which have shown that they abide by the democratic process.

In the Communiqué of 28 February, both Governments expressed the hope that all political parties with an electoral mandate will be able to participate in all-party negotiations. However, both Governments are also agreed that the resumption of Ministerial dialogue with Sinn Fein, and their participation in negotiations, requires the unequivocal restoration of the ceasefire of August 1994.

4. If these requirements continue not to be met by Sinn Fein, the Government is nonetheless determined to carry forward the process with the current participants.

5. Against this background, the Government's approach to the four issues identified by Sinn Fein is set out.

*Confidence building*

6. The Government is committed to a continuing programme to build trust and confidence among both unionists and nationalists. Its approach is based on the principles of equality of opportunity, equity of treatment and parity of esteem irrespective of political, cultural or religious affiliation or gender. It supports, with equal respect, the varied cultural traditions of both communities including the Irish language. This approach

is intended to secure just and equal treatment for the identity, ethos and aspirations of both communities.

7. The Government has already announced its commitment, in the Queen's Speech and elsewhere, to:

- protecting human rights, including by incorporating of the ECHR into the domestic law of the UK as a whole;
- combating discrimination in the labour market by taking forward the Employment Equality Review in the light of SACHR's report due in June this year;
- a major review of training so as to enhance employment opportunities, especially for young people;
- easing tensions over parades by upholding the rule of law and bringing forward legislation in the autumn to implement the North report recommendations, with care and sensibility for the right to march and the responsibility to take account of the concerns of those who live in areas through which marches pass;
- increasing confidence across the community in the police, including a start on reform of the structure and style of policing by implementing Labour's May 1996 proposals and the recommendations in the Hayes Report on police complaints;
- reviewing legislation against terrorism.

8. Confidence building is a two-way street. A genuine and lasting IRA ceasefire is the single most pressing step required to rebuild confidence across the community. This would enable the Government, as the threat reduced, to respond imaginatively by addressing the issues identified for the Government in Chapter VII of the International Body's Report.

9. On the other side, as the Report notes, "The early termination of parliamentary activities, including surveillance and targeting, would demonstrate a commitment to peaceful methods and so to build trust among other parties and alleviate the fears and anxieties of the general population. So, too, would the provision of information on the status of missing persons, and the return of those who have been forced to leave their communities under threat."

*Entry to negotiations*

10. The Government's objective is inclusive negotiations in a peaceful environment, involving all those parties with an electoral mandate which
establish a commitment to exclusively peaceful methods and which have
shown that they abide by the democratic process. As agreed with the
Irish Government in the communiqué of 28 February 1996, Sinn Fein's
participation requires an unequivocal restoration of the IRA ceasefire of
August 1994.

11. As soon as the Secretary of State considers these requirements are met,
then under the legislation she must and will invite Sinn Fein to participate.
Any ceasefire must be reflected in both word and deed. She will reach a
view on whether or not the statutory requirements are met, in the light of
all the relevant information and making a political judgement of all the
circumstances in the round.

12. Following a ceasefire declaration, some time would be required to establish that this was reflected in both word and deed. During this period
the Government would:

- ask Senator Mitchel to adjourn the talks process for a period to
  allow consideration of the ceasefire and its consequences for the
  negotiations;
- have Ministerial meetings with Sinn Fein to explore with them
  what assurances could be given and what confidence building
  measures established;
- invite Sinn Fein to make an early total and absolute commitment
  to the Mitchell principles of democracy and non-violence in a
  meeting with both the British and Irish Governments, together
  with such other talks participants and the independent Chairmen
  as wish to attend, at Castle Buildings, Stormont;
- consult the Irish Government as to whether it considers the agreed
  requirements for entry to negotiations are met;
- undertake bilateral and other consultations with all the parties to
  consider the implications for the negotiations and how they could
  most constructively be advanced once they resume.

13. The Government seeks no unnecessary delay. The period needed will be affected by the extent of terrorist activities prior to any declaration. But if an unequivocal restoration of the IRA ceasefire were declared (now/in the next fortnight) and was reflected in both word and deed so that the statutory requirements were met, then Sinn Fein would be invited to join a plenary session of the negotiations (in the first week of September).

14. From their entry into the negotiations onwards, Sinn Fein would, in common with all the other participants, be subject to all the agreed provisions and rules of procedure. These include those governing the contingency where any participant is no longer entitled to participate on the grounds that they have demonstrably dishonoured the Mitchell principles of democracy and non-violence.

*The negotiations*

15. Beyond the unequivocal restoration of the IRA ceasefire, these negotiations are without preconditions. Each participant will be able to raise any significant issue of concern to them, and to receive a fair hearing for those concerns, without this being subject to the veto of any party. Any aspect can be raised, including constitutional issues and any other matter which any party considers relevant. No negotiated outcome is either predetermined or excluded in advance or limited by anything other than the need for agreement.

16. Among the crucial issues is decommissioning. This must be resolved to the satisfaction of the participants, without blocking the negotiations. In their report, the International Body said the parties should consider an approach under which some decommissioning would take place during the process of all-party negotiations. Both the British and Irish Governments support the International Body's compromise approach. Agreement needs to be reached on how to take it forward, so that the process of decommissioning is not a block to progress in the negotiations, but can be used to build confidence one step at a time during them. Both Governments will be looking for the commitment of all participants to work constructively during the negotiations to implement all aspects of

the International Body's report. They will bring forward proposals to implement all aspects of the report and on the basis of these proposals, which
will require sufficient consensus for adoption, work to secure the launch
of the three strands of political negotiations by the (end of September).

17. The proposals they envisage will reflect common ground already established in the discussions so far and will include:

- the commitment of each participant to work constructively during
  the negotiations to implement all aspects of the international
  Body's report;
- the establishment, in parallel with the launch of the three
  strands, of an independent Commission as recommended in the
  International Body's report;
- a dedicated Committee of the plenary, possibly with sub-
  committees on specific issues, to advance the implementation of
  all aspects of the International Body's report;
- a mechanism to enable all the participants to review developments
  across the whole spectrum of the negotiations.

18. The aim of the two Governments in these proposals will be to secure
agreement to structural mechanisms to give effect to the International
Body's compromise approach which envisaged mutual progress on political issues and decommissioning as helping to create a progressive pattern
of mutual trust and confidence.

*Timeframe for the negotiations*

19. The Government does not expect the current process to continue beyond the end of May 1998, the date set by law when the Northern Ireland
Forum ceases to exist. The Government will encourage and facilitate
agreement but cannot guarantee it: agreement depends upon a sufficient
consensus among the participants. In the absence of agreement by the
time these negotiations end, the Government would continue to work, in
co-operation with the Irish Government and with the political parties of

Northern Ireland, to secure an overall political settlement based on consent and which commands the support of the unionists and nationalists and is endorsed by the people of Northern Ireland in a referendum.

20. If it is helpful, the Government will bring forward proposals for adoption by the participants of an agreed indicative time frame and calendar for the conduct of the negotiations until the end of May 1998. In any event, the British and Irish Governments expect to review their approach to the negotiations at regular intervals. The two Prime Ministers expect to do so in a Summit before the (end of this year).

*Conclusion*

21. The Government has set out its clear position on the issues identified by Sinn Fein. But there is an equal need for absolute clarity on other issues. It is now for the IRA to restore its cessation of August 1994 so that it is genuinely unequivocal and reflected in words and deeds, offering a clear and unambiguous commitment to peaceful and democratic means which provides confidence that it is genuine and irreversible.

# Document 81  British Government Policy on the Northern Ireland Talks

10 Downing Street, 25 May 1997

The Government has made clear its approach to the search for peace in Northern Ireland on many occasions. But we continue to be asked about this or that aspect, particularly about the multi-party negotiations which started on 10 June in Belfast. There has been continued speculation about a new IRA ceasefire, despite the no-warning attack on Thiepval barracks, Lisburn and various arms finds, including the huge find in London. This has renewed questions about what effect this would have on the negotiations, and our approach to these negotiations. It may therefore be helpful to spell out our position again.

The purpose of the negotiations is to achieve a new beginning for relationships within Northern Ireland, within the island of Ireland and between the peoples of these islands. The negotiations have one overriding aim: to reach an overall political settlement, achieved through agreement and founded on consent.

They will therefore address all the issues relevant to a settlement. Inclusive in nature, they involve both the British and Irish Governments and all the relevant political parties with the necessary democratic mandate and commitment to exclusively peaceful methods.

It is important to emphasise that all parties are treated equally in the negotiations, in accordance with the scale of their democratic mandate and the need for sufficient consensus. But no one party can prevent the negotiations continuing by withdrawing from them. No party has an undemocratic advantage. Both Governments intend that the outcome of these negotiations will be submitted for democratic ratification through referendums, North and South.

The prospects for success in these negotiations will obviously be much greater if they take place in a peaceful environment. The loyalist ceasefire has made an important contribution. It made it possible for the loyalist parties to join the negotiations. They are now playing their part in shaping Northern Ireland's future, as I have acknowledged by meeting their leaders.

The British and Irish Governments agree that, beyond the unequivocal restoration of the IRA ceasefire, these negotiations are without preconditions. But in the light of the breaking of the ceasefire and the events since then, assurances are obviously needed that any new ceasefire would be intended to be genuinely unequivocal, i.e., lasting and not simply a tactical device. Consistent with this, the process set out below would follow the declaration by the IRA of an unequivocal restoration of the ceasefire with the stated purpose of the conflict being permanently ended.

The successful conclusion of this process would depend on whether words, actions and all the circumstances were consistent with a lasting ceasefire. For example, how far the declaration of a new ceasefire was convincingly unequivocal and intended to be lasting would be an important indicator. Whether or not any parliamentary activity, including surveillance, targeting and weapons preparation, continued would also be directly relevant. Developments which were inconsistent with an unequivocal restoration of the ceasefire or Sinn Fein's commitment to the Mitchell principles of democracy and non-violence would affect consideration adversely. Sufficient time would have to be taken to ensure the requirements of paragraphs 8 and 9 of Command Paper 3232 were accordingly met before Sinn Fein were invited to participate in negotiations.

We envisage that the process would involve:

- meetings with Sinn Fein at various levels to explore with them what assurances could be given and what confidence-building measures established;
- the British and Irish Governments would invite Sin Fein to meet them together for the purpose of making an early total and absolute commitment to the Mitchell principles of democracy and non-violence;
- the two Governments would then propose bilateral and other consultations with all the parties to seek to determine how, if this process were successfully concluded, the negotiations could most constructively be advanced, including the issue of the participants adopting an agreed indicative time frame for taking stock of their progress;
- following a successful conclusion of the process set out above, including due time for consideration, the two Governments would expect the independent chairmen to convene a plenary session for all participants, with Sinn Fein invited formally to participate, to consider the outcome of these consultations and the future programme of work.

From their entry into negotiations onwards, Sinn Fein would, in common with all the other participants, be subject to all the agreed provisions and rules of procedure. These include those governing the contingency where any participant is no longer entitled to participate on the grounds that they have demonstrably dishonoured the principles of democracy and non-violence.

The range of issues on which an overall agreement will depend means that the negotiations will be on the basis of a comprehensive agenda. This will be adopted by agreement. Each participant will be able to raise any significant issue of concern to them, and to receive a fair hearing for those concerns, without this being subject to the veto of any other party. Any aspect can be raised, including constitutional issues and any other matter which any party considers relevant. No negotiated outcome is either pre-determined or excluded in advance or limited by anything other than the need for agreement.

Among the crucial issues is decommissioning. So the opening plenary is addressing the International Body's proposals on decommissioning of illegal arms. In their report, the International Body said the parties should consider an approach under which some decommissioning would take place during the process of all-party negotiations. We and the Irish Government support this compromise approach. Agreement needs to be reached on how to take it forward, so that the process of decommissioning is not seen as a block to progress in the negotiations, but can be used to build confidence one step at a time during them. So both Governments have already said they will be looking for the commitments of all participants to work constructively during the negotiations to implement all aspects of the International Body's report.

It is essential that all participants negotiate in good faith, seriously address all areas of the agreed agenda and make every effort to reach a comprehensive agreement. For their part, the two Governments are committed to ensure that all items on the comprehensive agenda are fully addressed. They will do so themselves with a view to overcoming any obstacles which may arise.

For our part, we are wholly committed to upholding our responsibility to encourage, facilitate and enable agreement over a period through the negotiations. This must be based on full respect for the rights and identities of both traditions. We want to see peace, stability and reconciliation established by agreement.

We are also determined to see these negotiations through successfully, as speedily as possible. This is in line with the hopes and aspirations of people in both the United Kingdom and the Irish Republic. These have already given momentum to a process which will always have difficulties. We will encourage the adoption by the participants of an agreed indicative time frame for the conduct of the negotiations and, if it would be helpful, will bring forward proposals for this. We have already proposed that a plenary meeting should be held in December to take stock of progress in the negotiations as a whole. The two Governments will also review progress at regular intervals. I will be meeting the Taoiseach on 9 December and the Secretary of State regularly meets the Tanaiste. Progress will be reviewed again by the end of of May 1997, a date set in the legislation.

Meanwhile we are committed to raising confidence, both through the talks and through a range of other measures alongside them. The International Body's report itself proposes a process of mutual confidence-building.

So we will continue to pursue social and economic policies based on the principles of equality of opportunity, equity of treatment and parity of esteem irrespective of political, cultural or religious affiliation or gender. We support, with equal respect, the varied cultural traditions of both communities. We are also committed to developing policing arrangements so that the police service should enjoy the support of the entire community.

It is worth recalling that, in response to the ceasefires of Autumn 1994 and the changed level of threat, we undertook a series of confidence-building measures. These included changed arrangements for release of prisoners in Northern Ireland under the Northern Ireland (Remission of Sentences) Act 1995, security force redeployment, a review of emergency legislation and others. If the threat reduces again, the opportunity for further confidence-building measures returns.

But confidence-building is a two-way street. Support for the use of violence is incompatible with participation in the democratic process. An end to punishment beatings and other paramilitary activities, including surveillance and targeting, would demonstrate real commitment to peaceful methods and help build trust.

The opportunity for progress has never been greater. The process of peace and reconciliation has received valuable economic support from the United States, the European Union and through the International Fund. The negotiations are widely supported internationally and benefit from the USA, Canada and Finland. They also have the overwhelming support of the people throughout these islands. They want them to take place in a peaceful environment, free of all violence. That is our aim too.

## Document 82 The Secretary of State for Northern Ireland to Meet the Bloody Sunday Relatives

10 Downing Street
London SW1A 2AA

From the Private Secretary

27 May 1997

Don Mullan Esq

Thank you for your letters of 15 and 23 May to the Prime Minister regarding the visit to Westminster by the families of some of those killed on 30 January 1972 in Londonderry. As I am sure you can imagine, the pressures on the Prime Minister's time at the moment are enormous. He will not, unfortunately be able to meet the families on 2 June. The Prime Minister has, however, asked Dr Mowlam, the Secretary of State for Northern Ireland, to meet the relatives on his behalf.

Please rest assured that the Prime Minister is very aware of the continuing grief felt by the families of those killed. He is determined that the lessons of that day are not forgotten and to work with others to ensure that such a tragedy should never happen again.

Philip Barton

## Document 83 Liaison Group Meeting, 27 May

From: D A Lavery, Central Secretariat

29 May 1997

cc:
PS/Secretary of State (B&L)
PS/Mr Murphy (B&L)
PS/Mr Ingram (B&L)
PS/PUS(B&L)
PS/ Sir David Fell
PS/Mr Thomas (B&L)
Mr Steel
Mr Stephens
Mr Bell
Mr Watkins
Mr Wood (B&L)
Mr Beeton
Mr Brooker
Mr Hill (B&L)
Mr Priestly
Mr Maccabe
Mr Whysall
Ms Mapstone
Miss Bharucha
Miss Benson
Mr Budd, Cabinet Office (via IPL)
HMA Dublin
Mr Tebitt, RID
Mr Lamont, RID
Mr Warner

(enclosure issued separately)

1. A Liaison Group meeting with Irish officials took place in Dublin on Tuesday. The "away team" was led by Mr Thomas, supported by HMA, Mr Stephens, Mr Bell, Mr Sanderson, Mr Hill, Mr Warner and Mr Lavery. Mr O'hUiginn led for the Irish side supported by Mr Kirwan, Mr Donoghue, Mr Cooney, Mr Montgomery, Mr Hare, Mr Callaghan and Mr Keown.

*Summary*

2. A meeting dominated by discussion of the Irish side's paper of 26 May ("An Approach to the Decommissioning Roadblock") which the British side had only received that morning (copy attached). A lengthy discussion (which continued at a working lunch) exposed some significant weaknesses in the Irish paper and concluded with the British side undertaking to prepare a first draft of a new paper combining the best features of our own paper of 7 April and the Irish paper of 26 May. The new paper will be further considered by officials, ad referendum to Ministers. Further consideration to be given as to how, and when, such a paper might be deployed with the Talks participants. The lunchtime discussion included Mr O'hUiginn's advice on handling Sinn Fein, including the symbolic importance for them of the timescale of entry to the Talks process (with Mr O'hUiginn cautioning that a possible consequence of deferring Sinn Fein's entry until the autumn could be that any new ceasefire would similarly be deferred), and the importance for Sinn Fein of not being treated differently from other participants. Looking forward to Thursday's Adare meeting between the Secretary of State and the Tanaiste, decommissioning and the handling of the resumption of the Talks on 3 June were identified as likely agenda items.

3. The main points to emerge in the course of the discussion were as follows.

(a) *Decommissioning*

4. The British side were allowed time to read the Irish paper of 26 May, which had only just become available.

5. Regarding the status of the paper, Mr O'hUiginn explained that it had not been cleared with Irish Ministers. However, officials had endeavoured to consult widely in developing the ideas reflected in the paper, and some of its central ideas, if not the actual drafting, had been discussed with Ministers.

6. Mr O'hUiginn conceded that the drafting of the paper had proved difficult. They had previously explained the difficulties they had with the British side's paper of 7 April. He suggested that both Governments shared a common

position on the need to address the substance of decommissioning, the key to which would be the implementation of the report of the International Body. Assuming that both Governments agreed that implementation of the Report was the best way forward, it would be necessary to find a way to decouple this objective from the tactical use of decommissioning as an issue to keep Sinn Fein out of the Talks process. The Irish side was particularly anxious that the interplay of the substantive political discussion in the Talks and the need to address decommissioning did not have the effect of obstructing progress. For this reason, the Irish side were reluctant to endorse those ideas in the British side's paper, (e.g. "communication cord") which might have the effect of obstructing progress.

7. Against this background, the Irish side's paper sought to balance the objective of an engagement on the substance of decommissioning with sufficient measures to sufficiently address the concerns of the Unionists. Among the principal measures intended to reassured the Unionists were the following:

(a) an emphasis on the good faith of both Governments in their commitment to the implementation of the International Body's Report – hence the idea that the Governments would give a formal pledge of this commitment;

(b) provision for mechanisms to take decommissioning forward – this would be achieved through the establishment of a sub-committee with an emphasis on the implementation of the International Body's Report in its entirety;

(c) a guarantee that the Government's proposals on taking the issue of decommissioning forward would not be open to re-negotiation if Sinn Fein were to join the process; and

(d) a commitment to establish an Independent Commission to oversee decommissioning – the Commission could be established once the Talks process becomes inclusive on the entry of Sinn Fein.

8. Mr O'hUiginn explained that the paper envisaged the Talks resuming with an opportunity for the participants to engage in a limited round

of further discussion on decommissioning. The Government would then need to reach an early determination as to whether a sufficient consensus could be secured on a commitment to implement the International Body's Report.

9. Paragraph 6 (iii) of the paper contemplated a situation where the Independent Chairmen concluded that a party was not prepared to work in good faith to implement the Mitchell Report but where this refusal did not appear to amount to a fundamental contradiction of the Report (so as to leave open the possibility that this reserve would be capable of resolution in the course of the negotiations). This procedural device was intended to allow the Independent Chairmen to "shelter" the UUP where their attitude to the Mitchell Report stopped short of its complete rejection. This reflected the Irish side's uncertainty as to how to read the UUP's commitment to the Mitchell Report – unlike the position of, say, the Loyalists, it did not seem to the Irish side that a refusal by the UUP to give a commitment to implement the Mitchell Report would necessarily be conclusive. Unlike the position of, say, the Loyalist parties, such a refusal would be unlikely to constitute a breach of the Mitchell Principles.

10. Finally, Mr O'hUiginn explained that the paper contemplated (at paragraph 11) that, where there was not sufficient consensus for the launch of the 3 Strands, the Chairmen might initiate preparatory discussion on some of the substantive issues to the extent that the participants were agreeable to this.

11. Responding to this, and noting that both sides shared a good deal of common ground (including recognition of the need to make a play on decommissioning soon), Mr Thomas said there were important differences in the approaches of the two Governments to this issue. Central among these was the British side's conviction that it was necessary to look at the issue of decommissioning not merely as an analytical exercise, but in a way which recognised the political context to the current impasse. One important consideration was that not all of the participants accepted the Mitchell Report and it was unlikely, therefore, that they would be prepared to make a commitment to its full implementation. He suggested it might be possible, and indeed preferable, to find a way forward on decommissioning which was consistent with the Mitchell Report, and which acknowledged

the concerns of a number of the participants on decommissioning, but which stopped short of confronting the participants with a requirement to make a commitment to implement the Report.

12. Mr Thomas said that if the Governments were to make a play on decommissioning, their stance in relation to the Unionists should be such as to clearly indicate that a purely tactical reserve on decommissioning would not be acceptable, while at the same time acknowledging that the Unionists do have genuine concerns regarding decommissioning. Mr Thomas suggested that the Unionists' concern was that they could find themselves engaged in negotiations with Sinn Fein and, in doing so, it was essential that they would not appear to their supporters to have compromised their principles by negotiating on equal terms with a party which retained its own private army.

13. Mr Thomas acknowledged that a requirement to give a commitment to implement the Mitchell Report must not be such as would predictably have the consequence of preventing Sinn Fein's entry to the Talks process – it was self-evident that decommissioning would only be possible, if at all, once Sinn Fein had entered the process. What was required was a political construct which would allow us to enter the substantive political process bringing all of the participants with us – once in the substantive process, we would be in a position to test the Mitchell Report's proposition that a benign dynamic could be created. His principal concern with the Irish side's paper was that it was less sound as a political construct than the British side's paper of 7 April.

14. Turning to the detail of the Irish paper, Mr Thomas sought clarification of the proposed "formal intergovernmental guarantee" (that "the decommissioning issue must be resolved to the satisfaction of the participants as an indispensable part of the process") as contemplated in paragraph 6(i)(c). He wondered what this might amount to in practice? Although finding it superficially attractive, it was a more forward position than anything contemplated in the British side's paper, which was couched in terms of the Governments' expectation that some parallel decommissioning might take place. Mr Stephens suggested that the UUP were quite likely to ask whether this "guarantee" amounted to a commitment to secure actual

decommissioning, or merely a commitment that some "consideration" might be given to this.

15. Visibly uncomfortable, Mr O'hUiginn sought to argue that although the Irish Government wished to see actual decommissioning taking place, they had a problem in making the entire process hostage to this expectation. He argued that too categorical an expression of the expectation on the part of the Governments could cause difficulties, not least for the UUP. This aspect of the paper was intended to address the Unionists' apparent distrust of the Governments' commitment to decommissioning – but he acknowledged that the idea of a guarantee could become a hostage to fortune.

16. Mr Thomas cautioned that if the Governments were to use language which suggested a formal guarantee, in time they might well be asked whether they regarded their responsibility in this regard as having been discharged. The guarantee could come to be regarded either as false-talk or, alternatively, the parties would seek to hold the Governments to it. A further difficulty with the approach suggested in the Irish paper was that it required the Independent Chairmen to ascertain whether the participants were committed to implementing the Mitchell Report – this could well lead to the Chairmen being asked to explain what their Report contemplated on decommissioning.

17. Mr O'hUiginn said that the Irish side's approach to this issue amounted to saying, in terms:

- we are serious about this process;
- we do not want to make a particular interpretation of the Mitchell Report a condition of entry to the process;
- we do not want to raise so specific an expectation regarding decommissioning as to store-up difficulty for the process ahead.

18. Mr Thomas suggested that a softer commitment on the part of the Governments' reading of decommissioning might be more advisable. The idea that the Independent Chairmen might reach a judgement as to when decommissioning should start was one possible way of structuring participants' expectations on this difficult issue.

19. Mr Stephens noted that paragraph 6(iii) of the Irish paper invited the Independent Chairmen [to assess] whether the participants were prepared to work constructively to implement the Mitchell Report. The draft also contemplated that the Independent Chairmen might conclude that a participant's objection to this was not of a fundamental nature. While recognising that this formula was intended to meet unionist reservations regarding aspects of the Mitchell Report, he thought it quite likely that the Unionists would choose to read this provision as a means of allowing Sinn Fein to fudge the issue of decommissioning. The current draft could also cause difficulty with a party such as the DUP who have such an unambiguous position on the Mitchell Report.

20. Mr Thomas wondered whether a "package deal" approach might not be needed, based on the Governments' best judgement of what could be achievable. Such an approach would almost certainly have to be forced through by tabling a paper and pushing for sufficient consensus. This might be preferable as both the British side's paper and the Irish paper involved a sequence of commitments that the parties might not be prepared to make.

21. Mr O'hUiginn explained that paragraph 8 was intended to be helpful to the unionists in that it prevented any renegotiation of the Governments' proposals on decommissioning.

22. Mr Thomas noted that paragraph 9 combined decommissioning and confidence-building in a single sub-committee notwithstanding known unionist objections to this. He wondered whether this was wise – he suggested the Government should try to deny the unionists grounds for rejecting this proposal.

23. On paragraph 11, Mr Thomas wondered how realistic the idea of preparatory discussion was? He thought it quite likely that if a move into substantive negotiations was not possible, it might be better to default to a new "Plan B" if such could be found.

24. Concluding this part of the discussion, Mr Thomas said that the British side would endeavour to produce a draft of a possible joint paper for presentation in the Talks. Although such a paper was unlikely to be ready in time for the Adare meeting, he thought that officials might have an opportunity to discuss the new draft at Castle Buildings next week. Mr

O'hUinginn said that any such paper would have to meet the dual test of not only getting people into Talks process, but also sustaining the Talks.

(b) *Sinn Fein Entry*

25. Various possible scenarios were discussed, including the possibility that the decommissioning impasse could be resolved before the Summer break, with the launch of the 3 Strands in September, coinciding with Sinn Fein's entry to the process. Mr Thomas noted the likelihood that a ceasefire would necessitate a pause in the Talks to allow the parties to take stock.

26. Mr O'hUiginn said it was his assumption that there was no prospect of a ceasefire ahead of the Irish General Election on 6 June. But he believed there were signs of a willingness to "do business" quite soon afterwards. However, it was unclear to what extend Sinn Fein/IRA were factoring into their assessment and keeping their options open. He cautioned that if the political horizon was formally transferred to September, tactical considerations could well come into play so that Sinn Fein/IRA might defer any formal ceasefire until then.

27. Mr O'hUiginn said that Sinn Fein/IRA appeared to place particular reliance on having a reliable sense where the two Governments wanted to get to in the process. He thought that the key issue was whether the timescale for Sinn Fein's entry could be got out of the way – it was not a matter of historical significance but was largely symbolic. He recognised that the Secretary of State would require some time to be satisfied regarding any new ceasefire, but any such time period would need to be limited. He appeared to suggest that a period of 4 weeks might be acceptable, and it would be important to avoid any suggestion of unequal treatment for Sinn Fein. There were important issues of symbolism and reassurance for both sides in all of this. In the case of Sinn Fein, it would be helpful to signal that the timescale for their entry on the process would be clear, manageable and brisk.

28. Mr Stephens said that the British side had told Sinn Fein that the idea of their immediate admission to the Talks following a ceasefire was not realistic. The Secretary of State would inevitably require some time to be

satisfied that words and deeds were consistent with a ceasefire. This time could be used to address matters which would help to develop confidence. In time, the Minister of State and the Secretary of State might be prepared to hold meetings with Sinn Fein. Sinn Fein would also be likely to have access to Castle Buildings.

(c) *The Loyalist Parties*

29. It was noted that the situation with the loyalist's cease-fire was a potential source of difficulty when the Talks resumed. The Alliance Party had indicated they intended to raise this issue. There were also the activities of the LVF. Mr O'hUiginn argued that it would be wrong to make those at the Talks table hostage to the actions of groups outside the process, Mr Thomas cautioned that a difficulty could arise in relation to the concept of mutual decommissioning if splinter groups were active.

　　D A Lavery
　　SC 28196

# Document 84　Meeting between Sinn Fein and NIO Officials – Wednesday 28 May

From C G Maccabe
Political Affairs Division

28 May 1997

cc:
PS/Mr Ingram (B&L)
PS/Mr Murphy (B&L)
PS/PUS (B&L)
PS/Sir David Fell
Mr Thomas
Mr Steele
Mr Ray

Mr Bell
Mr Stephens
Mr Leach
Mr Watkins
Mr Hill
Mr Brooker
Mr Perry
Mr Beeton
Mr Lavery
Mr Warner
Mr Holmes, No 10
Mr Budd, CO
Mr Lamont, RID
HMA, Dublin
PS/Secretary of State (B&L) – O

Today's meeting with Sinn Fein began at 12.10 pm and ended at 3.20 pm. Once again it was held in Stormont Castle and Sinn Fein were represented by Martin McGuinness, Gerry Kelly, Caoimhghin o Caolain and Siobhan O'Hanlon. Quentin Thomas, Jonathan Stephens and I comprised the Government team.

*Summary*
2. This was a less fruitful meeting than that on 21 May. Although the Sinn Fein delegation were reasonably friendly, the delivery and demeanour of Mr McGuinness – who did most of the talking – were reminiscent of Exploratory Dialogue. Sinn Fein laboured a lot of points. As at our first meeting, discussion centred on confidence-building measures, decommissioning, a time frame for Talks, and Sinn Fein's entry into them. Despite repeated assurances of the Government's wish to see them included in negotiations as quickly as possible after the unequivocal restoration of the IRA ceasefire, and a helpful description of how we saw things proceeding after a ceasefire, Sinn Fein expressed dissatisfaction and disappointment. They had come expecting us to put flesh on the

bones of our earlier remarks about their four principal areas of concern, and complained repeatedly that we had failed to do so. We defended our position in robust terms and the meeting ended with both sides agreeing to reflect on what had been said. Sinn Fein are to come back to us about a further meeting – subject to events on the ground – at the end of next week.

*Detail*

3. Welcoming Sinn Fein, Mr Thomas said he was glad events on the ground had made the meeting possible. Mr McGuinness reciprocated. He said the Secretary of State's recent trip to the United States had generated a lot of optimism, but while style was important, the substance behind it was much more so. Substance was what they wanted to hear from us.

4. Mr Thomas asked what Sinn Fein saw as the end product of our meetings. Was it an outcome where Gerry Adams was able to present an analysis to the IRA that would bring another ceasefire? Was it enough to hear explanations of our position across the table, or would some text or a Ministerial speech be more helpful? Mr McGuinness did not offer an option. What Sinn Fein wanted, he said, was real, meaningful and inclusive peace negotiations alongside substantial confidence-building measures. This was, however, without prejudice to Sinn Fein's absolute right to equality of treatment with other political parties. It could not be otherwise as their electoral mandate was now 45% of the Nationalist vote. No matter how much others wished it were not so, there was no hope of the peace train reaching its destination without them. In Sinn Fein's opinion, this destination was an end to British jurisdiction in Ireland, and national self-determination by all the people of the island. Sinn Fein needed to be convinced that meaningful negotiations were on offer; if they were they would go to the IRA and present an analysis that would hopefully lead to the end of violence. We said we believed such negotiations were on offer – following a ceasefire – and had no intention of extending the series of meetings any longer than absolutely necessary to do the business. As regards a time frame for Talks, we confirmed that both the British and Irish Governments did not see a problem with regular reviews of progress, probably every three months.

Sinn Fein appeared to be satisfied with this, although they insisted that the Talks should be limited to six months rather than ending in May 1998, as we had said they would at the earlier meeting. Moreover, they needed to be certain that both Governments would "move decisively" against any party that was deliberately stalling.

5. Mr Thomas said that he thought it was common ground between us that a way had to be found to bring the bulk of Unionists and the bulk of Nationalists into the project. Ideally, the vexed question of decommissioning could be dealt with satisfactorily to allow entry into the meat of three strands before the Summer break, but if this period proved impossible we might have to seek another way forward. Mr McGuinness looked unimpressed and suggested moving the discussion on to confidence-building measures.

6. We were reminded of the areas of most concern to Sinn Fein and Nationalists at large, namely equality of opportunity in economic, social and cultural affairs, democratic rights, parity of esteem, demilitarisation, prisoners, policing and emergency legislation. We were asked for details of initiatives we were prepared to take in these areas. For their part, Sinn Fein would return with a more specific list in due course. But they wanted to raise some prisoners' issues right away.

7. Mr Thomas said it was not appropriate to get into this sort of detail now. That was for the Talks. Mr McGuinness replied testily that it probably did not matter one way or the other, as we were well aware of the issues. Confidence-building measures were fundamental to the process, and could be dealt with outside the Talks. They were in a class of their own. The Government should formally recognise that fundamental, political and constitutional change had to take place. We reminded Sinn Fein that they had not answered our question about whether some text or a Ministerial speech might be helpful. For example, at some stage, the Government might state that the process we were involved in had the capacity to deliver historic change. Mr McGuinness appeared to signify assent. We said the Government were committed to change and cited "Frameworks" as proof of our intent. We said that we had also signalled our commitment to pressing on with the search for agreement, even though the current process failed to deliver. And, in the meantime, that we would continue to

introduce confidence-building measures that would meet the aspirations of both communities.

8. Mr McGuinness said he hoped Sinn Fein would soon be invited to sit down with the *political* representatives of the Government. Mr Thomas said that normalisation of relationships with Ministers could only begin after an unequivocal restoration of the IRA ceasefire. After further complaints by Mr McGuinness and Mr Kelly about the treatment of IRA prisoners in Great Britain and Northern Ireland, Mr Thomas repeated that while it was the Government's intention to go on looking at confidence-building measures, he could give no commitment to come forward with a programme of reforms as a result of this series of meetings. Mr McGuinness said he was profoundly disappointed. Queen's Speeches were all very well, but vague promises in them meant nothing to the people of Crossmaglen or Coalisland. They did not think they were on the threshold of significant changes to their lives. At that point he suggested, abruptly, moving on to decommissioning.

9. We reminded Sinn Fein that both the British and Irish Governments were committed to implementation of the Mitchell report in all respects, but in a way that did not block progress in the Talks. We asked them how they imagined decommissioning might be played in a situation where the Talks had moved into the three strands, and seemed to be heading for a satisfactory conclusion. Mr McGuiness ducked the question and fell back on Sinn Fein's traditional position: they have always wanted to see the removal of all guns from Ireland, but decommissioning must not be allowed to block the negotiations. He added that they had come to the meeting expecting to hear how we planned to get everyone over the hurdle.

10. Mr Kelly said it was not a matter for Sinn Fein, but for the British and Irish Governments. We explained that both Governments were working together, and neither were expecting prior decommissioning or a schedule of instalments. But Mitchell did embrace the concept of a *dynamic* process. Mr McGuinness said it sounded to him as if we were just moving decommissioning down the road a bit, delaying the crunch as it were. Mr Thomas repeated that, together with the Irish, we would do our best, but success could not be guaranteed. Sinn Fein kept pressing for a definitive answer and seemed keen to know if we were prepared to proceed in the absence of sufficient consensus.

11. After some circular discussion, during which we reminded the delegation that Unionists were fearful of finding themselves negotiating with Sinn Fein in the three strands when decommissioning [was] turning out to be illusory, this part of the meeting ended with Mr McGuinness demanding that the Government disabuse David Trimble and the UUP of the notion that they could "strangle" the process. The meeting broke for lunch at 1.35 pm and resumed again at 2.05 pm.

12. Mr McGuinness opened by demanding Sinn Fein's immediate entry into Talks, following an unequivocal restoration of the IRA ceasefire. He went on to ask how the General Election in the Irish Republic was affecting the process. We did our best to allay his apparent concern that developments in the Republic following the Election may delay or derail the train. As further reassurance, Mr Thomas explained what would probably happen following restoration of the ceasefire. First, some time would be needed to see if the IRA's words and deeds were consistent; the absence of pre-ceasefire activity would be relevant here. The Secretary of State would then make a political judgement in all the circumstances in the round, and there would be no unnecessary delay. What others, including the Unionist parties, thought would be immaterial.

13. He continued that it was likely that the imminent arrival of Sinn Fein at the Talks table would induce paralysis in some of the other participants, and in anticipation of this the Governments might invite Senator Mitchell to propose an adjournment. More or less in parallel, Ministers would want to meet Sinn Fein to explore their position on various issues and other parties might want to engage in bi-lateral and tri-lateral meetings with them. During this period, the Party would be invited to take up rooms in Castle Buildings. All being well, in accordance with the law, they would be invited to join the Talks process. A lot of thought was going into preparing the way for Sinn Fein's entry into the Talks and in the right circumstances we would not be found wanting. Mr McGuinness' grudging reply was that this could last for years. Mr Thomas said this was nonsense and that he would try to give a more specific indication of the likely timescale at any subsequent meeting. He repeated that Ministers wanted Sinn Fein in the process because it was in their interest to have them in. He could envisage

a Government statement that on X date, if certain conditions were met, Sinn Fein could be in the Talks by Y date. Mr Guinness said this would be helpful, but added the now familiar rider about Sinn Fein's inalienable right to be in Talks immediately after a ceasefire, without precondition. Mr Thomas again asked if Sinn Fein would see advantage in having something written down. Mr McGuinness said that he would like to have a full and comprehensive description of how the Government were going to deal with the four issues of principal concern to them. There had been a distinct lack of substance in both meetings and this caused difficulties for the delegation. Mr Thomas reminded Sinn Fein that the purpose of the meetings was to ensure the Government's position was clearly understood, and challenged the assertion that the meetings had been without substance. He said several of the things Sinn Fein had been told were very helpful to them: it would be very helpful to us if they were willing to reply in kind. During an extended exchange in this vein, Mr Thomas stressed that:

- we looked forward to all-inclusive, meaningful negotiations and that we had made it pretty clear what timetable we envisaged;
- we were working with the Irish Government to find a solution to decommissioning;
- we had set out clearly the sequence of events we envisaged following an unequivocal restoration of the IRA ceasefire;
- we had noted everything Sinn Fein had to say about confidence-building measures and had had some useful things to say in response.

14. Mr Thomas continued to press for some indication of how close, or far apart, Sinn Fein thought they and we were. He needed to be able to tell Ministers that the gap was bridgeable, and what was needed to fill it. Mr McGuinness replied that they had heard very little about confidence-building measures, especially prisoners; that they had noted that we did not expect the Talks to run beyond May 1998; and on decommissioning that they had sensed the UUP might have a veto on the basis of "sufficient consensus". Mr Thomas said that in this respect, everyone had a veto.

Mr McGuinness complained that despite the potentially helpful idea that the two Governments would work together to drive the process forward, "consent" and "sufficient consensus" kept cropping up. "Let's be serious", he said, "decommissioning has strangled the Talks. Sooner or later the two Governments will have to drive the process forward". Mr Thomas repeated that, *without sufficient consensus*, the Governments could not force something through in the face of UUP dissent. If Sinn Fein wanted a categorical assurance that decommissioning would not be an impediment, they could not have it. Changing tack slightly, Sinn Fein said they sensed the period between the declaration of a ceasefire and their entry could be described as yet another period of "decontamination". Mr Thomas denied this and asked again for Sinn Fein's assessment of how far apart our two sides were. Mr McGuinness responded by summarising the criticisms of the inadequacy of our responses he had already made. He again asked for an adjournment which lasted from 2.43 pm until 3.13 pm. On Sinn Fein's return, Mr McGuinness said that the delegation were very disappointed with the meeting. It was absolutely essential to have clarity on all the issues they had raised. They needed meat on the bones. The Government must face up to their responsibilities in the four main areas of concern to Sinn Fein so that they would have "some evidence that meaningful negotiations were on offer". They had heard nothing that provided them with any consolation.

15. Mr Thomas said he was very disappointed that Sinn Fein were disappointed. He reminded the delegation of the Hume/Adams document of 10 October 1996 which John Hume had said was a firm platform for movement by the IRA. He argued that on three of the four matters of concern to Sinn Fein – the fourth being a certain date for entry into Talks – we had been more forward than the 10 October document had required. And even on a date for entry, we had indicated the Government's preparedness, in principle, for rapid progress. In view of this, he wondered if Sinn Fein were serious about their commitment to peace and their professed desire to enter into Talks.

16. Sinn Fein seemed rather shaken by this, but quickly regained their composure. Mr McGuinness said again that our responses had been inadequate and did not convince the delegation that a credible and meaningful process was on offer. From what they had heard, they were doubtful if the Government really were prepared to offer Sinn Fein parity of esteem or to recognise their mandate. Nevertheless, all was not lost and they would continue to seek a way forward with the British and Irish Governments.

Apparently feeling the need to have the last word, Mr McGuinness said he wanted to put on record Sinn Fein's requirement for a six-month limit on the Talks; his concern that we accepted David Trimble and the UUP had a veto on progress; and the delegation's interpretation of our remarks about Sinn Fein's entry to Talks after a ceasefire to mean that they would have to undergo a decontamination period. Mr Thomas said he disagreed with the last two points,

17. The meeting ended with a brief discussion of each side's proposed, and bland, press lines; and agreement to meet again on a date to be arranged after the Sinn Fein delegation returned from South Africa at the end of the next week, subject as always to events on the ground.

C G Maccabe
SH Ext 27086

## Document 85  Dealings with Sinn Fein

From: John Holmes

Date: 28 May 1997

Prime Minister
cc:
Jonathan Powell
Alastair Campbell
Philip Barton

Officials had their second meeting with Sinn Fein today. It went reasonably well in tone, but Sinn Fein pushed harder. There is now a need to get into more detail about Sinn Fein's concerns, e.g. on CBMs and decommissioning, and about ours, on the durability of any ceasefire. This inevitably raises the question of a text setting out our understanding of the position – Sinn Fein have no trust in us (nor we in them) and always want written reassurances. They can also show this to their hardliners to demonstrate that Sinn Fein have gained something in exchange for a ceasefire.

This is of course where it gets difficult. Any HMG text will be (rightly) seen as the result of discussions with Sinn Fein – so much for not negotiating the terms of a ceasefire. It is not entirely easy to justify an effectively joint text with the political wing of the IRA. We don't negotiate such texts with the constitutional political parties. So why are we running after Sinn Fein? Surely, they should just declare a ceasefire without having to be offered inducements to do so.

On the other hand, if a text which gives nothing of substance away is required to achieve a ceasefire, save lives and give the best chance to the talks, why not? The last government was negotiating such a text (the Hume draft of 10 October was part of this process) and published a version of it on 28 November last year when the terms could not be agreed. Mo Mowlam and the NIO are clear we will need to agree some kind of text, and show it in advance to the Americans and Irish, as well as Sinn Fein.

NIO have sent us a draft of such a text – attached, with their covering letter. I have made various comments on it in manuscript. Also attached for comparison are the texts published by the last government on 28 November 1996 and the Hume/Adams text of 10 October. You will see that there are many similarities with both. But the new draft is greener in tone than the 28 November text, and moves more towards the kind of language Sin Fein wants. This is perhaps inevitable, but if the principle of a text is accepted, it is questionable whether we should shift so much towards Sinn Fein at the beginning. They will pocket this and ask more.

Meanwhile the Unionists are not happy. The local election results did not go their way, with Sinn Fein doing well and the nationalists' vote overall up. They lost Belfast. They believe Mo has been showing a nationalist bias in her words and actions, despite her protestations to the contrary. As we discussed, we need to invite Trimble in before too long to cuddle him (although the substance of the discussion may not be easy to handle).

On other points, the loyalist ceasefire is increasingly questioned, and hence their participation in the talks, while the prospects for the marching season do not look good, despite Mo's efforts. The problem remains that the two factions on the ground in the sensitive areas will not talk to each other.

That is all background. The question for now is: are you content for a text on the lines of the one attached to be deployed in the next round of talks with Sinn Fein, probably next week, perhaps with a few modifications on the lines of any comments?

You may want to discuss.
John Holmes

## Document 86 Dealings with Sinn Fein

10 Downing Street
London SW1A 2AA

29 May 1997

From the Private Secretary
to
Ken Lindsay, Esq.,
Northern Ireland Office

Dear Ken,

Thank you for your letter of 23 May, and the enclosed possible text to be deployed with Sinn Fein at an appropriate moment.

Having seen the draft, the Prime Minister has significant reservations about becoming involved in negotiation of such a text. He believes that this could cause us unnecessary difficulties with the Unionists, and is a process which tempts Sinn Fein into adding conditions and keeping the pressure on us. The Prime Minister's own preference would therefore be to make a speech at an appropriate moment which could offer Sinn Fein entry into the talks on a particular date, assuming an early and satisfactory ceasefire. The speech would also cover Sinn Fein's concerns, but not in agreed language, and not necessarily in the kind of terms they have been seeking. He believes that an offer of this kind would put Sinn Fein on the spot and would be very hard for them to refuse, particularly if the Americans and the Irish rode in behind very hard. He thinks President Clinton would certainly be ready to do so.

As far as the content of the draft text is concerned, and leaving aside the desirability of tabling it, the Prime Minister also has some concerns. It is very long and very obviously a joint text with Sinn Fein. More specifically:

(i) he does not like the formulation in the second tiret of paragraph 2 about whether the people of Northern Ireland prefer to support the Union or a sovereign united Ireland. The tiret would be better ended after " … people of Northern Ireland".

(ii) the Prime Minister is nervous about the fifth tiret of paragraph 7 on police reform. He thinks this needs to be defined very tightly to make clear that we are not talking about radical change to the RUC. The following tiret about legislation against terrorism also needs to be very carefully formulated to make clear that this is not code for becoming softer on terrorists;

(iii) the Prime Minister is not persuaded of the necessity for the first tiret of paragraph 12 about a possible adjournment of the talks process. He understands that this would make any "decontamination period" easier for Sinn Fein to swallow, but equally it could go down very badly with the Unionists. They could argue that it was unacceptable to be told that they could not continue discussions without Sinn Fein, just because a ceasefire whose genuineness was still to be proved had been declared;

(iv) the Prime Minister does not like the second sentence of paragraph 16. It is ambiguous and worrying to Unionists to whom decommissioning remains important. The point is covered better in the fourth sentence of the same paragraph.

As I mentioned to you, the Prime Minister would like to discuss this with Dr Mowlam and one or two others, probably after the call by Senator Mitchell on Monday 2 June. This would also be an opportunity to move forward to the resumption of the talks the following day and the problems likely to come up there. We will be in touch to separately confirm the time.

I am copying this letter to William Ehrman (Foreign and Commonwealth Office) and Jan Polley (Cabinet Office).

Yours ever,
John Holmes

## Document 87  Visit of President Clinton, 29 May: Northern Ireland

10 Downing Street
London SW1A 2AA
29 May 1997

From the Private Secretary
to
Ken Lindsay, Esq.
Northern Ireland Office

Dear Ken,

This letter reports the conversation on Northern Ireland in a pre-lunch session. I am recording separately the lengthy discussion on Bosnia in the same session, while Philip Barton is recording the foreign policy conversation over lunch. The President was accompanied by Ambassador Crowe, Sandy Berger and Mary Ann Peters (NSC). Sir John Kerr, Jonathan Powell and I were present.

*Northern Ireland*

*President Clinton* said that he had found the Government's early moves very encouraging. He wanted to be helpful. If he could say something useful, publicly or privately, on any issue, whether it was a ceasefire, decommissioning or whatever, he would be delighted to do so. The US had a certain position with the republican movement and some debts to call in. They were ready to do so at the right moment.

*The Prime Minister* said that our strategy was to reassure the Unionists about where we were going, and about the importance of the consent principle, while trying to bring in Sinn Fein through talking to them at official level and urging on them a new ceasefire. He wanted Sinn Fein in the talks sooner rather than later in order to force them to make the choice between the democratic path and their current position. All the parties in Northern Ireland and the Irish Republic accepted the consent principle except Sinn Fein. Sinn Fein had to decide to negotiate without keeping open the option of violence. He would be as reasonable as he could in facilitating Sinn Fein's entry into talks, but he had to be careful. If the Unionists walked away, the process would be no further forward. If and when he made an offer to Sinn Fein, he would want to see great pressure put on them to accept it. He wanted to avoid a position where Sinn Fein kept adding new conditions. If the Unionists thought that we were in the process of making concessions, it would be very hard to keep them in.

The *Prime Minister* continued that the parades issue for the summer looked very difficult. Anything Sinn Fein could do to be reasonable in their approach would be helpful. Drumcree had done enormous damage last year. There was now a little more optimism but it was very fragile. *President Clinton* repeated that he was ready to help, and would reflect on what could be done about parades. As far as a political settlement was concerned, he wondered whether a solution existed which all parties could accept. The *Prime Minister* said that a united Ireland was unlikely for the foreseeable future. The need was to produce a devolved government in Northern Ireland, which had genuine respect for both traditions, together with some form of North/South cooperation. Most people accepted this basic approach, although there were significant differences about what the North/South arrangements should look like in practice. Paradoxically, the outlines of the solution could be seen, but it remained extremely difficult to get there.

*President Clinton* said that he had sensed from his own visit to Belfast that the people were ahead of their leaders in looking for a settlement. The Paisleys of this world, conditioned by a lifetime of conflict, were unlikely to be part of the solution. *Admiral Crowe* commented that there was something in this. However, at the time of Drumcree the supposed mass of reasonable people in the centre had been nowhere in sight. The *Prime Minister* said that one of his aims was to put pressure on the business community in

Northern Ireland to intervene more in the political process. After all they had most to lose from violence and the absence of a settlement.

*President Clinton* agreed, and said he would go on trying to get US investment into Northern Ireland. But there was a need to find a political place for the party leaders to go, so that they did not simply define their identity by preventing the British Government from moving forward. People like Paisely had to find a role in a settlement somewhere. On the republican side, there were a lot of tough questions which Sinn Fein had not had to answer hitherto, because they had not been in negotiations. If they got into negotiations, they would have to decide what they would settle for. He guessed they would need some kind of guarantee of a connection to Ireland.

I commented that it might be necessary, in arriving at a settlement, to leave the extrem[ists] of both sides behind. We might be able to achieve a settlement which did not have their active support, but with which they could live in practice. Meanwhile, one attraction of a settlement for the Unionists was the chance to become genuine politicians with a role in governing Northern Ireland, rather than simply speech makers. *Berger* commented that the Americans could play a role with the Unionists too. He had talked to Trimble recently. *President Clinton* added that he found Trimble impressive. The *Prime Minister* said that, at the end of the day, the key might lie in agreement between Trimble and Hume.

*President Clinton* concluded that we should keep the Americans in mind constantly in formulating our approach. They were ready to help wherever they could. He repeated that he was impressed by the start the new Government had made. He had also been watching Dr Mowlam on CNN the previous night, and had been most impressed by her solid, down to earth approach. He thought this would inspire confidence.

## Comment

This was a largely analytical discussion, with a notable absence of policy pressure on us from the American side. President Clinton played straight down the line in response to several questions about Northern Ireland at the subsequent press conference.

I am copying this letter to William Ehrman (Foreign and Commonwealth Office), Jan Polley (Cabinet Office), Sir John Kerr (Washington) and Veronica Sutherland (Dublin).

Yours ever
John Holmes


## Document 88   Great Irish Famine Event: Message from Prime Minister


Foreign & Commonwealth Office
London SW1A 2AH

30 May 1997

John Holmes Esq.
10 Downing Street

Dear John,

Your letter of 28 May asked for a draft message from the Prime Minister for use at the Great Irish Famine Event on Saturday 31 May (full details in my letter to you of 22 May). We consider that a Prime Ministerial message (rather than a video message from the Foreign Secretary or Northern Ireland Secretary, for example) is the best option to make the required impact and to avoid any impression of a snub. A number of other heads of Government have contributed, either on video or in written form.

The exact use of the Prime Minister's message (draft attached) will be clarified by the organisers today. It will probably appear on a large screen at the event or may be read out by the British Ambassador, Mrs Veronica Sutherland, who is attending the commemoration.

I enclose a sample text sent by the organisers of the kind of message they hope world leaders will send. The text of President Clinton's video message is also enclosed. The draft prepared for the Prime Minister is a little fuller than either, but the Irish would probably expect this, given our role 150 years ago.

The text explicitly acknowledges British failings of the time while making clear that the famine began as a natural disaster. The Irish should welcome this tone – the organisers have been keen that the event approaches the famine in a spirit of reconciliation rather than recrimination, but any attempt by us to skate over the very considerable failings of official policies of the time would be quickly seized upon by Irish commentators. The text includes positive references to the Irish diaspora and to Irish work in the humanitarian field which should be welcomed by an Irish audience.

As you will appreciate, timing is short. I would be most grateful if you would fax the approved text direct to the Embassy in Dublin, as well as sending it back here.

Yours ever,
Fiona Mylchreest
*Private Secretary*

## Document 89   Draft Message from Prime Minister on Occasion of the Great Irish Famine Event: 31 May-1 June 1997

I am glad to have this opportunity to join with you in commemorating all those who suffered and died during the Great Irish Famine.

The Famine was a defining event in the history of Ireland and of Britain. It has left deep scars. That one million people should have died in what was then part of the richest and most powerful nation in the world is something that still causes pain as we reflect on it today. We must not forget such an immense human tragedy and must draw lessons from it.

While remembering with humility the devastation of the Famine, it is also right that we should pay tribute to the ways in which the Irish people have triumphed in the face of such a catastrophe. By 1861 there were over 800,000 Irish-born people in England, Scotland and Wales as a result of mass emigration from Ireland. Now, more people of Irish descent live in Britain than live in the Irish Republic. Britain has benefited immeasurably from the skills and talents of Irish people, not only in areas such as music, the arts and the caring professions, but across the whole spectrum of our political, economic and social life.

Let us therefore today celebrate the resilience and courage of those Irish men and women who were able to forge another life outside Ireland, and give thanks for the rich culture and vitality they brought with them. Britain, the US and many Commonwealth countries, home to the majority of the Irish diaspora, are richer for their presence and the contribution they have made.

One hundred and fifty years ago, those who governed in London failed the people of these islands by adhering too strictly to economic dogma. What then began as a crop failure culminated in human tragedy. There are countries today facing natural disasters which threaten to overwhelm them. Particularly in the light of our history and experience, we, the British and Irish peoples, must help tackle these problems with imagination, flexibility and compassion.

I know that the Irish people, catalysed by their own famine history, have long been particularly active in fighting poverty and hunger throughout the world. My government too has given a strong pledge to combat world poverty. I hope that this event, which commemorates a tragedy in our shared history, will give inspiration to all our peoples who strive for these shared goals.

## Document 90   Northern Ireland: Moving the Process Forward

From Marjorie Mowlam

30 May 1997

Prime Minister
We are to meet on Monday. We have made an excellent start in setting a new style, demonstrating commitment to confidence building and making clear our determination to put new momentum into the process.

But we face key challenges in the next two months:

- We must quickly conclude our exchanges with Sinn Fein: they must *not* turn into open-ended negotiations. That means achieving a *ceasefire* or putting an offer to Sinn Fein so reasonable it attracts the US and Irish Government's support and ensures that the SDLP are prepared to move forward without them if it is spurned;
- Making real progress in the talks: that means getting an agreement on *decommissioning* satisfactory to both unionists and nationalists. Without it the talks will collapse;
- Getting through the *marching season* with the least possible damage. The prospects don't look good; we need all the help we can get.

*The single step most likely to help all these challenges, and to deliver the sort of momentum we seek, is a renewed and unequivocal IRA ceasefire.* I think we have a genuine opportunity to achieve one. But we need to act decisively now to bring it about sooner rather than later.

*Date for entry*

We should set ourselves to achieve:

- *an IRA ceasefire in mid-June*, building on the two months of undecided ceasefire since the last (real, as opposed to hoax) IRA attack on 10 April;
- *Sinn Fein's formal admission to the talks by the end of July*, to make their formal commitment to the Mitchell principles, some three and a half months after the start of the undeclared ceasefire and six weeks or so after a formal ceasefire declaration:
- adjourn for the summer with the aim of starting the *real political negotiations in September*. So the first actual negotiations involving Sinn Fein, at which we hope at least some unionists would be present, would be *five months* after the start of the declared ceasefire.

I am seriously worried that any slower timetable would mean there would be no ceasefire in place before the marching season, leaving the real possibility that either loyalists or republicans resort to violence then, which might destroy the opportunity for some months if not years. *Postponing the entry date for Sinn Fein means postponing, or losing altogether, the ceasefire.* Nor am I optimistic that the talks will make much progress, while Sinn Fein are so obviously hanging around the entrance. So any slower timetable merely risks wasting the summer months in the talks, further discrediting the process and leaving the dynamic to the streets.

As you have so powerfully put it, both to President Clinton and the Taoiseach, we want to get Sinn Fein in quickly, we want to hold them in the process and then put them to the *test* of real political negotiations.

The timetable I have outlined is not without risks. At our last meeting we accepted that unionists were very likely to walk out whenever Sinn Fein comes in, but the benefits of a ceasefire and getting Sinn Fein in the political process made this worthwhile. We must reckon they will do so if Sinn Fein come in at the end of July. But the long summer break before real negotiations start offer some prospect that the UUP at least could be enticed back, provided of course that over that period the ceasefire holds and the Government is seen to remain firm on its declared even-handed approach.

We shall have to work hard to *reassure unionists*. I have deliberately held back on implementing Grand Committee reforms as these are a unionist-friendly move to play in at the right time. We shall work hard on identifying similar issues to run alongside repeated reassurance on consent, the Union, words and deeds etc. But moving quickly can also be presented as having attractions for unionists: the issue of whether Sinn Fein are in or out will be resolved quickly and the talks can go forward, with or without them.

*A possible text*

There have been exchanges about a possible text. What I intended may have been misunderstood. I think we are agreed that:

- At the right time *something needs to be said in public* to Sinn Fein about a date and the other issues they have raised. That means we need a set of words of some sort, whether for a speech, an article, a statement, an open letter or whatever;

- We want to rally the maximum support to any position which we set out, including *crucially the Irish and US Governments*. That means showing them these words well in advance and listening seriously to any concerns they may have. As was clear at the time, the last Government failed to consult the Irish Government adequately at crucial moments, including its response to the Mitchell report and its statement of 28 November. The result was a public split between the two Governments and all pressure on Sinn Fein was lost;

- We are working seriously to create the conditions in which there is a *good prospect of the IRA calling a ceasefire*. Although we must keep an eye on the possibility that they won't, *we are not simply playing for tactical advantage over Sinn Fein*. That means also showing any words to Sinn Fein in advance, as the previous Government sought to do in a similar situation, though through intermediaries, last Autumn. If we slap down a public challenge to Sinn Fein without any warning, they will have no time to prepare the movement or consider their response. In such circumstances, they are most likely to revert to what is familiar for them: condemnation of HMG and a resort to violence. But if we give Adams and McGuinness the means to assure their movement that their concerns are being taken seriously and HMG is in good faith then a ceasefire is a real possibility;

- We want to make whatever position we take as defensible as possible with respect to *unionists* and public opinion generally. That points to any set of words being seen to be consistent with the underlying approach of the last Government, while containing the new elements (such as the date) designed to bridge the gap they failed to close.

This points decisively in my view to a developed set of words which is shown to the Irish and US Governments, as well as Sinn Fein. John Holmes' letter of 29 May may be based on two possible misinterpretations:

- *That we intend to negotiate any text with Sinn Fein.* We don't. We
see no realistic prospect of agreed language with Sinn Fein on the
issues they have been raising. Our suggested wording certainly
does *not* offer reassurances in the kind of terms they have been
seeking. But I do believe it to be highly desirable to show Sinn
Fein in advance the sort of words we have in mind to use, so as to
establish whether they are prepared to acquiesce in it and use it as
a basis for declaring a ceasefire;
- *That we have ruled out these words being made public in the form of
a speech.* We have not. There are a number of options as to how it
could be made public. Anything in your words would carry enormous weight.

I start with a strong preference for simple, direct language which sets out
our position in our terms. But we must also use some established language both to demonstrate to Sinn Fein, the Irish and US Governments
that we have moved beyond the position of the last Government *and* to
reassure unionists that we have not abandoned fundamental positions of
principle.

It is also helpful to use language which can be compared to the Hume/
Adams text of 10 October 1996. Since Sinn Fein have publicly emphasised
their acceptance of that text, it will be difficult for them to reject anything
which goes as far, if not further. Especially in the eyes of those already in
possession of the Hume/Adams text: John Hume, the American and Irish
Governments.

I have examined the attached text carefully. It is not a "green" text. It
offers a balanced account of the Government's position, based on familiar
principles but offering subtle, but significant advances.

We don't have much time if we are to achieve the timetable I believe
is necessary. So I propose to send the text to Sinn Fein, with a copy to
the Irish and US Governments *next week*. Anything slower risks losing
the chance of a summer ceasefire. We could, if we wished, still hold back the
specific date of end July while signalling to the Irish and US Governments
that that is the sort of timescale we have in mind.

*Textual details*

On the specific worries raised by John Holmes:

(i) The formulation in the second tiret of paragraph 2 is a quote from the opening sentence of paragraph 4 of the Downing Street Declaration which we have said we support. Anything less will reinforce worries among the nationalists that we are reneging on one side of the principle of consent. A united Ireland is not realistic in the foreseeable future, but nationalists – and republicans in particular – need to be reassured regularly that it is not the British Government that is standing in their way, but the majority wish of the people of Northern Ireland.

(ii) The SDLP are clear that there *will* need to be radical restructuring of the RUC at some or a part of any political settlement. Nationalists generally have taken comfort from our commitment to reform. We must not excite unionists unduly, but nor must we be seen to disappoint the expectations we have raised. We are also committed to correct the flaws in the existing legislation against terrorism and, in the long term, develop new counter-terrorist legislation which is UK-wide and responds to the changing nature of terrorism;

(iii) *An adjournment of the talks* after a ceasefire is both critical to the prospects of a ceasefire and simply a recognition of reality. Sinn Fein will not accept a "decontamination period" (a term to be avoided in public) in which, after a ceasefire, they are seen to be excluded from talks which carry on without them. In their eyes this would deny their electoral mandate and their claim to equal treatment. *It is a break point for them* (and most likely the Irish Government and possibly the US Government too). In fact, when a ceasefire is declared, we expect all the current participants to be mesmerised by the prospect of Sinn Fein's entry so that no significant business is done. An adjournment would simply recognise the reality. In public, it would be defended as reflecting the need for a period to test the ceasefire and as acknowledging the reality that the talks could not, and sensibly should not, proceed in the meantime. We could make it explicit that the *Forum*, to which unionists attach much importance, would *not* be suspended.

(iv) The second sentence at paragraph 16 offers a careful balance which it will be difficult for unionists or Sinn Fein to challenge. The first part – "this must be resolved to the satisfaction of the participants" – is the most forward position Sinn Fein have ever adopted on decommissioning and a pretty positive statement as far as unionists are concerned as well. The second half – "without blocking the negotiations" – is a quote from the last Prime Minister to which the SDLP and the Irish Government, as well as Sinn Fein, attach much significance. The point is that everyone accepts that decommissioning has to be resolved. But nationalists fear, not without some justification, that unionists are using it merely as a deliberate blocking tactic to keep Sinn Fein out and to avoid real negotiations. They want a clear signal from the two Governments that they will not allow this to happen.

I attach a *revised text* which tries to make these points clearer.

*The Talks*

On Monday, I can describe in greater detail our preparations for the start of talks on Tuesday. The issue on the table is decommissioning. We need to show at an early stage that we are determined to find a way through this issue into political negotiations. That requires a joint approach with the Irish Government. In the first week or so, at least, of the talks we don't know which Irish Government we are likely to face.

The real position on decommissioning is that it is essentially a political issue. It is clear that even substantial decommissioning would not affect the paramilitaries' capability to return to violence. The best assessment, shared by the police, security and intelligence agencies and my Department, as well as by the SDLP, the Irish Government, and – in moments of candour – by many unionists, is that decommissioning is of little *military* significance and is unlikely to occur from either loyalists or republicans until shortly before, or at the same time as, a political settlement.

But, while working in the knowledge of that reality, we need in the meantime to find some political mechanism which enables unionists to move beyond this issue into political negotiations. I can explain on Monday in greater detail our thoughts on how to do this.

A copy goes to Sir Robin Butler.
Approved by the Secretary of Statement
and signed in her absence

K Lindsay

# Document 91   Call by Senator Mitchell, 1100, 2 June

Northern Ireland Office
11 Millbank
London Sw1P 4QE

From: The Private Secretary
30 May 1997

Philip Barton Esq.
Private Secretary
No 10 Downing Street

Dear Philip,
Your letter of 15 May asked for briefing for the Prime Minister's meeting with Senator Mitchell on Monday. The other two Talks Chairmen, General de Chastelain and Mr Holkeri will also be in attendance. I understand from our Embassy in Washington that Senator Mitchell will also be accompanied by two of his staffers, Martha Pope and Kelly Currie. My Secretary of State and Mr Murphy stand ready to attend this meeting. They will have had meetings themselves with the Senator earlier that day.

2. The main objectives of this meeting, which takes place at Senator Mitchell's request might be:

- to establish personal contact with the Senator and the other two chairmen and assure them of the new government's commitment to achieving a political settlement;
- to make clear HMG's gratitude for their commitment to the process; our appreciation of their skills; and to encourage them in their difficult task as chairmen;
- to demonstrate HMG's determination to see early progress in the talks;
- to let them know that the 2 Governments are working hard to develop agreed proposals on decommissioning with a view to tabling soon after 3 June;
- to hear their views on the proposals for the talks.

3. A *speaking note* for the meeting is attached at *Annex A*. The Senator will go straight on to Dublin for meetings with the Taoiseach and Mr Ahern, before travelling to Belfast.
*Press Line*

4. The meeting, which takes place the day before the Northern Ireland talks resume, provides an ideal opportunity for the Prime Minister to make a public restatement of his wish to see the talks make early, positive progress. He could do so either in the form of a short written attached at *Annex B* – or perhaps a short photocall with the three Chairmen at the end of the meeting. This could be particularly effective in Northern Ireland; there may not be much other political comment about the talks on Monday because most of the senior Northern Ireland politicians are away at a conference in South Africa. Alternatively, the Secretary could do a brief photocall with the Chairmen, after the meeting, to complement a written statement by the Prime Minister.

5. The draft statement attached is deliberately drafted in measured tones. It would be wrong to strike too optimistic a note since the parties still have to overcome the formidable hurdle of decommissioning. The best course would be to call on the parties to show renewed vigour and determination to press on with the negotiations and overcome any obstacles; this would echo the language of the Independent Chairmens' statement to the talks when they were suspended before the general election.

Yours ever
W K. Lindsay

**ANNEX A**
**Speaking Note**
*General*

- value this opportunity to meet today;
- grateful for the very great *personal commitment* which each of you have made and continue to make to the talks process;
- pleased that the talks will again benefit from your skilled and fair chairmanship;

*New government/Resumption of Talks*

- Northern Ireland will continue to be *a high priority* for this government and for me personally. I had a very useful discussion with the President.
- want to see *early progress* onto issues of substance in the talks;
- this means injecting *new momentum* into the process and finding a way through on decommissioning as a matter of urgency. The 2 Governments are endeavouring to work up *joint proposals* for early submission to the parties;
- the UUP vote held up well in the general election and they won an extra seat. Hope this will give them *fresh confidence* in the talks;
- want to see *Sinn Fein* in the talks – on the same basis as the other participants;
- we have said that no party can have a veto on progress at the talks;
- Loyalists – concerned about recent attacks attributed to Loyalists – this will need to be handled carefully in the talks – importance of the government acting justly, and with principle.

*Sinn Fein*

- have authorised meetings between and officials, subject to events on the ground;

- hope that this new initiative will result in them making themselves eligible to join the talks soon;
- if not, will have no hesitation in *moving ahead without them* – they cannot hold the democratic process to ransom;
- the President's personal involvement has been vital: will continue to work closely with the Administration to achieve the peaceful and honourable settlement which we all want to see;
- officials have reported some encouraging signs from their two meetings with Sinn Fein;
- they are negotiating hard on issues of interest to them, particularly the question of how soon they could enter talks after a ceasefire;
- in the event of an unequivocal restoration of the ceasefire, and consistency of words and deeds, there would be no unnecessary delay to their entry to talks.

*Decommissioning*

- would like the two governments together to make an early attempt to break out of the decommissioning impasse and set a date for the launch of substantive negotiations;
- agreement between the two governments increases the pressure on the UUP to acquiesce;
- also need to give the UPP cover;
- would value any help you can give in moving this forward with the Irish and UUP;
- aware of Irish concerns but the reality is that unless both governments are committed to work to bring about decommissioning during the negotiations and to creating the mechanisms for this, the UPP will not engage;
- interested in your views on this and the other issues?

## ANNEX B
**Speaking Note/Press Statement**
In advance of the resumption of multi-party talks in Northern Ireland on Tuesday 3 June, the Prime Minister (and the Secretary of State for

Northern Ireland) today met the Talks Chairmen, Senator Mitchell, General de Chastelain and Mr Holkeri.

- The meeting provided a valuable and timely opportunity to exchange views on the talks process. All agreed that it was important that all the participants returned to the table with the necessary will and desire to see the talks process through to a successful conclusion.
- The Prime Minister reiterated his desire to see an inclusive talks process, but again made it clear that it was for Sinn Fein to decide whether they wished to play their part in determining the future of Northern Ireland. The door remained open to them, but only if there were an unequivocal ceasefire by the IRA, reflected in words and deeds, and a firm commitment to democratic principles.

The Prime Minister said:

- There is no alternative to democratic dialogue. Terrorism and democracy do not, and cannot, go hand in hand.
- I ask all the parties who are meeting again tomorrow to return to the negotiations with a renewed sense of purpose and a firm determination to drive the process through to a successful conclusion. A great deal rests on their shoulders and I, for one, do not underestimate the task that lies ahead of them. I hope that by approaching the issues in a positive frame of mind and by showing a willingness to recognise the views of others it will be possible for real progress to be made. This is a new opportunity for everyone involved in the talks to prove the value of political dialogue to the Northern Ireland people and to create a better future for all parts of the community. I wish the participants well.

# Document 92  Call by George Mitchell

From: John Holmes

Date: 30 May 1997

Prime Minister

cc:

Jonathan Powell

Alastair Campbell

Philip Barton

Mitchell will be accompanied by the other two talks chairmen, General de Chastelain from Canada and Harri Holkeri, a former Finnish Prime Minister. All three are good news. Despite the controversy over his appointment, Mitchell has impressed everyone with his neutrality. There has been some criticism of him for lack of firm chairmanship, but this is because he is rightly careful not to be seen as a US mediator making proposals of his own. There may come a time when he needs to take a more pro-active role on one or two issues, but it is important that this is only when we want him to. He was very frustrated by the lack of progress in the talks before the Elections, but is ready to give it one more go. He believes that movement forward is possible, although he has a good appreciation of the difficulties after his time as chairman (and has usefully fed this back to those in Washington inclined to take a simplistic view).

NIO briefing for the meeting is attached. The main point is to encourage the three Chairmen, thank them for their efforts, and make clear your own personal commitment to early progress if at all possible. You should not go into details with them about our strategy with Sinn Fein. But you can usefully discuss with them how they think decommissioning could be taken forward successfully, and how to keep the Loyalists in the talks without justifying accusations of double standards.

There will be a photo-call. The NIO have also suggested that you issue a statement afterwards and have provided a draft. I see no need for this, and it would be rather artificial. The main point – your strong commitment to get the talks moving quickly – can be effectively made in press briefing afterwards, as well as by Mo in interviews she is bound to be giving as the talks resume.

John Holmes

# Document 93  Messages to David Trimble

**1.**

10 Downing Street
London SW1A 2AA

From the Private Secretary

30 May 1997
David Trimble Esq MP

Dear David,
We spoke about the desirability of a further meeting between yourself and the Prime Minister. Can I propose 17.30 on Wednesday 4 June for 30 minutes or so? This would be a useful opportunity to compare notes about where to go next.

You have also been talking to the NIO about arrangements for a group of representatives of the Orange Order, and they are helping you with this. To avoid misunderstanding, I hope it is clear that the meeting with the Prime Minister is for you (and one or two of your UUP colleagues if you wish) and not the Orange Order representatives. Perhaps you can confirm whether these arrangements suit you, either from South Africa or on your return?

Yours ever,
John Holmes

**2.**

10 Downing Street
London SW1A 2AA

From the Private Secretary

30 May 1997

Miss M G Fort CMG
British High Commission
Pretoria

*Message to David Trimble*
I would be grateful if you could somehow contrive to get the attached message from me to David Trimble, if necessary by telephone. I hope this does not prove too difficult.

Many thanks for your help in advance.
Yours ever,
John Holmes

## Document 94  Northern Ireland

From: John Holmes
Date: 30 May 1997

The Prime Minister
cc:
Jonathan Powell
Philip Barton

Pat McFadden

I have arranged a 45-minute meeting with Mo Mowlam, Paul Murphy, John Chilcott and Quentin Thomas on Monday morning, immediately before you see George Mitchell. The aim is to talk through the next steps with Sinn Fain, and to look at the handling of the talks which resume the following day.
    As background I attach:

   – a minute from Mo received late this evening which sets out at some length the NIO strategy, including tabling a text with Sinn Fein and the Irish and US Governments, and a much earlier end-July date for Sinn Fein's entry into talks;

- my letter recording your views on the previous draft NIO text, which you will detect have not gone down well in the NIO!
- the record of the latest meeting between NIO officials and Sinn Fein. This conveys well the flavour of the exchanges, in particular the way in which Sinn Fein always tries to put the onus on us to meet their demands;
- the NIO "game plan" for the resumption of the talks. This helps to bring out the main issues: above all, decommissioning; the delicate position of the Loyalists; and how to spin out the process convincingly in the period Sinn Fein enter (if they do), when there may be no Irish Government in place for some weeks.

The key issue for decision at Monday's meeting is whether to table a text at the next meeting with Sinn Fein, as very strongly recommended by Mo, or to go down your preferred route of a speech. A third option worth exploring, which could be combined with the second, is using the Americans to reinforce our oral assurances to Sinn Fein that we understand their concerns and can respond to them, at least up to a point, once a genuine ceasefire is in place. It is worth noting that Sinn Fein have not asked to table a new text, although they may still do.

A speech from you with an explicit offer to Sinn Fein of a date, and some reassurance but in your own words, not agreed ones, has the advantage of putting the onus on them, where it belongs. In my view Clinton would have no option but to give you strong support. It would go down much better with the Unionists than a suspicious looking text obviously negotiated with Sinn Fein. But the NIO are right to point out that the risks of not achieving a ceasefire are higher.

Mo's minute is well argued. It represents a coherent approach. She could well be right, and what she suggests may well be worth trying. It would certainly call Sinn Fein's bluff. But I have to say it also represents very much an Irish view of the world, including something of an obsession with a new ceasefire as an end in itself, and a belief that at the end of the day the Unionists will just have to lump it. It does not bring out enough the real risks of the Unionists giving up on you altogether because you have moved too precipitately. For example, it mentions the dangers of the marching season – but the real risk in the marching season is from Unionists making the Province ungovernable.

I have made a few other comments in manuscript. But I find myself in a difficult position as someone inevitably associated with the last government's position, which *did* fail to achieve a renewal of the ceasefire. The NIO paper seems to me somewhat pointed about this, and I detect that I am clearly suspected of influencing you in the wrong direction.

Whatever the truth of this, you will want to test the NIO case with some tough questioning. If you go down their suggested route, you will be warmly applauded by the US and Irish Governments, and may well achieve a new ceasefire. Reaction in the media here will inevitably be mixed, but you can get away with it. The *key test* is not whether the Unionists are angry – they will be even if we go a bit slower, and they are by nature unreasonable – but whether they can be drawn back into the process afterwards, because they will have to deal with you for at least five years. And the *key judgment* is whether we are in a political position such that we have in effect to meet Sinn Fein's demands, or whether they are themselves in difficulties and can be pushed to accept a tougher approach from us, with US help.

The other issue you may wish to explore a bit further in the meeting is decommissioning. There are endless complicated papers about this but they serve mostly to confuse. The NIO are supposedly producing a fresh proposal for the talks. You may like to ask Quentin Thomas to explain this to you.

However complicated the papers, the issue is fairly simple. The Unionists want guarantees, before they get into serious political negotiations, that real deommissioning will take place, because they believe that otherwise Sinn Fein is always retaining the violent option. We are also committed to the Mitchell approach of parallel decommissioning, but we are relatively flexible about implementation. Sinn Fein's view, covertly supported by the Irish, is that there is no question of serious decommisssioning before a settlement is agreed. Can these positions be reconciled? If they can't be reconciled in substance, as is likely, is there a procedural way through, which [does] not in effect concede that no decommissioning is likely to happen during the talks? No one has yet found a convincing answer to this conundrum.

I agree with you that we should not be on this decommissioning hook, but we are – and we can't simply move away from it without seriously threatening our relations with the Unionists. That is why we have to find a subtle way through, if we can.

Finally, on the subject of Unionists, I have a meeting with Trimble on Wednesday afternoon. He and others are currently in South Africa, to learn how the ANC and National Party did it, until Monday evening. Sinn Fein are also there, but sealed off from the Unionists, which has caused much wry media comment about the new apartheid.

John Holmes

# Document 95 The Great Irish Famine Event

10 Downing Street
London SW1A 2AA

The Prime Minister

I am glad to have this opportunity to join with you in commemorating all those who suffered and died during the Great Irish Famine.

The Famine was a defining event in the history of Ireland and of Britain. It has left deep scars. That one million people should have died in what was then part of the richest and most powerful nation in the world is something that still causes pain as we reflect on it today. Those who governed in London at the time failed their people through standing by while a crop failure turned into a massive human tragedy. We must not forget such a dreadful event.

It is also right that we should pay tribute to the ways in which the Irish people have triumphed in the face of the catastrophe. Britain in particular has benefited immeasurably from the skills and talents of Irish people, not only in areas such as music, the arts and the caring professions but across the whole spectrum of our political, economic and social life.

Let us therefore today not only remember those who died but also celebrate the resilience and courage of those Irish men and women who were able to forge another life outside Ireland, and the rich culture and vitality they brought with them. Britain, the US and many Commonwealth countries are richer for their presence.

31 May 1997
I hope this does not cause you any problems. It should go down well
with the Irish, and I cannot see anyone here or in Northern Ireland seriously
objecting. Clinton's video recorded message is attached for comparison.

John Holmes

## Document 96   President Clinton's Speech re: The
Candlelighting Ceremony, 30 May 1997

I am pleased to join this commemoration of the great Irish Famine. An
event that transformed both Ireland and America and linked our two nations forever.

1 million of Ireland's sons and daughters died in the course of the terrible blight that ravaged the crops 150 years ago. But 2 million more fled
their native land in a desperate quest to survive. The famine was the greatest
disaster in the history of Ireland.

Yet out of that horrible tragedy there emerged a blessing for our nation.
The men, women and children who crossed the ocean to build new lives
in America. Today our cities, our society, our culture reflect the skill and
determination of these immigrants and their descendants. Irish-Americans
have excelled in every profession. From industry and government to the
arts. They have enriched America's way of life with the values of their heritage, their love of family, faith and hard work, devotion to community and
compassion for those in need.

Perhaps the haunting memory of the famine helps to explain thei remarkable generosity of the Irish at home and all around the world. Irish
troops have stood watch for peace from Lebanon to Cyprus to Haiti.
Renewing hope in the future and helping others to help themselves. As
America joins in the remembrance of the famine, we share your commitment to fight poverty and hunger everywhere and we draw inspiration from
Ireland's example in making this world a much better place.

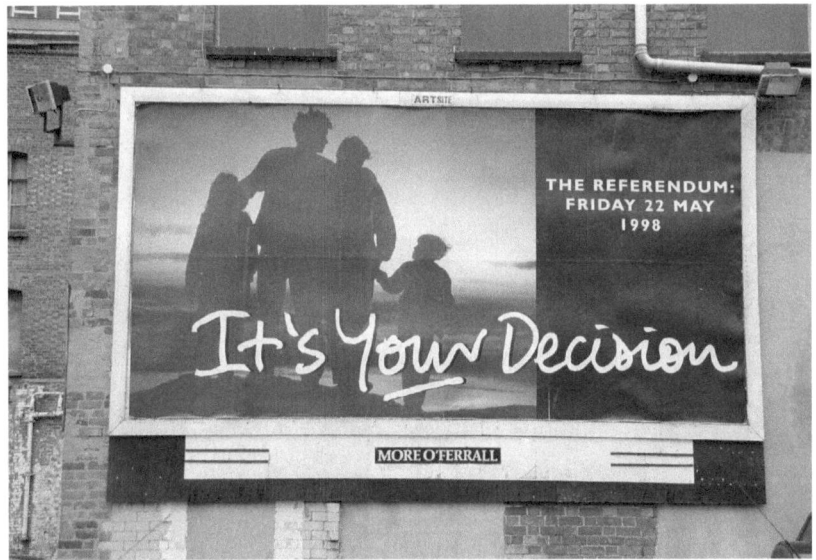

Referendum.

Photograph by Martin Melaugh

Referendum "Yes" campaign , no1.

Photograph by Martin Melaugh

Referendum poster, no 2.

Photograph by Martin Melaugh

Hunger Strike Memorial no 1 (25 July 2000).

Photograph by Martin Melaugh

Crossmaglen Hunger Strike Memorial , 28 Oct. 2001, no.1.

Photograph by Martin Melaugh

Derry: Bloody Sunday March 30 Jan. 2011, nos 11+ 12.

Photograph by Martin Melaugh

Protest against British Army petro, no. F8P12.

Photograph by Eamon Melaugh

Children in the city walls (1968), no. F1P1.

Photograph by Eamon Melaugh

Belfast County officers, 12 July 1993.

Photograph by Neil Jarman

British Army: Taking a break, no. F2P7, 31 July 1972.

Photograph by Eamon Melaugh

Internment camp.

Photograph by Martin Melaugh

Demilitarisation no 1 (28 Oct. 2001).

Photograph by Martin Melaugh

Hungerstrike.

Photograph by Martin Melaugh

Loyalist mural, no 5.

Photograph by Michael Melaugh

Loyalist mural, no 6.

Photograph by Michael Melaugh

# TOWARDS THE NORTHERN IRELAND ACT

The documents presented in this volume all come from the very first month of Tony Blair's "New Labour" government, which was simultaneously working on devolution plans for Scotland and Wales. As can be seen, May 1997 was an intensely busy month in the negotiations. Major Irish party leaders, mostly from Northern Ireland, came to visit the British Prime Minister. In his conversations Tony Blair seems to have followed Samuel Johnson's dictum where there is a controversy concerning national interests, that "a man may treat his antagonist with politeness and even respect".

The bargaining was not easy when he met David Trimble, John Hume or Ian Paisley. The purpose of the negotiations was to reach an overall political settlement, "achieved through agreement and founded on consent". The British government intended to address all the issues relevant to a settlement. It was important that these negotiations took place in a peaceful environment; so the loyalist ceasefire, as well as the declaration of an unequivocal ceasefire by the IRA, would be an important indicator of how they might proceed. Sinn Fein would be formally invited to participate in the discussions only after it had committed to the principles of democracy and non-violence. The crucial issue was the decommissioning of illegal arms. This, it was eventually decided, should take place during the process of all-party negotiations. Here the government was "looking for the commitment of all participants to work constructively during the negotiations to implement all aspects of the International Body's report".

In 1995 George Mitchell, a United States Senator, accepted the position of special advisor to President Bill Clinton to help broker peace in Northern Ireland. Along with John de Chastelain, former Canadian Chief-of-Staff and ambassador to the US, and Harri Holkeri, former Prime Minister of Finland, Mitchell created an International Committee on arms decommissioning, which he chaired. The Committee came up with its proposals on 22 January 1996. These laid down the principles that would lead the paramilitary groups to give up their weapons.

The Blair government welcomed the Mitchell report, advising the Northern Ireland parties that they should do the same. Gerry Adams welcomed the report too, saying that it provided "a basis for moving forward so that all matters can be settled to the satisfaction of all sides as part of the process".[1] The Unionists were sceptical at the beginning, but they mostly joined in acceptance later on.

The talks-process went on for a further full year, when on 19 April 1998, the Good Friday Agreement (also known as the Belfast Agreement) was signed.[2] In this process, George Mitchell played a very significant role. He crossed the Atlantic more than a hundred times to mediate in the Northern Ireland conflict. A referendum on the Agreement was held in Northern Ireland on 22 May 1998. Over 81% of the population turned out to vote: 71.1 % approved the Agreement; 28.9 % voted against it. Since the Good Friday Agreement was overwhelmingly approved by the people of Northern Ireland, it was now made the basis for the Northern Ireland Act of 1998.[3] The Act provided Northern Ireland with a democratic constitution, which the country had never had before.

Yet Northern Ireland continued to be a *dependent* nation – dependent on the United Kingdom. It remained "part of the United Kingdom and shall not cease to be so without the consent of a majority of the people of Northern Ireland". According to the terms of the Northern Ireland Act, the country would elect its own Assembly, but the bills passed by it had to receive Royal Assent. The Acts of the Assembly would not "affect the power of the Parliament of the United Kingdom to make laws for Northern Ireland". Her Majesty may by Order of Council specify certain functions. The Secretary of State, a member of the British government, possessed dissenting powers, and consent from this official was needed whenever international relations, defence and national security collided

---

1    Gerry Adams, *op. cit.*, p. 324.
2    Complete text is attached below.
3    Complete text is attached below.

with Westminster. The executive power continued to be vested in Her [His] Majesty's Government. The Assembly could elect its own First Minister and Deputy Minister, and yet the Secretary of State kept continual watch. The devolved powers to the Assembly were limited. The Assembly had legislative authority for "transferred matters", but none for "excepted matters", such as "matters of British national importance".

Almost since its outset, devolution to Northern Ireland has been in trouble. The Secretary of State had to suspend the Assembly in 2000 and 2002 because of party differences, and direct rule from Westminster was restored.[4] Further discussion on this problem is outside the scope of the present work, but the documents it presents do show how much patient work and preparedness to accept the points of view of people with contrary opinions had to go into the reconciliation process and how much could be damagingly lost if divisions and suspicions were resurrected.

4    For details, see Russell Deacon & Alan Sandry, *Devolution in the United Kingdom* (Edinburgh University Press: Edinburgh, 2007), pp. 173–78.

4

# Documents 97 And 98: Report of the International Body on Arms Decommissioning, 22 January 1996 & The Belfast Agreement as originally enacted

Document 97  Report of the International Body on Arms Decommissioning, 22 January 1996

## I. INTRODUCTION[1]

1. On 28 November, 1995, the British and Irish Governments issued a Communiqué which announced the launching in Northern Ireland of a "twin track" process to make progress in parallel on the decommissioning issue and on all-party negotiations.

2. One track was "to invite the parties to intensive preparatory talks with a remit to reach widespread agreement on the basis, participation, structure, format and agenda to bring all parties together for substantive negotiations aimed at a political settlement based on consent". This has become known as the political track.

3. The other track concerned the decommissioning of arms and was set forth as follows in the Communiqué:
   [Point 4 is missing in the original.]

5. In parallel, the two Governments have agreed to establish an International Body to provide an independent assessment of the decommissioning issue.

1   Source: CAIN Web Service.

6. Recognising the widely expressed desire to see all arms removed from Irish politics, the two Governments will ask the International Body to report on the arrangements necessary for the removal from the political equation of arms silenced by virtue of the welcome decisions taken last summer and autumn by those organisations that previously supported the use of arms for political purposes.

7. In particular, the two Governments will ask the Body to:

  – identify and advise on a suitable and acceptable method for full and verifiable decommissioning; and
  – report whether there is a clear commitment on the part of those in possession of such arms to work constructively to achieve that.

8. It will be for the International Body to determine its own procedures. The two Governments expect it to consult widely, to invite relevant parties to submit their analysis of matters relevant to the decommissioning issue and, in reaching its conclusions within its remit, to consider such evidence on its merits.

4. We are that Body. This is our report. We have no stake in Northern Ireland other than an interest in seeing an end to the conflict and in the ability of its people to live in peace. Our role is to bring an independent perspective to the issue. We are motivated solely by our wish to help. This assessment represents our best and our independent judgment. We are unanimous in our views. There are no differences of opinion among us.

5. To provide us with sufficient information to meet our remit, we held two series of meetings in Belfast, Dublin and London: the first, 15th through 18th December, 1995: the second, 11th through 22nd January, 1996.

In addition, we held an organisational meeting in New York on December 9th, 1995.

6. In the course of our meetings we heard orally and in writing from dozens of government officials, political leaders, church officials and representatives of other organisations and institutions. We received hundreds of letters and telephone calls from members of the public and met with many others. We thank all for their submissions.

Contributions from those who suffered losses during the time of troubles but are strongly committed to the peace process were especially moving. All the submissions have been carefully reviewed and considered.

## II. DISCUSSION

7. Our examination of the issues and of the facts, and the perspectives brought to us by those who briefed us or who made written representations to us, convince us that while there is no simple solution to the conflict in Northern Ireland, the factors on which a process for peace must be based are already known. We can indicate the way we believe these factors should be addressed so that decommissioning of arms and all-party negotiations can proceed, but only resolute action by the parties themselves will produce progress.

8. That noted, we are aware of the enormous contribution already made by individuals and groups in advancing the process of peace in Northern Ireland to its current stage. The tireless and courageous efforts of Prime Minister John Major and Taoiseach John Bruton (and before him Albert Reynolds) have been essential to the peace process. They have been joined by other political leaders, institutions, organisations and individuals in the promotion of peace.

9. We considered our task in the light of our responsibility to all of the people of Northern Ireland; the need for the people to be reassured that their democratic and moral expectations can be realised; and in the spirit of serious efforts made by the British and Irish Governments to advance the peace process.

10. For nearly a year and a half the guns have been silent in Northern Ireland. The people want that silence to continue. They want lasting peace in a just society in which paramilitary violence plays no part.

That was the dominant theme expressed in the many letters and calls we received from those in the North and South, Unionist and Nationalist, Catholic and Protestant, Loyalist and Republican.

11. Notwithstanding reprehensible 'punishment' killings and beatings, the sustained observance of the ceasefires should not be devalued. It is a significant factor which must be given due weight in assessing the commitment

of the paramilitaries to "work constructively to achieve" full and verifiable decommissioning.

12. Since the ceasefires, the political debate has focused largely on the differences that have prevented the commencement of all-party negotiations intended to achieve an agreed political settlement. This circumstance has obscured the widespread agreement that exists – so widespread that it tends to be taken for granted. In fact, members of both traditions may be less far apart on the resolution of their differences than they believe.

13. No one should underestimate the value of the consensus for peace, and the fact that no significant group is actively seeking to end it.

14. In paragraph five of the Communiqué we were asked "to provide an independent assessment of the decommissioning issue". It is a serious issue. It is also a symptom of a larger problem: the absence of trust. Common to many of our meetings were arguments, steeped in history, as to why the other side cannot be trusted. As a consequence, even well-intentioned acts are often viewed with suspicion and hostility.

15. But a resolution of the decommissioning issue – or any other issue – will not be found if the parties resort to their vast inventories of historical recrimination. Or, as it was put to us several times, what is really needed is the decommissioning of mind-sets in Northern Ireland.

16. We have asked ourselves how those who have suffered during the many years of internal strife can accept the fact that the establishment of a lasting peace will call for reconciliation with those they hold responsible for their loss and pain. Surely the continued suffering and bereavement of individuals and of families should never be forgotten.

But if the focus remains on the past, the past will become the future, and that is something no one can desire.

17. Everyone with whom we spoke agrees in principle with the need to decommission. There are differences on the timing and context – indeed, those differences led to the creation of this Body – but they should not obscure the nearly universal support which exists for the total and verifiable disarmament of all paramilitary organisations. That must continue to be a principal objective.

18. However the issue of decommissioning is resolved, that alone will not lead directly to all-party negotiations. Much work remains on the many issues involved in the political track. The parties should address those issues with urgency.

## III. RECOMMENDATIONS: PRINCIPLES OF DEMOCRACY AND NON-VIOLENCE

19. To reach an agreed political settlement and to take the gun out of Irish politics, there must be commitment and adherence to fundamental principles of democracy and non-violence. Participants in all-party negotiations should affirm their commitment to such principles.

20. Accordingly, we recommend that the parties to such negotiations affirm their total and absolute commitment:

a. To democratic and exclusively peaceful means of resolving political issues;

b. To the total disarmament of all paramilitary organisations;

c. To agree that such disarmament must be verifiable to the satisfaction of an independent commission;

d. To renounce for themselves, and to oppose any effort by others, to use force, or threaten to use force, to influence the course or the outcome of all-party negotiations;

e. To agree to abide by the terms of any agreement reached in all-party negotiations and to resort to democratic and exclusively peaceful methods in trying to alter any aspect of that outcome with which they may disagree; and,

f. To urge that "punishment" killings and beatings stop and to take effective steps to prevent such actions.

21. We join the Governments, religious leaders and many others in condemning "punishment" killings and beatings. They contribute to the fear that those who have used violence to pursue political objectives in the

past will do so again in the future. Such actions have no place in a lawful society.

22. Those who demand decommissioning prior to all-party negotiations do so out of concern that the paramilitaries will use force, threaten to use force, to influence the negotiations, or to change any aspect of the outcome of negotiations with which they disagree.

Given the history of Northern Ireland, this is not an unreasonable concern. The principles we recommend address those concerns directly.

23. These commitments, when made and honoured, would remove the threat of force before, during and after all-party negotiations. They would focus all concerned on what is ultimately essential if the gun is to be taken out of Irish politics: an agreed political settlement and the total and verifiable disarmament of all paramilitary organisations. That should encourage the belief that the peace process will truly be an exercise in democracy, not one influenced by the threat of violence.

## IV. COMMITMENT TO DECOMMISSIONING

24. The second of the specific questions in paragraph seven of the Communiqué asks us "to report whether there is a clear commitment on the part of those in possession of such arms to work constructively to achieve" full and verifiable decommissioning.

25. We have concluded that there is a clear commitment on the part of those in possession of such arms to work constructively to achieve full and verifiable decommissioning as part of the process of all-party negotiations; but that commitment does not include decommissioning prior to such negotiations.

26. After careful consideration, on the basis of intensive discussions with the Governments, the political parties, religious leaders, the security forces, and many others, we have concluded that the paramilitary organisations will not decommission any arms prior to all-party negotiations. That was the unanimous and emphatically expressed view of the representatives of the political parties close to paramilitary organisations on both sides. It was also the view of the vast majority of the organisations and individuals

who made oral and written submissions. It is not that they are all opposed to prior decommissioning. To the contrary, many favour it. But they are convinced that it will not happen. That is the reality with which all concerned must deal.

27. Competing views were advanced on prior decommissioning. One was that decommissioning of arms must occur prior to all-party negotiations. We were told that the clearest demonstration of adherence to democratic principles, and of a permanent end to the use of violence, is the safe removal and disposal of paramilitary arms, and that at this time only a start to decommissioning will provide the confidence necessary for all-party negotiations to commence. In this view, all parties were aware of the need for prior decommissioning before the ceasefires were announced and should not now be able to avoid that requirement.

28. In the competing view we were told that decommissioning of arms prior to all-party negotiations was not requested before the announcement of the ceasefires, and that had it been, there would have been no ceasefires; that those who entered into ceasefires did so in the belief they would lead immediately to all-party negotiations; and that the request for prior decommissioning, seriously pursued for the first time months after the ceasefires were declared, is merely a tactic to delay or deny such negotiations. In this view, the ceasefires having been maintained for nearly a year and a half, all-party negotiations should begin immediately with no further requirements.

29. We believe that each side of this argument reflects a core of reasonable concern which deserves to be understood and addressed by the other side.

30. Those who insist on prior decommissioning need to be reassured that the commitment to peaceful and democratic means by those formerly supportive of politically motivated violence is genuine and irreversible, and that the threat or use of such violence will not be invoked to influence the process of negotiations or to change any agreed settlement.

31. Those who have been persuaded to abandon violence for the peaceful political path need to be reassured that a meaningful and inclusive process of negotiation is genuinely being offered to address the legitimate concerns of their traditions and the need for new political arrangements with which all can identify.

32. Clearly, new approaches must be explored to overcome this impasse. That is the purpose of the six principles we recommend. They invoke a comprehensive commitment to democracy and non-violence that is intended to reassure all parties to the negotiations.

## V. DECOMMISSIONING DURING ALL-PARTY NEGOTIATIONS

33. One side has insisted that some decommissioning of arms must take place before all-party negotiations can begin. The other side has insisted that no decommissioning can take place until the end of the process, after an agreed settlement has been reached. This has resulted in the current impasse.

34. The parties should consider an approach under which some decommissioning would take place during the process of all-party negotiations, rather than before or after as the parties now urge. Such an approach represents a compromise. If the peace process is to move forward, the current impasse must be overcome. While both sides have been adamant in their positions, both have repeatedly expressed the desire to move forward. This approach provides them that opportunity.

35. In addition, it offers the parties an opportunity to use the process of decommissioning to build confidence one step at a time during negotiations. As progress is made on political issues, even modest mutual steps on decommissioning could help create the atmosphere needed for further steps in a progressive pattern of mounting trust and confidence.

## VI. RECOMMENDATIONS: GUIDELINES ON THE MODALITIES OF DECOMMISSIONING

36. The first of the specific questions in paragraph seven of the Communiqué asks us "to identify and advise on a suitable and acceptable method for full and verifiable decommissioning".

37. We recommend the following guidelines on the modalities of decommissioning. These recommendations are realistic in light of the nature and scale of the arsenals in question, estimates of which were provided to us by the Governments and their security forces. We believe these estimates to be accurate.

38. Decommissioning should receive a high priority in all-party negotiations. The details of decommissioning, including supporting confidence-building measures, timing and sequencing, have to be determined by the parties themselves.

The decommissioning process should suggest neither victory nor defeat.

39. The ceasefires and the peace process are products not of surrender but rather of a willingness to address differences through political means. This essential fact should be reflected clearly in the modalities of the decommissioning process, which should not require that any party be seen to surrender.

The decommissioning process should take place to the satisfaction of an independent commission.

40. The decommissioning process should take place to the satisfaction of an independent commission acceptable to all parties. The commission would be appointed by the British and Irish Governments on the basis of consultations with the other parties to the negotiating process.

41. The commission should be able to operate independently in both jurisdictions, and should enjoy appropriate legal status and immunity.

42. In addition to having available to it independent sources of legal and technical advice and adequate field resources to receive and audit armaments and to observe and verify the decommissioning process, the commission should be able to call upon the resources and the relevant technical expertise of the British and Irish Armies, when it is appropriate.

The decommissioning process should result in the complete destruction of armaments in a manner that contributes to public safety.

43. The decommissioning process should result in the complete destruction of the armaments. Procedures for destruction would include the cutting up or

chipping of small arms and other weapons, the controlled explosion of ammunition and explosives, and other forms of conventional munitions disposal.

44. The decommissioning process could encompass a variety of methods, subject to negotiation, including:

- the transfer of armaments to the commission or to the designated representatives of either Government, for subsequent destruction;
- the provision of information to the commission or to designated representatives of either Government, leading to the discovery of armaments for subsequent destruction; and,
- the depositing of armaments for collection and subsequent destruction, by the commission or by representatives of either Government.

Parties should also have the option of destroying their weapons themselves.

45. Priority should be accorded throughout to ensuring that armaments are safely handled and stored, and are not misappropriated.
The decommissioning process should be fully verifiable.

46. Whatever the options chosen for the destruction of armaments, including the destruction of weapons by the parties themselves, verification must occur to the satisfaction of the commission.

47. The commission would record information required to monitor the process effectively. The commission should have available to it the relevant data of the Garda Siochana and the Royal Ulster Constabulary. It would report periodically to relevant parties on progress achieved in the decommissioning process.
The decommissioning process should not expose individuals to prosecution.

48. Individuals involved in the decommissioning process should not be prosecuted for the possession of those armaments; amnesties should be established in law in both jurisdictions. Armaments made available for decommissioning, whether directly or indirectly, should be exempt under law from forensic examination, and information obtained as a result of the decommissioning process should be inadmissible as evidence in courts of law in either jurisdiction.

49. Groups in possession of illegal armaments should be free to organise their participation in the decommissioning process as they judge appropriate, e.g. groups may designate particular individuals to deposit armaments on their behalf.

The decommissioning process should be mutual.

50. Decommissioning would take place on the basis of the mutual commitment and participation of the paramilitary organisations.

This offers the parties another opportunity to use the process of decommissioning to build confidence one step at a time during negotiations.

## VII. FURTHER CONFIDENCE-BUILDING

51. It is important for all participants to take steps to build confidence throughout the peace process. In the course of our discussions, many urged that certain actions other than decommissioning be taken to build confidence. We make no recommendations on them since they are outside our remit, but we believe it appropriate to comment on some since success in the peace process cannot be achieved solely by reference to the decommissioning of arms.

52. Support for the use of violence is incompatible with participation in the democratic process. The early termination of paramilitary activities, including surveillance and targeting, would demonstrate a commitment to peaceful methods and so build trust among other parties and alleviate the fears and anxieties of the general population. So, too, would the provision of information on the status of missing persons, and the return of those who have been forced to leave their communities under threat.

53. Continued action by the Governments on prisoners would bolster trust. So would early implementation of the proposed review of emergency legislation, consistent with the evolving security situation.

54. Different views were expressed as to the weapons to be decommissioned. In the Communiqué, the Governments made clear their view that our remit is limited to those weapons held by paramilitary organisations. We accept and share that view. There is no equivalence between such weapons and

those held by security forces. However, in the context of building mutual confidence, we welcome the commitment of the Governments, as stated in paragraph nine of the Communiqué, "to continue to take responsive measures, advised by their respective security authorities, as the threat reduces".

55. We share the hope, expressed by many on all sides, that policing in Northern Ireland can be normalised as soon as the security situation permits. A review of the situation with respect to legally registered weapons and the use of plastic bullets, and continued progress toward more balanced representation in the police force would contribute to the building of trust.

56. Several oral and written submissions raised the idea of an elected body. We note the reference in paragraph three of the Communiqué to "whether and how an elected body could play a part". Elections held in accordance with democratic principles express and reflect the popular will. If it were broadly acceptable, with an appropriate mandate, and within the three-strand structure, an elective process could contribute to the building of confidence.

57. Finally, the importance of further progress in the social and economic development of Northern Ireland and its communities was emphasised time and again in our meetings, in the context of building confidence and establishing a lasting peace.

## VIII. CONCLUDING REMARKS

58. Last week we stood in Belfast and looked at a thirty foot high wall and at barriers topped with iron and barbed wire. The wall, which has ironically come to be known as the "peace line", is a tangible symbol of the division of the people of Northern Ireland into two hostile communities. To the outsider both are warm and generous. Between themselves they are fearful and antagonistic.

59. Yet, it is now clear beyond doubt that the vast majority of the people of both traditions want to turn away from the bitter past. There is a powerful desire for peace in Northern Ireland. It is that desire which creates the present opportunity.

60. This is a critical time in the history of Northern Ireland. The peace process will move forward or this society could slip back to the horror of the past quarter century.

61. Rigid adherence by the parties to their past positions will simply continue the stalemate which has already lasted too long. In a society as deeply divided as Northern Ireland, reaching across the "peace line" requires a willingness to take risks for peace.

62. The risk may seem high but the reward is great: a future of peace, equality and prosperity for all the people of Northern Ireland.
    George J. Mitchell; John de Chastelain; Harri Holkeri.
    January 22nd, 1996

# Document 98    The Belfast Agreement:

**An Agreement Reached at the Multi-Party Talks on Northern Ireland**

**Presented to Parliament**

**by the Secretary of State for Northern Ireland by Command of Her Majesty**

**April 1998**

Cm 3883

TABLE OF CONTENTS

*Strand Two*:
  North/South Ministerial Council
*Strand Three*:
  British - Irish Council
  British - Irish Intergovernmental Conference
*Rights, Safeguards and Equality of Opportunity*
  Human Rights
    United Kingdom Legislation
    New Institutions in Northern Ireland
    Comparable Steps by the Irish Government
    A Joint Committee
    Reconciliation and Victims of Violence
  Economic, Social and Cultural Issues
*Decommissioning*
*Security*
*Policing and Justice*
  Annex A: Commission on Policing for Northern Ireland
  Annex B: Review of the Criminal Justice System
*Prisoners*
*Validation, Implementation and Review*
  Validation and Implementation
  Review Procedures Following Implementation

ANNEX:

Agreement between the Government of the United Kingdom of Great
  Britain and Northern Ireland and the Government of Ireland.

DECLARATION OF SUPPORT

1. We, the participants in the multi-party negotiations, believe that the
agreement we have negotiated offers a truly historic opportunity for a
new beginning.

2. The tragedies of the past have left a deep and profoundly regrettable legacy
of suffering. We must never forget those who have died or been injured,
and their families. But we can best honour them through a fresh start, in
which we firmly dedicate ourselves to the achievement of reconciliation,

tolerance, and mutual trust, and to the protection and vindication of the human rights of all.

3. We are committed to partnership, equality and mutual respect as the basis of relationships within Northern Ireland, between North and South, and between these islands.

4. We reaffirm our total and absolute commitment to exclusively democratic and peaceful means of resolving differences on political issues, and our opposition to any use or threat of force by others for any political purpose, whether in regard to this agreement or otherwise.

5. We acknowledge the substantial differences between our continuing, and equally legitimate, political aspirations. However, we will endeavour to strive in every practical way towards reconciliation and rapprochement within the framework of democratic and agreed arrangements. We pledge that we will, in good faith, work to ensure the success of each and every one of the arrangements to be established under this agreement. It is accepted that all of the institutional and constitutional arrangements – an Assembly in Northern Ireland, a North/South Ministerial Council, implementation bodies, a British-Irish Council and a British-Irish Intergovernmental Conference and any amendments to British Acts of Parliament and the Constitution of Ireland – are interlocking and interdependent and that in particular the functioning of the Assembly and the North/South Council are so closely inter-related that the success of each depends on that of the other.

6. Accordingly, in a spirit of concord, we strongly commend this agreement to the people, North and South, for their approval.

CONSTITUTIONAL ISSUES

1. The participants endorse the commitment made by the British and Irish Governments that, in a new British-Irish Agreement replacing the Anglo-Irish Agreement, they will:

(i) recognise the legitimacy of whatever choice is freely exercised by a majority of the people of Northern Ireland with regard to its status, whether they prefer to continue to support the Union with Great Britain or a sovereign united Ireland;

(ii) recognise that it is for the people of the island of Ireland alone, by agreement between the two parts respectively and without external impediment, to exercise their right of self-determination on the basis of consent, freely and concurrently given, North and South, to bring about a united Ireland, if that is their wish, accepting that this right must be achieved and exercised with and subject to the agreement and consent of a majority of the people of Northern Ireland;

(iii) acknowledge that while a substantial section of the people in Northern Ireland share the legitimate wish of a majority of the people of the island of Ireland for a united Ireland, the present wish of a majority of the people of Northern Ireland, freely exercised and legitimate, is to maintain the Union and, accordingly, that Northern Ireland's status as part of the United Kingdom reflects and relies upon that wish; and that it would be wrong to make any change in the status of Northern Ireland save with the consent of a majority of its people;

(iv) affirm that if, in the future, the people of the island of Ireland exercise their right of self-determination on the basis set out in sections (i) and (ii) above to bring about a united Ireland, it will be a binding obligation on both Governments to introduce and Support in their respective Parliaments legislation to give effect to that wish;

(v) affirm that whatever choice is freely exercised by a majority of the people of Northern Ireland, the power of the sovereign government with jurisdiction there shall be exercised with rigorous impartiality on behalf of all the people in the diversity of their identities and traditions and shall be founded on the principles of full respect for, and equality of, civil, political, social and cultural rights, of freedom from discrimination for all citizens, and of parity of esteem and of just and equal treatment for the identity, ethos, and aspirations of both communities;

(vi) recognise the birthright of all the people of Northern Ireland to identify themselves and be accepted as Irish or British, or both, as they may so choose, and accordingly confirm that their right to hold both British and Irish citizenship is accepted by both Governments and would not be affected by any future change in the status of Northern Ireland.

2. The participants also note that the two Governments have accordingly undertaken in the context of this comprehensive political agreement, to propose and support changes in, respectively, the Constitution of Ireland and in British legislation relating to the constitutional status of Northern Ireland.

## ANNEX A

## DRAFT CLAUSES/SCHEDULES FOR INCORPORATION IN BRITISH LEGISLATION

1 (1) It is hereby declared that Northern Ireland in its entirety remains part of the United Kingdom and shall not cease to be so without the consent of a majority of the people of Northern Ireland voting in a poll held for the purposes of this section in accordance with Schedule 1.

(2) But if the wish expressed by a majority in such a poll is that Northern Ireland should cease to be part of the United Kingdom and form part of a united Ireland, the Secretary of State shall lay before Parliament such proposals to give effect to that wish as may be agreed between Her Majesty's Government in the United Kingdom and the Government of Ireland.

The Government of Ireland Act 1920 is repealed; and this Act shall have effect notwithstanding any other previous enactment.

## SCHEDULE 1

## POLLS FOR THE PURPOSE OF SECTION 1

2 The Secretary of State may by order direct the holding of a poll for the purposes of section 1 on a date specified in the order.

3 Subject to paragraph 3, the Secretary of State shall exercise the power under paragraph 1 if at any time it appears likely to him

that a majority of those voting would express a wish that Northern
Ireland should cease to be part of the United Kingdom and form
part of a united Ireland.

4     The Secretary of State shall not make an order under paragraph 1
      earlier than seven years after the holding of a previous poll under
      this Schedule.

5     (Remaining paragraphs along the lines of paragraphs 2 and 3 of
      existing Schedule 1 to 1973 Act.)

## ANNEX B

## IRISH GOVERNMENT DRAFT LEGISLATION TO AMEND
## THE CONSTITUTION

Add to Article 29 the following sections:

7.

1. The State may consent to be bound by the British-Irish Agreement done
at Belfast on the day of 1998, hereinafter called the Agreement.

2. Any institution established by or under the Agreement may exercise
the powers and functions thereby conferred on it in respect of all or any
part of the island of Ireland notwithstanding any other provision of this
Constitution conferring a like power or function on any person or any
organ of State appointed under or created or established by or under this
Constitution. Any power or function conferred on such an institution in
relation to the settlement or resolution of disputes or controversies may be
in addition to or in substitution for any like power or function conferred
by this Constitution on any such person or organ of State as aforesaid.

3. If the Government declare that the State has become obliged, pursuant
to the Agreement, to give effect to the amendment of this Constitution referred to therein, then, notwithstanding Article 46 hereof, this Constitution
shall be amended as follows:

      i. the following Articles shall be substituted for Articles 2 and 3 of
         the Irish text:
         "2. [Irish text to be inserted here]

3. [Irish text to be inserted here]"

ii. the following Articles shall be substituted for Articles 2 and 3 of the English text:

"Article 2

It is the entitlement and birthright of every person born in the island of Ireland, which includes its islands and seas, to be part of the Irish nation. That is also the entitlement of all persons otherwise qualified in accordance with law to be citizens of Ireland. Furthermore, the Irish nation cherishes its special affinity with people of Irish ancestry living abroad who share its cultural identity and heritage.

Article 3

1. It is the firm will of the Irish nation, in harmony and friendship, to unite all the people who share the territory of the island of Ireland, in all the diversity of their identities and traditions, recognising that a united Ireland shall be brought about only by peaceful means with the consent of a majority of the people, democratically expressed, in both jurisdictions in the island. Until then, the laws enacted by the Parliament established by this Constitution shall have the like area and extent of application as the laws enacted by the Parliament that existed immediately before the coming into Operation of this Constitution.

2. Institutions with executive powers and functions that are shared between those jurisdictions may be established by their respective responsible authorities for stated purposes and may exercise powers and functions in respect of all or any part of the island."

iii. the following section shall be added to the Irish text of this Article:

"8. [Irish text to be inserted here]"

and

iv. the following section shall be added to the English text of this Article:

"8. The State may exercise extra-territorial jurisdiction in accordance with the generally recognised principles of international law."

4. If a declaration under this section is made, this subsection and subsection 3, other than the amendment of this Constitution effected thereby, and subsection 5 of this section shall be omitted from every official text of this Constitution published thereafter, but notwithstanding such omission this section shall continue to have the force of law.

5. If such a declaration is not made within twelve months of this section being added to this Constitution or such longer period as may be provided for by law, this section shall cease to have effect and shall be omitted from every official text of this Constitution published thereafter.

STRAND ONE

DEMOCRATIC INSTITUTIONS IN NORTHERN IRELAND

1. This agreement provides for a democratically elected Assembly in Northern Ireland which is inclusive in its membership, capable of exercising executive and legislative authority, and subject to safeguards to protect the rights and interests of all sides of the community.

*The Assembly*

2. A 108-member Assembly will be elected by PR(STV) from existing Westminster constituencies.

3. The Assembly will exercise full legislative and executive authority in respect of those matters currently within the responsibility of the six Northern Ireland Government Departments, with the possibility of taking on responsibility for other matters as detailed elsewhere in this agreement.

4. The Assembly – operating where appropriate on a cross-community basis – will be the prime source of authority in respect of all devolved responsibilities.

*Safeguards*

5. There will be safeguards to ensure that all sections of the community can participate and work together successfully in the operation of these institutions and that all sections of the community are protected, including:

   (a) allocations of Committee Chairs, Ministers and Committee membership in proportion to party strengths;

(b) the European Convention on Human Rights (ECHR) and any Bill of Rights for Northern Ireland supplementing it, which neither the Assembly nor public bodies can infringe, together with a Human Rights Commission;

(c) arrangements to provide that key decisions and legislation are proofed to ensure that they do not infringe the ECHR and any Bill of Rights for Northern Ireland;

(d) arrangements to ensure key decisions are taken on a cross-community basis;

   (i) either parallel consent, i.e. a majority of those members present and voting, including a majority of the unionist and nationalist designations present and voting;

   (ii) or a weighted majority (60%) of members present and voting, including at least 40% of each of the nationalist and unionist designations present and voting.

Key decisions requiring cross-community support will be designated in advance, including election of the Chair of the Assembly, the First Minister and Deputy First Minister, standing orders and budget allocations. In other cases such decisions could be triggered by a petition of concern brought by a significant minority of Assembly members (30/108).

(e) an Equality Commission to monitor a statutory obligation to promote equality of opportunity in specified areas and parity of esteem between the two main communities, and to investigate individual complaints against public bodies.

*Operation of the Assembly*

6. At their first meeting, members of the Assembly will register a designation of identity – nationalist, unionist or other – for the purposes of measuring cross-community support in Assembly votes under the relevant provisions above.

7. The Chair and Deputy Chair of the Assembly will be elected on a cross-community basis, as set out in paragraph 5(d) above.

8. There will be a Committee for each of the main executive functions of the Northern Ireland Administration. The Chairs and Deputy Chairs of the Assembly Committees will be allocated proportionally, using the d'Hondt system. Membership of the Committees will be in broad proportion to party strengths in the Assembly to ensure that the opportunity of Committee places is available to all members.

9. The Committees will have a scrutiny, policy development and consultation role with respect to the Department with which each is associated, and will have a role in initiation of legislation. They will have the power to:

- consider and advise on Departmental budgets and Annual Plans in the context of the overall budget allocation;
- approve relevant secondary legislation and take the Committee stage of relevant primary legislation;
- call for persons and papers;
- initiate enquiries and make reports;
- consider and advise on matters brought to the Committee by its Minister.

10. Standing Committees other than Departmental Committees may be established as may be required from time to time.

11. The Assembly may appoint a special Committee to examine and report on whether a measure or proposal for legislation is in conformity with equality requirements, including the ECHR/Bill of Rights. The Committee shall have the power to call people and papers to assist in its consideration of the matter. The Assembly shall then consider the report of the Committee and can determine the matter in accordance with the cross-community consent procedure.

12. The above special procedure shall be followed when requested by the Executive Committee, or by the relevant Departmental Committee, voting on a cross-community basis.

13. When there is a petition of concern as in 5(d) above, the Assembly shall vote to determine whether the measure may proceed without reference to

this special procedure. If this fails to achieve support on a cross-community basis, as in 5(d)(i) above, the special procedure shall be followed.

*Executive Authority*

14. Executive authority to be discharged on behalf of the Assembly by a First Minister and Deputy First Minister and up to ten Ministers with Departmental responsibilities.

15. The First Minister and Deputy First Minister shall be jointly elected into office by the Assembly voting on a cross-community basis, according to 5(d)(i) above.

16. Following the election of the First Minister and Deputy First Minister, the posts of Ministers will be allocated to parties on the basis of the d'Hondt system by reference to the number of seats each party has in the Assembly.

17. The Ministers will constitute an Executive Committee, which will be convened, and presided over, by the First Minister and Deputy First Minister.

18. The duties of the First Minister and Deputy First Minister will include, inter alia, dealing with and co-ordinating the work of the Executive Committee and the response of the Northern Ireland administration to external relationships.

19. The Executive Committee will provide a forum for the discussion of, and agreement on, issues which cut across the responsibilities of two or more Ministers, for prioritising executive and legislative proposals and for recommending a common position where necessary (e.g. in dealing with external relationships).

20. The Executive Committee will seek to agree each year, and review as necessary, a programme incorporating an agreed budget linked to policies and programmes, subject to approval by the Assembly, after scrutiny in Assembly Committees, on a cross-community basis.

21. A party may decline the opportunity to nominate a person to serve as a Minister or may subsequently change its nominee.

22. All the Northern Ireland Departments will be headed by a Minister. All Ministers will liaise regularly with their respective Committee.

23. As a condition of appointment, Ministers, including the First Minister and Deputy First Minister, will affirm the terms of a Pledge of Office (Annex A) undertaking to discharge effectively and in good faith all the responsibilities attaching to their office.

24. Ministers will have full executive authority in their respective areas of responsibility, within any broad programme agreed by the Executive Committee and endorsed by the Assembly as a whole.

25. An individual may be removed from office following a decision of the Assembly taken on a cross-community basis, if (s)he loses the confidence of the Assembly, voting on a cross-community basis, for failure to meet his or her responsibilities including, inter alia, those set out in the Pledge of Office. Those who hold office should use only democratic, non-violent means, and those who do not should be excluded or removed from office under these provisions.

*Legislation*

26. The Assembly will have authority to pass primary legislation for Northern Ireland in devolved areas, subject to:

  (a) the ECHR and any Bill of Rights for Northern Ireland supplementing it which, if the courts found to be breached, would render the relevant legislation null and void;

  (b) decisions by simple majority of members voting, except when decision on a cross-community basis is required;

  (c) detailed scrutiny and approval in the relevant Departmental Committee;

  (d) mechanisms, based on arrangements proposed for the Scottish Parliament, to ensure suitable co-ordination, and avoid disputes, between the Assembly and the Westminster Parliament;

  (e) option of the Assembly seeking to include Northern Ireland provisions in United Kingdom-wide legislation in the Westminster Parliament, especially on devolved issues where parity is normally maintained (e.g. social security, company law).

27. The Assembly will have authority to legislate in reserved areas with the approval of the Secretary of State and subject to Parliamentary control.

28. Disputes over legislative competence will be decided by the Courts.

29. Legislation could be initiated by an individual, a Committee or a Minister.

*Relations with other institutions*

30. Arrangements to represent the Assembly as a whole, at Summit level and in dealings with other institutions, will be in accordance with paragraph 18, and will be such as to ensure cross-community involvement.

31. Terms will be agreed between appropriate Assembly representatives and the Government of the United Kingdom to ensure effective co-ordination and input by Ministers to national policy-making, including on EU issues.

32. Role of Secretary of State:

(a) to remain responsible for NIO matters not devolved to the Assembly, subject to regular consultation with the Assembly and Ministers;

(b) to approve and lay before the Westminster Parliament any Assembly legislation on reserved matters;

(c) to represent Northern Ireland interests in the United Kingdom Cabinet;

(d) to have the right to attend the Assembly at their invitation.

33. The Westminster Parliament (whose power to make legislation for Northern Ireland would remain unaffected) will:

(a) legislate for non-devolved issues, other than where the Assembly legislates with the approval of the Secretary of State and subject to the control of Parliament;

(b) to legislate as necessary to ensure the United Kingdom's international obligations are met in respect of Northern Ireland;

(c) scrutinise, including through the Northern Ireland Grand and Select Committees, the responsibilities of the Secretary of State.

34. A consultative Civic Forum will be established. It will comprise representatives of the business, trade union and voluntary sectors, and such other sectors as agreed by the First Minister and the Deputy First

Minister. It will act as a consultative mechanism on social, economic and cultural issues. The First Minister and the Deputy First Minister will by agreement provide administrative support for the Civic Forum and establish guidelines for the selection of representatives to the Civic Forum.

*Transitional Arrangements*

35. The Assembly will meet first for the purpose of organisation, without legislative or executive powers, to resolve its standing orders and working practices and make preparations for the effective functioning of the Assembly, the British-Irish Council and the North/South Ministerial Council and associated implementation bodies. In this transitional period, those members of the Assembly serving as shadow Ministers shall affirm their commitment to non-violence and exclusively peaceful and democratic means and their opposition to any use or threat of force by others for any political purpose; to work in good faith to bring the new arrangements into being; and to observe the spirit of the Pledge of Office applying to appointed Ministers.

*Review*

36. After a specified period there will be a review of these arrangements, including the details of electoral arrangements and of the Assembly's procedures, with a view to agreeing any adjustments necessary in the interests of efficiency and fairness.

ANNEX A

PLEDGE OF OFFICE

To pledge:

(a) to discharge in good faith all the duties of office;
(b) commitment to non-violence and exclusively peaceful and democratic means;
(c) to serve all the people of Northern Ireland equally, and to act in accordance with the general obligations on government to promote equality and prevent discrimination;

(d) to participate with colleagues in the preparation of a programme for government;

(e) to operate within the framework of that programme when agreed within the Executive Committee and endorsed by the Assembly;

(f) to support, and to act in accordance with, all decisions of the Executive Committee and Assembly;

(g) to comply with the Ministerial Code of Conduct.

## CODE OF CONDUCT
Ministers must at all times:

- observe the highest standards of propriety and regularity involving impartiality, integrity and objectivity in relationship to the stewardship of public funds;
- be accountable to users of services, the community and, through the Assembly, for the activities within their responsibilities, their stewardship of public funds and the extent to which key performance targets and objectives have been met;
- ensure all reasonable requests for information from the Assembly, users of services and individual citizens are complied with; and that Departments and their staff conduct their dealings with the public in an open and responsible way;
- follow the seven principles of public life set out by the Committee on Standards in Public Life;
- comply with this code and with rules relating to the use of public funds;
- operate in a way conducive to promoting good community relations and equality of treatment;
- not use information gained in the course of their service for personal gain; nor seek to use the opportunity of public service to promote their private interests;
- ensure they comply with any rules on the acceptance of gifts and hospitality that might be offered;

- declare any personal or business interests which may conflict with their responsibilities. The Assembly will retain a Register of Interests. Individuals must ensure that any direct or indirect pecuniary interests which members of the public might reasonably think could influence their judgement are listed in the Register of Interests;

## STRAND TWO
## NORTH/SOUTH MINISTERIAL COUNCIL

1. Under a new British/Irish Agreement dealing with the totality of relationships, and related legislation at Westminster and in the Oireachtas, a North/South Ministerial Council to be established to bring together those with executive responsibilities in Northern Ireland and the Irish Government, to develop consultation, co-operation and action within the island of Ireland – including through implementation on an all-island and cross-border basis – on matters of mutual interest within the competence of the Administrations, North and South.

2. All Council decisions to be by agreement between the two sides. Northern Ireland to be represented by the First Minister, Deputy First Minister and any relevant Ministers, the Irish Government by the Taoiseach and relevant Ministers, all operating in accordance with the rules for democratic authority and accountability in force in the Northern Ireland Assembly and the Oireachtas respectively. Participation in the Council to be one of the essential responsibilities attaching to relevant posts in the two Administrations. If a holder of a relevant post will not participate normally in the Council, the Taoiseach in the case of the Irish Government and the First and Deputy First Minister in the case of the Northern Ireland Administration to be able to make alternative arrangements.

3. The Council to meet in different formats:

  (i) in plenary format twice a year, with Northern Ireland representation led by the First Minister and Deputy First Minister and the Irish Government led by the Taoiseach;
  (ii) in specific sectoral formats on a regular and frequent basis with each side represented by the appropriate Minister;

(iii) in an appropriate format to consider institutional or cross-sectoral matters (including in relation to the EU) and to resolve disagreement.

4. Agendas for all meetings to be settled by prior agreement between the two sides, but it will be open to either to propose any matter for consideration or action.

5. The Council:

(i) to exchange information, discuss and consult with a view to co-operating on matters of mutual interest within the competence of both Administrations, North and South;

(ii) to use best endeavours to reach agreement on the adoption of common policies, in areas where there is a mutual cross-border and all-island benefit, and which are within the competence of both Administrations, North and South, making determined efforts to overcome any disagreements;

(iii) to take decisions by agreement on policies for implementation separately in each jurisdiction, in relevant meaningful areas within the competence of both Administrations, North and South;

(iv) to take decisions by agreement on policies and action at an all-island and cross-border level to be implemented by the bodies to be established as set out in paragraphs 8 and 9 below.

6. Each side to be in a position to take decisions in the Council within the defined authority of those attending, through the arrangements in place for co-ordination of executive functions within each jurisdiction. Each side to remain accountable to the Assembly and Oireachtas respectively, whose approval, through the arrangements in place on either side, would be required for decisions beyond the defined authority of those attending.

7. As soon as practically possible after elections to the Northern Ireland Assembly, inaugural meetings will take place of the Assembly, the British/

Irish Council and the North/South Ministerial Council in their transitional forms. All three institutions will meet regularly and frequently on this basis during the period between the elections to the Assembly, and the transfer of powers to the Assembly, in order to establish their modus operandi.

8. During the transitional period between the elections to the Northern Ireland Assembly and the transfer of power to it, representatives of the Northern Ireland transitional Administration and the Irish Government operating in the North/South Ministerial Council will undertake a work programme, in consultation with the British Government, covering at least 12 subject areas, with a view to identifying and agreeing by 31 October 1998 areas where co-operation and implementation for mutual benefit will take place. Such areas may include matters in the list set out in the Annex.

9. As part of the work programme, the Council will identify and agree at least 6 matters for co-operation and implementation in each of the following categories:

(i) Matters where existing bodies will be the appropriate mechanisms for co-operation in each separate jurisdiction;

(ii) Matters where the co-operation will take place through agreed implementation bodies on a cross-border or all-island level.

10. The two Governments will make necessary legislative and other enabling preparations to ensure, as an absolute commitment, that these bodies, which have been agreed as a result of the work programme, function at the time of the inception of the British-Irish Agreement and the transfer of powers, with legislative authority for these bodies transferred to the Assembly as soon as possible thereafter. Other arrangements for the agreed co-operation will also commence contemporaneously with the transfer of powers to the Assembly.

11. The implementation bodies will have a clear operational remit. They will implement on an all-island and cross-border basis policies agreed in the Council.

12. Any further development of these arrangements to be by agreement in the Council and with the specific endorsement of the Northern Ireland Assembly and Oireachtas, subject to the extent of the competences and responsibility of the two Administrations.

13. It is understood that the North/South Ministerial Council and the Northern Ireland Assembly are mutually inter-dependent, and that one cannot successfully function without the other.

14. Disagreements within the Council to be addressed in the format described at paragraph 3(iii) above or in the plenary format. By agreement between the two sides, experts could be appointed to consider a particular matter and report.

15. Funding to be provided by the two Administrations on the basis that the Council and the implementation bodies constitute a necessary public function.

16. The Council to be supported by a standing joint Secretariat, staffed by members of the Northern Ireland Civil Service and the Irish Civil Service.

17. The Council to consider the European Union dimension of relevant matters, including the implementation of EU policies and programmes and proposals under consideration in the EU framework. Arrangements to be made to ensure that the views of the Council are taken into account and represented appropriately at relevant EU meetings.

18. The Northern Ireland Assembly and the Oireachtas to consider developing a joint parliamentary forum, bringing together equal numbers from both institutions for discussion of matters of mutual interest and concern.

19. Consideration to be given to the establishment of an independent consultative forum appointed by the two Administrations, representative of civil society, comprising the social partners and other members with expertise in social, cultural, economic and other issues.

## ANNEX

Areas for North/South cooperation and implementation may include the following:

1. Agriculture - animal and plant health.
2. Education - teacher qualifications and exchanges.
3. Transport – strategic transport planning.

4. Environment – environmental protection, pollution, water quality, and waste management.
5. Waterways – inland waterways.
6. Social Security/Social Welfare – entitlements of cross-border workers and fraud control.
7. Tourism – promotion, marketing, research, and product development.
8. Relevant EU Programmes such as SPPR, INTERREG, Leader II and their successors.
9. Inland Fisheries.
10. Aquaculture and marine matters
11. Health: accident and emergency services and other related cross-border issues.
12. Urban and rural development.

Others to be considered by the shadow North/South Council.

STRAND THREE
BRITISH-IRISH COUNCIL

1. A British-Irish Council (BIC) will be established under a new British-Irish Agreement to promote the harmonious and mutually beneficial development of the totality of relationships among the peoples of these islands.

2. Membership of the BIC will comprise representatives of the British and Irish Governments, devolved institutions in Northern Ireland, Scotland and Wales, when established, and, if appropriate, elsewhere in the United Kingdom, together with representatives of the Isle of Man and the Channel Islands.

3. The BIC will meet in different formats: at summit level, twice per year; in specific sectoral formats on a regular basis, with each side represented by the appropriate Minister; in an appropriate format to consider cross-sectoral matters.

4. Representatives of members will operate in accordance with whatever procedures for democratic authority and accountability are in force in their respective elected institutions.

5. The BIC will exchange information, discuss, consult and use best endeavours to reach agreement on cooperation on matters of mutual interest within the competence of the relevant Administrations. Suitable issues for early discussion in the BIC could include transport links, agricultural issues, environmental issues, cultural issues, health issues, education issues and approaches to EU issues. Suitable arrangements to be made for practical co-operation on agreed policies.

6. It will be open to the BIC to agree common policies or common actions. Individual members may opt not to participate in such common policies and common action.

7. The BIC normally will operate by consensus. In relation to decisions on common policies or common actions, including their means of implementation, it will operate by agreement of all members participating in such policies or actions.

8. The members of the BIC, on a basis to be agreed between them, will provide such financial support as it may require.

9. A secretariat for the BIC will be provided by the British and Irish Governments in coordination with officials of each of the other members.

10. In addition to the structures provided for under this agreement, it will be open to two or more members to develop bilateral or multilateral arrangements between them. Such arrangements could include, subject to the agreement of the members concerned, mechanisms to enable consultation, co-operation and joint decision-making on matters of mutual interest; and mechanisms to implement any joint decisions they may reach. These arrangements will not require the prior approval of the BIC as a whole and will operate independently of it.

11. The elected institutions of the members will be encouraged to develop interparliamentary links, perhaps building on the British-Irish Interparliamentary Body.

12. The full membership of the BIC will keep under review the workings of the Council, including a formal published review at an appropriate time after the Agreement comes into effect, and will contribute as appropriate to any review of the overall political agreement arising from the multiparty negotiations.

## BRITISH-IRISH INTERGOVERNMENTAL CONFERENCE

1. There will be a new British-Irish Agreement dealing with the totality of relationships. It will establish a standing British-Irish Intergovernmental Conference, which will subsume both the Anglo-Irish Intergovernmental Council and the Intergovernmental Conference established under the 1985 Agreement.

2. The Conference will bring together the British and Irish Governments to promote bilateral cooperation at all levels on all matters of mutual interest within the competence of both Governments.

3. The Conference will meet as required at Summit level (Prime Minister and Taoiseach). Otherwise, Governments will be represented by appropriate Ministers. Advisers, including police and security advisers, will attend as appropriate.

4. All decisions will be by agreement between both Governments. The Governments will make determined efforts to resolve disagreements between them. There will be no derogation from the sovereignty of either Government.

   In recognition of the Irish Government's special interest in Northern Ireland and of the extent to which issues of mutual concern arise in relation to Northern Ireland, there will be regular and frequent meetings of the Conference concerned with non-devolved Northern Ireland matters, on which the Irish Government may put forward views and proposals. These meetings, to be co-chaired by the Minister for Foreign Affairs and the Secretary of State for Northern Ireland, would also deal with all-island and cross-border co-operation on non-devolved issues.

6. Cooperation within the framework of the Conference will include facilitation of cooperation in security matters. The Conference also will address, in particular, the areas of rights, justice, prisons and policing in Northern Ireland (unless and until responsibility is devolved to a Northern Ireland administration) and will intensify cooperation between the two Governments on the all-island or cross-border aspects of these matters.

   Relevant executive members of the Northern Ireland Administration will be involved in meetings of the Conference, and in the reviews referred to in paragraph 9 below to discuss non-devolved Northern Ireland matters.

8. The Conference will be supported by officials of the British and Irish Governments, including by a standing joint Secretariat of officials dealing with non-devolved Northern Ireland matters.

9. The Conference will keep under review the workings of the new British-Irish Agreement and the machinery and institutions established under it, including a formal published review three years after the Agreement comes into effect. Representatives of the Northern Ireland Administration will be invited to express views to the Conference in this context. The Conference will contribute as appropriate to any review of the overall political agreement arising from the multi-party negotiations but will have no power to override the democratic arrangements set up by this Agreement.

## RIGHTS, SAFEGUARDS AND EQUALITY OF OPPORTUNITY

## HUMAN RIGHTS

1. The parties affirm their commitment to the mutual respect, the civil rights and the religious liberties of everyone in the community. Against the background of the recent history of communal conflict, the parties affirm in particular:

- the right of free political thought;
- the right to freedom and expression of religion;
- the right to pursue democratically national and political aspirations;
- the right to seek constitutional change by peaceful and legitimate means;
- the right to freely choose one's place of residence;
- the right to equal opportunity in all social and economic activity, regardless of class, creed, disability, gender or ethnicity;
- the right to freedom from sectarian harassment; and
- the right of women to full and equal political participation.

*United Kingdom Legislation*

2. The British Government will complete incorporation into Northern Ireland law of the European Convention on Human Rights (ECHR), with direct access to the courts, and remedies for breach of the Convention,

including power for the courts to overrule Assembly legislation on grounds of inconsistency.

3. Subject to the outcome of public consultation underway, the British Government intends, as a particular priority, to create a statutory obligation on public authorities in Northern Ireland to carry out all their functions with due regard to the need to promote equality of opportunity in relation to religion and political opinion; gender; race; disability; age; marital status; dependants; and sexual orientation. Public bodies would be required to draw up statutory schemes showing how they would implement this obligation. Such schemes would cover arrangements for policy appraisal, including an assessment of impact on relevant categories, public consultation, public access to information and services, monitoring and timetables.

4. The new Northern Ireland Human Rights Commission (see paragraph 5 below) will be invited to consult and to advise on the scope for defining, in Westminster legislation, rights supplementary to those in the European Convention on Human Rights, to reflect the particular circumstances of Northern Ireland, drawing as appropriate on international instruments and experience. These additional rights to reflect the principles of mutual respect for the identity and ethos of both communities and parity of esteem, and – taken together with the ECHR – to constitute a Bill of Rights for Northern Ireland. Among the issues for consideration by the Commission will be:

- the formulation of a general obligation on government and public bodies fully to respect, on the basis of equality of treatment, the identity and ethos of both communities in Northern Ireland; and
- a clear formulation of the rights not to be discriminated against and to equality of opportunity in both the public and private sectors.

*New Institutions in Northern Ireland*

5. A new Northern Ireland Human Rights Commission, with membership from Northern Ireland reflecting the community balance, will be established by Westminster legislation, independent of Government, with an extended and enhanced role beyond that currently exercised by the

Standing Advisory Commission on Human Rights, to include keeping under review the adequacy and effectiveness of laws and practices, making recommendations to Government as necessary; providing information and promoting awareness of human rights; considering draft legislation referred to them by the new Assembly; and, in appropriate cases, bringing court proceedings or providing assistance to individuals doing so.

6. Subject to the outcome of public consultation currently underway, the British Government intends a new statutory Equality Commission to replace the Fair Employment Commission, the Equal Opportunities Commission (NI), the Commission for Racial Equality (NI) and the Disability Council. Such a unified Commission will advise on, validate and monitor the statutory obligation and will investigate complaints of default.

7. It would be open to a new Northern Ireland Assembly to consider bringing together its responsibilities for these matters into a dedicated Department of Equality.

8. These improvements will build on existing protections in Westminster legislation in respect of the judiciary, the system of justice and policing.

*Comparable Steps by the Irish Government*

9. The Irish Government will also take steps to further strengthen the protection of human rights in its jurisdiction. The Government will, taking account of the work of the All-Party Oireachtas Committee on the Constitution and the Report of the Constitution Review Group, bring forward measures to strengthen and underpin the constitutional protection of human rights. These proposals will draw on the European Convention on Human Rights and other international legal instruments in the field of human rights and the question of the incorporation of the ECHR will be further examined in this context. The measures brought forward would ensure at least an equivalent level of protection of human rights as will pertain in Northern Ireland. In addition, the Irish Government will:

  – establish a Human Rights Commission with a mandate and remit equivalent to that within Northern Ireland;

- proceed with arrangements as quickly as possible to ratify the Council of Europe Framework Convention on National Minorities (already ratified by the UK);
- implement enhanced employment equality legislation;
- introduce equal status legislation; and
- continue to take further active steps to demonstrate its respect for the different traditions in the island of Ireland.

*A Joint Committee*

10. It is envisaged that there would be a joint committee of representatives of the two Human Rights Commissions, North and South, as a forum for consideration of human rights issues in the island of Ireland. The joint committee will consider, among other matters, the possibility of establishing a charter, open to signature by all democratic political parties, reflecting and endorsing agreed measures for the protection of the fundamental rights of everyone living in the island of Ireland.

*Reconciliation and Victims of Violence*

11. The participants believe that it is essential to acknowledge and address the suffering of the victims of violence as a necessary element of reconciliation. They look forward to the results of the work of the Northern Ireland Victims Commission.

12. It is recognised that victims have a right to remember as well as to contribute to a changed society. The achievement of a peaceful and just society would be the true memorial to the victims of violence. The participants particularly recognise that young people from areas affected by the troubles face particular difficulties and will support the development of special community-based initiatives based on international best practice. The provision of services that are supportive and sensitive to the needs of victims will also be a critical element and that support will need to be channelled through both statutory and community-based voluntary organisations facilitating locally-based self-help and support networks. This will require the allocation of sufficient resources, including statutory funding as necessary, to meet the needs of victims and to provide for community-based support programmes.

13. The participants recognise and value the work being done by many organisations to develop reconciliation and mutual understanding and respect between and within communities and traditions, in Northern Ireland and between North and South, and they see such work as having a vital role in consolidating peace and political agreement. Accordingly, they pledge their continuing support to such organisations and will positively examine the case for enhanced financial assistance for the work of reconciliation. An essential aspect of the reconciliation process is the promotion of a culture of tolerance at every level of society, including initiatives to facilitate and encourage integrated education and mixed housing.

RIGHTS, SAFEGUARDS AND EQUALITY OF OPPORTUNITY
ECONOMIC, SOCIAL AND CULTURAL ISSUES

1. Pending the devolution of powers to a new Northern Ireland Assembly, the British Government will pursue broad policies for sustained economic growth and stability in Northern Ireland and for promoting social inclusion, including in particular community development and the advancement of women in public life.

2. Subject to the public consultation currently under way, the British Government will make rapid progress with:

(i) a new regional development strategy for Northern Ireland, for consideration in due course by the Assembly, tackling the problems of a divided society and social cohesion in urban, rural and border areas, protecting and enhancing the environment, producing new approaches to transport issues, strengthening the physical infrastructure of the region, developing the advantages and resources of rural areas and rejuvenating major urban centres;

(ii) a new economic development strategy for Northern Ireland, for consideration in due course by a the Assembly, which would provide for short and medium term economic planning linked as appropriate to the regional development strategy; and

(iii) measures on employment equality included in the recent White Paper ("Partnership for Equality") and covering the extension and strengthening of anti-discrimination legislation, a review of the national security aspects of the present fair employment legislation at the earliest possible time, a new more focused Targeting Social Need initiative and a range of measures aimed at combating unemployment and progressively eliminating the differential in unemployment rates between the two communities by targeting objective need.

3. All participants recognise the importance of respect, understanding and tolerance in relation to linguistic diversity, including in Northern Ireland, the Irish language, Ulster-Scots and the languages of the various ethnic communities, all of which are part of the cultural wealth of the island of Ireland.

4. In the context of active consideration currently being given to the UK signing the Council of Europe Charter for Regional or Minority Languages, the British Government will in particular in relation to the Irish language, where appropriate and where people so desire it:

- take resolute action to promote the language;
- facilitate and encourage the use of the language in speech and writing in public and private life where there is appropriate demand;
- seek to remove, where possible, restrictions which would discourage or work against the maintenance or development of the language;
- make provision for liaising with the Irish language community, representing their views to public authorities and investigating complaints;
- place a statutory duty on the Department of Education to encourage and facilitate Irish medium education in line with current provision for integrated education;
- explore urgently with the relevant British authorities, and in cooperation with the Irish broadcasting authorities, the scope for achieving more widespread availability of Teilifís na Gaeilige in Northern Ireland;

- seek more effective ways to encourage and provide financial support for Irish language film and television production in Northern
Ireland; and
- encourage the parties to secure agreement that this commitment
will be sustained by a new Assembly in a way which takes account
of the desires and sensitivities of the community.

5. All participants acknowledge the sensitivity of the use of symbols
and emblems for public purposes, and the need in particular in creating the new institutions to ensure that such symbols and emblems are
used in a manner which promotes mutual respect rather than division.
Arrangements will be made to monitor this issue and consider what action might be required.

DECOMMISSIONING

1. Participants recall their agreement in the Procedural Motion adopted
on 24 September 1997 "that the resolution of the decommissioning issue
is an indispensable part of the process of negotiation", and also recall the
provisions of paragraph 25 of Strand 1 above.

2. They note the progress made by the Independent International Commission
on Decommissioning and the Governments in developing schemes which
can represent a workable basis for achieving the decommissioning of
illegally-held arms in the possession of paramilitary groups.

3. All participants accordingly reaffirm their commitment to the total
disarmament of all paramilitary organisations. They also confirm their
intention to continue to work constructively and in good faith with the
Independent Commission, and to use any influence they may have, to
achieve the decommissioning of all paramilitary arms within two years
following endorsement in referendums North and South of the agreement
and in the context of the implementation of the overall settlement.

4. The Independent Commission will monitor, review and verify progress
on decommissioning of illegal arms, and will report to both Governments
at regulär intervals.
     [Point 5 is missing from the original.]

6. Both Governments will take all necessary steps to facilitate the decommissioning process to include bringing the relevant schemes into force by the end of June.

SECURITY

1. The participants note that the development of a peaceful environment on the basis of this agreement can and should mean a normalisation of security arrangements and practices.

2. The British Government will make progress towards the objective of as early a return as possible to normal security arrangements in Northern Ireland, consistent with the level of threat and with a published overall strategy, dealing with:

(i) the reduction of the numbers and role of the Armed Forces deployed in Northern Ireland to levels compatible with a normal peaceful society;
(ii) the removal of security installations;
(iii) the removal of emergency powers in Northern Ireland; and
(iv) other measures appropriate to and compatible with a normal peaceful society.

3. The Secretary of State will consult regularly on progress, and the response to any continuing paramilitary activity, with the Irish Government and the political parties, as appropriate.

4. The British Government will continue its consultation on firearms regulation and control on the basis of the document published on 2 April 1998.

5. The Irish Government will initiate a wide-ranging review of the Offences Against the State Acts 1939–85 with a view to both reform and dispensing with those elements no longer required as circumstances permit.

POLICING AND JUSTICE

1. The participants recognise that policing is a central issue in any society. They equally recognise that Northern Ireland's history of deep divisions has made it highly emotive, with great hurt suffered and sacrifices made by many individuals and their families, including those in the RUC and

other public servants. They believe that the agreement provides the opportunity for a new beginning to policing in Northern Ireland with a police service capable of attracting and sustaining support from the community as a whole. They also believe that this agreement offers a unique opportunity to bring about a new political dispensation which will recognise the full and equal legitimacy and worth of the identities, senses of allegiance and ethos of all sections of the community in Northern Ireland. They consider that this opportunity should inform and underpin the development of a police service representative in terms of the make-up of the community as a whole and which, in a peaceful environment, should be routinely unarmed.

2. The participants believe it essential that policing structures and arrangements are such that the police service is professional, effective and efficient, fair and impartial, free from partisan political control; accountable, both under the law for its actions and to the community it serves; representative of the society it polices, and operates within a coherent and cooperative criminal justice system, which conforms with human rights norms. The participants also believe that those structures and arrangements must be capable of maintaining law and order including responding effectively to crime and to any terrorist threat and to public order problems. A police service which cannot do so will fail to win public confidence and acceptance. They believe that any such structures and arrangements should be capable of delivering a policing service, in constructive and inclusive partnerships with the community at all levels, and with the maximum delegation of authority and responsibility, consistent with the foregoing principles. These arrangements should be based on principles of protection of human rights and professional integrity and should be unambiguously accepted and actively supported by the entire community.

3. An independent Commission will be established to make recommendations for future policing arrangements in Northern Ireland including means of encouraging widespread community support for these arrangements within the agreed framework of principles reflected in the paragraphs above and in accordance with the terms of reference at Annex A. The Commission will be broadly representative with expert and international representation among its membership and will be asked to consult widely and to report no later than Summer 1999.

4. The participants believe that the aims of the criminal justice system are to:

- deliver a fair and impartial system of justice to the community;
- be responsive to the community's concerns, and encouraging community involvement where appropriate;
- have the confidence of all parts of the community; and
- deliver justice efficiently and effectively.

5. There will be a parallel wide-ranging review of criminal justice (other than policing and those aspects of the system relating to the emergency legislation) to be carried out by the British Government through a mechanism with an independent element, in consultation with the political parties and others. The review will commence as soon as possible, will include wide consultation, and a report will be made to the Secretary of State no later than Autumn 1999. Terms of Reference are attached at Annex B.

6. Implementation of the recommendations arising from both reviews will be discussed with the political parties and with the Irish Government.

7. The participants also note that the British Government remains ready in principle, with the broad support of the political parties, and after consultation, as appropriate, with the Irish Government, in the context of ongoing implementation of the relevant recommendations, to devolve responsibility for policing and justice issues.

ANNEX A

COMMISSION ON POLICING FOR NORTHERN IRELAND

*Terms of Reference*

Taking account of the principles on policing as set out in the agreement, the Commission will inquire into policing in Northern Ireland and, on the basis of its findings, bring forward proposals for future policing structures and arrangements, including means of encouraging widespread community support for those arrangements.

Its proposals on policing should be designed to ensure that policing arrangements, including composition, recruitment, training, culture, ethos and symbols, are such that in a new approach Northern Ireland has a police service that can enjoy widespread support from, and is seen as an integral part of, the community as a whole.

Its proposals should include recommendations covering any issues such as re-training, job placement and educational and professional development required in the transition to policing in a peaceful society.

Its proposals should also be designed to ensure that:

- the police service is structured, managed and resourced so that it can be effective in discharging its full range of functions (including proposals on any necessary arrangements for the transition to policing in a normal peaceful society);
- the police service is delivered in constructive and inclusive partnerships with the community at all levels with the maximum delegation of authority and responsibility;
- the legislative and constitutional framework requires the impartial discharge of policing functions and conforms with internationally accepted norms in relation to policing standards;
- the police operate within a clear framework of accountability to the law and the community they serve, so:
  - they are constrained by, accountable to and act only within the law;
  - their powers and procedures, like the law they enforce, are clearly established and publicly available;
  - there are open, accessible and independent means of investigating and adjudicating upon complaints against the police;
  - there are clearly established arrangements enabling local people, and their political representatives, to articulate their views and concerns about policing and to establish publicly policing priorities and influence policing policies, subject to safeguards to ensure police impartiality and freedom from partisan political control;

- there are arrangements for accountability and for the effective, efficient and economic use of resources in achieving policing objectives;
- there are means to ensure independent professional scrutiny and inspection of the police service to ensure that proper professional standards are maintained;
- the scope for structured co-operation with the Garda Siochana and other police forces is addressed; and
- the management of public order events which can impose exceptional demands on policing resources is also addressed.

The Commission should focus on policing issues, but if it identifies other aspects of the criminal justice system relevant to its work on policing, including the role of the police in prosecution, then it should draw the attention of the Government to those matters.

The Commission should consult widely, including with non-governmental expert organisations, and through such focus groups as they consider it appropriate to establish.

The Government proposes to establish the Commission as soon as possible, with the aim of it starting work as soon as possible and publishing its final report by Summer 1999.

## ANNEX B

## REVIEW OF THE CRIMINAL JUSTICE SYSTEM

*Terms of Reference*

Taking account of the aims of the criminal justice system as set out in the Agreement, the review will address the structure, management and resourcing of publicly funded elements of the criminal justice system and will bring forward proposals for future criminal justice arrangements (other than policing and those aspects of the system relating to emergency legislation, which the Government is considering separately) covering such issues as:

- the arrangements for making appointments to the judiciary and magistracy, and safeguards for protecting their independence;

- the arrangements for the organisation and supervision of the prosecution process, and for safeguarding its independence;
- measures to improve the responsiveness and accountability of, and any lay participation in the criminal justice system;
- mechanisms for addressing law reform;
- the scope for structured cooperation between the criminal justice agencies on both parts of the island; and
- the structure and organisation of criminal justice functions that might be devolved to an Assembly, including the possibility of establishing a Department of Justice, while safeguarding the essential independence of many of the key functions in this area.

The Government proposes to commence the review as soon as possible, consulting with the political parties and others, including non-governmental expert organisations. The review will be completed by Autumn 1999.

## PRISONERS

1. Both Governments will put in place mechanisms to provide for an accelerated programme for the release of prisoners, including transferred prisoners, convicted of scheduled offences in Northern Ireland or, in the case of those sentenced outside Northern Ireland, similar offences (referred to hereafter as qualifying prisoners). Any such arrangements will protect the rights of individual prisoners under national and international law.

2. Prisoners affiliated to organisations which have not established or are not maintaining a complete and unequivocal ceasefire will not benefit from the arrangements. The situation in this regard will be kept under review.

3. Both Governments will complete a review process within a fixed time frame and set prospective release dates for all qualifying prisoners. The review process would provide for the advance of the release dates of qualifying prisoners while allowing account to be taken of the seriousness of the offences for which the person was convicted and the need to protect the community. In addition, the intention would be that should the circumstances allow it, any qualifying prisoners who remained in custody two years after the commencement of the scheme would be released at that point.

4. The Governments will seek to enact the appropriate legislation to give effect to these arrangements by the end of June 1998.

5. The Governments continue to recognise the importance of measures to facilitate the reintegration of prisoners into the community by providing support both prior to and after release, including assistance directed towards availing of employment opportunities, re-training and/or re-skilling, and further education.

## VALIDATION, IMPLEMENTATION AND REVIEW

## VALIDATION AND IMPLEMENTATION

1. The two Governments will as soon as possible sign a new British-Irish Agreement replacing the 1985 Anglo-Irish Agreement, embodying understandings on constitutional issues and affirming their solemn commitment to support and, where appropriate, implement the agreement reached by the participants in the negotiations which shall be annexed to the British-Irish Agreement.

2. Each Government will organise a referendum on 22 May 1998. Subject to Parliamentary approval, a consultative referendum in Northern Ireland, organised under the terms of the Northern Ireland (Entry to Negotiations, etc.) Act 1996, will address the question: "Do you support the agreement reached in the multi-party talks on Northern Ireland and set out in Command Paper 3883?". The Irish Government will introduce and support in the Oireachtas a Bill to amend the Constitution as described in paragraph 2 of the section "Constitutional Issues" and in Annex B, as follows: (a) to amend Articles 2 and 3 as described in paragraph 8.1 in Annex B above and (b) to amend Article 29 to permit the Government to ratify the new British-Irish Agreement. On passage by the Oireachtas, the Bill will be put to referendum.

3. If majorities of those voting in each of the referendums support this agreement, the Governments will then introduce and support, in their respective Parliaments, such legislation as may be necessary to give effect to all aspects of this agreement, and will take whatever ancillary steps as may be required, including the holding of elections on 25 June, subject

to parliamentary approval, to the Assembly, which would meet initially in a "shadow" mode. The establishment of the North-South Ministerial Council, implementation bodies, the British-Irish Council and the British-Irish Intergovernmental Conference and the assumption by the Assembly of its legislative and executive powers will take place at the same time on the entry into force of the British-Irish Agreement.

4. In the interim, aspects of the implementation of the multi-party agreement will be reviewed at meetings of those parties relevant in the particular case (taking into account, once Assembly elections have been held, the results of those elections), under the chairmanship of the British Government or the two Governments, as may be appropriate; and representatives of the two Governments and all relevant parties may meet under independent chairmanship to review implementation of the agreement as a whole.

*Review procedures following implementation*

5. Each institution may, at any time, review any problems that may arise in its Operation and, where no other institution is affected, take remedial action in consultation as necessary with the relevant Government or Governments. It will be for each institution to determine its own procedures for review.

6. If there are difficulties in the operation of a particular institution, which have implications for another institution, they may review their operations separately and jointly and agree on remedial action to be taken under their respective authorities.

7. If difficulties arise which require remedial action across the range of institutions, or otherwise require amendment of the British-Irish Agreement or relevant legislation, the process of review will fall to the two Governments in consultation with the parties in the Assembly. Each Government will be responsible for action in its own jurisdiction.

8. Notwithstanding the above, each Institution will publish an annual report on its operations. In addition, the two Governments and the parties in the Assembly will convene a Conference 4 years after the agreement comes into effect, to review and report on its operation.

## AGREEMENT BETWEEN THE GOVERNMENT OF THE UNITED KINGDOM OF GREAT BRITAIN AND NORTHERN IRELAND AND THE GOVERNMENT OF IRELAND

*The British and Irish Governments:*

Welcoming the strong commitment to the Agreement reached on 10th April 1998 by themselves and other participants in the multi-party talks and set out in Annex 1 to this Agreement (hereinafter "the Multi-Party Agreement");

Considering that the Multi-Party Agreement offers an opportunity for a new beginning in relationships within Northern Ireland, within the island of Ireland and between the peoples of these islands;

Wishing to develop still further the unique relationship between their peoples and the close Cooperation between their countries as friendly neighbours and as partners in the European Union;

Reaffirming their total commitment to the principles of democracy and non-violence which have been fundamental to the multi-party talks;

Reaffirming their commitment to the principles of partnership, equality and mutual respect and to the protection of civil, political, social, economic and cultural rights in their respective jurisdictions;

Have agreed as follows:

### ARTICLE 1

*The two Governments:*

(i) recognise the legitimacy of whatever choice is freely exercised by a majority of the people of Northern Ireland with regard to its status, whether they prefer to continue to support the Union with Great Britain or a sovereign united Ireland;

(ii) recognise that it is for the people of the island of Ireland alone, by agreement between the two parts respectively and without external impediment, to exercise their right of self-determination on the basis of consent, freely and concurrently given, North and South, to bring about a united Ireland, if that is their wish, accepting that this right must be achieved and exercised with and subject to the agreement and consent of a majority of the people of Northern Ireland;

(iii) acknowledge that while a substantial section of the people in Northern Ireland share the legitimate wish of a majority of the people of the island of Ireland for a united Ireland, the present wish of a majority of the people of Northern Ireland, freely exercised and legitimate, is to maintain the Union and accordingly, that Northern Ireland's status as part of the United Kingdom reflects and relies upon that wish; and that it would be wrong to make any change in the status of Northern Ireland save with the consent of a majority of its people;

(iv) affirm that, if in the future, the people of the island of Ireland exercise their right of self-determination on the basis set out in sections (i) and (ii) above to bring about a united Ireland, it will be a binding obligation on both Governments to introduce and support in their respective Parliaments legislation to give effect to that wish;

(v) affirm that whatever choice is freely exercised by a majority of the people of Northern Ireland, the power of the sovereign government with jurisdiction there shall be exercised with rigorous impartiality on behalf of all the people in the diversity of their identities and traditions and shall be founded on the principles of full respect for, and equality of, civil, political, social and cultural rights, of freedom from discrimination for all citizens, and of parity of esteem and of just and equal treatment for the identity, ethos and aspirations of both communities;

(vi) recognise the birthright of all the people of Northern Ireland to identify themselves and be accepted as Irish or British, or both, as they may so choose, and accordingly confirm that their right to hold both British and Irish citizenship is accepted by both Governments and would not be affected by any future change in the status of Northern Ireland.

## ARTICLE 2

The two Governments affirm their solemn commitment to support, and where appropriate implement, the provisions of the Multi-Party Agreement. In particular there shall be established in accordance with the provisions of the Multi-Party Agreement immediately on the entry into force of this Agreement, the following institutions:

(i)  a North/South Ministerial Council;
(ii)  the implementation bodies referred to in paragraph 9 (ii) of the section entitled "Strand Two" of the Multi-Party Agreement;
(iii)  a British-Irish Council;
(iv)  a British-Irish Intergovernmental Conference.

## ARTICLE 3

(1)  This Agreement shall replace the Agreement between the British and Irish Governments done at Hillsborough on 15th November 1985 which shall cease to have effect on entry into force of this Agreement.
(2)  The Intergovernmental Conference established by Article 2 of the aforementioned Agreement done on 15th November 1985 shall cease to exist on entry into force of this Agreement.

## ARTICLE 4

(1)  It shall be a requirement for entry into force of this Agreement that:

(a)  British legislation shall have been enacted for the purpose of implementing the provisions of Annex A to the section entitled "Constitutional Issues" of the Multi-Party Agreement;
(b)  the amendments to the Constitution of Ireland set out in Annex B to the section entitled "Constitutional Issues" of

the Multi-Party Agreement shall have been approved by Referendum;

(c) such legislation shall have been enacted as may be required to establish the institutions referred to in Article 2 of this Agreement.

(2) Each Government shall notify the other in writing of the completion, so far as it is concerned, of the requirements for entry into force of this Agreement. This Agreement shall enter into force on the date of the receipt of the later of the two notifications.

(3) Immediately on entry into force of this Agreement, the Irish Government shall ensure that the amendments to the Constitution of Ireland set out in Annex B to the section entitled "Constitutional Issues" of the Multi-Party Agreement take effect.

In witness thereof the undersigned, being duly authorised thereto by the respective Governments, have signed this Agreement.

Done in two originals at Belfast on the 10th day of April 1998.

For the Government of the United      For the Government of Ireland
Kingdom of Great Britain and
Northern Ireland

# ANNEX 1

The Agreement Reached

in the Multi-Party Talks

ANNEX 2

Declaration on the Provisions of

Paragraph (vi) of Article 1

In Relationship to Citizenship

The British and Irish Governments declare that it is their joint under-standing that the term "the people of Northern Ireland" in paragraph (vi) of Article 1 of this Agreement means, for the purposes of giving effect to this provision, all persons born in Northern Ireland and having, at the time of their birth, at least one parent who is a British citizen, an Irish citizen or is otherwise entitled to reside in Northern Ireland without any restriction on their period of residence.

# THE NORTHERN IRELAND ACT 1998
as originally enacted

## Northern Ireland Act 1998

### 1998 CHAPTER 47

An Act to make new provision for the government of Northern Ireland for the purpose of implementing the agreement reached at multi-party talks on Northern Ireland set out in Command Paper 3883. [19th November 1998]

Be it enacted by the Queen's most Excellent Majesty, by and with the advice and consent of the Lords Spiritual and Temporal, and Commons, in this present Parliament assembled, and by the authority of the same, as follows:—

## PART I

### PRELIMINARY

1 **Status of Northern Ireland**

(1) It is hereby declared that Northern Ireland in its entirety remains part of the United Kingdom and shall not cease to be so without the consent of a majority of the people of Northern Ireland voting in a poll held for the purposes of this section in accordance with Schedule 1.

(2) But if the wish expressed by a majority in such a poll is that Northern Ireland should cease to be part of the United Kingdom and form part of a united Ireland, the Secretary

of State shall lay before Parliament such proposals to give effect to that wish as may be agreed between Her Majesty's Government in the United Kingdom and the Government of Ireland.

**2 Previous enactments**
The Government of Ireland Act 1920 is repealed; and this Act shall have effect notwithstanding any other previous enactment.

**3 Devolution order**
(1) If it appears to the Secretary of State that sufficient progress has been made in implementing the Belfast Agreement, he shall lay before Parliament the draft of an Order in Council appointing a day for the commencement of Parts II and III ("the appointed day").
(2) If the draft Order laid before Parliament under subsection (1) is approved by resolution of each House of Parliament, the Secretary of State shall submit it to Her Majesty in Council and Her Majesty in Council may make the Order.

**4 Transferred, excepted and reserved matters**
(1) In this Act—
"excepted matter" means any matter falling within a description specified in Schedule 2;
"reserved matter" means any matter falling within a description specified in Schedule 3;
"transferred matter" means any matter which is not an excepted or reserved matter.
(2) If at any time after the appointed day it appears to the Secretary of State—
(a) that any reserved matter should become a transferred matter; or
(b) that any transferred matter should become a reserved matter,

he may, subject to subsection (3), lay before Parliament the draft of an Order in Council amending Schedule 3 so that the matter ceases to be or, as the case may be, becomes a reserved matter with effect from such date as may be specified in the Order.

(3) The Secretary of State shall not lay the draft of an Order before Parliament under subsection (2) unless the Assembly has passed with cross-community support a resolution praying that the matter concerned should cease to be or, as the case may be, should become a reserved matter.

(4) If the draft of an Order laid before Parliament under subsection (2) is approved by resolution of each House of Parliament, the Secretary of State shall submit it to Her Majesty in Council and Her Majesty in Council may make the Order.

(5) In this Act—

"the Assembly" means the New Northern Ireland Assembly, which after the appointed day shall be known as the Northern Ireland Assembly;

"cross-community support", in relation to a vote on any matter, means—

(a) the support of a majority of the members voting, a majority of the designated Nationalists voting and a majority of the designated Unionists voting; or

(b) the support of 60 per cent of the members voting, 40 per cent of the designated Nationalists voting and 40 per cent of the designated Unionists voting; "designated Nationalist" means a member designated as a Nationalist in accordance with standing orders of the Assembly and "designated Unionist" shall be construed accordingly.

## PART II

## LEGISLATIVE POWERS

*General*

### 5  Acts of the Northern Ireland Assembly

(1)  Subject to sections 6 to 8, the Assembly may make laws, to be known as Acts.

(2)  A Bill shall become an Act when it has been passed by the Assembly and has received Royal Assent.

(3)  A Bill receives Royal Assent at the beginning of the day on which Letters Patent under the Great Seal of Northern Ireland signed with Her Majesty's own hand signifying Her Assent are notified to the Presiding Officer.

(4)  The date of Royal Assent shall be written on the Act by the Presiding Officer, and shall form part of the Act.

(5)  The validity of any proceedings leading to the enactment of an Act of the Assembly shall not be called into question in any legal proceedings.

(6)  This section does not affect the power of the Parliament of the United Kingdom to make laws for Northern Ireland, but an Act of the Assembly may modify any provision made by or under an Act of Parliament in so far as it is part of the law of Northern Ireland.

### 6  Legislative competence

(1)  A provision of an Act is not law if it is outside the legislative competence of the Assembly.

(2)  A provision is outside that competence if any of the following paragraphs apply—

   (a)  it would form part of the law of a country or territory other than Northern Ireland, or confer or remove functions exercisable otherwise than in or as regards Northern Ireland;

(b) it deals with an excepted matter and is not ancillary to other provisions (whether in the Act or previously enacted) dealing with reserved or transferred matters;

(c) it is incompatible with any of the Convention rights;

(d) it is incompatible with Community law;

(e) it discriminates against any person or class of person on the ground of religious belief or political opinion;

(f) it modifies an enactment in breach of section 7.

(3) For the purposes of this Act, a provision is ancillary to other provisions if it is a provision—

(a) which provides for the enforcement of those other provisions or is otherwise necessary or expedient for making those other provisions effective; or

(b) which is otherwise incidental to, or consequential on, those provisions;

and references in this Act to provisions previously enacted are references to provisions contained in, or in any instrument made under, other Northern Ireland legislation or an Act of Parliament.

(4) Her Majesty may by Order in Council specify functions which are to be treated, for such purposes of this Act as may be specified, as being, or as not being, functions which are exercisable in or as regards Northern Ireland.

(5) No recommendation shall be made to Her Majesty to make an Order in Council under subsection (4) unless a draft of the Order has been laid before and approved by resolution of each House of Parliament.

## 7 Entrenched enactments

(1) Subject to subsection (2), the following enactments shall not be modified by an Act of the Assembly or subordinate legislation made, confirmed or approved by a Minister or Northern Ireland department—

(a) the European Communities Act 1972;

(b) the Human Rights Act 1998; and

(c) section 43(1) to (6) and (8), section 67, sections 84 to 86, section 95(3) and (4) and section 98.

(2) Subsection (1) does not prevent an Act of the Assembly or subordinate legislation modifying section 3(3) or (4) or 11(1) of the European Communities Act 1972.

(3) In this Act "Minister", unless the context otherwise requires, means the First Minister, the deputy First Minister or a Northern Ireland Minister.

## 8  Consent of Secretary of State required in certain cases

The consent of the Secretary of State shall be required in relation to a Bill which contains—

(a) a provision which deals with an excepted matter and is ancillary to other provisions (whether in the Bill or previously enacted) dealing with reserved or transferred matters; or

(b) a provision which deals with a reserved matter. *Scrutiny and stages of Bills*

## 9  Scrutiny by Ministers

(1) A Minister in charge of a Bill shall, on or before introduction of it in the Assembly, make a statement to the effect that in his view the Bill would be within the legislative competence of the Assembly.

(2) The statement shall be in writing and shall be published in such manner as the Minister making the statement considers appropriate.

## 10  Scrutiny by Presiding Officer

(1) Standing orders shall ensure that a Bill is not introduced in the Assembly if the Presiding Officer decides that any provision of it would not be within the legislative competence of the Assembly.

(2) Subject to subsection (3)—

(a) the Presiding Officer shall consider a Bill both on its introduction and before the Assembly enters on its final stage; and

(b) if he considers that the Bill contains—

(i) any provision which deals with an excepted matter and is ancillary to other provisions (whether in the Bill or previously enacted) dealing with reserved or transferred matters; or

(ii) any provision which deals with a reserved matter,

he shall refer it to the Secretary of State; and

(c) the Assembly shall not proceed with the Bill or, as the case may be, enter on its final stage unless—

(i) the Secretary of State's consent to the consideration of the Bill by the Assembly is signified;

or (ii) the Assembly is informed that in his opinion the Bill does not contain any such provision as is mentioned in paragraph (b)(i) or (ii).

(3) Subsection (2)(b) and (c) shall not apply—

(a) where, in the opinion of the Presiding Officer, each provision of the Bill which deals with an excepted or reserved matter is ancillary to other provisions (whether in the Bill or previously enacted) dealing with transferred matters only; or

(b) on the introduction of a Bill, where the Bill has been endorsed with a statement that the Secretary of State has consented to the Assembly considering the Bill.

(4) In this section and section 14 "final stage", in relation to a Bill, means the stage in the Assembly's proceedings at which the Bill falls finally to be passed or rejected.

## 11 Scrutiny by the Judicial Committee

(1) The Attorney General for Northern Ireland may refer the question of whether a provision of a Bill would be within the legislative competence of the Assembly to the Judicial Committee for decision.

(2) Subject to subsection (3), he may make a reference in relation to a provision of a Bill at any time during—

(a) the period of four weeks beginning with the passing of the Bill; and

(b) the period of four weeks beginning with any subsequent approval of the Bill in accordance with standing orders made by virtue of section 13(6).

(3) If he notifies the Presiding Officer that he does not intend to make a reference in relation to a provision of a Bill, he shall not make such a reference unless, after the notification, the Bill is approved as mentioned in subsection (2)(b).

(4) If the Judicial Committee decide that any provision of a Bill would be within the legislative competence of the Assembly, their decision shall be taken as applying also to that provision if contained in the Act when enacted.

**12 Reconsideration where reference made to ECJ**

(1) This section applies where—

(a) a reference has been made under section 11 in relation to a provision of a Bill;

(b) a reference for a preliminary ruling has been made by the Judicial Committee in connection with that reference; and

(c) neither of the references has been decided or otherwise disposed of.

(2) If the Assembly resolves that it wishes to reconsider the Bill—

(a) the Presiding Officer shall notify the Attorney General for Northern Ireland and the Attorney General of that fact; and

(b) the Attorney General for Northern Ireland shall request the withdrawal of the reference under section 11.

(3) In this section "reference for a preliminary ruling" means a reference of a question to the European Court of Justice under—

(a) Article 177 of the Treaty establishing the European Community;

(b) Article 41 of the Treaty establishing the European Coal and Steel Community; or

(c) Article 150 of the Treaty establishing the European Atomic Energy Community.

## 13  Stages of Bills

(1) Standing orders shall include provision—

(a) for general debate on a Bill with an opportunity for members to vote on its general principles;

(b) for the consideration of, and an opportunity for members to vote on, the details of a Bill; and

(c) for a final stage at which a Bill can be passed or rejected but not amended.

(2) Standing orders may, in relation to different types of Bill, modify provisions made in pursuance of subsection (1)(a) or (b).

(3) Standing orders—

(a) shall include provision for establishing such a committee as is mentioned in paragraph 11 of Strand One of the Belfast Agreement;

(b) may include provision for the details of a Bill to be considered by the committee in such circumstances as may be specified in the orders.

(4) Standing orders shall include provision—

(a) requiring the Presiding Officer to send a copy of each Bill, as soon as reasonably practicable after introduction, to the Northern Ireland Human Rights Commission; and

(b) enabling the Assembly to ask the Commission, where the Assembly thinks fit, to advise whether a Bill is compatible with human rights (including the Convention rights).

(5) Standing orders shall provide for an opportunity for the re-consideration of a Bill after its passing if (and only if)—

(a) the Judicial Committee decide that any provision of the Bill would not be within the legislative competence of the Assembly;

(b) a reference made in relation to a provision of the Bill under section 11 has been withdrawn following a request for withdrawal under section 12;

(c) a decision is made in relation to the Bill under section 14(4) or (5); or

(d) a motion under section 15(1) is passed by either House of Parliament.

(6) Standing orders shall, in particular, ensure that any Bill amended on reconsideration is subject to a final stage at which it can be approved or rejected but not amended.

(7) References in subsection (5) and other provisions of this Act to the passing of a Bill shall, in the case of a Bill which has been amended on reconsideration, be read as references to the approval of the Bill.

*Royal Assent*

**14 Submission by Secretary of State**

(1) It shall be the Secretary of State who submits Bills for Royal Assent.

(2) The Secretary of State shall not submit a Bill for Royal Assent at any time when—

(a) the Attorney General for Northern Ireland is entitled to make a reference in relation to a provision of the Bill under section 11; or

(b) any such reference has been made but has not been decided or otherwise disposed of by the Judicial Committee.

(3) If—

(a) the Judicial Committee have decided that any provision of a Bill would not be within the legislative competence of the Assembly; or

(b) a reference made in relation to a provision of the Bill under section 11 has been withdrawn following a request for withdrawal under section 12,

the Secretary of State shall not submit the Bill in its un-amended form for Royal Assent.

(4) The Secretary of State may, unless he consents to it, decide not to submit for Royal Assent a Bill containing a provision—

(a) which the Secretary of State considers deals with an excepted matter and is ancillary to other provisions (whether in the Bill or previously enacted) dealing with reserved or transferred matters; or

(b) which the Secretary of State considers deals with a reserved matter,

if the Bill has not been referred to him under subsection (2) of section 10 (whether by virtue of subsection (3)(a) of that section or otherwise) before the Assembly enters on its final stage.

(5) The Secretary of State may decide not to submit for Royal Assent a Bill which contains a provision which he considers—

(a) would be incompatible with any international obligations, with the interests of defence or national security or with the protection of public safety or public order; or

(b) would have an adverse effect on the operation of the single market in goods and services within the United Kingdom.

### 15 Parliamentary control where consent given

(1) Subject to subsections (2) and (3), a Bill to which the Secretary of State has consented under this Part shall not be submitted by him for Royal Assent unless he has first laid it before Parliament and either—

(a) the period of 20 days beginning with the date on which it is laid has expired without notice having been given in

either House of a motion that the Bill shall not be submitted for Royal Assent; or

(b) if notice of such a motion is given within that period, the
motion has been rejected or withdrawn.

(2) Subsection (1) shall not apply to a Bill if the Secretary of State
considers that it contains no provision which deals with an
excepted or reserved matter except a provision which is ancillary to other provisions (whether in the Bill or previously
enacted) dealing with transferred matters only.

(3) Subsection (1) shall not apply to a Bill if the Secretary of State
considers that by reason of urgency it should be submitted
for Royal Assent without first being laid before Parliament.

(4) Any Bill submitted by virtue of subsection (3) shall, if given
Royal Assent, be laid before Parliament by the Secretary of
State after Royal Assent, and if—

(a) within the period of 20 days beginning with the date on
which it is laid notice is given in either House of a motion praying that the Act of the Assembly shall cease to
have effect; and

(b) that motion is carried,

Her Majesty may by Order in Council repeal that Act with
effect from such date as may be specified in the Order.

(5) An Order in Council under subsection (4) may make such
consequential and transitional provisions and such savings in
connection with the repeal as appear to Her Majesty to be
necessary or expedient.

(6) Any notice of motion for the purposes of subsection (1) or
(4) must be signed by not less than 20 members of the House
in which it is given; and the period mentioned in that subsection shall be computed, in relation to each House, by reference only to days on which that House sits.

## PART III

## EXECUTIVE AUTHORITIES

*Authorities*

16 **First Minister and deputy First Minister**
(1) Each Assembly shall, within a period of six weeks beginning with its first meeting, elect from among its members the First Minister and the deputy First Minister.
(2) Each candidate for either office must stand for election jointly with a candidate for the other office.
(3) Two candidates standing jointly shall not be elected to the two offices without the support of a majority of the members voting in the election, a majority of the designated Nationalists voting and a majority of the designated Unionists voting.
(4) The First Minister and the deputy First Minister—
   (a) shall not take up office until each of them has affirmed the terms of the pledge of office; and
   (b) subject to the provisions of this Part, shall hold office until the conclusion of the next election for First Minister and deputy First Minister.
(5) The holder of the office of First Minister or deputy First Minister may by notice in writing to the Presiding Officer designate a Northern Ireland Minister to exercise the functions of that office—
   (a) during any absence or incapacity of the holder; or
   (b) during any vacancy in that office arising otherwise than under subsection (7)(a); but a person shall not have power to act by virtue of paragraph (a) for a continuous period exceeding 6 weeks.
(6) The First Minister or the deputy First Minister—
   (a) may at any time resign by notice in writing to the Presiding Officer; and

(b) shall cease to hold office if he ceases to be a member of the Assembly otherwise than by virtue of a dissolution.

(7) If either the First Minister or the deputy First Minister ceases to hold office at any time, whether by resignation or otherwise, the other—

(a) shall also cease to hold office at that time; but

(b) may continue to exercise the functions of his office until the election required by subsection (8).

(8) Where the offices of the First Minister and the deputy First Minister become vacant at any time an election shall be held under this section to fill the vacancies within a period of six weeks beginning with that time.

(9) Standing orders may make provision with respect to the holding of elections under this section.

(10) In this Act "the pledge of office" means the pledge of office which, together with the code of conduct to which it refers, is set out in Annex A to Strand One of the Belfast Agreement (the text of which Annex is reproduced in Schedule 4).

**17  Ministerial offices**

(1) The First Minister and the deputy First Minister acting jointly may at any time, and shall where subsection (2) applies, determine—

(a) the number of Ministerial offices to be held by Northern Ireland Ministers; and

(b) the functions to be exercisable by the holder of each such office.

(2) This subsection applies where provision is made by an Act of the Assembly for establishing a new Northern Ireland department or dissolving an existing one.

(3) In making a determination under subsection (1), the First Minister and the deputy First Minister shall ensure that the functions exercisable by those in charge of the different Northern Ireland departments existing at the date of the

determination are exercisable by the holders of different Ministerial offices.

(4) The number of Ministerial offices shall not exceed 10 or such greater number as the Secretary of State may by order provide.

(5) A determination under subsection (1) shall not have effect unless it is approved by a resolution of the Assembly passed with cross-community support.

## 18 Northern Ireland Ministers

(1) Where—

(a) an Assembly is elected under section 31 or 32;

(b) a determination under section 17(1) takes effect;

(c) a resolution which causes one or more Ministerial offices to become vacant is passed under section 30(2);

(d) the period of exclusion imposed by a resolution under section 30(2) comes to an end; or

(e) such other circumstances obtain as may be specified in standing orders,

all Northern Ireland Ministers shall cease to hold office and the Ministerial offices shall be filled by applying subsections (2) to (6) within a period so specified.

(2) The nominating officer of the political party for which the formula in subsection (5) gives the highest figure may select a Ministerial office and nominate a person to hold it who is a member of the party and of the Assembly.

(3) If—

(a) the nominating officer does not exercise the power conferred by subsection (2) within a period specified in standing orders; or

(b) the nominated person does not take up the selected Ministerial office within that period,

that power shall become exercisable by the nominating officer of the political party for which the formula in subsection (5) gives the next highest figure.

(4)  Subsections (2) and (3) shall be applied as many times as may be necessary to secure that each of the Ministerial offices is filled.

(5)  The formula is—

$$\frac{S}{1 + M}$$

where—

S= the number of seats in the Assembly which were held by members of the party on the day on which the Assembly first met following its election;

M= the number of Ministerial offices (if any) which are held by members of the party.

(6)  Where the figures given by the formula for two or more political parties are equal, each of those figures shall be recalculated with S being equal to the number of first preference votes cast for the party at the last general election of members of the Assembly.

(7)  The holding of office as First Minister or deputy First Minister shall not prevent a person being nominated to hold a Ministerial office.

(8)  A Northern Ireland Minister shall not take up office until he has affirmed the terms of the pledge of office.

(9)  A Northern Ireland Minister shall cease to hold office if—

(a)  he resigns by notice in writing to the First Minister and the deputy First Minister;

(b)  he ceases to be a member of the Assembly otherwise than by virtue of a dissolution; or

(c)  he is dismissed by the nominating officer who nominated him (or that officer's successor) and the Presiding Officer is notified of his dismissal.

(10)  Where a Ministerial office is vacant otherwise than by virtue of subsection (1), the nominating officer of the party on whose behalf the previous incumbent was nominated may nominate a person to hold the office who is a member of the party and of the Assembly.

(11) If—

(a) the nominating officer does not exercise the power conferred by subsection (10) within a period specified in standing orders; or

(b) the nominated person does not take up the office within that period,

the vacancy shall be filled by applying subsections (2) to (6) within a period specified in standing orders.

(12) Where—

(a) the Assembly has resolved under section 30(2) that a political party does not enjoy its confidence; and

(b) the party's period of exclusion has not come to an end,

the party shall be disregarded for the purposes of any application of subsections (2) to (6).

(13) In this section "nominating officer"—

(a) in relation to a party registered under the Registration of Political Parties Act 1998, means the registered nominating officer or a member of the Assembly nominated by him for the purposes of this section;

(b) in relation to any other political party, means the person who appears to the Presiding Officer to be the leader of the party, or a member of the Assembly nominated by that person for the purposes of this section.

## 19 Junior Ministers

(1) The First Minister and the deputy First Minister acting jointly may at any time determine—

(a) that a number of members of the Assembly specified in the determination shall be appointed as junior Ministers in accordance with such procedures for their appointment as are so specified; and

(b) that the functions exercisable by virtue of each junior Ministerial office shall be those specified in relation to that office in the determination.

(2) Procedures specified in a determination under this section may apply such formulae or other rules as the First Minister and the deputy First Minister consider appropriate.

(3) A determination under this section shall—

(a) make provision as to the circumstances in which a junior Minister shall cease to hold office, and for the filling of vacancies; and

(b) provide that a junior Minister shall not take up office until he has affirmed the terms of the pledge of office.

(4) A determination under this section shall not take effect until it has been approved by a resolution of the Assembly.

(5) Where a determination under this section takes effect—

(a) any junior Ministers previously appointed shall cease to hold office; and

(b) the procedures specified in the determination shall be applied within a period specified in standing orders.

## 20 The Executive Committee

(1) There shall be an Executive Committee of each Assembly consisting of the First Minister, the deputy First Minister and the Northern Ireland Ministers.

(2) The First Minister and the deputy First Minister shall be chairmen of the Committee.

(3) The Committee shall have the functions set out in paragraphs 19 and 20 of Strand One of the Belfast Agreement

## 21 Northern Ireland departments

(1) Subject to subsection (2), the Northern Ireland departments existing on the appointed day shall be the Northern Ireland departments for the purposes of this Act.

(2) Provision may be made by Act of the Assembly for establishing new Northern Ireland departments or dissolving existing ones.

(3) If an Act of the Assembly which establishes a new Northern Ireland department provides for it to be in the charge of the First Minister and the deputy First Minister acting jointly—

(a) the department shall not be regarded as a Northern Ireland department for the purposes of subsection (2) or (3) of section 17; and

(b) the office held by those Ministers as the head of the department shall not be regarded as a Ministerial office for the purposes of subsection (4) of that section or section 18.

*Functions*

22 **Statutory functions**

(1) An Act of the Assembly or other enactment may confer functions on a Minister (but not a junior Minister) or a Northern Ireland department by name.

(2) Functions conferred on a Northern Ireland department by an enactment passed or made before the appointed day shall, except as provided by an Act of the Assembly or other subsequent enactment, continue to be exercisable by that department.

23 **Prerogative and executive powers**

(1) The executive power in Northern Ireland shall continue to be vested in Her Majesty.

(2) As respects transferred matters, the prerogative and other executive powers of Her Majesty in relation to Northern Ireland shall, subject to subsection (3), be exercisable on Her Majesty's behalf by any Minister or Northern Ireland department.

(3) As respects the Northern Ireland Civil Service and the Commissioner for Public Appointments for Northern Ireland, the prerogative and other executive powers of Her Majesty in relation to Northern Ireland shall be exercisable on Her Majesty's behalf by the First Minister and the deputy First Minister acting jointly.

(4) The First Minister and deputy First Minister acting jointly may by prerogative order under subsection (3) direct that

such of the powers mentioned in that subsection as are specified in the order shall be exercisable on Her Majesty's behalf by a Northern Ireland Minister or Northern Ireland department so specified.

## 24  Community law, Convention rights etc

(1) A Minister or Northern Ireland department has no power to make, confirm or approve any subordinate legislation, or to do any act, so far as the legislation or act—

(a) is incompatible with any of the Convention rights;

(b) is incompatible with Community law;

(c) discriminates against a person or class of person on the ground of religious belief or political opinion;

(d) in the case of an act, aids or incites another person to discriminate against a person or class of person on that ground; or

(e) in the case of legislation, modifies an enactment in breach of section 7.

(2) Subsection (1)(c) and (d) does not apply in relation to any act which is unlawful by virtue of the Fair Employment (Northern Ireland) Act 1976, or would be unlawful but for some exception made by virtue of Part V of that Act.

## 25  Excepted and reserved matters

(1) If any subordinate legislation made, confirmed or approved by a Minister or Northern Ireland department contains a provision dealing with an excepted or reserved matter, the Secretary of State may by order revoke the legislation.

(2) An order made under subsection (1) shall recite the reasons for revoking the legislation and may make provision having retrospective effect.

## 26  International obligations

(1) If the Secretary of State considers that any action proposed to be taken by a Minister or Northern Ireland department

would be incompatible with any international obligations, with the interests of defence or national security or with the protection of public safety or public order, he may by order direct that the proposed action shall not be taken.

(2) If the Secretary of State considers that any action capable of being taken by a Minister or Northern Ireland department is required for the purpose of giving effect to any international obligations, of safeguarding the interests of defence or national security or of protecting public safety or public order, he may by order direct that the action shall be taken.

(3) In subsections (1) and (2), "action" includes making, confirming or approving subordinate legislation and, in subsection (2), includes introducing a Bill in the Assembly.

(4) If any subordinate legislation made, confirmed or approved by a Minister or Northern Ireland department contains a provision which the Secretary of State considers—

(a) would be incompatible with any international obligations, with the interests of defence or national security or with the protection of public safety or public order; or

(b) would have an adverse effect on the operation of the single market in goods and services within the United Kingdom,

the Secretary of State may by order revoke the legislation.

(5) An order under this section shall recite the reasons for making the order and may make provision having retrospective effect.

### 27 Quotas for purposes of international etc obligations

(1) A Minister of the Crown may make an order containing provision such as is specified in subsection (2) where—

(a) an international obligation or an obligation under Community law is an obligation to achieve a result defined by reference to a quantity (whether expressed as an amount, proportion or ratio or otherwise); and

(b) the quantity relates to the United Kingdom (or to an area including the United Kingdom or to an area consisting of a part of the United Kingdom which is or includes the whole or part of Northern Ireland).

(2) The provision referred to in subsection (1) is provision for the achievement by a Minister or Northern Ireland department (in the exercise of his or its functions) of so much of the result to be achieved under the international obligation or obligation under Community law as is specified in the order.

(3) The order may specify the time by which any part of the result to be achieved by the Minister or department is to be achieved.

(4) Where an order under subsection (1) is in force in relation to an international obligation or an obligation under Community law, the obligation shall have effect for the purposes of this Act as if it were an obligation to achieve so much of the result to be achieved under the obligation as is specified in the order by the time or times so specified.

(5) No order shall be made by a Minister of the Crown under subsection (1) unless he has consulted the Minister or department concerned.

**28 Agency arrangements between UK and NI departments**
(1) Arrangements may be made between—
(a) any department of the Government of the United Kingdom or any public body, or holder of a public office, in the United Kingdom; and
(b) any Northern Ireland department,
for any functions of one of them to be discharged by, or by officers of, the other.

(2) No such arrangements shall affect the responsibility of the person on whose behalf any functions are discharged.

(3) In this section—
   (a) references to a department of the Government of the United Kingdom include references to any Minister of the Crown; and
   (b) references to a Northern Ireland department include references to a Minister.

*Miscellaneous*

## 29 Statutory committees

(1) Standing orders shall make provision—
   (a) for establishing committees of members of the Assembly ("statutory committees") to advise and assist each Northern Ireland Minister in the formulation of policy with respect to matters within his responsibilities as a Minister;
   (b) for enabling a committee to be so established either in relation to a single Northern Ireland Minister or in relation to more than one; and
   (c) conferring on the committees the powers described in paragraph 9 of Strand One of the Belfast Agreement.

(2) Standing orders shall provide that—
   (a) the nominating officer of the political party for which the formula in subsection (3) gives the highest figure may select a statutory committee and nominate as its chairman or deputy chairman a person who is a member of the party and of the Assembly;
   (b) if the nominating officer does not exercise the power conferred by paragraph (a) within a period specified in standing orders, or the nominated person does not take up the selected office within that period, that power shall be exercisable instead by the nominating officer of the political party for which the formula in subsection (3) gives the next highest figure; and

(c) paragraphs (a) and (b) shall be applied as many times as may be necessary to secure that a chairman and deputy chairman are nominated for each of the statutory committees.

(3) The formula is—

$$\frac{S}{1 + C}$$

where—

S= the number of seats in the Assembly which were held by members of the party on the day on which the Assembly first met following its election;

C = the number of chairmen and deputy chairmen of statutory committees (if any) who are members of the party.

(4) Standing orders shall provide that, where the figures given by the formula for two or more political parties are equal, each of those figures shall be recalculated with S being equal to the number of first preference votes cast for the party at the last general election of members of the Assembly.

(5) Standing orders shall provide that—

(a) a Minister or junior Minister may not be the chairman or deputy chairman of a statutory committee; and

(b) in making a selection under the provision made by virtue of subsection (2)(a), a nominating officer shall prefer a committee in which he does not have a party interest to one in which he does.

(6) For the purposes of subsection (5) a nominating officer has a party interest in a committee if it is established to advise and assist a Northern Ireland Minister who is a member of his party.

(7) Standing orders shall provide that a chairman or deputy chairman shall cease to hold office if—

(a) he resigns by notice in writing to the Presiding Officer;

(b) he ceases to be a member of the Assembly; or

(c) he is dismissed by the nominating officer who nominated him (or that officer's successor) and the Presiding Officer is notified of his dismissal.

(8) Standing orders shall provide that, where an office of chairman or deputy chairman is vacant, the nominating officer of the party on whose behalf the previous incumbent was nominated may nominate a person to hold the office who is a member of the party and of the Assembly.

(9) Standing orders shall provide that if—

    (a) the nominating officer does not exercise the power conferred by subsection (8) within a period specified in standing orders; or

    (b) the nominated person does not take up the selected office within that period,

the vacancy shall be filled by applying the provision made by virtue of subsections (2) to (5).

(10) In this section "nominating officer" has the same meaning as in section 18.

## 30 Exclusion of Ministers from office

(1) If the Assembly resolves that a Minister or junior Minister no longer enjoys the confidence of the Assembly—

    (a) because he is not committed to non-violence and exclusively peaceful and democratic means; or

    (b) because of any failure of his to observe any other terms of the pledge of office,

he shall be excluded from holding office as a Minister or junior Minister for a period of twelve months beginning with the date of the resolution.

(2) If the Assembly resolves that a political party does not enjoy the confidence of the Assembly—

    (a) because it is not committed to non-violence and exclusively peaceful and democratic means; or

(b) because it is not committed to such of its members as are or might become Ministers or junior Ministers observing the other terms of the pledge of office,

members of that party shall be excluded from holding office as Ministers or junior Ministers for a period of twelve months beginning with the date of the resolution.

(3) The Assembly may, before a period of exclusion comes to an end, resolve to extend it for twelve months beginning with the date of the resolution.

(4) A period of exclusion shall come to an end if the Assembly—

(a) is dissolved; or

(b) resolves to bring the exclusion to an end.

(5) A motion for a resolution under this section shall not be moved unless—

(a) it is supported by at least 30 members of the Assembly;

(b) it is moved by the First Minister and the deputy First Minister acting jointly; or

(c) it is moved by the Presiding Officer in pursuance of a notice under subsection (6).

(6) If the Secretary of State is of the opinion that the Assembly ought to consider—

(a) a resolution under subsection (1)(a) in relation to a Minister or junior Minister; or

(b) a resolution under subsection (2)(a) in relation to a political party,

he shall serve a notice on the Presiding Officer requiring him to move a motion for such a resolution.

(7) In forming an opinion under subsection (6), the Secretary of State shall in particular take into account whether the Minister or junior Minister or the political party—

(a) is committed to the use now and in the future of only democratic and peaceful means to achieve his or its objectives;

(b) has ceased to be involved in any acts of violence or of preparation for violence;

(c) is directing or promoting acts of violence by other persons;

(d) is co-operating fully with any Commission of the kind referred to in section 7 of the Northern Ireland Arms Decommissioning Act 1997 in implementing the Decommissioning section of the Belfast Agreement.

(8) A resolution under this section shall not be passed without cross-community support.

## PART IV

## THE NORTHERN IRELAND ASSEMBLY

*Elections etc*

**31 Dates of elections and dissolutions**

(1) Subject to subsection (2), the date of the poll for the election of each Assembly shall be the first Thursday in May in the fourth calendar year following that in which its predecessor was elected; and the predecessor shall be dissolved at the beginning of the minimum period which ends with that date.

(2) The date of the poll for the election of the Assembly next following the Assembly elected under section 2 of the Northern Ireland (Elections) Act 1998 shall be 1st May 2003; and the Assembly elected under that section shall be dissolved at the beginning of the minimum period which ends with that date.

(3) The Secretary of State may at any time by order direct that the date of the poll for the election of the next Assembly shall, instead of being that specified in subsection (1) or (2), be a date specified in the order being a date falling not more than two months before or after the date specified in that subsection.

(4) An Assembly elected under this section or section 32 shall meet within the period of eight days beginning with the day of the poll at which it is elected.

(5) For the purposes of subsection (4), a Saturday, a Sunday, Christmas Day, Good Friday and any day which is a bank holiday in Northern Ireland shall be disregarded.

(6) In this section "minimum period" means a period determined in accordance with an order of the Secretary of State.

## 32 Extraordinary elections

(1) If the Assembly passes a resolution that it should be dissolved the Secretary of State shall propose a date for the poll for the election of the next Assembly.

(2) A resolution under subsection (1) shall not be passed without the support of a number of members of the Assembly which equals or exceeds two thirds of the total number of seats in the Assembly.

(3) If the period mentioned in section 16(1) or (8) ends without a First Minister and a deputy First Minister having been elected, the Secretary of State shall propose a date for the poll for the election of the next Assembly.

(4) If the Secretary of State proposes a date under subsection (1) or (3), Her Majesty may by Order in Council—

  (a) direct that the date of the poll for the election of the next Assembly shall, instead of being determined in accordance with section 31, be the date proposed; and

  (b) provide for the Assembly to be dissolved on a date specified in the Order.

## 33 Constituencies and numbers of members

(1) The members of the Assembly shall be returned for the parliamentary constituencies in Northern Ireland.

(2) Each constituency shall return six members.

(3) An Order in Council under the Parliamentary Constituencies Act 1986 changing a parliamentary constituency

in Northern Ireland shall have effect for the purposes of this Act in relation to—

(a) the first election under section 31 or 32 which takes place after the Order comes into force; and

(b) later elections under that section and by-elections.

**34 Elections and franchise**

(1) This section applies to elections of members of the Assembly, including by-elections.

(2) Each vote in the poll at an election shall be a single transferable vote.

(3) A single transferable vote is a vote—

(a) capable of being given so as to indicate the voter's order of preference for the candidates for election as members for the constituency; and

(b) capable of being transferred to the next choice when the vote is not needed to give a prior choice the necessary quota of votes or when a prior choice is eliminated from the list of candidates because of a deficiency in the number of votes given for him.

(4) The Secretary of State may by order make provision about elections or any matter relating to them.

(5) In particular, an order under subsection (4) may make—

(a) provision as to the persons entitled to vote at an election and the registration of such persons;

(b) provision for securing that no person stands as a candidate for more than one constituency at a general election;

(c) provision for determining the date of the poll at a by-election;

(d) provision about deposits.

(6) An order under subsection (4) may apply (with or without modifications) any provision of, or made under, any enactment.

## 35 Vacancies

(1) The Secretary of State may by order make provision for the filling of vacancies occurring in the Assembly's membership.

(2) Such provision may be made by reference to by-elections or substitutes or such other method of filling vacancies as the Secretary of State thinks fit.

(3) If a seat becomes vacant, the Presiding Officer shall as soon as reasonably practicable inform the Chief Electoral Officer for Northern Ireland.

(4) The validity of any proceedings of the Assembly is not affected by any vacancy in its membership.

(5) An order under subsection (1) may apply (with or without modifications) any provision of, or made under, any enactment.

*Disqualification*

## 36 Disqualification

(1) The Northern Ireland Assembly Disqualification Act 1975 shall have effect as if any reference to the Assembly established under section 1 of the Northern Ireland Assembly Act 1973 were a reference to the Assembly.

(2) No recommendation shall be made to Her Majesty to make an Order in Council under section 3(1) of the Northern Ireland Assembly Disqualification Act 1975 (power to amend Schedule 1) without the consent of the Secretary of State.

(3) A person who is Her Majesty's Lord-Lieutenant or Lieutenant for a county or county borough in Northern Ireland is disqualified for membership of the Assembly for a constituency comprising the whole or part of the county or county borough.

(4) A person is disqualified for membership of the Assembly if he is disqualified for membership of the House of

Commons otherwise than under the House of Commons Disqualification Act 1975.

(5) A person is not disqualified for membership of the Assembly by virtue of subsection (1) by reason only that he is a member of the Seanad Eireann (Senate of Ireland).

(6) A person is not disqualified for membership of the Assembly by virtue of subsection (4) by reason only that—

(a) he is a peer (other than a Lord of Appeal in Ordinary); or

(b) he is ordained or is a minister of any religious denomination.

(7) A person is not disqualified for membership of the Assembly by virtue of subsection (4) by reason only that he is disqualified under section 3 of the Act of Settlement (certain persons born out of the Kingdom) if he is a citizen of the European Union.

## 37  Effect of disqualification and provision for relief

(1) Subject to any order made by the Assembly under this section—

(a) if any person disqualified by virtue of section 36 is returned as a member of the Assembly, his return shall be void; and

(b) if any person being a member of the Assembly becomes disqualified by virtue of that section, his seat shall be vacated.

(2) If, in a case which falls or is alleged to fall within subsection (1) otherwise than by virtue of section 36(4), it appears to the Assembly—

(a) that the grounds of disqualification or alleged disqualification which subsisted or arose at the material time have been removed; and

(b) that it is otherwise proper so to do,

the Assembly may by order direct that any such disqualification incurred on those grounds at that time shall be disregarded for the purposes of this section.

(3) No order under subsection (2) shall affect the proceedings
on any election petition or any determination of an election
court.

(4) Subsection (1)(b) has effect subject to section 141 of the
Mental Health Act 1983 (mental illness) and section 427
of the Insolvency Act 1986 (bankruptcy etc); and where, in
consequence of either of those sections, the seat of a disqualified member of the Assembly has not been vacated—

(a) he shall not participate in any proceedings of the
Assembly; and

(b) any of his other rights and privileges as a member of
the Assembly may be withdrawn by a resolution of the
Assembly.

(5) The validity of any proceedings of the Assembly is not affected by the disqualification of any person from being a
member of the Assembly or from being a member for the
constituency for which he purports to sit.

## 38 Disqualification: judicial proceedings

(1) Any person who claims that a person purporting to be a
member of the Assembly—

(a) is disqualified; or

(b) was disqualified when, or at any time since, he was
returned,

may apply to the High Court of Justice in Northern Ireland
for a declaration to that effect.

(2) On an application—

(a) the person in respect of whom the application is made
shall be the respondent;

(b) the applicant shall give such security for costs, not exceeding £5,000, as the court may direct; and

(c) the decision of the court shall be final.

(3) A declaration made in accordance with this section shall be certified in writing to the Secretary of State by the court.

(4) No such declaration shall be made in respect of a person on any grounds if an order has been made by the Assembly under subsection (2) of section 37 directing that any disqualification incurred by him on those grounds shall be disregarded for the purposes of that section.

(5) No declaration shall be made in respect of any person on grounds which subsisted when he was elected if an election petition is pending or has been tried in which his disqualification on those grounds is or was in issue.

(6) The Secretary of State may by order substitute for the amount specified in subsection (2)(b) such other amount as may be specified in the order.

*Presiding Officer and Commission*

## 39 Presiding Officer

(1) Each Assembly shall as its first business elect from among its members a Presiding Officer and deputies.

(2) A person elected Presiding Officer or deputy shall hold office until the conclusion of the next election for Presiding Officer under subsection (1) unless—

(a) he previously resigns;

(b) he ceases to be a member of the Assembly otherwise than by virtue of a dissolution; or

(c) the Assembly elects from among its members a person to hold office as Presiding Officer or deputy in his place.

(3) If the Presiding Officer or a deputy ceases to hold office (otherwise than under subsection (2)(c)) before the Assembly is dissolved, the Assembly shall elect another from among its members to fill his place.

(4) The Presiding Officer's functions may be exercised by a deputy if the office of Presiding Officer is vacant or the Presiding Officer is for any reason unable to act.

(5) The Presiding Officer may (subject to standing orders) authorise a deputy to exercise functions on his behalf.

(6) Standing orders may include provision as to the participation (including voting) of the Presiding Officer and deputies in the proceedings of the Assembly.

(7) A person shall not be elected under subsections (1) to (3) without cross-community support.

### 40 Commission

(1) There shall be a body corporate, to be known as the Northern Ireland Assembly Commission ("the Commission"), to perform—

(a) the functions conferred on the Commission by virtue of any enactment; and

(b) any functions conferred on the Commission by resolution of the Assembly.

(2) The members of the Commission shall be—

(a) the Presiding Officer; and

(b) the prescribed number of members of the Assembly appointed in accordance with standing orders.

(3) In subsection (2) "the prescribed number" means 5 or such other number as may be prescribed by standing orders.

(4) The Commission shall provide the Assembly, or ensure that the Assembly is provided, with the property, staff and services required for the Assembly's purposes.

(5) The Assembly may give special or general directions to the Commission for the purpose of or in connection with the exercise of the Commission's functions.

(6) Proceedings by or against the Assembly (other than proceedings on the Crown side of the Queen's Bench Division) shall be instituted by or against the Commission on behalf of the Assembly.

(7) Any property or liabilities acquired or incurred in relation to matters within the general responsibility of the Commission to which (apart from this subsection) the Assembly would be entitled or subject shall be treated for all purposes as property or liabilities of the Commission.

(8) Any expenses of the Commission shall be defrayed out of money appropriated by Act of the Assembly.

(9) Any sums received by the Commission shall be paid into the Consolidated Fund of Northern Ireland, subject to any provision made by Act of the Assembly for the disposal of or accounting for such sums.

(10) Schedule 5 (which makes further provision about the Commission) shall have effect.

*Proceedings etc.*

## 41 Standing orders

(1) The proceedings of the Assembly shall be regulated by standing orders.

(2) Standing orders shall not be made, amended or repealed without cross-community support.

(3) Schedule 6 (which makes provision as to how certain matters are to be dealt with by standing orders) shall have effect.

## 42 Petitions of concern

(1) If 30 members petition the Assembly expressing their concern about a matter which is to be voted on by the Assembly, the vote on that matter shall require cross-community support.

(2) Standing orders shall make provision with respect to the procedure to be followed in petitioning the Assembly under this section, including provision with respect to the period of notice required.

(3) Standing orders shall provide that the matter to which a petition under this section relates may be referred, in accordance with paragraphs 11 and 13 of Strand One of the Belfast Agreement, to the committee established under section 13(3)(a).

### 43 Members' interests

(1) Standing orders shall include provision for a register of interests of members of the Assembly, and for—
   (a) registrable interests (as defined in standing orders) to be registered in it; and
   (b) the register to be published and made available for public inspection.

(2) Standing orders shall include provision requiring that any member of the Assembly who has—
   (a) a financial interest (as defined in standing orders) in any matter; or
   (b) any other interest, or an interest of any other kind, specified in standing orders in any matter,
   declares that interest before taking part in any proceedings of the Assembly relating to that matter.

(3) Standing orders made in pursuance of subsection (1) or (2) may include provision for preventing or restricting the participation in proceedings of the Assembly of a member with a registrable interest, or an interest mentioned in subsection (2), in a matter to which the proceedings relate.

(4) Standing orders shall include provision prohibiting a member of the Assembly from—
   (a) advocating or initiating any cause or matter on behalf of any person, by any means specified in standing orders, in consideration of any payment or benefit in kind of a description so specified; or
   (b) urging, in consideration of any such payment or benefit in kind, any other member of the Assembly to advocate

or initiate any cause or matter on behalf of any person by any such means.

(5) Standing orders may include provision—

(a) for excluding from proceedings of the Assembly any member who fails to comply with, or contravenes, any provision made in pursuance of subsections (1) to (4); and

(b) for withdrawing his rights and privileges as a member for the period of his exclusion.

(6) Any member of the Assembly who—

(a) takes part in any proceedings of the Assembly without having complied with, or in contravention of, any provision made in pursuance of subsections (1) to (3); or

(b) contravenes any provision made in pursuance of subsection (4),

is guilty of an offence.

(7) A person guilty of an offence under subsection (6) is liable on summary conviction to a fine not exceeding level 5 on the standard scale.

(8) Proceedings for an offence under subsection (6) shall not be taken without the consent of the Director of Public Prosecutions for Northern Ireland.

## 44 Power to call for witnesses and documents

(1) The Assembly may require any person—

(a) to attend its proceedings for the purpose of giving evidence; or

(b) to produce documents in his custody or under his control, relating to any of the matters mentioned in subsection (2).

(2) Those matters are—

(a) transferred matters concerning Northern Ireland;

(b) other matters in relation to which statutory functions are exercisable by Ministers or the Northern Ireland departments.

(3) The power in subsection (1) is exercisable in relation to a person outside Northern Ireland only in connection with the discharge by him of functions relating to matters within subsection (2).

(4) That power is not exercisable in relation to a person who is or has been a Minister of the Crown, or a person who is or has been in Crown employment within the meaning of Article 236 of the Employment Rights (Northern Ireland) Order 1996, in connection with the discharge of any functions prior to the appointed day.

(5) That power is not exercisable in relation to—

(a) a person discharging functions of any body whose functions relate to excepted matters, in connection with the discharge by him of those functions;

(b) a person discharging functions of any body whose functions relate to reserved matters, in connection with the discharge by him of those functions;

(c) a judge of any court or a member of any tribunal which exercises the judicial power of the State.

(6) That power may be exercised by a committee of the Assembly only if the committee is expressly authorised to do so by standing orders.

(7) The Presiding Officer shall give the person in question notice in writing specifying—

(a) the time and place at which the person is to attend and the particular matters relating to which he is required to give evidence; or

(b) the documents, or types of documents, which he is to produce, the date by which he is to produce them and the particular matters to which they are to relate.

(8) Such notice shall be given—

(a) in the case of an individual, by sending it, by registered post or the recorded delivery service, addressed to him at his usual or last known address or, where he has given an address for service, at that address;

(b) in any other case, by sending it, by registered post or the recorded delivery service, addressed to the person at the person's registered or principal office.

(9) A person is not obliged under this section to answer any question or produce any document which he would be entitled to refuse to answer or produce in proceedings in a court in Northern Ireland.

(10) In this section "statutory functions" means functions conferred by virtue of any enactment.

### 45 Witnesses and documents: offences

(1) Subject to subsection (9) of section 44, any person to whom a notice under subsection (7) of that section has been given who—

(a) refuses or fails to attend proceedings as required by the notice;

(b) refuses or fails, when attending proceedings as required by the notice, to answer any question relating to the matters specified in the notice;

(c) deliberately alters, suppresses, conceals or destroys any document which he is required to produce by the notice; or

(d) refuses or fails to produce any such document, is guilty of an offence and liable on summary conviction to a fine not exceeding level 5 on the standard scale or to imprisonment for a period not exceeding three months.

(2) It is a defence for a person charged with an offence under subsection (1)(a), (b) or (d) to prove that he had a reasonable excuse for the refusal or failure.

(3) Where an offence under this section which has been committed by a body corporate is proved to have been committed with the consent or connivance of, or to be attributable to any neglect on the part of—

(a) a director, manager, secretary or other similar officer of the body corporate; or

(b) any person who was purporting to act in any such capacity,

he, as well as the body corporate, is guilty of that offence and liable to be proceeded against accordingly.

(4) Proceedings for an offence under this section shall not be taken without the consent of the Director of Public Prosecutions for Northern Ireland.

(5) For the purposes of section 44 and this section, a person shall be taken to comply with a requirement to produce a document if he produces a copy of, or an extract of the relevant part of, the document.

**46 Witnesses: oaths**

(1) The Presiding Officer or such other person as may be authorised by standing orders may—

(a) administer an oath to any person giving evidence in proceedings of the Assembly; and

(b) require him to take the oath.

(2) Any person who refuses to take an oath when required to do so under subsection (1)(b) is guilty of an offence.

(3) A person guilty of an offence under this section is liable on summary conviction to a fine not exceeding level 5 on the standard scale or to imprisonment for a period not exceeding three months.

*Remuneration and pensions*

**47 Remuneration of members**

(1) The Assembly shall pay to members of the Assembly such salaries as the Assembly may from time to time determine.

(2) The Assembly may pay to members of the Assembly such allowances as the Assembly may from time to time determine.

(3) A determination under this section may provide—
- (a) for higher salaries to be payable to members of the Assembly—
  - (i) holding office as a Minister or junior Minister;
  - (ii) holding office as Presiding Officer or deputy;
  - (iii) holding office as a member of the Northern Ireland Assembly Commission; or
  - (iv) holding an office specified in standing orders; and
- (b) for different salaries to be payable to members of the Assembly holding different such offices.

(4) A determination under this section shall provide that, if a salary is payable to a member of the Assembly as a member of either House of Parliament or of the European Parliament, his salary as a member of the Assembly shall be reduced—
- (a) to a proportion of what it would otherwise be or to a particular amount; or
- (b) by the amount of the other salary payable to him, by a proportion of that amount or by some other amount.

(5) A determination under this section may provide for different allowances for different cases.

(6) A determination under this section may provide for salaries or allowances to change from time to time by reference to other amounts or specified formulas.

(7) The Assembly may not delegate the function of making a determination under this section.

(8) Standing orders must include provision for the publication of every determination under this section.

(9) For the purposes of this section—
- (a) a person's membership of the Assembly begins on the day on which he takes his seat in accordance with standing orders; and
- (b) a person's holding of such an office as is mentioned in subsection (3)(a) begins on the day on which he takes up office.

(10) For the purposes of this section, a person who is a member of the Assembly immediately before the Assembly is dissolved shall be treated—

  (a) if he continues to hold such an office as is mentioned in subsection (3)(a)(i) to (iii), as if he were a member of the Assembly until the end of the day on which he ceases to hold the office; and

  (b) if he does not fall within paragraph (a) but is nominated as a candidate at the subsequent general election, as if he were a member of the Assembly until the end of the day of the poll for that election.

(11) Any expenditure incurred by the Assembly under this section shall be defrayed out of money appropriated by Act of the Assembly.

**48  Pensions of members**

(1) The Assembly may make provision for the payment of pensions, gratuities or allowances to, or in respect of, any person who—

  (a) has ceased to be a member of the Assembly; or

  (b) has ceased to hold such an office as is mentioned in section 47(3)(a) but continues to be a member of the Assembly.

(2) Such provision may, in particular, include provision for—

  (a) contributions or payments towards provision for such pensions, gratuities or allowances;

  (b) the establishment and administration (whether by the Commission or otherwise) of one or more pension schemes.

(3) In this section—

"the Commission" means the Northern Ireland Assembly Commission;

"provision" includes provision—

   (a) by an Act of the Assembly; or

   (b) by a resolution of the Assembly conferring functions on the Commission.

(4) Any expenditure incurred by the Assembly under this section shall be defrayed out of money appropriated by Act of the Assembly.

*Miscellaneous*

**49 Letters Patent etc**

(1) Her Majesty may by Order in Council make provision as to—

   (a)   the form and manner of preparation; and

   (b)   the publication,

of Letters Patent signed with Her Majesty's own hand signifying Her Assent to a Bill passed by the Assembly.

(2) If the First Minister and the deputy First Minister acting jointly so direct, impressions with the same device as the Great Seal of Northern Ireland shall be taken in such manner, of such size and on such material as is specified in the direction.

(3) Each such impression—

   (a)   shall be known as a Wafer Great Seal of Northern Ireland; and

   (b)   shall be kept in accordance with directions of the First Minister and the deputy First Minister acting jointly.

(4) If a Wafer Great Seal of Northern Ireland has been applied to Letters Patent mentioned in subsection (1), the document has the same validity as if it had passed under the Great Seal of Northern Ireland.

**50  Privilege**

(1)  For the purposes of the law of defamation, absolute privilege shall attach to—

(a)  the making of a statement in proceedings of the Assembly; and

(b)  the publication of a statement under the Assembly's authority.

(2)  A person is not guilty of contempt of court under the strict liability rule as the publisher of any matter—

(a)  in the course of proceedings of the Assembly which relate to a Bill or subordinate legislation; or

(b)  to the extent that it consists of a fair and accurate report of such proceedings which is made in good faith.

(3)  In this section—

"statement" has the same meaning as in the Defamation Act 1996;

"the strict liability rule" has the same meaning as in the Contempt of Court Act 1981.

**51  Resignation of members**

A member of the Assembly may at any time resign his seat by notice in writing to the Presiding Officer.

**PART V**

**NSMC, BIC, BIIC ETC.**

**52  North-South Ministerial Council and British-Irish Council**

(1)  The First Minister and the deputy First Minister acting jointly shall make such nominations of Ministers and junior Ministers (including where appropriate alternative nominations) as they consider necessary to ensure—

(a)  such cross-community participation in the North-South Ministerial Council as is required by the Belfast Agreement; and

(b) such cross-community participation in the British-Irish Council as is so required.

(2) It shall be a Ministerial responsibility of a Minister or junior Minister nominated under subsection (1)(a) or (b) to participate in the Council concerned in such meetings or activities as are specified in the nomination.

(3) Without prejudice to the operation of section 24, such a Minister or junior Minister shall act in accordance with any decisions of the Assembly or the Executive Committee which are relevant to his participation in the Council concerned.

(4) A Minister may in writing authorise a Minister or junior Minister who has been nominated under subsection (1)(a) or (b) to enter into agreements or arrangements in respect of matters for which he is responsible.

(5) The First Minister and the deputy First Minister acting jointly shall, as far in advance of each meeting of either Council as is reasonably practicable, give to the Executive Committee and to the Assembly the following information in relation to the meeting—

(a) the date;

(b) the agenda; and

(c) nominations made under subsection (1) for the purposes of the meeting.

(6) A Minister or junior Minister who participates in a meeting of either Council by reason of a nomination under this section shall, as soon as reasonably practicable after the meeting, make a report—

(a) to the Executive Committee; and

(b) to the Assembly.

(7) A report under subsection (6)(b) shall be made orally unless standing orders authorise it to be made in writing.

(8) The Northern Ireland contributions towards the expenses of the Councils shall be defrayed as expenses of the Department of Finance and Personnel.

(9) In this section "participate" shall be construed—

(a) in relation to the North-South Ministerial Council, in accordance with paragraphs 5 and 6 of Strand Two of the Belfast Agreement;

(b) in relation to the British-Irish Council, in accordance with the first paragraph 5 of Strand Three of that Agreement.

### 53 Agreements etc. by persons participating in Councils

(1) This section applies to any agreement or arrangement entered into by a Minister or junior Minister participating, by reason of a nomination under section 52, in a meeting of the North-South Ministerial Council or the British-Irish Council.

(2) Provision may be made by Act of the Assembly for giving effect to any agreement or arrangement to which this section applies, including provision—

(a) for transferring to any body designated by or constituted under the agreement or arrangement any functions which would otherwise be exercisable by any Minister or Northern Ireland department;

(b) for transferring to a Minister or Northern Ireland department any functions which would otherwise be exercisable by any authority outside Northern Ireland.

(3) Subsection (2) has effect notwithstanding anything in subsection (2)(a) of section 6; but it does not affect—

(a) the operation of subsection (2)(b) to (f) of that section; or

(b) the operation of section 8 or 15 in relation to the enactment of any Act of the Assembly.

(4) No agreement or arrangement to which this section applies entered into for the establishment after the appointed day of an implementation body shall come into operation without the approval of the Assembly.

(5) In subsection (4) "implementation body" means a body for implementing, on the basis mentioned in paragraph 11 of

Strand Two of the Belfast Agreement, policies agreed in the North-South Ministerial Council.

## 54 British-Irish Intergovernmental Conference

(1) This section applies where excepted or reserved matters relating to Northern Ireland are to be discussed at a meeting of the British-Irish Intergovernmental Conference.

(2) The First Minister and the deputy First Minister acting jointly shall ensure that there is such cross-community attendance by Ministers and junior Ministers at the meeting as is required by the Belfast Agreement.

## 55 Implementation bodies

(1) The Secretary of State may make an order about any body—
   (a) which he considers to be an implementation body; and
   (b) which is, or is to be, established on or before the appointed day.

(2) An order under this section may make any such provision as may be made (after the appointed day) by Act of the Assembly and may in particular—
   (a) confer on the body the legal capacities of a body corporate;
   (b) confer on the body any function which the Secretary of State considers necessary or expedient for the purpose for which it is, or is to be, established;
   (c) confer on a Northern Ireland department power to make grants to the body out of money appropriated by Act of the Assembly;
   (d) make provision as to the accounting and audit arrangements which are to apply in relation to the body; and
   (e) make consequential or supplementary provisions, including provisions amending or repealing any Northern Ireland legislation, or any instrument made under such legislation.

(3) In this section "implementation body" means a body for implementing, on the basis mentioned in paragraph 11 of Strand Two of the Belfast Agreement, policies agreed in the North-South Ministerial Council.

**56 Civic Forum**

(1) The First Minister and the deputy First Minister acting jointly shall make arrangements for obtaining from the Forum its views on social, economic and cultural matters.

(2) The arrangements so made shall not take effect until after they have been approved by the Assembly.

(3) The expenses of the Forum shall be defrayed as expenses of the Department of Finance and Personnel.

(4) In this section "the Forum" means the consultative Civic Forum established in pursuance of paragraph 34 of Strand One of the Belfast Agreement by the First Minister and the deputy First Minister acting jointly.

## PART VI

## FINANCIAL PROVISIONS

*Consolidated Fund*

**57 Consolidated Fund of Northern Ireland**

(1) The Consolidated Fund of Northern Ireland shall continue to exist.

(2) Sums forming part of the Fund—

(a) shall be appropriated to the public service of Northern Ireland by Act of the Assembly; and

(b) shall not be applied for any purpose for which they are not appropriated.

(3) Subsection (2) is subject to section 59 and to any provision which charges sums on the Fund and is made—

(a) by or under an Act of Parliament; or

(b) by an Act of the Assembly or other Northern Ireland legislation.

**58 Payments into the Fund**

The Secretary of State shall from time to time make payments into the Consolidated Fund of Northern Ireland out of money provided by Parliament of such amounts as he may determine.

**59 Payments out of Fund without appropriation Act**

(1) If an Act is not passed at least three working days before the end of a financial year ("year 1") authorising the issue out of the Consolidated Fund of Northern Ireland of sums for the service of the next financial year ("year 2")—

(a) the authorised officer of the Department of Finance and Personnel may, subject to any Act subsequently passed, authorise the issue of sums out of that Fund for the service of year 2; and

(b) the sums so issued shall be appropriated for such services and purposes as the officer may direct.

(2) The aggregate of the sums issued under subsection (1) for the service of year 2 shall not exceed 75 per cent of the total amount appropriated by Act for the service of year 1.

(3) If an Act is not passed before the end of July in any financial year authorising the issue out of the Consolidated Fund of Northern Ireland of sums for the service of the year—

(a) the authorised officer of the Department of Finance and Personnel may, subject to any Act subsequently passed, authorise the issue of sums out of that Fund for the service of the year; and

(b) the sums so issued shall be appropriated for such services and purposes as the officer may direct.

(4) The aggregate of the sums issued under subsection (3), and (where applicable) the sums issued under subsection (1), for the service of any financial year shall not exceed 95 per cent of the total amount appropriated by Act for the service of the preceding financial year.

(5) In this section—

"Act" means an Act of the Assembly or, in relation to any time before the appointed day, an Order in Council under Schedule 1 to the Northern Ireland Act 1974;

"authorised officer", in relation to the Department of Finance and Personnel, means the Permanent Secretary or such other officer as may be nominated by him for the purpose.

**60  Financial control, accounts and audit**

(1) In so far as such provision has not been made, an Act of the Assembly or other Northern Ireland legislation shall make provision—

(a) for proper accounts to be prepared by the Northern Ireland departments, and by other persons to whom sums are paid directly out of the Consolidated Fund of Northern Ireland, of their expenditure and receipts;

(b) for the Department of Finance and Personnel to prepare an account of payments into and out of the Fund;

(c) for the Comptroller and Auditor General for Northern Ireland to exercise, or ensure the exercise by other persons of, the functions mentioned in subsection (2);

(d) for access by persons exercising those functions to such documents as they may reasonably require;

(e) for members of the Northern Ireland Civil Service designated for the purpose to be answerable to the Assembly in respect of the expenditure and receipts of each of the Northern Ireland departments; and

(f) for the publication of accounts prepared in pursuance of paragraphs (a) and (b), and of reports on such accounts, and for the laying of such accounts and reports before the Assembly.

(2) The functions referred to in subsection (1)(c) are—

  (a) issuing credits for the payment of sums out of the Fund;

  (b) examining accounts prepared in pursuance of subsection (1)(a) and (b) (which includes determining whether sums paid out of the Fund have been paid out and applied in accordance with section 57), and certifying and reporting on them;

  (c) carrying out examinations into the economy, efficiency and effectiveness with which the Northern Ireland departments have used their resources in discharging their functions; and

  (d) carrying out examinations into the economy, efficiency and effectiveness with which other persons determined under Northern Ireland legislation to whom sums are paid directly out of the Fund have used those sums in discharging their functions.

(3) Standing orders shall make provision for establishing a committee of members of the Assembly to consider accounts, and reports on accounts, laid before the Assembly in pursuance of this section or any other enactment.

(4) Persons (other than the Comptroller and Auditor General for Northern Ireland) charged with the exercise of any function under subsection (2) or other like function conferred by Northern Ireland legislation shall not, in the exercise of that or any ancillary function, be subject to the direction or control of any Minister or Northern Ireland department or of the Assembly.

(5) Subsection (2)(b) does not apply to accounts prepared by the Comptroller and Auditor General for Northern Ireland.

*Advances*

### 61 Advances to Secretary of State

(1) The Secretary of State may advance to the Department of Finance and Personnel sums required for the purpose of—

(a) meeting a temporary excess of sums to be paid out of the Consolidated Fund of Northern Ireland over sums paid into the Fund; or

(b) providing a working balance in the Fund.

(2) The Treasury may issue to the Secretary of State out of the National Loans Fund any sum which he requires for the making of an advance under this section.

(3) The aggregate at any time outstanding in respect of the principal of sums advanced under this section shall not exceed £250 million.

(4) Sums advanced under this section shall be repaid to the Secretary of State at such times and by such methods, and interest on them shall be paid to him at such rates and at such times, as the Treasury may determine.

(5) Sums received by the Secretary of State under subsection (4) shall be paid into the National Loans Fund.

(6) Amounts required for the repayment of, or the payment of interest on, sums advanced under this section shall be charged on the Consolidated Fund of Northern Ireland.

(7) The Secretary of State may by order, with the consent of the Treasury, substitute for the amount specified in subsection (3) such increased amount as may be specified in the order.

## 62 Accounts

(1) The Secretary of State shall, for each financial year—

(a) prepare, in such form and manner as the Treasury may direct, an account of sums paid and received by him under section 61; and

(b) send the account to the Comptroller and Auditor General not later than the end of November in the following financial year.

(2) The Comptroller and Auditor General shall— (a) examine, certify and report on the account; and (b) lay copies of it and his report before each House of Parliament.

*Miscellaneous*

**63 Financial acts of the Assembly**

(1) The Assembly may not pass a vote, resolution or Act to which this subsection applies except in pursuance of a recommendation which—

(a) is made by the Minister of Finance and Personnel; and

(b) is signified to the Assembly by him or on his behalf.

(2) Subsection (1) applies to a vote, resolution or Act which—

(a) imposes or increases a charge on the Consolidated Fund of Northern Ireland;

(b) appropriates a sum out of that Fund or increases a sum to be appropriated;

(c) releases or compounds a debt owed to the Crown; or

(d) imposes or increases a tax.

(3) Standing orders shall provide that a vote, resolution or Act which—

(a) appropriates a sum out of the Consolidated Fund of Northern Ireland or increases a sum to be appropriated; or

(b) imposes or increases a tax,

shall not be passed without cross-community support.

**64 Draft budgets**

(1) The Minister of Finance and Personnel shall, before the beginning of each financial year, lay before the Assembly a draft budget, that is to say, a programme of expenditure proposals for that year which has been agreed by the Executive Committee in accordance with paragraph 20 of Strand One of the Belfast Agreement.

(2) The Assembly may, with cross-community support, approve a draft budget laid before them with or without modification.

**65 Audit**

(1) The Comptroller and Auditor General for Northern Ireland
shall be appointed by Her Majesty on the nomination of the
Assembly.

(2) A recommendation shall not be made to Her Majesty for
the removal from office of the Comptroller and Auditor
General for Northern Ireland unless—

(a) the Assembly so resolves; and

(b) the resolution is passed with the support of a number of
members of the Assembly which equals or exceeds two
thirds of the total number of seats in the Assembly.

(3) The Comptroller and Auditor General for Northern Ireland
shall not, in the exercise of any of his functions, be subject to
the direction or control of any Minister or Northern Ireland
department or of the Assembly; but this subsection does not
apply in relation to any function conferred on him of preparing accounts.

(4) The accounts of the Consolidated Fund of Northern Ireland
shall be audited by the Comptroller and Auditor General
for Northern Ireland in accordance with the Exchequer and
Audit Act Northern Ireland) 1921.

(5) Subsection (4) is subject to any provision of an Act of the
Assembly or other Northern Ireland legislation.

(6) The Assembly shall not have power under Article 4(1) of the
Audit (Northern Ireland) Order 1987 to pass at any time
a resolution which reduces the salary payable to a person
holding the office of Comptroller and Auditor General for
Northern Ireland at that time.

**66 Expenses of Northern Ireland Audit Office**

(1) Standing orders shall make provision for establishing a committee of members of the Assembly to exercise, in place of
the Department of Finance and Personnel, the functions
conferred on that Department by Article 6(2) of the Audit

(Northern Ireland) Order 1987 (expenses of Northern Ireland Audit Office).

(2) No more than one member of the committee established under subsection (3) of section 60 may be a member of the committee established under this section.

(3) The committee established under this section shall, in discharging its functions, have regard to the advice of the committee established under that subsection and of the Department of Finance and Personnel.

## 67 Provision of information to Treasury

(1) The Treasury may require the Northern Ireland Ministers and departments to provide, within such period as the Treasury may specify, such information, in such form and prepared in such manner, as the Treasury may specify.

(2) If the information is not in their possession or under their control, their duty under subsection (1) is to take all reasonable steps to comply with the requirement.

## PART VII

## HUMAN RIGHTS AND EQUAL OPPORTUNITIES

*Human rights*

## 68 The Northern Ireland Human Rights Commission

(1) There shall be a body corporate to be known as the Northern Ireland Human Rights Commission.

(2) The Commission shall consist of a Chief Commissioner and other Commissioners appointed by the Secretary of State.

(3) In making appointments under this section, the Secretary of State shall as far as practicable secure that the Commissioners, as a group, are representative of the community in Northern Ireland.

(4) Schedule 7 (which makes supplementary provision about the Commission) shall have effect.

### 69 The Commission's functions

(1) The Commission shall keep under review the adequacy and effectiveness in Northern Ireland of law and practice relating to the protection of human rights.

(2) The Commission shall, before the end of the period of two years beginning with the commencement of this section, make to the Secretary of State such recommendations as it thinks fit for improving—

(a) its effectiveness;

(b) the adequacy and effectiveness of the functions conferred on it by this Part; and

(c) the adequacy and effectiveness of the provisions of this Part relating to it.

(3) The Commission shall advise the Secretary of State and the Executive Committee of the Assembly of legislative and other measures which ought to be taken to protect human rights—

(a) as soon as reasonably practicable after receipt of a general or specific request for advice; and

(b) on such other occasions as the Commission thinks appropriate.

(4) The Commission shall advise the Assembly whether a Bill is compatible with human rights—

(a) as soon as reasonably practicable after receipt of a request for advice; and

(b) on such other occasions as the Commission thinks appropriate.

(5) The Commission may—

(a) give assistance to individuals in accordance with section 70; and

(b) bring proceedings involving law or practice relating to the protection of human rights.

(6) The Commission shall promote understanding and awareness of the importance of human rights in Northern
Ireland; and for this purpose it may undertake, commission
or provide financial or other assistance for—
(a) research; and
(b) educational activities.

(7) The Secretary of State shall request the Commission to
provide advice of the kind referred to in paragraph 4 of the
Human Rights section of the Belfast Agreement.

(8) For the purpose of exercising its functions under this section
the Commission may conduct such investigations as it considers necessary or expedient.

(9) The Commission may decide to publish its advice and the
outcome of its research and investigations.

(10) The Commission shall do all that it can to ensure the establishment of the committee referred to in paragraph 10 of
that section of that Agreement.

(11) In this section—
(a) a reference to the Assembly includes a reference to a
committee of the Assembly;
(b) "human rights" includes the Convention rights.

## 70 Assistance by Commission

(1) This section applies to—
(a) proceedings involving law or practice relating to the
protection of human rights which a person in Northern
Ireland has commenced, or wishes to commence; or
(b) proceedings in the course of which such a person relies,
or wishes to rely, on such law or practice.

(2) Where the person applies to the Northern Ireland Human
Rights Commission for assistance in relation to proceedings to which this section applies, the Commission may
grant the application on any of the following grounds—
(a) that the case raises a question of principle;

(b) that it would be unreasonable to expect the person to deal with the case without assistance because of its complexity, or because of the person's position in relation to another person involved, or for some other reason;

(c) that there are other special circumstances which make it appropriate for the Commission to provide assistance.

(3) Where the Commission grants an application under subsection (2) it may—

(a) provide, or arrange for the provision of, legal advice;

(b) arrange for the provision of legal representation;

(c) provide any other assistance which it thinks appropriate.

(4) Arrangements made by the Commission for the provision of assistance to a person may include provision for recovery of expenses from the person in certain circumstances.

## 71 Restrictions on application of rights

(1) Nothing in section 6(2)(c), 24(1)(a) or 69(5)(b) shall enable a person—

(a) to bring any proceedings in a court or tribunal on the ground that any legislation or act is incompatible with the Convention rights; or

(b) to rely on any of the Convention rights in any such proceedings,

unless he would be a victim for the purposes of article 34 of the Convention if proceedings in respect of the legislation or act were brought in the European Court of Human Rights.

(2) Subsection (1) does not apply to the Attorney General, the Attorney General for Northern Ireland, the Advocate General for Scotland or the Lord Advocate.

(3) Section 6(2)(c)—

(a) does not apply to a provision of an Act of the Assembly if the passing of the Act is, by virtue of subsection (2) of section 6 of the Human Rights Act 1998, not unlawful under subsection (1) of that section; and

    (b)  does not enable a court or tribunal to award in respect of the passing of an Act of the Assembly any damages which it could not award on finding the passing of the Act unlawful under that subsection.

(4)  Section 24(1)(a)—

    (a)  does not apply to an act which, by virtue of subsection (2) of section 6 of the Human Rights Act 1998, is not unlawful under subsection (1) of that section; and

    (b)  does not enable a court or tribunal to award in respect of an act any damages which it could not award on finding the act unlawful under that subsection.

(5)  In this section "the Convention" has the same meaning as in the Human Rights Act 1998.

## 72 Standing Advisory Commission on Human Rights: dissolution

(1)  The Standing Advisory Commission on Human Rights is hereby dissolved.

(2)  The Secretary of State may by order make such supplemental, incidental or consequential provision as appears to him to be appropriate as a result of subsection (1).

(3)  In particular, an order may include provision—

    (a)  amending an enactment;

    (b)  for the transfer of rights and liabilities;

    (c)  for payments into the Consolidated Fund or to a specified person.

*Equality of opportunity*

## 73 The Equality Commission for Northern Ireland

(1)  There shall be a body corporate to be known as the Equality Commission for Northern Ireland.

(2)  The Commission shall consist of not less than 14 nor more than 20 Commissioners appointed by the Secretary of State.

(3) The Secretary of State shall appoint—
   (a) one Commissioner as Chief Commissioner; and
   (b) at least one Commissioner as Deputy Chief Commissioner.
(4) In making appointments under this section, the Secretary of State shall as far as practicable secure that the Commissioners, as a group, are representative of the community in Northern Ireland.
(5) Schedule 8 (which makes supplementary provision about the Commission) shall have effect.

**74 The Commission's principal functions**
   (1) The functions exercisable by the bodies listed in subsection (2) shall instead be exercisable by the Equality Commission; and the bodies listed are hereby dissolved.
   (2) Those bodies are—
   (a) the Fair Employment Commission for Northern Ireland;
   (b) the Equal Opportunities Commission for Northern Ireland;
   (c) the Commission for Racial Equality for Northern Ireland;
   (d) the Northern Ireland Disability Council.
   (3) In exercising its functions the Equality Commission shall—
   (a) aim to secure an appropriate division of resources between the functions previously exercisable by each of the bodies listed in subsection (2); and
   (b) have regard to advice offered by a consultative council.
   (4) In subsection (3) "consultative council" means a group of persons selected by the Commission to advise in relation to the functions previously exercisable by one of the bodies listed in subsection (2) or in relation to the Commission's functions under Schedule 9.

(5) The Secretary of State may by order make such supplemental, incidental or consequential provision as appears to him to be appropriate as a result of subsections (1) and (2).

(6) In particular, an order may include provision—
  (a) amending an enactment;
  (b) for the transfer of rights and liabilities;
  (c) for payments into the Consolidated Fund or to a specified person.

## 75 Statutory duty on public authorities

(1) A public authority shall in carrying out its functions relating to Northern Ireland have due regard to the need to promote equality of opportunity—
  (a) between persons of different religious belief, political opinion, racial group, age, marital status or sexual orientation;
  (b) between men and women generally;
  (c) between persons with a disability and persons without; and
  (d) between persons with dependants and persons without.

(2) Without prejudice to its obligations under subsection (1), a public authority shall in carrying out its functions relating to Northern Ireland have regard to the desirability of promoting good relations between persons of different religious belief, political opinion or racial group.

(3) In this section "public authority" means—
  (a) any department, corporation or body listed in Schedule 2 to the Parliamentary Commissioner Act 1967 (departments, corporations and bodies subject to investigation) and designated for the purposes of this section by order made by the Secretary of State;
  (b) any body (other than the Equality Commission) listed in Schedule 2 to the Commissioner for Complaints (Northern Ireland) Order 1996 (bodies subject to investigation);

(c) any department or other authority listed in Schedule 2 to the Ombudsman (Northern Ireland) Order 1996 (departments and other authorities subject to investigation);

(d) any other person designated for the purposes of this section by order made by the Secretary of State.

(4) Schedule 9 (which makes provision for the enforcement of the duties under this section) shall have effect.

(5) In this section—

"disability" has the same meaning as in the Disability Discrimination Act 1995;

and "racial group" has the same meaning as in the Race Relations (Northern Ireland) Order 1997.

### 76 Discrimination by public authorities

(1) It shall be unlawful for a public authority carrying out functions relating to Northern Ireland to discriminate, or to aid or incite another person to discriminate, against a person or class of person on the ground of religious belief or political opinion.

(2) An act which contravenes this section is actionable in Northern Ireland at the instance of any person adversely affected by it; and the court may—

(a) grant damages;

(b) subject to subsection (3), grant an injunction restraining the defendant from committing, causing or permitting further contraventions of this section.

(3) Without prejudice to any other power to grant an injunction, a court may grant an injunction under subsection (2) only if satisfied that the defendant—

(a) contravened this section on the occasion complained of and on more than one previous occasion; and

(b) is likely to contravene this section again unless restrained by an injunction.

(4) This section does not apply in relation to any act or omission which is unlawful by virtue of the Fair Employment

(Northern Ireland) Act 1976, or would be unlawful but for some exception made by virtue of Part V of that Act.

(5) Subsection (1) applies to the making, confirmation or approval of subordinate legislation only if—

(a) the legislation contains a provision which discriminates against a person or class of person on the ground of religious belief or political opinion; and

(b) the provision extends only to the whole or any part of Northern Ireland.

(6) Where it is alleged that subsection (1) applies to the making, confirmation or approval of subordinate legislation, subsection (2) shall not apply but the contravention may be relied upon in legal proceedings relating to the validity of the subordinate legislation.

(7) The following are public authorities for the purposes of this section—

(a) a Minister of the Crown;

(b) any department, corporation or body listed in Schedule 2 to the Parliamentary Commissioner Act 1967 (departments, corporations and bodies subject to investigation);

(c) any body listed in Schedule 2 to the Commissioner for Complaints (Northern Ireland) Order 1996 (bodies subject to investigation);

(d) any authority (other than a Northern Ireland department) listed in Schedule 2 to the Ombudsman (Northern Ireland) Order 1996 (departments and other authorities subject to investigation);

(e) the Police Authority for Northern Ireland, the Royal Ulster Constabulary and the Royal Ulster Constabulary Reserve;

(f) the Probation Board for Northern Ireland; and

(g) the Post Office.

**77 Unlawful oaths etc**

(1) Subject to subsections (2) and (3), an authority or body to which this section applies may not require a person to take an oath or make a declaration as a condition of—

(a) being appointed to the authority or body;

(b) acting as a member of the authority or body; or

(c) serving with or being employed by the authority or body.

(2) Subsection (1) shall not prevent a person being required to take an oath, or make a declaration, which is expressly required or authorised by the law in force immediately before this section comes into force.

(3) Subsection (1) shall not prevent a person being required to make a declaration—

(a) of acceptance of office;

(b) that he is qualified to act, serve or be employed in a capacity; or

(c) that he is not disqualified from acting, serving or being employed in a capacity.

(4) This section applies to—

(a) the Assembly;

(b) the Northern Ireland Assembly Commission;

(c) any body listed in Schedule 2 to the Commissioner for Complaints (Northern Ireland) Order 1996 (bodies subject to investigation);

(d) any authority (other than a Northern Ireland department) listed in Schedule 2 to the Ombudsman (Northern Ireland) Order 1996 (departments and other authorities subject to investigation); and

(e) the Probation Board for Northern Ireland.

(5) Subsections (1) to (3) apply with the necessary modifications to a Minister and a Northern Ireland department.

(6) An act which contravenes this section is actionable in Northern Ireland at the instance of any person adversely affected by it; and the court may—

(a)  grant damages;

(b)  subject to subsection (7), grant an injunction restraining the defendant from committing, causing or permitting further contraventions of this section.

(7)  Without prejudice to any other power to grant an injunction, a court may grant an injunction under subsection (6) only if satisfied that the defendant—

(a)  contravened this section on the occasion complained of and on more than one previous occasion; and

(b)  is likely to contravene this section again unless restrained by an injunction.

(8)  In this section a reference to a declaration includes a reference to any kind of undertaking or affirmation, by whatever name.

## 78 Removal of restrictions on investigation into maladministration

(1)  The provisions mentioned in subsection (2) (which preclude an investigation when the person aggrieved has or had a remedy by way of proceedings in a court of law) shall not apply to an investigation of a complaint alleging maladministration involving—

(a)  discrimination, or aiding or inciting any person to discriminate, on the ground of religious belief or political opinion; or

(b)  a requirement in contravention of section 77 to take an oath or make a declaration (within the meaning of that section).

(2)  The provisions are—

(a)  section 5(2)(b) of the Parliamentary Commissioner Act 1967;

(b)  Article 9(3)(b) of the Commissioner for Complaints (Northern Ireland) Order 1996; and

(c)  Article 10(3)(b) of the Ombudsman (Northern Ireland) Order 1996.

# PART VIII

# MISCELLANEOUS

*Judicial scrutiny*

**79 Devolution issues**
Schedule 10 (which makes provision in relation to devolution issues) shall have effect.

**80 Legislative power to remedy ultra vires acts**
(1) The Secretary of State may by order make such provision as he considers necessary or expedient in consequence of—
  (a) any provision of an Act of the Assembly which is not, or may not be, within the legislative competence of the Assembly; or
  (b) any purported exercise by a Minister or Northern Ireland department of his or its functions which is not, or may not be, a valid exercise of those functions.
(2) An order under this section may—
  (a) make provision having retrospective effect;
  (b) make consequential or supplementary provision, including provision amending or repealing any Northern Ireland legislation, or any instrument made under such legislation;
  (c) make transitional or saving provision.

**81 Powers of courts or tribunals to vary retrospective decisions**
(1) This section applies where any court or tribunal decides that—
  (a) any provision of an Act of the Assembly is not within the legislative competence of the Assembly; or
  (b) a Minister or Northern Ireland department does not have the power to make, confirm or approve a provision

of subordinate legislation that he or it has purported to make, confirm or approve.

(2) The court or tribunal may make an order—

(a) removing or limiting any retrospective effect of the decision; or

(b) suspending the effect of the decision for any period and on any conditions to allow the defect to be corrected.

(3) In deciding whether to make an order under this section, the court or tribunal shall (among other things) have regard to the extent to which persons who are not parties to the proceedings would otherwise be adversely affected.

(4) Where a court or tribunal is considering whether to make an order under this section, it shall order notice of that fact to be given to—

(a) the Attorney General for Northern Ireland; and

(b) where the decision mentioned in subsection (1) relates to a devolution issue (within the meaning of Schedule 10), the appropriate authority,

unless the person to whom the notice would be given is a party to the proceedings.

(5) A person to whom notice is given under subsection (4) or, where such notice is given to the First Minister and the deputy First Minister, those Ministers acting jointly may take part as a party in the proceedings so far as they relate to the making of the order.

(6) Paragraphs 37 and 38 of Schedule 10 apply with necessary modifications for the purposes of subsections (4) and (5) as they apply for the purposes of that Schedule.

(7) In this section "the appropriate authority" means—

(a) in relation to proceedings in Northern Ireland, the First Minister and the deputy First Minister;

(b) in relation to proceedings in England and Wales, the Attorney General;

(c) in relation to proceedings in Scotland, the Lord Advocate and the Advocate General for Scotland.

**82  The Judicial Committee**

(1) Any decision of the Judicial Committee in proceedings under this Act shall be stated in open court and shall be binding in all legal proceedings (other than proceedings before the Committee).

(2) No member of the Judicial Committee shall sit and act as a member of the Committee in proceedings under this Act unless he holds or has held—

(a) the office of a Lord of Appeal in Ordinary; or

(b) high judicial office as defined in section 25 of the Appellate Jurisdiction Act 1876 (ignoring for this purpose section 5 of the Appellate Jurisdiction Act 1887).

(3) Her Majesty may by Order in Council—

(a) confer on the Judicial Committee in relation to proceedings under this Act such powers as Her Majesty considers necessary or expedient;

(b) apply the Judicial Committee Act 1833 in relation to proceedings under this Act with exceptions or modifications;

(c) make rules for regulating the procedure in relation to proceedings under this Act before the Judicial Committee.

(4) A statutory instrument containing an Order in Council under subsection (3)(a) or (b) shall be subject to annulment in pursuance of a resolution of either House of Parliament.

(5) In this section "proceedings under this Act" means proceedings on a question referred to the Judicial Committee under section 11 or proceedings under Schedule 10.

**83  Interpretation of Acts of the Assembly etc**

(1) This section applies where—

(a) any provision of an Act of the Assembly, or of a Bill for such an Act, could be read either—

      (i)  in such a way as to be within the legislative compe-
tence of the Assembly; or

      (ii)  in such a way as to be outside that competence; or

(b)  any provision of subordinate legislation made, confirmed or approved, or purporting to be made, confirmed or approved, by a Northern Ireland authority
could be read either—

      (i)  in such a way as not to be invalid by reason of
section 24 or, as the case may be, section 76; or

      (ii)  in such a way as to be invalid by reason of that
section.

(2)  The provision shall be read in the way which makes it within
that competence or, as the case may be, does not make
it invalid by reason of that section, and shall have effect
accordingly.

(3)  In this section "Northern Ireland authority" means a
Minister, a Northern Ireland department or a public authority (within the meaning of section 76) carrying out
functions relating to Northern Ireland.

*Power to make provision by Order in Council*

**84 Provision with respect to certain matters relating to Northern
Ireland**

(1)  Her Majesty may by Order in Council make provision with
respect to elections (but not the franchise) and boundaries
in respect of district councils in Northern Ireland.

(2)  Her Majesty may by Order in Council make such amendments of the law of any part of the United Kingdom as
appear to Her Majesty to be necessary or expedient in consequence of any provision made by or under—

(a)  Northern Ireland legislation; or

(b)  any Act of Parliament passed before this Act in so far as
the provision is part of the law of Northern Ireland.

(3) An Order in Council under subsection (1) or (2) may contain such consequential and supplemental provisions as appear to Her Majesty to be necessary or expedient.

(4) No recommendation shall be made to Her Majesty to make an Order in Council under this section unless a draft of the Order has been laid before and approved by resolution of each House of Parliament.

**85  Provision dealing with certain reserved matters**

(1) Her Majesty may by Order in Council make provision dealing with any matter falling within a description specified in any of paragraphs 9 to 17 of Schedule 3 (a "relevant matter"), including—

    (a) provision having retrospective effect;

    (b) provision for the delegation of functions;

    (c) provision amending or repealing any provision made by or under any Act of Parliament or Northern Ireland legislation.

(2) An Order in Council under this section may—

    (a) make provision ancillary to provisions (whether in the Order or previously enacted) which deal with any relevant matter;

    (b) make such consequential, incidental, supplemental, or transitional provision as appears to Her Majesty to be necessary or expedient.

(3) No recommendation shall be made to Her Majesty to make an Order in Council under this section unless a draft of the Order has been laid before and approved by resolution of each House of Parliament.

(4) No draft may be laid under subsection (3) unless—

    (a) the Secretary of State has laid before Parliament a document which contains a draft of the proposed Order;

    (b) the Secretary of State has referred the document to the Assembly for its consideration; and

(c) the period of 60 days beginning with the day on which the document was laid before Parliament has ended.

(5) The Assembly may report to the Secretary of State the views expressed in the Assembly on the proposed Order and shall do so if the Secretary of State so requests.

(6) The draft laid under subsection (3) must be accompanied—

(a) if representations have been made during the period mentioned in subsection (4), by a statement containing a summary of the representations;

(b) if a report has been made to the Secretary of State under subsection (5) during that period, by a copy of the report; and

(c) if, as a result of any representations or report so made, the proposed Order has been changed, by a statement containing details of the changes.

(7) Subsection (3) does not apply to an Order in Council which declares that it has been made to appear to Her Majesty that by reason of urgency the Order requires to be made without a draft having been approved as mentioned in that subsection.

(8) Where an Order in Council contains a declaration such as is mentioned in subsection (7)—

(a) the Order shall be laid before Parliament after being made; and

(b) if at the end of the period of 40 days after the date on which the Order is made it has not been approved by resolution of each House, it shall then cease to have effect (but without prejudice to anything previously done under it or to the making of a new Order).

(9) In reckoning the periods mentioned in subsections (4) and (8), no account shall be taken of any time during which Parliament is dissolved or prorogued or during which both Houses are adjourned for more than four days.

(10) References to Acts of the Assembly in any enactment or instrument shall, so far as the context permits, be deemed to include references to Orders in Council under this section.

(11) Orders in Council under this section may be omitted from any annual edition of statutory instruments made by virtue of section 8 of the Statutory Instruments Act 1946.

(12) In this section "representations" means representations about a proposed Order in Council under this section made to the Secretary of State and includes—

(a) any relevant resolution of either House of Parliament or of the Assembly; and

(b) any relevant report or resolution of any committee of either House of Parliament or of the Assembly.

## 86 Provision for purposes consequential on Act etc

(1) Her Majesty may by Order in Council make such provision, including provision amending the law of any part of the United Kingdom, as appears to Her Majesty to be necessary or expedient in consequence of, or for giving full effect to, this Act or any Order under section 4 or 6.

(2) Orders under subsection (1) may make provision for transferring to a United Kingdom authority, with effect from any date specified in the Order—

(a) any functions which immediately before that date are exercisable by a Northern Ireland authority and appear to Her Majesty to be concerned with a matter which is an excepted or reserved matter (whether by virtue of an Order under section 4 or otherwise);

(b) any functions which immediately before that date are exercisable by a Northern Ireland authority and appear to Her Majesty not to be exercisable in or as regards Northern Ireland by virtue of an Order under section 6.

(3) Orders under subsection (1) may make provision for transferring to a Northern Ireland authority, with effect from any date specified in the Order—

(a) any functions which immediately before that date are exercisable by a United Kingdom authority and appear to Her Majesty to be concerned with a matter which is a transferred matter (whether by virtue of an Order under section 4 or otherwise);

(b) any functions which immediately before that date are exercisable by a United Kingdom authority and appear to Her Majesty to be exercisable in or as regards Northern Ireland by virtue of an Order under section 6.

(4) An Order under subsection (1) may make provision, to such extent as may appear to Her Majesty to be necessary or expedient in consequence of, or for giving full effect to, this Act or any Order under section 4 or 6—

(a) for transferring or apportioning any property, rights or liabilities;

(b) for substituting any authority for any other authority in any charter, contract or other document or in any legal proceedings;

(c) for any other transitional or consequential matter.

(5) Where such provision as is mentioned in subsection (3)(b) has been made by Order in Council under subsection (1), Her Majesty may, if it appears to Her necessary or expedient to do so, by Order in Council—

(a) provide that the functions transferred to the Northern Ireland authority shall be exercisable by a United Kingdom authority, either alone or concurrently with the Northern Ireland authority; and

(b) make such provision as is mentioned in subsection (4)(a) to (c).

(6) No recommendation shall be made to Her Majesty to make an Order under this section unless a draft of it has been laid before and approved by resolution of each House of Parliament.

(7) In this section "Northern Ireland authority" means—
   (a) a Minister or a Northern Ireland department;
   (b) the Comptroller and Auditor General for Northern Ireland; or
   (c) any other public body or holder of public office in Northern Ireland.
(8) In this section "United Kingdom authority" means—
   (a) the Privy Council;
   (b) any Minister of the Crown;
   (c) the Defence Council;
   (d) the Commissioners of Inland Revenue;
   (e) the Commissioners of Customs and Excise;
   (f) the Comptroller and Auditor General; or
   (g) any other public body or holder of public office in the United Kingdom.

*Social security, child support and pensions*

**87 Consultation and co-ordination**
(1) The Secretary of State and the Northern Ireland Minister having responsibility for social security ("the Northern Ireland Minister") shall from time to time consult one another with a view to securing that, to the extent agreed between them, the legislation to which this section applies provides single systems of social security, child support and pensions for the United Kingdom.
(2) Without prejudice to section 28, the Secretary of State with the consent of the Treasury, and the Northern Ireland Minister with the consent of the Department of Finance and Personnel, may make—
   (a) arrangements for co-ordinating the operation of the legislation to which this section applies with a view to securing that, to the extent allowed for in the arrangements, it provides single systems of social security, child support and pensions for the United Kingdom; and

(b) reciprocal arrangements for co-ordinating the operation of so much of the legislation as operates differently in relation to Great Britain and in relation to Northern Ireland.

(3) Such arrangements as are mentioned in subsection (2)(a) or (b) may include provision for making any necessary financial adjustments, other than adjustments between the National Insurance Fund and the Northern Ireland National Insurance Fund.

(4) The Secretary of State may make regulations for giving effect to arrangements under subsection (2); and any such regulations may for the purposes of the arrangements provide—

(a) for adapting legislation (including subordinate legislation) for the time being in force in Great Britain;

(b) without prejudice to paragraph (a) above, for securing that acts, omissions and events having any effect for the purposes of the enactments in force in Northern Ireland have a corresponding effect in relation to Great Britain (but not so as to confer any double benefit); and

(c) for determining, in cases where rights accrue both in relation to Great Britain and in relation to Northern Ireland, which of those rights shall be available to the person concerned.

(5) The Northern Ireland department having responsibility for social security may make regulations for giving effect to arrangements under subsection (2); and any such regulations may for the purposes of the arrangements provide—

(a) for adapting legislation (including subordinate legislation) for the time being in force in Northern Ireland;

(b) without prejudice to paragraph (a) above, for securing that acts, omissions and events having any effect for the purposes of the enactments in force in Great Britain have a corresponding effect in relation to Northern Ireland (but not so as to confer any double benefit); and

(c) for determining, in cases where rights accrue both in relation to Northern Ireland and in relation to Great Britain, which of those rights shall be available to the person concerned.

(6) This section applies to—

(a) the Social Security Contributions and Benefits Act 1992 and the Social Security Contributions and Benefits (Northern Ireland) Act 1992;

(b) the Social Security Administration Act 1992 and the Social Security Administration (Northern Ireland) Act 1992;

(c) the Child Support Act 1991 and the Child Support (Northern Ireland) Order 1991;

(d) the Social Security Pensions Act 1975 and the Social Security Pensions (Northern Ireland) Order 1975;

(e) the Social Security Act 1989 and the Social Security (Northern Ireland) Orer 1989;

(f) the Disability (Grants) Act 1993;

(g) the Pension Schemes Act 1993 and the Pensions Schemes (Northern Ireland) Act 1993;

(h) the Social Security (Incapacity for Work) Act 1994 and the Social Security (Incapacity for Work) (Northern Ireland) Order 1994;

(i) the Jobseekers Act 1995 and the Jobseekers (Northern Ireland) Order 1995

(j) he Pensions Act 1995 and the Pensions (Northern Ireland) Order 1995;

(k) the Child Support Act 1995 and the Child Support (Northern Ireland) Order 1995;

(l) the Social Security (Recovery of Benefits) Act 1997 and the Social Security (Recovery of Benefits) (Northern Ireland) Order 1997;

(m) the Social Security Act 1998 and the Social Security (Northern Ireland) Order 1998.

(7) Her Majesty may by Order in Council make any modifications of subsection (6) which She considers necessary or expedient.

(8) The following provisions (which are superseded by this section and section 88) shall cease to have effect—

   (a) sections 177 and 178 of the Social Security Administration Act 1992 (co-ordination and reciprocity with Northern Ireland);

   (b) sections 153 and 154 of the Social Security Administration (Northern Ireland) Act 1992 (co-ordination and reciprocity with Great Britain);

   (c) section 56(2) to (4) of the Child Support Act 1991 (co-ordination with Northern Ireland);

   (d) Article 49(2) and (3) of the Child Support (Northern Ireland) Order 1991 (co-ordination with Great Britain);

   (e) section 29(2) to (4) of the Child Support Act 1995 (co-ordination with Northern Ireland);

   (f) Article 20 of the Child Support (Northern Ireland) Order 1995 (co-ordination with Great Britain).

(9) Section 189 of the Social Security Administration Act 1992 (regulations and orders: general) shall apply in relation to the power conferred by subsection (4) as it applied in relation to the power conferred by section 177(4) of that Act.

(10) The power conferred by subsection (5) shall be construed as if it had been conferred by an Act of the Assembly; and section 165 of the Social Security Administration (Northern Ireland) Act 1992 (regulations and orders: general) shall apply in relation to that power as it applied in relation to the power conferred by section 153(3) of that Act.

(11) A statutory instrument containing an Order in Council under subsection (7) shall be subject to annulment in pursuance of a resolution of either House of Parliament.

**88 The Joint Authority**

(1) The Joint Authority continued in being by section 177(2) of the Social Security Administration Act 1992—

(a) shall consist of the Secretary of State, the Northern Ireland Minister having responsibility for social security and the Chancellor of the Exchequer; and

(b) shall continue in being by the name of the Social Security, Child Support and Pensions Joint Authority for the purposes of the legislation to which section 87 applies.

(2) The responsibility of the Joint Authority shall include that of giving effect to arrangements under section 87(2), with power to discharge such functions as may be provided under the arrangements.

(3) The Joint Authority shall also have power to make any necessary financial adjustments, including adjustments between the National Insurance Fund and the Northern Ireland National Insurance Fund.

(4) The Joint Authority shall continue—

(a) to be a body corporate; and

(b) to have an official seal which shall be officially and judicially noticed;

and the seal of the Authority may be authenticated by any member of, or the secretary to, the Authority, or by any person authorised by the Authority to act on behalf of the secretary.

(5) Any member of the Joint Authority shall be entitled, subject to and in accordance with any rules laid down by the Authority, to appoint a deputy to act for him at meetings of the Authority.

(6) The Documentary Evidence Act 1868 shall apply to the Joint Authority as if the Authority were included in the first column of the Schedule to that Act and—

(a) as if any member or the secretary, or any person authorised to act on behalf of the secretary, of the Authority were mentioned in the second column of that Schedule; and

(b) as if the regulations referred to in that Act included any document issued by the Authority.

## 89 Industrial Injuries Advisory Council

(1) For subsection (1) of section 149 of the Social Security Administration (Northern Ireland) Act 1992 (Social Security Advisory Committee) substitute—

"(1) The Department may from time to time—

(a) refer to the Social Security Advisory Committee for consideration and advice such questions relating to the operation of any of the relevant enactments as the Department thinks fit (including questions as to the advisability of amending any of them);

(b) refer to the Industrial Injuries Advisory Council for consideration and advice such questions as the Department thinks fit relating to industrial injuries benefit or its administration."

(2) After subsection (2) of that section insert—

"(2A) Subject—

(a) to subsection (3) below; and

(b) to section 150 below,

where the Department proposes to make regulations relating only to industrial injuries benefit or its administration, it shall refer the proposals, in the form of draft regulations or otherwise, to the Industrial Injuries Advisory Council for consideration and advice."

(3) At the end of subsection (3) of that section insert "; and subsection (2A) above does not apply to the regulations specified in Schedule 5A to this Act".

(4) After that subsection insert—

"(3A) The Industrial Injuries Advisory Council may also give advice to the Department on any other matter relating to industrial injuries benefit or its administration."

(5) In subsections (1), (2) and (5) of section 150 of that Act (cases in which consultation not required), after "the Committee", in each place, insert "or the Council".

(6) In subsection (3) of that section—

(a) after "the Committee", in the first place, insert "or the Council"; and

(b) after "the Committee has made its report" insert "or, as the case may be, the Council has given its advice".

(7) In subsection (6) of that section, after the definition of "the Committee" insert—

""the Council" means the Industrial Injuries Advisory Council;".

(8) After Schedule 5 to that Act insert—

"SCHEDULE 5A
REGULATIONS NOT REQUIRING PRIOR SUBMISSION
TO INDUSTRIAL INJURIES ADVISORY COUNCIL

1 Regulations under section 120(1)(b) of the Contributions and Benefits Act.

2 Regulations which state that they contain only provisions in consequence of an order under section 129 or 132 above.

3 Regulations made within a period of 6 months from the passing of any Act passed after this Act and directed to be construed as one with this Act, where—

(a) the regulations state that they contain only regulations to make provision consequential on the passing of the Act; and

(b) the Act does not exclude this paragraph in respect of the regulations;

and in this paragraph "Act" includes an Act of the Northern Ireland Assembly.

4  Regulations which state that they contain only regulations making with respect to industrial injuries benefit or its administration the same or substantially the same provision as has been, or is to be, made with respect to other benefit as defined in section 121(1) of the Contributions and Benefits Act or its administration.

5  Regulations which state that the only provision with respect to industrial injuries benefit or its administration that is made by the regulations is the same or substantially the same as provision made by the instrument with respect to other benefit as defined in section 121(1) of the Contributions and Benefits Act or its administration.

6  Regulations made for the purpose only of consolidating other regulations revoked by them.

7  Regulations making only provision corresponding to provision contained in regulations made by the Secretary of State or the Lord Chancellor in relation to Great Britain."

(9)  In section 192(5) of the Social Security Administration Act 1992, after the entry relating to section 170 (with Schedule 5) insert— "section 171 (with Schedule 6);".

*Discrimination: certificates by Secretary of State*

## 90  Effect of certificates

(1)  This section applies where in any proceedings—

(a)  a person claims that an act discriminated against him in contravention of section 24 or 76; and

(b)  the person against whom the claim is made proposes to rely on a certificate purporting to be signed by or on behalf of the Secretary of State and certifying—

(i) that an act specified in the certificate was done for the purpose of safeguarding national security or protecting public safety or public order; and

(ii) that the doing of the act was justified by that purpose.

(2) The claimant may, in accordance with rules made by the Lord Chancellor, appeal against the certificate to the Tribunal, that is to say, the tribunal established under section 91.

(3) If on an appeal under subsection (2) the Tribunal determines—

(a) that the act specified in the certificate was done for the certified purpose; and

(b) that the doing of the act was justified by that purpose,

the Tribunal shall uphold the certificate; in any other case, the Tribunal shall quash the certificate.

(4) If—

(a) the claimant does not appeal against the certificate; or

(b) the certificate is upheld on appeal,

the certificate shall be conclusive evidence of the matters certified by it.

(5) In this section "act" does not include the making, confirmation or approval of a provision of subordinate legislation.

## 91 The Tribunal

(1) There shall be a tribunal in relation to which Schedule 11 shall have effect.

(2) The Lord Chancellor may make rules—

(a) for regulating the exercise of rights of appeal to the Tribunal;

(b) for prescribing the practice and procedure to be followed on or in connection with appeals to the Tribunal, including the mode and burden of proof and admissibility of evidence on such appeals; and

(c) for other matters preliminary or incidental to or arising out of such appeals.

(3) Rules under this section may provide that—
   (a) a party to any proceedings before the Tribunal on an appeal; and
   (b) where the Secretary of State is not party to any such proceedings,

the Secretary of State, has the right to be legally represented in the proceedings, subject to any power conferred on the Tribunal by such rules.

(4) Rules under this section may, in particular—
   (a) make provision enabling proceedings before the Tribunal to take place without a party being given full particulars of the reasons for the issue of the certificate which is the subject of the appeal;
   (b) make provision enabling the Tribunal to hold proceedings in the absence of any person, including a party and any legal representative appointed by a party;
   (c) make provision about the functions in proceedings before the Tribunal of persons appointed under subsection (7); and
   (d) make provision enabling the Tribunal to give a party a summary of any evidence taken in his absence.

(5) Rules under this section may also include provision—
   (a) enabling any functions of the Tribunal which relate to matters preliminary or incidental to an appeal to be performed by a single member of the Tribunal; or
   (b) conferring on the Tribunal such ancillary powers as the Lord Chancellor thinks necessary for the purposes of the exercise of its functions.

(6) In making rules under this section, the Lord Chancellor shall have regard, in particular, to—
   (a) the need to secure that certificates which are the subject of appeals are properly reviewed; and
   (b) the need to secure that information is not disclosed contrary to the public interest.

(7) The Attorney General for Northern Ireland may appoint a person to represent the interests of a party to proceedings before the Tribunal in any proceedings from which he and any legal representative of his are excluded.

(8) A person appointed under subsection (7)—
  (a) shall be a member of the Bar of Northern Ireland;
  (b) shall not be responsible to the party whose interests he represents.

(9) In this section and section 92 "party", in relation to proceedings on appeal, means the appellant or the person proposing to rely on the certificate which is the subject of the appeal.

## 92 Appeals from the Tribunal

(1) Where the Tribunal has determined an appeal under section 90—
  (a) any party to the appeal; or
  (b) where the Secretary of State was not a party to the appeal, the Secretary of State,

  may bring a further appeal to the Court of Appeal in Northern Ireland on any question of law material to the Tribunal's determination.

(2) An appeal under this section may be brought only with the leave of the Tribunal or, if such leave is refused, with the leave of the Court of Appeal in Northern Ireland.

(3) The Lord Chancellor may make rules regulating, and prescribing the procedure to be followed on, applications to the Tribunal for leave to appeal under this section.

(4) Rules under this section may include provision enabling an application for leave to appeal to be heard by a single member of the Tribunal.

*Miscellaneous*

## 93 Parliament Buildings etc

(1) Subject to subsection (2), property in relation to which section 31(4) of the Northern Ireland Constitution Act 1973

had effect (property held in trust for Parliament of Northern Ireland etc.) shall on and after the commencement of this section be applied for the purposes of the Assembly or such other purposes as the Department of the Environment ("the Department") may determine.

(2) The Secretary of State may require the Department to make available to him in any premises comprised in the property mentioned in subsection (1) (other than the Parliament Buildings at Stormont) such accommodation and facilities as he may specify.

(3) The Secretary of State shall in consideration of the use of any such accommodation and facilities make to the Department such payments out of money provided by Parliament as he and the Department may agree.

(4) In so far as any of the property mentioned in subsection (1) was not immediately before the commencement of this section vested in the Department it shall vest in the Department at that commencement; and subsections (1) and (2) shall have effect notwithstanding anything in any deed or other instrument relating to the property to which those subsections apply.

## 94 Land purchase annuities etc

(1) Subject to subsection (2), land purchase annuities shall be collected by the Department of Agriculture and paid into the Consolidated Fund of Northern Ireland.

(2) A land purchase annuity may be extinguished by, or redeemed with the agreement of, the Department of Agriculture.

(3) The Irish Land Purchase Fund shall be wound up and the money standing to its credit shall be paid into the Consolidated Fund of the United Kingdom.

(4) In this section "land purchase annuities" means annuities for the repayment of advances made under any enactment relating to land purchase in Northern Ireland.

## PART IX

## SUPPLEMENTAL

**95  Savings for existing laws**
(1) Except so far as otherwise provided by or under this Act, nothing in this Act shall affect the operation in or in relation to Northern Ireland of any law in force on the appointed day or passed or made before that day, including in particular Orders in Council made under—

(a) section 69 of the Government of Ireland Act 1920;

(b) section 1(3) of the Northern Ireland (Temporary Provisions) Act 1972;

(c) section 38 or 39 of the Northern Ireland Constitution Act 1973; or

(d) Schedule 1 to the Northern Ireland Act 1974.

(2) The laws continued by section 61 of the Government of Ireland Act 1920 shall continue to have effect to the extent provided for by that section (but with any modification necessary for adapting them to this Act).

(3) No law made by the Assembly shall have effect so as to prejudice or diminish the rights or privileges of any pensioned officer of a local authority under the provisions of the Local Government (Ireland) Acts 1898 to 1919.

(4) No provision of this Act shall—

(a) affect the operation before the coming into force of that provision of any Northern Ireland legislation; or

(b) render unlawful anything required or authorised to be done by any Act of Parliament, whenever passed.

(5) Schedule 12 (which provides for the construction of certain references in existing laws) shall have effect, but subject to any provision made by or under this Act or by any Act of the Assembly.

## 96 Orders and regulations

(1) An order under section 17(4), 25, 26, 27, 31(3) or (6), 38(6), 72(2) or 74(5) shall be made by statutory instrument which shall be subject to annulment in pursuance of a resolution of either House of Parliament.

(2) An order under section 34(4), 35(1), 55, 75(3)(a) or (d) or 80 or Schedule 1—

(a) shall be made by statutory instrument; and

(b) shall not be made unless a draft has been laid before and approved by resolution of each House of Parliament.

(3) Regulations under section 87(4) shall be made by statutory instrument which shall be subject to annulment in pursuance of a resolution of the House of Commons.

(4) An order under section 61(7)—

(a) shall be made by statutory instrument; and

(b) shall not be made unless a draft has been laid before and approved by resolution of the House of Commons.

(5) Regulations under section 87(5) shall be subject to negative resolution (within the meaning given by section 41(6) of the Interpretation Act Northern Ireland) 1954).

(6) Rules under section 91 or 92—

(a) shall be made by statutory instrument; and

(b) shall not be made unless a draft has been laid before and approved by resolution of each House of Parliament.

## 97 Financial provision

Any expenditure of the Secretary of State in consequence of this Act shall be paid out of money provided by Parliament.

## 98 Interpretation

(1) In this Act—

"the appointed day" has the meaning given by section 3(1);

"the Assembly" has the meaning given by section 4(5);

"the Belfast Agreement" means the agreement reached at multi-party talks on Northern Ireland set out in Command Paper 3883;

"Community law" means—

(a) all rights, powers, liabilities, obligations and restrictions created or arising by or under the Community Treaties; and

(b) all remedies and procedures provided for by or under those Treaties;

"the Convention rights" has the same meaning as in the Human Rights Act 1998;

"cross-community support" has the meaning given by section 4(5);

"designated Nationalist" and "designated Unionist" have the meanings given by section 4(5);

"document" includes anything in which information is recorded in any form;

"enactment" includes any provision of this Act and any provision of, or of any instrument made under, Northern Ireland legislation;

"excepted matter" has the meaning given by section 4(1);

"financial year", unless the context otherwise requires, means a year ending with 31st March;

"functions" includes powers and duties, and "confer", in relation to functions, includes impose;

"international obligations" means any international obligations of the United Kingdom other than obligations to observe and implement Community law or the Convention rights;

"Judicial Committee" means the Judicial Committee of the Privy Council;

"Minister", unless the context otherwise requires, has the meaning given by section 7(3);

"Minister of the Crown" includes the Treasury; "modify", in relation to an enactment, includes amend or repeal;

"Northern Ireland" includes so much of the internal waters and territorial sea of the United Kingdom as are adjacent to Northern Ireland;

"Northern Ireland legislation" means—

(a) Acts of the Parliament of Ireland;
(b) Acts of the Parliament of Northern Ireland;
(c) Orders in Council under section 1(3) of the Northern Ireland (Temporary Provisions) Act 1972;
(d) Measures of the Northern Ireland Assembly established under section 1 of the Northern Ireland Assembly Act 1973;
(e) Orders in Council under Schedule 1 to the Northern Ireland Act 1974;
(f) Acts of the Assembly; and
(g) Orders in Council under section 85;

"the Northern Ireland zone" means the sea within British fishery limits which is adjacent to Northern Ireland;
"the pledge of office" has the meaning given by section 16(10);
"political opinion" and "religious belief" shall be construed in accordance with section 57(2) and (3) of the Fair Employment (Northern Ireland) Act 1976;
"proceedings", in relation to the Assembly, includes proceedings of any committee;
"property" includes rights and interests of any description;
"reserved matter" has the meaning given by section 4(1);
"subordinate legislation" has the same meaning as in the Interpretation Act 1978 and also includes an instrument made under Northern Ireland legislation;
"transferred matter" has the meaning given by section 4(1).

(2) For the purposes of this Act, a provision of any enactment, Bill or subordinate legislation deals with the matter, or each of the matters, which it affects otherwise than incidentally.

(3) For the purposes of this Act, a provision of any Act or Bill which modifies a provision of—

(a) the Agricultural Wages (Regulation) (Northern Ireland) Order 1977;

(b) the Employment Rights (Northern Ireland) Order 1996; or

(c) the Industrial Tribunals (Northern Ireland) Order 1996, which is amended or applied by or under the National Minimum Wage Act 1998 shall not be treated as dealing with a matter falling within the subject-matter of that Act if the modification affects the national minimum wage and other employment matters in the same way.

(4) For the purposes of this Act, a provision of an Act of the Assembly or of subordinate legislation discriminates against any person or class of persons if it treats that person or that class less favourably in any circumstances than other persons are treated in those circumstances by the law for the time being in force in Northern Ireland.

(5) For those purposes a person discriminates against another person or a class of persons if he treats that other person or that class less favourably in any circumstances than he treats or would treat other persons in those circumstances.

(6) No provision of an Act of the Assembly or of subordinate legislation, and no making, confirmation or approval of a provision of subordinate legislation, shall be treated for the purposes of this Act as discriminating if the provision has the effect of safeguarding national security or protecting public safety or public order.

(7) No other act done by any person shall be treated for the purposes of this Act as discriminating if—

(a) the act is done for the purpose of safeguarding national security or protecting public safety or public order; and

(b) the doing of the act is justified by that purpose.

(8) Her Majesty may by Order in Council determine, or make provision for determining, for such purposes of this Act as may be specified, any boundary between—

(a) the waters or parts of the sea which are to be treated as adjacent to Northern Ireland; and

(b) those which are not,

and may make different determinations or provisions for different purposes.

(9) No recommendation shall be made to Her Majesty to make an Order in Council under subsection (8) unless a draft of the Order has been laid before and approved by resolution of each House of Parliament.

## 99 Minor and consequential amendments

The enactments mentioned in Schedule 13 shall have effect subject to the amendments there specified, being minor amendments and amendments consequential on the provisions of this Act.

## 100 Transitional provisions, savings and repeals

(1) The transitional provisions and savings contained in Schedule 14 shall have effect; but nothing in this subsection shall be taken as prejudicing the operation of sections 16 and 17 of the Interpretation Act 1978 (which relate to the effect of repeals).

(2) The enactments specified in Schedule 15, which include some that are spent, are hereby repealed to the extent specified in the third column of that Schedule.

## 101 Short title and commencement

(1) This Act may be cited as the Northern Ireland Act 1998.

(2) The following provisions shall come into force on the day on which this Act is passed—

(a) sections 3, 55, 86, 93, 96 and 98;

(b) paragraph 20 of Schedule 13 and section 99 so far as relating to that paragraph;

(c) in Schedule 15, the repeal of section 31(4) to (6) of the Northern Ireland Constitution Act 1973 and section 100(2) so far as relating to that repeal; and

(d) this section.

(3) The remaining provisions of this Act (except Parts II and III) shall come into force on such day as the Secretary of State may by order made by statutory instrument appoint; and different days may be appointed for different purposes.

## SCHEDULES

## SCHEDULE 1 Section 1(1)

### POLLS FOR THE PURPOSES OF SECTION 1

1  The Secretary of State may by order direct the holding of a poll for the purposes of section 1 on a date specified in the order.

2  Subject to paragraph 3, the Secretary of State shall exercise the power under paragraph 1 if at any time it appears likely to him that a majority of those voting would express a wish that Northern Ireland should cease to be part of the United Kingdom and form part of a united Ireland.

3  The Secretary of State shall not make an order under paragraph 1 earlier than seven years after the holding of a previous poll under this Schedule.

4 (1) An order under this Schedule directing the holding of a poll shall specify—

(a)  the persons entitled to vote; and

(b)  the question or questions to be asked.

(2) An order—

(a)  may include any other provision about the poll which the Secretary of State thinks expedient (including the creation of criminal offences); and

(b)  may apply (with or without modification) any provision of, or made under, any enactment.

**SCHEDULE 2** Section 4(1)

## EXCEPTED MATTERS

1 The Crown, including the succession to the Crown and a regency, but not—

(a) functions of the First Minister and deputy First Minister, the Northern Ireland Ministers or the Northern Ireland departments, or functions in relation to Northern Ireland of any Minister of the Crown;

(b) property belonging to Her Majesty in right of the Crown or belonging to a government department or held in trust for Her Majesty for the purposes of a government department (other than property used for the purposes of the armed forces of the Crown or the Ministry of Defence Police);

(c) the foreshore or the sea bed or subsoil or their natural resources so far as vested in Her Majesty in right of the Crown.

2 The Parliament of the United Kingdom; parliamentary elections, including the franchise; disqualifications for membership of that Parliament.

3 International relations, including relations with territories outside the United Kingdom, the European Communities (and their institutions) and other international organisations, and international development assistance and cooperation, but not—

(a) the surrender of fugitive offenders between Northern Ireland and the Republic of Ireland;

(b) the exercise of legislative powers so far as required for giving effect to any agreement or arrangement entered into—

(i) by a Minister or junior Minister participating, by reason of a nomination under section 52, in a meeting of the North-South Ministerial Council or the British-Irish Council; or

(ii) by, or in relation to the activities of, any body established for implementing, on the basis mentioned in paragraph 11

of Strand Two of the Belfast Agreement, policies agreed
in the North-South Ministerial Council;

(c) observing and implementing international obligations, obligations under the Human Rights Convention and obligations
under Community law.

In this paragraph "the Human Rights Convention" means the
following as they have effect for the time being in relation to
the United Kingdom—

(a) the Convention for the Protection of Human Rights and
Fundamental Freedoms, agreed by the Council of Europe
at Rome on 4th November 1950; and

(b) any Protocols to that Convention which have been ratified by the United Kingdom.

4 The defence of the realm; trading with the enemy; the armed
forces of the Crown but not any matter within paragraph 10 of
Schedule 3; war pensions; the Ministry of Defence Police.

5 Control of nuclear, biological and chemical weapons and other
weapons of mass destruction.

6 Dignities and titles of honour.

7 Treason but not powers of arrest or criminal procedure.

8 Nationality; immigration, including asylum and the status
and capacity of persons in the United Kingdom who are not
British citizens; free movement of persons within the European
Economic Area; issue of travel documents.

9 The following matters—

(a) taxes or duties under any law applying to the United Kingdom
as a whole;

(b) stamp duty levied in Northern Ireland before the appointed
day; and

(c) taxes or duties substantially of the same character as those
mentioned in sub-paragraph (a) or (b).

10 The following matters—

(a) national insurance contributions;

(b) the control and management of the Northern Ireland National Insurance Fund and payments into and out of that Fund;

(c) reductions in and deductions from national insurance contributions;

(d) national insurance rebates;

(e) payments out of public money to money purchase pension schemes;

(f) contributions equivalent premiums;

(g) rights to return to the state pension scheme.

Sub-paragraph (a) includes the determination, payment, collection and return of national insurance contributions and matters incidental to those matters.

Sub-paragraph (b) does not include payments out of the Northern Ireland National Insurance Fund which relate to—

(i) the benefits mentioned in section 143(1) of the Social Security Administration (Northern Ireland) Act 1992, or benefits substantially of the same character as those benefits; or

(ii) administrative expenses incurred in connection with matters not falling within sub-paragraphs (a) to (g).

Sub-paragraphs (b) and (e) do not include payments out of or into the Northern Ireland National Insurance Fund under—

(i) section 172(1)(b), (2)(a) or (7)(c) of the Pension Schemes (Northern Ireland) Act 1993; or

(ii) Article 202, 227, 234 or 252 of the Employment Rights (Northern Ireland) Order 1996.

In this paragraph "contributions equivalent premium" has the meaning given by section 51(2) of the Pension Schemes (Northern Ireland) Act 1993.

11 The appointment and removal of judges of the Supreme Court of Judicature of Northern Ireland, holders of offices listed in column 1 of Schedule 3 to the Judicature (Northern Ireland) Act 1978, county court judges, recorders, resident magistrates, justices of the peace, members of juvenile court panels, coroners, the

Chief and other Social Security Commissioners for Northern
Ireland, the Chief and other Child Support Commissioners for
Northern Ireland and the President and other members of the
Lands Tribunal for Northern Ireland.

12  Elections, including the franchise, in respect of the Northern
    Ireland Assembly, the European Parliament and district councils.

13  The registration of political parties.

14  Coinage, legal tender and bank notes

15  The National Savings Bank.

16  The subject-matter of the Protection of Trading Interests
    Act 1980.

17  National security (including the Security Service, the Secret
    Intelligence Service and the Government Communications
    Headquarters); special powers and other provisions for dealing
    with terrorism or subversion; the subject-matter of—

    (a)  the Official Secrets Acts 1911 and 1920;

    (b)  the Interception of Communications Act 1985, except so far
         as relating to the prevention or detection of serious crime
         (within the meaning of that Act); and

    (c)  the Official Secrets Act 1989, except so far as relating to any
         information, document or other article protected against
         disclosure by section 4(2) (crime) and not by any other pro-
         vision of sections 1 to 4.

18  Nuclear energy and nuclear installations, including nuclear safety,
    security and safeguards, and liability for nuclear occurrences, but
    not the subject-matter of—

    (a)  section 3(5) to (7) of the Environmental Protection Act 1990
         (emission limits); or

    (b)  the Radioactive Substances Act 1993.

19  Regulation of sea fishing outside the Northern Ireland zone (ex-
    cept in relation to Northern Ireland fishing boats). In this para-
    graph "Northern Ireland fishing boat" means a fishing vessel
    which is registered in the register maintained under section 8 of
    the Merchant Shipping Act 1995 and whose entry in the register

specifies a port in Northern Ireland as the port to which the vessel is to be treated as belonging.

20  Regulation of activities in outer space.

21  Any matter with which a provision of the Northern Ireland Constitution Act 1973 solely or mainly deals.

22  Any matter with which a provision of this Act falling within the following sub-paragraphs solely or mainly deals—

(a)  Parts I and II;

(b)  Part III except sections 19, 20, 22, 23(2) to (4) and 28;

(c)  Part IV except sections 40, 43, 44(8) and 50 and Schedule 5;

(d)  in Part V, sections 52 and 54;

(e)  Part VI except sections 57(1) and 67;

(f)  Part VII except sections 73, 74(1) to (4), 75 and 77 and Schedules 8 and 9;

(g)  in Part VIII, sections 79 to 83 and Schedule 10. This paragraph does not apply to—

(i)  any matter in respect of which it is stated by this Act that provision may be made by Act of the Assembly;

(ii)  any matter to which a description specified in this Schedule or Schedule 3 is stated not to apply; or

(iii)  any matter falling within a description specified in Schedule 3.

**SCHEDULE 3** Section 4(1)

## RESERVED MATTERS

1  The conferral of functions in relation to Northern Ireland on any Minister of the Crown.

2  Property belonging to Her Majesty in right of the Crown or belonging to a department of the Government of the United Kingdom or held in trust for Her Majesty for the purposes of such

a department (other than property used for the purposes of the armed forces of the Crown or the Ministry of Defence Police).

3  Navigation, including merchant shipping, but not harbours or inland waters.

4  Civil aviation but not aerodromes.

5  The foreshore and the sea bed and subsoil and their natural resources (except so far as affecting harbours); submarine pipe-lines; submarine cables, including any land line used solely for the purpose of connecting one submarine cable with another.

6  Domicile.

7  The Post Office, posts (including postage stamps, postal orders and postal packets) and the regulation of postal services.

8  Disqualification for membership of the Assembly; privileges, powers and immunities of the Assembly, its members and committees greater than those conferred by section 50.

9  The following matters—

(a)  the criminal law;

(b)  the creation of offences and penalties;

(c)  the prevention and detection of crime and powers of arrest and detention in connection with crime or criminal proceedings;

(d)  prosecutions;

(e)  the treatment of offenders (including children and young persons, and mental health patients, involved in crime);

(f)  the surrender of fugitive offenders between Northern Ireland and the Republic of Ireland;

(g)  compensation out of public funds for victims of crime. Sub-paragraphs (a) to (c) do not include any matter within paragraph 17 of Schedule 2. Sub-paragraph (e) includes, in particular, prisons and other institutions for the treatment or detention of persons mentioned in that sub-paragraph.

Sub-paragraphs (a) to (c) do not include any matter within paragraph 17 of Schedule 2.

Sub-paragraph (c) includes, in particular, prisons and other institutions for the treatment or detention of persons mentioned in that sub-paragraph.

10  The maintenance of public order, including the conferring of powers, authorities, privileges or immunities for that purpose on constables, members of the armed forces of the Crown and other persons (other than the Ministry of Defence Police), but not any matter within paragraph 17 of Schedule 2; the Parades Commission for Northern Ireland.

11  The establishment, organisation and control of the Royal Ulster Constabulary and of any other police force (other than the Ministry of Defence Police); the Police Authority for Northern Ireland; traffic wardens.

12  Firearms and explosives.

13  Civil defence.

14  The subject-matter of the Emergency Powers Act Northern Ireland) 1926.

15  All matters, other than those specified in paragraph 11 of Schedule 2, relating to the Supreme Court of Judicature of Northern Ireland, county courts, courts of summary jurisdiction (including magistrates' courts and juvenile courts) and coroners, including procedure, evidence, appeals, juries, costs, legal aid and the registration, execution and enforcement of judgments and orders but not—

(a)  bankruptcy, insolvency, the winding up of corporate and unincorporated bodies or the making of arrangements or compositions with creditors;

(b)  the regulation of the profession of solicitors.

16  The functions and procedures of the Civil Service Commissioners for Northern Ireland.

17  All matters (including procedure and appeals) relating to—

(a)  the Chief and other Social Security Commissioners for Northern Ireland; or

(b)  the Chief and other Child Support Commissioners for Northern Ireland, but not any matter within paragraph 11 of Schedule 2.

18  The subject-matter of sections 149 to 151 of and Schedules 5 and 5A to the Social Security Administration (Northern Ireland) Act 1992 (Social Security Advisory Committee and Industrial Injuries Advisory Council).

19  The subject-matter of the Vaccine Damage Payment Scheme.

20  Import and export controls and trade with any place outside the United Kingdom but not—

(a)  the furtherance of the trade of Northern Ireland or the protection of traders in Northern Ireland against fraud;

(b)  services in connection with, or the regulation of, the quality, insurance, transport, marketing or identification of agricultural or food products, including livestock;

(c)  the prevention of disease or the control of weeds and pests;

(d)  aerodromes and harbours;

(e)  any matter within paragraph 4 of Schedule 2.

21  The subject-matter of the National Minimum Wage Act 1998.

22  The subject-matter of the following provisions of the Pension Schemes Act 1993—

(a)  section 6(1), (2)(a)(i), (iii) and (iv) and (b), (3), (4) and (8) (registration of occupational and personal pension schemes);

(b)  section 145 (Pensions Ombudsman).

23  The following matters—

(a)  financial services, including investment business, banking and deposit-taking, collective investment schemes and insurance;

(b)  financial markets, including listing and public offers of securities and investments, transfer of securities and insider dealing.

This paragraph does not include the subject-matter of—

(a)  the Industrial and Provident Societies Act Northern Ireland) 1969;

(b)  the Credit Unions (Northern Ireland) Order 1985;

(c)  the Companies (Northern Ireland) Order 1986;

(d)  the Insolvency (Northern Ireland) Order 1989;

(e)  the Companies (Northern Ireland) Order 1990;

(f)  the Companies (No.2) (Northern Ireland) Order 1990;

(g)  the Open-Ended Investment Companies (Investment Companies with Variable Capital) Regulations (Northern Ireland) 1997.

24  The subject-matter of—

(a)  the Building Societies Act 1986;

(b)  the Friendly Societies Act 1992.

25  The subject-matter of the Money Laundering Regulations 1993, but in relation to any type of business.

26  Regulation of anti-competitive practices and agreements; abuse of dominant position; monopolies and mergers.

27  Intellectual property but not the subject-matter of Parts I and II of the Plant Varieties Act 1997 (plant varieties and the Plant Varieties and Seeds Tribunal).

28  Units of measurement and United Kingdom primary standards.

29  Telecommunications; wireless telegraphy; the provision of programme services (within the meaning of the Broadcasting Act 1990); internet services; electronic encryption; the subject matter of Part II of the Wireless Telegraphy Act 1949 (electromagnetic disturbance).

30  The National Lottery (except in so far as any matter within Schedule 2 is concerned).

31  Xenotransplantation.

32  Surrogacy arrangements, within the meaning of the Surrogacy Arrangements Act 1985, including the subject-matter of that Act.

33  The subject-matter of the Human Fertilisation and Embryology Act 1990.

34  Human genetics.

35  Research Councils within the meaning of the Science and Technology Act 1965.

36  Areas in which industry may qualify for assistance under Part III of the Industrial Development Act 1982.

37  Consumer safety in relation to goods.

38 Technical standards and requirements in relation to products in pursuance of an obligation under Community law but not standards and requirements in relation to food, agricultural or horticultural produce, fish or fish products, seeds, animal feeding stuffs, fertilisers or pesticides.

39 The subject-matter of section 3(5) to (7) of the Environmental Protection Act 1990 (emission limits); the environmental protection technology scheme for research and development in the United Kingdom.

40 The subject-matter of—

(a) the Data Protection Act 1984;

(b) the Data Protection Act 1998; and

(c) Council Directive 95/46/EC (protection of individuals with regard to the processing of personal data and free movement of such data).

41 Oaths and declarations (including all undertakings and affirmations, by whatever name) other than those within section 77(3).

42 Any matter with which a provision of this Act falling within the following sub-paragraphs solely or mainly deals—

(a) in Part III, sections 19, 20 and 28;

(b) in Part VII, sections 73, 74(3) and (4), 75 and 77(1), (2) and (4) to (8) and Schedules 8 and 9;

(c) in Part VIII, sections 90 to 93 and Schedule 11.

This paragraph does not apply to—

(i) any matter in respect of which it is stated by this Act that provision may be made by Act of the Assembly; or

(ii) any matter to which a description specified in this Schedule or Schedule 2 is stated not to apply.

**SCHEDULE 4** Section 16(10).

## ANNEX A TO STRAND ONE OF BELFAST AGREEMENT

### PLEDGE OF OFFICE

To pledge:

(a) to discharge in good faith all the duties of office;

(b) commitment to non-violence and exclusively peaceful and democratic means;

(c) to serve all the people of Northern Ireland equally, and to act in accordance with the general obligations on government to promote equality and prevent discrimination;

(d) to participate with colleagues in the preparation of a programme for government;

(e) to operate within the framework of that programme when agreed within the Executive Committee and endorsed by the Assembly;

(f) to support, and act in accordance with, all decisions of the Executive Committee and Assembly;

(g) to comply with the Ministerial Code of Conduct.

### CODE OF CONDUCT

Ministers must at all times:

observe the highest standards of propriety and regularity involving impartiality, integrity and objectivity in relationship to the stewardship of public funds;

be accountable to users of services, the community and, through the Assembly, for the activities within their responsibilities, their stewardship of public funds and the extent to which key performance targets and objectives have been met; ensure all reasonable requests for information from the Assembly, users of services and individual citizens are complied with; and that Departments and their staff conduct their dealings with the public in an open and responsible way;

follow the seven principles of public life set out by the Committee on Standards in Public Life;

comply with this code and with rules relating to the use of public funds;

operate in a way conducive to promoting good community relations and equality of treatment;

not use information gained in the course of their service for personal gain; nor seek to use the opportunity of public service to promote their private interests;

ensure they comply with any rules on the acceptance of gifts and hospitality that might be offered;

declare any personal or business interests which may conflict with their responsibilities. The Assembly will retain a Register of Interests. Individuals must ensure that any direct or indirect pecuniary interests which members of the public might reasonably think could influence their judgement are listed in the Register of Interests.

**SCHEDULE 5** Section 40(10)

## NORTHERN IRELAND ASSEMBLY COMMISSION

*Membership*

1 A person appointed under standing orders made under section 40(2)(b) shall hold office until another member of the Assembly is appointed in his place, unless he previously resigns or ceases to be a member of the Assembly otherwise than by virtue of a dissolution.

*Staff*

2 (1) The Commission may appoint staff.

(2) The persons appointed by the Commission are referred to in this Act as the staff of the Assembly.

(3) It is for the Commission to determine the terms and conditions of appointment of the staff of the Assembly, including

arrangements for the payment of pensions, gratuities or allowances to, or in respect of, any person who has ceased to be a member of the staff of the Assembly.

(4) Accordingly, the Commission may—
  (a) make contributions or payments towards provision for such pensions, gratuities or allowances;
  (b) establish and administer one or more pension schemes.

(5) The power conferred by sub-paragraph (1) includes power to make arrangements for administrative, secretarial or other assistance to be provided for the Commission by officers of the civil service of Northern Ireland or the civil service; and the reference in sub-paragraph (2) to persons appointed by the Commission shall be construed accordingly.

*Powers*

3 (1) Subject to sub-paragraph (4), the Commission may do anything which appears to it to be necessary or expedient for the purpose of or in connection with the discharge of its functions.

(2) That includes, in particular—
  (a) holding property;
  (b) charging for goods or services;
  (c) entering into contracts;
  (d) investing sums not immediately required in relation to the discharge of its functions; and
  (e) accepting gifts.

(3) The Commission may sell goods or provide services, and may make arrangements for the sale of goods or provision of services, to the public.

(4) The Commission may borrow sums in sterling by way of overdraft or otherwise for the purpose of meeting a temporary excess of expenditure over sums otherwise available to meet that expenditure.

(5) The Commission may borrow money only under sub-paragraph (4) and may borrow under that sub-paragraph only with the special or general approval of the Assembly.

## *Delegation*

4  The Commission may delegate any of its functions to the Presiding Officer or a member of the staff of the Assembly.

## *Proceedings and business*

5  (1)  The validity of any acts of the Commission shall not be affected by any vacancy among the members, or by any defect in the appointment, or qualification for membership, of any member.

(2)  The Commission may determine its own procedure.

(3)  The Presiding Officer shall preside at meetings of the Commission, but the Commission may appoint another of its members to preside if the office of Presiding Officer is vacant or the Presiding Officer is for any reason unable to act.

## *Crown status*

6  (1)  Her Majesty may by Order in Council provide for the Commission to be treated to any extent as a Crown body for the purposes of any enactment.

(2)  In particular, the Order may for the purposes of any enactment provide—

(a)  for employment under the Commission to be treated as employment under the Commission as a Crown body;

(b)  for land held, used or managed by the Commission, or operations carried out by or on behalf of the Commission, to be treated (as the case may be) as land held, used or managed, or operations carried out by or on behalf of, the Commission as a Crown body.

(3)  For the purposes of this paragraph, "Crown body" means a body which is the servant or agent of the Crown, and includes a government department.

(4) A statutory instrument containing an Order in Council under this paragraph shall be subject to annulment in pursuance of a resolution of either House of Parliament.

**SCHEDULE 6** Section 41(3)

STANDING ORDERS: FURTHER PROVISION

*Preservation of order*

1 (1) The standing orders shall include provision for preserving order in the proceedings of the Assembly, including provision for—
   (a) preventing conduct which would constitute a criminal offence or contempt of court; and
   (b) a sub judice rule.
(2) Such provision may provide for excluding a member of the Assembly from proceedings and for withdrawing his rights and privileges as a member for the period of his exclusion.

*Proceedings to be in public*

2 (1) The standing orders shall include provision requiring the proceedings of the Assembly to be held in public, except in such circumstances as the standing orders may provide.
(2) The standing orders may include provision as to the conditions to be complied with by any member of the public attending the proceedings, including provision for excluding from the proceedings any member of the public who does not comply with those conditions.

*Reporting and publishing proceedings*

3 The standing orders shall include provision for reporting the proceedings of the Assembly and for publishing the reports.

*Committees*

4 (1)  The standing orders shall include provision for ensuring that, in appointing members to committees, regard is had to the balance of parties in the Assembly.

(2)  The standing orders may include provision for excluding from the proceedings of a committee a member of the Assembly who is not a member of the committee.

**SCHEDULE 7** Section 68(4)

## THE NORTHERN IRELAND HUMAN RIGHTS COMMISSION

*Introductory*

1  In this Schedule "the Commission" means the Northern Ireland Human Rights Commission.

*Commissioners' tenure*

2 (1)  Subject to the provisions of this Schedule, a Commissioner shall hold office in accordance with the terms of his appointment.

(2)  A Commissioner shall not be appointed—

(a)  in the case of the Chief Commissioner, for more than five years at a time; and

(b)  in any other case, for more than three years at a time.

(3)  A person may resign as a Commissioner or as Chief Commissioner by notice in writing to the Secretary of State.

(4)  The Secretary of State may dismiss a person from his office as Commissioner or Chief Commissioner if satisfied—

(a)  that he has without reasonable excuse failed to discharge his functions for a continuous period of three months beginning not earlier than six months before the day of dismissal;

(b) that he has been convicted of a criminal offence;

(c) that a bankruptcy order has been made against him, or his estate has been sequestrated, or he has made a composition or arrangement with, or granted a trust deed for, his creditors; or

(d) that he is unable or unfit to carry out his functions.

*Commissioners' salary etc.*

3 (1) The Commission shall pay to or in respect of Commissioners—

(a) remuneration;

(b) allowances and fees; and

(c) sums for the provision of pensions,

in accordance with directions of the Secretary of State.

(2) Where a person who by reference to any office or employment is a participant in a scheme under section 1 of the Superannuation Act 1972 becomes a Commissioner or the Chief Commissioner, the Minister for the Civil Service may, notwithstanding any provision made under sub-paragraph (1)(c), determine that the person's service as Commissioner or Chief Commissioner shall be treated for the purposes of the scheme as service in that office or employment.

*Staff*

4 (1) The Commission may employ staff subject to the approval of the Secretary of State as to numbers and as to remuneration and other terms and conditions of employment.

(2) Employment with the Commission shall be included among the kinds of employment to which a superannuation scheme under section 1 of the Superannuation Act 1972 can apply, and

accordingly in Schedule 1 to that Act (in which those kinds of employment are listed) after "Commission for Racial Equality" insert—

"Northern Ireland Human Rights Commission".

(3) The Commission shall pay to the Minister for the Civil Service, at such times as he may direct, such sums as he may determine in respect of any increase attributable to sub-paragraph (2) in the sums payable out of money provided by Parliament under the Superannuation Act 1972.

*Annual report*

5 (1) The Commission shall, as soon as reasonably practicable after the end of each year, make a report to the Secretary of State on the performance of its functions during the year.

(2) The Secretary of State shall lay a copy of the report before each House of Parliament.

*Money*

6 The Secretary of State may make grants to the Commission out of money provided by Parliament.

7 (1) The Commission shall keep proper accounts and financial records.

(2) The Commission shall—

(a) prepare a statement of accounts in respect of each financial year containing such information, and in such form, as the Secretary of State with the consent of the Treasury directs; and

(b) send a copy to the Secretary of State and to the Comptroller and Auditor General within such period after the end of the financial year as the Secretary of State directs.

(3) The Comptroller and Auditor General shall—

(a) examine, certify and report on the statement of accounts; and

(b) lay a copy of the statement of accounts and of his report before each House of Parliament.

(4) For the purposes of this paragraph—

(a) a financial year is a period of twelve months ending on 31st March; but

(b) the first financial year is the period beginning with the day on which section 68 comes into force and ending with the first 31st March which falls at least six months after that day.

*Procedure*

8 (1) In determining its own procedure the Commission may, in particular, make provision about—

(a) the discharge of its functions by committees (which may include persons who are not Commissioners);

(b) a quorum for meetings of the Commission or a committee.

(2) The validity of any proceedings of the Commission or a committee shall not be affected by—

(a) a vacancy in the office of Chief Commissioner; or

(b) a defect in the appointment of a Commissioner.

*Disqualification*

9 In Part III of Schedule 1 to the House of Commons Disqualification Act 1975 (other disqualifying offices) at the appropriate place insert— "Northern Ireland Human Rights Commissioner".

10  In Part III of Schedule 1 to the Northern Ireland Assembly
Disqualification Act 1975 (other disqualifying offices) at the appro-
priate place insert—
"Northern Ireland Human Rights Commissioner".

*Status*

11  The Commission shall not be regarded as the servant or agent of the
Crown or as enjoying any status, immunity or privilege of the Crown;
and property of the Commission shall not be regarded as property of,
or held on behalf of, the Crown.


**SCHEDULE 8** Section 73(5)

THE EQUALITY COMMISSION FOR NORTHERN IRELAND

*Introductory*

1  In this Schedule "the Commission" means the Equality Commission
for Northern Ireland.


*Commissioners' tenure*

2  (1)  Subject to the provisions of this Schedule, a Commissioner shall
hold office in accordance with the terms of his appointment.
(2)  A Commissioner shall not be appointed—
(a)  in the case of the Chief Commissioner, for more than five
years at a time; and
(b)  in any other case, for more than three years at a time.
(3)  A person may resign as a Commissioner, as the Chief
Commissioner or as a Deputy Chief Commissioner by notice in
writing to the Secretary of State.

(4) The Secretary of State may dismiss a person from his office of Commissioner, Chief Commissioner or Deputy Chief Commissioner if satisfied—

(a) that he has without reasonable excuse failed to discharge his functions for a continuous period of three months beginning not earlier than six months before the day of dismissal;

(b) that he has been convicted of a criminal offence;

(c) that a bankruptcy order has been made against him, or his estate has been sequestrated, or he has made a composition or arrangement with, or granted a trust deed for, his creditors; or

(d) that he is unable or unfit to carry out his functions.

### Commissioners' salary etc.

3   The Department of Economic Development may with the approval of the Department of Finance and Personnel pay to or in respect of Commissioners—

(a) remuneration;

(b) allowances and fees; and

(c) sums for the provision of pensions.

### Staff

4   (1) The Commission may with the approval of the Department of Economic Development and the Department of Finance and Personnel as to numbers and as to remuneration and other terms and conditions of employment—

(a) employ such staff as the Commission considers necessary;

(b) employ the services of such other persons as the Commission considers expedient for any particular purpose.

(2) The Commission may, in the case of such of its staff as may be determined by it with the approval of the Department of Economic

Development and the Department of Finance and Personnel, pay such pensions, allowances and gratuities, or provide and maintain such pension schemes, as may be determined.

(3) Payments made or expenses incurred under this paragraph shall be defrayed out of money appropriated by Act of the Assembly.

*Annual report*

5  (1) The Commission shall, as soon as reasonably practicable after the end of each year, make a report to the Department of Economic Development—

   (a) on the performance of its functions during the year; and

   (b) on any steps which, during the year, have been taken by it and other public authorities to promote such equality of opportunity as is mentioned in section 75(1).

(2) The report shall, in particular, give details of how resources have been divided between the functions previously exercisable by each of the bodies listed in section 74(2).

(3) The Department shall lay a copy of the report before the Assembly and send a copy of the report to the Secretary of State.

(4) The Secretary of State shall lay a copy of the report before each House of Parliament.

*Money*

6  (1) Expenditure incurred by the Commission may be defrayed as expenses of the Department of Economic Development if authorised by that Department and the Department of Finance and Personnel.

(2) Expenditure defrayed under this paragraph shall be defrayed out of money appropriated by Act of the Assembly and an

authorisation for the purposes of this paragraph may be general or specific.

7 (1) The Commission shall keep accounts and financial records in a form approved by the Department of Economic Development.

(2) The Commission shall—

(a) prepare a statement of accounts in respect of each financial year containing such information, and in such form, as is directed by the Department of Economic Development with the consent of the Department of Finance and Personnel; and

(b) send a copy to the Department of Economic Development and to the Comptroller and Auditor General for Northern Ireland within such period after the end of the financial year as the Department directs.

(3) The Comptroller and Auditor General for Northern Ireland shall—

(a) examine, certify and report on the statement of accounts; and

(b) send a copy of the statement of accounts and of his report to the Department of Economic Development.

(4) The Department shall lay a copy of the statement of accounts and the Comptroller and Auditor General's report before the Assembly.

(5) For the purposes of this paragraph—

(a) a financial year is a period of twelve months ending on 31st March; but

(b) the first financial year is the period beginning with the day on which section 73 comes into force and ending with the first 31st March which falls at least six months after that day.

*Procedure*

8 (1) In determining its own procedure the Commission may, in particular, make provision about—

(a) the discharge of its functions by committees (which may include persons who are not Commissioners);

(b) a quorum for meetings of the Commission or a committee.

(2) The validity of any proceedings of the Commission or a committee shall not be affected by—

(a) a vacancy in the office of Chief Commissioner or Deputy Chief Commissioner; or

(b) a defect in the appointment of a Commissioner.

*Disqualification*

9 In Part II of Schedule 1 to the House of Commons Disqualification Act 1975 (bodies whose members are disqualified) at the appropriate place insert—

"The Equality Commission for Northern Ireland".

10 In Part II of Schedule 1 to the Northern Ireland Assembly Disqualification Act 1975 (bodies whose members are disqualified) at the appropriate place insert—

"The Equality Commission for Northern Ireland".

*The Northern Ireland Commissioner for Complaints*

11 In Schedule 2 to the Commissioner for Complaints (Northern Ireland) Order 1996 (bodies subject to investigation) at the appropriate place insert—

"The Equality Commission for Northern Ireland".

*Status*

12 The Commission shall not be regarded as the servant or agent of the Crown or as enjoying any status, immunity or privilege of the Crown; and property of the Commission shall not be regarded as property of, or held on behalf of, the Crown.

**SCHEDULE 9** Section 75(4)

EQUALITY: ENFORCEMENT OF DUTIES

*The Equality Commission*

1  The Equality Commission for Northern Ireland shall—
(a) keep under review the effectiveness of the duties imposed by section 75;
(b) offer advice to public authorities and others in connection with those duties; and
(c) carry out the functions conferred on it by the following provisions of this Schedule.

*Equality schemes*

2  (1) A public authority to which this sub-paragraph applies shall, before the end of the period of six months beginning with the commencement of this Schedule or, if later, the establishment of the authority, submit a scheme to the Commission.
(2) Sub-paragraph (1) applies to any public authority except one which is notified in writing by the Commission that that sub-paragraph does not apply to it.

3  (1) Where it thinks appropriate, the Commission may—
(a) request a public authority to which paragraph 2(1) does not apply to make a scheme;
(b) request any public authority to make a revised scheme.
(2) A public authority shall respond to a request under this paragraph by submitting a scheme to the Commission before the end of the period of six months beginning with the date of the request.

4  (1)  A scheme shall show how the public authority proposes to fulfil the duties imposed by section 75 in relation to the relevant functions.

   (2)  A scheme shall state, in particular, the authority's arrangements—

      (a)  for assessing its compliance with the duties under section 75 and for consulting on matters to which a duty under that section is likely to be relevant (including details of the persons to be consulted);

      (b)  for assessing and consulting on the likely impact of policies adopted or proposed to be adopted by the authority on the promotion of equality of opportunity;

      (c)  for monitoring any adverse impact of policies adopted by the authority on the promotion of equality of opportunity;

      (d)  for publishing the results of such assessments as are mentioned in paragraph (b) and such monitoring as is mentioned in paragraph (c);

      (e)  for training staff;

      (f)  for ensuring, and assessing, public access to information and to services provided by the authority.

   (3)  A scheme shall—

      (a)  conform to any guidelines as to form or content which are issued by the Commission with the approval of the Secretary of State;

      (b)  specify a timetable for measures proposed in the scheme; and

      (c)  include details of how it will be published.

   (4)  In this paragraph—

      "equality of opportunity" means such equality of opportunity as is mentioned in section 75(1);

      "the relevant functions" means the functions of the public authority or, in the case of a scheme submitted in response to a request which specifies particular functions of the public authority, those functions.

5  Before submitting a scheme a public authority shall consult, in accordance with any directions given by the Commission—

(a) representatives of persons likely to be affected by the scheme; and

(b) such other persons as may be specified in the directions.

6 (1) On receipt of a scheme the Commission shall—

(a) approve it; or

(b) refer it to the Secretary of State.

(2) Where the Commission refers a scheme to the Secretary of State under sub-paragraph (1)(b), it shall notify the Assembly in writing that it has done so and send the Assembly a copy of the scheme.

7 (1) Where a scheme is referred to the Secretary of State he shall—

(a) approve it;

(b) request the public authority to make a revised scheme; or

(c) make a scheme for the public authority.

(2) A request under sub-paragraph (1)(b) shall be treated in the same way as a request under paragraph 3(1)(b).

(3) Where the Secretary of State—

(a) requests a revised scheme under sub-paragraph (1)(b); or

(b) makes a scheme under sub-paragraph (1)(c),

he shall notify the Assembly in writing that he has done so and, in a case falling within paragraph (b), send the Assembly a copy of the scheme.

8 (1) If a public authority wishes to revise a scheme it may submit a revised scheme to the Commission.

(2) A revised scheme shall be treated as if it were submitted in response to a request under paragraph 3(1)(b).

(3) A public authority shall, before the end of the period of five years beginning with the submission of its current scheme, or the latest review of that scheme under this sub-paragraph, whichever is the later, review that scheme and inform the Commission of the outcome of the review.

*Duties arising out of equality schemes*

9  (1)  In publishing the results of such an assessment as is mentioned
        in paragraph 4(2)(b), a public authority shall state the aims of
        the policy to which the assessment relates and give details of any
        consideration given by the authority to—
        (a)  measures which might mitigate any adverse impact of that
             policy on the promotion of equality of opportunity; and
        (b)  alternative policies which might better achieve the promo-
             tion of equality of opportunity.
   (2)  In making any decision with respect to a policy adopted or pro-
        posed to be adopted by it, a public authority shall take into
        account any such assessment and consultation as is mentioned in
        paragraph 4(2)(b) carried out in relation to the policy.
   (3)  In this paragraph "equality of opportunity" has the same meaning
        as in paragraph 4.

*Complaints*

10  (1)  If the Commission receives a complaint made in accordance with
        this paragraph of failure by a public authority to comply with a
        scheme approved or made under paragraph 6 or 7, it shall—
        (a)  investigate the complaint; or
        (b)  give the complainant reasons for not investigating.
   (2)  A complaint must be made in writing by a person who claims to
        have been directly affected by the failure.
   (3)  A complaint must be sent to the Commission during the period
        of 12 months starting with the day on which the complainant
        first knew of the matters alleged.
   (4)  Before making a complaint the complainant must—
        (a)  bring the complaint to the notice of the public authority;
             and
        (b)  give the public authority a reasonable opportunity to
             respond.

*Investigations*

11 (1) This paragraph applies to—
  (a) investigations required by paragraph 10; and
  (b) any other investigation carried out by the Commission where it believes that a public authority may have failed to comply with a scheme approved or made under paragraph 6 or 7.

(2) The Commission shall send a report of the investigation to—
  (a) the public authority concerned;
  (b) the Secretary of State; and
  (c) the complainant (if any).

(3) If a report recommends action by the public authority concerned and the Commission considers that the action is not taken within a reasonable time—
  (a) the Commission may refer the matter to the Secretary of State; and
  (b) the Secretary of State may give directions to the public authority in respect of any matter referred to him.

(4) Where the Commission—
  (a) sends a report to the Secretary of State under sub-paragraph (2)(b); or
  (b) refers a matter to the Secretary of State under sub-paragraph (3)(a),
  it shall notify the Assembly in writing that it has done so and, in a case falling within paragraph (a), send the Assembly a copy of the report.

(5) Where the Secretary of State gives directions to a public authority under sub-paragraph (3)(b), he shall notify the Assembly in writing that he has done so.

*Government departments*

12 (1) Paragraphs 6, 7 and 11(2)(b) and (3) do not apply to a govern-
     ment department which is such a public authority as is men-
     tioned in section 75(3)(a).
   (2) On receipt of a scheme submitted by such a government depart-
     ment under paragraph 2 or 3 the Commission shall—
     (a) approve it; or
     (b) request the department to make a revised scheme.
   (3) A request under sub-paragraph (2)(b) shall be treated in the
     same way as a request under paragraph 3(1)(b).
   (4) Where a request is made under sub-paragraph (2)(b), the gov-
     ernment department shall, if it does not submit a revised scheme
     to the Commission before the end of the period of six months
     beginning with the date of the request, send to the Commission
     a written statement of the reasons for not doing so.
   (5) The Commission may lay before Parliament and the Assembly
     a report of any investigation such as is mentioned in paragraph
     11(1) relating to a government department such as is mentioned
     in sub-paragraph (1).

**SCHEDULE** 10 Section 79

DEVOLUTION ISSUES

**PART I**

PRELIMINARY

1 In this Schedule "devolution issue" means—
   (a) a question whether any provision of an Act of the Assembly is
     within the legislative competence of the Assembly;

(b) a question whether a purported or proposed exercise of a function by a Minister or Northern Ireland department is, or would be, invalid by reason of section 24;

(c) a question whether a Minister or Northern Ireland department has failed to comply with any of the Convention rights, any obligation under Community law or any order under section 27 so far as relating to such an obligation; or

(d) any question arising under this Act about excepted or reserved matters.

2   A devolution issue shall not be taken to arise in any proceedings merely because of any contention of a party to the proceedings which appears to the court or tribunal before which the proceedings take place to be frivolous or vexatious.

## PART II

## PROCEEDINGS IN NORTHERN IRELAND

*Application of Part II*

3   This Part of this Schedule applies in relation to devolution issues in proceedings in Northern Ireland.

*Institution of proceedings*

4   (1)   Proceedings for the determination of a devolution issue may be instituted or defended by the Attorney General or the Attorney General for Northern Ireland.

(2)   The First Minister and the deputy First Minister acting jointly may defend any such proceedings.

(3) This paragraph is without prejudice to any power to institute or defend proceedings exercisable apart from this paragraph by any person.

## Notice of devolution issue

5 A court or tribunal shall order notice of any devolution issue which arises in any proceedings before it to be given to the Attorney General, the Attorney General for Northern Ireland, the First Minister and the deputy First Minister (unless the person to whom the notice would be given is a party to the proceedings).

6 A person to whom notice is given in pursuance of paragraph 5 or, where such notice is given to the First Minister and the deputy First Minister, those Ministers acting jointly may take part as a party in the proceedings, so far as they relate to a devolution issue.

## Reference of devolution issue to Court of Appeal

7 A court, other than the House of Lords or the Court of Appeal in Northern Ireland, may refer any devolution issue which arises in any proceedings before it to the Court of Appeal in Northern Ireland.

8 A tribunal from which there is no appeal shall refer any devolution issue which arises in any proceedings before it to the Court of Appeal in Northern Ireland; and any other tribunal may make such a reference.

## References from Court of Appeal to Judicial Committee

9 The Court of Appeal in Northern Ireland may refer any devolution issue which arises in proceedings before it (otherwise than on a reference under paragraph 7 or 8) to the Judicial Committee.

*Appeals from Court of Appeal to Judicial Committee*

10 An appeal against a determination of a devolution issue by the Court of Appeal in Northern Ireland on a reference under paragraph 7 or 8 shall lie to the Judicial Committee, but only with leave of the Court of Appeal in Northern Ireland or, failing such leave, with special leave of the Judicial Committee.

## PART III

## PROCEEDINGS IN ENGLAND AND WALES

*Application of Part III*

11 This Part of this Schedule applies in relation to devolution issues in proceedings in England and Wales.

*Institution of proceedings*

12 (1) Proceedings for the determination of a devolution issue may be instituted or defended by the Attorney General.

(2) The Attorney General for Northern Ireland or the First Minister and the deputy First Minister acting jointly may defend any such proceedings.

(3) This paragraph is without prejudice to any power to institute or defend proceedings exercisable apart from this paragraph by any person.

*Notice of devolution issue*

13  A court or tribunal shall order notice of any devolution issue which arises in any proceedings before it to be given to the Attorney General, the Attorney General for Northern Ireland, the First Minister and the deputy First Minister (unless the person to whom the notice would be given is a party to the proceedings).

14  A person to whom notice is given in pursuance of paragraph 13 or, where such notice is given to the First Minister and the deputy First Minister, those Ministers acting jointly may take part as a party in the proceedings, so far as they relate to a devolution issue.

*Reference of devolution issue to High Court or Court of Appeal*

15  A magistrates' court may refer any devolution issue which arises in proceedings (other than criminal proceedings) before it to the High Court.

16  (1) A court may refer any devolution issue which arises in proceedings (other than criminal proceedings) before it to the Court of Appeal.

(2) Sub-paragraph (1) does not apply to—

(a) a magistrates' court, the Court of Appeal or the House of Lords; or

(b) the High Court if the devolution issue arises in proceedings on a reference under paragraph 15.

17  A tribunal from which there is no appeal shall refer any devolution issue which arises in proceedings before it to the Court of Appeal; and any other tribunal may make such a reference.

18  A court, other than the House of Lords or the Court of Appeal, may refer any devolution issue which arises in criminal proceedings before it to—

(a)   the High Court (if the proceedings are summary proceedings); or

(b)   the Court of Appeal (if the proceedings are proceedings on indictment).

*References from Court of Appeal to Judicial Committee*

19   The Court of Appeal may refer any devolution issue which arises in proceedings before it (otherwise than on a reference under paragraph 16, 17 or 18) to the Judicial Committee.

*Appeals from superior courts to Judicial Committee*

20   An appeal against a determination of a devolution issue by the High Court or the Court of Appeal on a reference under paragraph 15, 16, 17 or 18 shall lie to the Judicial Committee, but only with leave of the High Court or the Court of Appeal or, failing such leave, with special leave of the Judicial Committee.

## PART IV

## PROCEEDINGS IN SCOTLAND

*Application of Part IV*

21   This Part of this Schedule applies in relation to devolution issues in proceedings in Scotland.

*Institution of proceedings*

22   (1)   Proceedings for the determination of a devolution issue may be instituted or defended by the Advocate General for Scotland.

(2)  The Attorney General for Northern Ireland or the First Minister and the deputy First Minister acting jointly may defend any such proceedings.

(3)  This paragraph is without prejudice to any power to institute or defend proceedings exercisable apart from this paragraph by any person.

### Intimation of devolution issue

23  Intimation of any devolution issue which arises in any proceedings before a court or tribunal shall be given to the Advocate General for Scotland, the Attorney General for Northern Ireland, the First Minister and the deputy First Minister (unless the person to whom the intimation would be given is a party to the proceedings).

24  A person to whom intimation is given in pursuance of paragraph 23 or, where such intimation is given to the First Minister and the deputy First Minister, those Ministers acting jointly may take part as a party in the proceedings, so far as they relate to a devolution issue.

### Reference of devolution issue to higher court

25  A court, other than the House of Lords or any court consisting of three or more judges of the Court of Session, may refer any devolution issue which arises in proceedings (other than criminal proceedings) before it to the Inner House of the Court of Session.

26  A tribunal from which there is no appeal shall refer any devolution issue which arises in proceedings before it to the Inner House of the Court of Session; and any other tribunal may make such a reference.

27  A court, other than any court consisting of two or more judges of the High Court of Justiciary, may refer any devolution issue which arises in criminal proceedings before it to the High Court of Justiciary.

*References from superior courts to Judicial Committee*

28 Any court consisting of three or more judges of the Court of Session may refer any devolution issue which arises in proceedings before it (otherwise than on a reference under paragraph 25 or 26) to the Judicial Committee.

29 Any court consisting of two or more judges of the High Court of Justiciary may refer any devolution issue which arises in proceedings before it (otherwise than on a reference under paragraph 27) to the Judicial Committee.

*Appeals from superior courts to Judicial Committee*

30 An appeal against a determination of a devolution issue by the Inner House of the Court of Session on a reference under paragraph 25 or 26 shall lie to the Judicial Committee.

31 An appeal against a determination of a devolution issue by—

(a) a court of two or more judges of the High Court of Justiciary (whether in the ordinary course of proceedings or on a reference under paragraph 27); or

(b) a court of three or more judges of the Court of Session from which there is no appeal to the House of Lords,

shall lie to the Judicial Committee, but only with leave of the court concerned or, failing such leave, with special leave of the Judicial Committee.

## PART V

## GENERAL

*Proceedings in the House of Lords*

32 Any devolution issue which arises in judicial proceedings in the House of Lords shall be referred to the Judicial Committee unless

the House considers it more appropriate, having regard to all the circumstances, that it should determine the issue.

*Direct references to Judicial Committee*

33   The Attorney General, the Attorney General for Northern Ireland, the First Minister and the deputy First Minister acting jointly or the Advocate General for Scotland may require any court or tribunal to refer to the Judicial Committee any devolution issue which has arisen in proceedings before it to which he is or they are a party.

34   The Attorney General, the Attorney General for Northern Ireland, the First Minister and the deputy First Minister acting jointly or the Advocate General for Scotland may refer to the Judicial Committee any devolution issue which is not the subject of proceedings.

35   (1) This paragraph applies where a reference is made under paragraph 34 in relation to a devolution issue which relates to the proposed exercise of a function by a Northern Ireland Minister or department.

(2) The person making the reference shall notify the Northern Ireland Minister or department of that fact.

(3) No Northern Ireland Minister or department shall exercise the function in the manner proposed during the period beginning with the receipt of the notification under sub-paragraph (2) and ending with the reference being decided or otherwise disposed of.

(4) Proceedings relating to any possible failure by a Northern Ireland Minister or department to comply with sub-paragraph (3) may be instituted by the Attorney General for Northern Ireland.

(5) Sub-paragraph (4) is without prejudice to any power to institute proceedings exercisable apart from that sub-paragraph by any person.

## Delegation by First Ministers

36 The First Minister and the deputy First Minister acting jointly may determine that a Minister or Northern Ireland department specified in the determination may exercise on their behalf, in relation to any proceedings under this Schedule so specified, any power conferred on them by this Schedule.

## Expenses

37 (1) A court or tribunal before which any proceedings take place may take account of any additional expense of the kind mentioned in sub-paragraph (3) in deciding any question as to costs or expenses.

(2) In deciding any such question, the court or tribunal may award the whole or part of the additional expense as costs or expenses to the party who incurred it (whatever the decision on the devolution issue).

(3) The additional expense is any additional expense which the court or tribunal considers that any party to the proceedings has incurred as a result of the participation of any person in pursuance of paragraph 6, 14 or 24.

## Procedure of courts and tribunals

38 Any power to make provision for regulating the procedure before any court or tribunal shall include power to make provision for the purposes of this Schedule including, in particular, provision—

(a) for prescribing the stage in the proceedings at which a devolution issue is to be raised or referred;

(b) for the staying or sisting of proceedings for the purpose of any proceedings under this Schedule; and

(c) for determining the manner in which and the time within which any notice or intimation is to be given.

*Bail and legal aid in criminal proceedings*

39 (1) Sub-paragraph (3) applies where a devolution issue arises in proceedings against a person ("the defendant") for an offence and the issue is referred to the Court of Appeal in Northern Ireland under paragraph 7.

(2) Sub-paragraphs (3) and (4) apply where such an issue arises in such proceedings and—

(a) the issue is referred by the Court to the Judicial Committee under paragraph 9 or 33; or

(b) the issue is determined by the Court under paragraph 7 and—

(i) an appeal to the Committee against the determination is brought under paragraph 10; or

(ii) an application for leave to bring such an appeal is made to the Court under that paragraph.

(3) The Court may, if it thinks fit, on the application of the defendant, admit him to bail pending the determination of the reference, appeal or application.

(4) The Court may at any time when it appears to the Court—

(a) that it is desirable in the interests of justice that the defendant should have legal aid; and

(b) that he has not sufficient means to obtain that aid,

assign to him a solicitor and counsel, or counsel only, in the reference, appeal or application.

(5) If, on a question of granting a person free legal aid under sub-paragraph (4), there is a doubt—

(a) whether it is desirable in the interests of justice that he should have legal aid; or

(b) whether he has sufficient means to obtain that aid,

the doubt shall be resolved in favour of granting him free legal aid.

(6) The fees of any counsel, and the expenses and fees of any solicitor, assigned to a person under sub-paragraph (4) shall be defrayed, up to an amount allowed by the Master (Taxing Office), by the Lord Chancellor out of money provided by Parliament.

40 Where a devolution issue arises as mentioned in sub-paragraph (1) of paragraph 39 and—

(a) the issue is referred to the Judicial Committee under paragraph 9 or 33; or

(b) the issue is determined by the Court of Appeal in Northern Ireland under paragraph 7 and—

(i) an appeal to the Committee against the determination is brought under paragraph 10; or

(ii) an application for special leave to bring such an appeal is made to the Committee under that paragraph,

sub-paragraphs (3) to (6) of paragraph 39 shall apply as if the references to the Court were references to the Committee.

*Interpretation*

41 Any duty or power conferred by this Schedule to refer a devolution issue to a court shall be construed as a duty or power to refer the issue to the court for decision.

## SCHEDULE 11

## TRIBUNAL ESTABLISHED UNDER SECTION 91

*Introductory*

1 In this Schedule "the Tribunal" means the tribunal established under section 91.

## Members

2  (1)  The Tribunal shall consist of such number of members appointed by the Lord Chancellor as he may determine.

   (2)  A member of the Tribunal shall hold and vacate office in accordance with the terms of his appointment and shall, on ceasing to hold office, be eligible for re-appointment.

   (3)  A member of the Tribunal may resign his office at any time by notice in writing to the Lord Chancellor.

## Chairman

3  (1)  The Lord Chancellor shall appoint one of the members of the Tribunal to be its chairman.

   (2)  The chairman may nominate a member as deputy chairman to act in his absence.

   (3)  A member may not be appointed as chairman or nominated as deputy chairman, unless he holds, or has held, office as a judge of the High Court, the High Court of Justice in Northern Ireland, the Court of Appeal or the Court of Appeal in Northern Ireland.

   (4)  The chairman may resign his office at any time by notice in writing to the Lord Chancellor.

## Payments to members

4  (1)  The Lord Chancellor may pay to the members of the Tribunal such remuneration and allowances as he may determine.

   (2)  The Lord Chancellor may, if he thinks fit in the case of any member of the Tribunal pay such pension, allowance or gratuity to or in respect of the member, or such sums towards the provision of such pension, allowance or gratuity, as he may determine.

   (3)  If a person ceases to be a member of the Tribunal and it appears to the Lord Chancellor that there are special circumstances which make it right that the person should receive compensation, he may pay to that person a sum of such amount as he may determine.

## *Proceedings*

5 The Tribunal shall sit at such times and in such places as the Lord Chancellor may direct.

6 The Tribunal shall be deemed to be duly constituted if it consists of the chairman or deputy chairman and two or more other members.

7 The chairman or, in his absence, the deputy chairman, shall preside at sittings of the Tribunal.

## *Staff*

8 The Lord Chancellor may appoint such officers and servants for the Tribunal as he thinks fit.

## *Expenses*

9 The Lord Chancellor shall defray the remuneration of persons appointed under paragraph 8 and such expenses of the Tribunal as he thinks fit.

## *Disqualification of Tribunal Members*

10 In Part II of Schedule 1 to the House of Commons Disqualification Act 1975 (bodies of which all members are disqualified) at the appropriate place insert—
"The Tribunal established under section 91 of the Northern Ireland Act 1998".

11 In Part II of Schedule 1 to the Northern Ireland Assembly Disqualification Act 1975 (bodies of which all members are disqualified) at the appropriate place insert—
"The Tribunal established under section 91 of the Northern Ireland Act 1998".

**SCHEDULE 12** Section 95(5)

CONSTRUCTION OF REFERENCES IN EXISTING LAWS

*Preliminary*

1  (1)  Enactments and instruments shall, except where the context otherwise requires, be construed in accordance with this Schedule.

(2)  In this Schedule "instruments" includes charters, contracts and other documents.

*The Parliament and the old Assembly*

2  (1)  References to the Parliament of Northern Ireland shall be construed as including references to—

(a)  the Assembly established under section 1 of the Northern Ireland Assembly Act 1973; and

(b)  the Assembly.

(2)  References to the Assembly established under section 1 of the Northern Ireland Assembly Act 1973 shall be construed as including references to the Assembly.

*Legislation etc of the Parliament or the old Assembly*

3  (1)  A reference to an Act or enactment of the Parliament of Northern Ireland shall be construed as including a reference to an Order in Council under section 1(3) of the Northern Ireland (Temporary Provisions) Act 1972.

(2)  A reference to an Act or enactment of, or a Bill in, the Parliament of Northern Ireland shall be construed as including a reference to—

(a)  a Measure or proposed Measure of the Assembly established under section 1 of the Northern Ireland Assembly Act 1973; and

(b)  an Act or Bill of the Assembly.

(3) A reference to a Measure or proposed Measure of the Assembly so established shall be construed as including a reference to an Act or Bill of the Assembly.

(4) A reference to a Measure of the Assembly so established shall be construed as including a reference to an Order in Council under paragraph 1 of Schedule 1 to the Northern Ireland Act 1974.

4  (1) A reference to a resolution or other decision of the Senate or the House of Commons of the Parliament of Northern Ireland, or of either House of that Parliament, shall be construed as including a reference to a resolution or decision of—

  (a) the Assembly established under section 1 of the Northern Ireland Assembly Act 1973; or

  (b) the Assembly.

(2) A reference to a resolution or other decision of the Assembly established under section 1 of the Northern Ireland Assembly Act 1973 shall be construed as a reference to a resolution or decision of the Assembly.

5  A reference to laying a document before, or presenting it to—

  (a) the Parliament of Northern Ireland or either House of that Parliament; or

  (b) the Assembly established under section 1 of the Northern Ireland Assembly Act 1973,

shall be construed as a reference to laying it before, or presenting it to, the Assembly.

6  Paragraphs 2 to 5 apply to enactments and instruments passed or made before the appointed day.

### *Money*

7  (1) A reference to—

  (a) money provided by the Parliament of Northern Ireland; or

  (b) money appropriated by Measure of the Assembly established under section 1 of the Northern Ireland Assembly Act 1973, shall be construed as a reference to money appropriated by Act of the Assembly.

(2) A reference to payment into or out of the Exchequer of Northern Ireland shall be construed as a reference to payment into or out of the Consolidated Fund of Northern Ireland.

(3) This paragraph applies to enactments and instruments passed or made before the appointed day.

*Office-holders and Ministers*

8  (1) A reference to—
   (a)  the Governor of Northern Ireland;
   (b)  the Governor of Northern Ireland in Council; or
   (c)  the making of an Order in Council by the Governor of Northern Ireland,
   shall be construed as a reference to the Secretary of State or, as the case may be, the making of an order by the Secretary of State.

   (2) This paragraph applies to enactments and instruments passed or made before 1st January 1974.

9  (1) A reference to—
   (a)  the Prime Minister of Northern Ireland; or
   (b)  the chief executive member,
   shall be construed as a reference to the First Minister and deputy First Minister acting jointly.

   (2) References to Northern Ireland executive authorities shall be construed as references to Ministers and the Northern Ireland departments.

   (3) A reference to—
   (a)  the Executive Committee for Northern Ireland; or
   (b)  the Northern Ireland Executive,
   shall be construed as a reference to the Executive Committee established by section 20.

   (4) This paragraph applies to enactments and instruments passed or made before the appointed day.

10  (1)  A reference to—
    (a)  a particular Ministry of Northern Ireland; or
    (b)  the Minister in charge of a particular Ministry,
    shall, in relation to a function, be construed as a reference to the Northern Ireland department which exercises that function or to the Northern Ireland Minister in charge of that department.

    (2)  A reference to an unspecified Ministry shall be construed as a reference to a Northern Ireland department.

    (3)  This paragraph applies to enactments and instruments passed or made before 1st January 1974.

11  (1)  A reference to—
    (a)  an unspecified Minister of Northern Ireland; or
    (b)  the head of a Northern Ireland department,
    shall be construed as a reference to a Northern Ireland Minister.

    (2)  A reference to the head of a specified Northern Ireland department shall, in relation to a function, be construed as a reference to the Northern Ireland Minister in charge of the department which exercises that function.

    (3)  In sub-paragraph (1) "Northern Ireland Minister" includes the First Minister and the deputy First Minister.

    (4)  This paragraph applies to enactments and instruments passed or made before the appointed day.

*Courts*

12  (1)  A reference to the Supreme Court of Judicature in Ireland shall be construed as a reference to the Supreme Court of Judicature of Northern Ireland.

    (2)  A reference to the High Court of Justice in Ireland shall be construed as a reference to the High Court of Justice in Northern Ireland.

    (3)  A reference to the Court of Appeal in Ireland shall be construed as a reference to the Court of Appeal in Northern Ireland.

(4) This paragraph applies to enactments and instruments passed or made before the passing of the Government of Ireland Act 1920.

*Equal opportunity bodies*

13 A reference to—
   (a) the Fair Employment Commission for Northern Ireland;
   (b) the Equal Opportunities Commission for Northern Ireland;
   (c) the Commission for Racial Equality for Northern Ireland; or
   (d) the Northern Ireland Disability Council,
   shall be construed as a reference to the Equality Commission for Northern Ireland.

(2) This paragraph applies to enactments and instruments passed or made before section 74 comes into force.

**SCHEDULE 13** Section 99

MINOR AND CONSEQUENTIAL AMENDMENTS

*Fair Employment (Northern Ireland) Act 1976 (c. 25)*

1 (1) The Fair Employment (Northern Ireland) Act 1976 shall be amended as follows.

(2) In section 1 (the Fair Employment Commission for Northern Ireland)—
   (a) for the words in subsection (1) before paragraph (a) substitute "The Commission shall have the duties of"; and
   (b) subsection (2) shall cease to have effect.

(3) In section 2 (educational functions) after "discharging its duties" insert "under section 1".

(4) In section 57(1) (interpretation), in the definition of "the Commission" for "the Fair Employment Commission for

Northern Ireland" substitute "the Equality Commission for Northern Ireland".

(5) Schedule 1 (the Fair Employment Commission for Northern Ireland) shall cease to have effect.

*Sex Discrimination (Northern Ireland) Order 1976 (S.I. 1976/1042 (N.I. 15))*

2 (1) The Sex Discrimination (Northern Ireland) Order 1976 shall be amended as follows.

(2) In Article 2(2) (interpretation), in the definition of "the Commission" for "the Equal Opportunities Commission for Northern Ireland" substitute "the Equality Commission for Northern Ireland".

(3) In Article 54(1) (establishment of Equal Opportunities Commission for Northern Ireland)—

(a) in paragraph (1) for the words before paragraph (a) substitute "The Commission shall have the following duties"; and

(b) paragraphs (2) to (4) shall cease to have effect.

(4) Schedule 3 (the Equal Opportunities Commission for Northern Ireland) shall cease to have effect.

*Interpretation Act 1978 (c. 30)*

3 In section 24(5) of the Interpretation Act 1978 (meaning of "Northern Ireland legislation"), for paragraphs (d) and (e) substitute—

"(d) Measures of the Northern Ireland Assembly established under section 1 of the Northern Ireland Assembly Act 1973;

(e) Orders in Council under Schedule 1 to the Northern Ireland Act 1974

(f) Acts of the Northern Ireland Assembly; and

(g) Orders in Council under section 85 of the Northern Ireland Act 1998."

*Statutory Rules (Northern Ireland) Order 1979 (S.I. 1979/1573 (N.I.12))*

4  In Part II of Schedule 1 to the Statutory Rules (Northern Ireland) Order 1979 (rule-making authorities), for "section 40 of and paragraph 4 of Schedule 5 to the Northern Ireland Constitution Act 1973" substitute "section 95(5) of and paragraph 8 of Schedule 12 to the Northern Ireland Act 1998".

*Mental Health Act 1983 (c. 20)*

5  (1) The Mental Health Act 1983 shall be amended as follows.
(2) In section 134(3)(a) (correspondence of patients), after "Parliament" insert "or of the Northern Ireland Assembly".
(3) In section 141 (members of the House of Commons suffering from mental illness), after subsection (9) insert—
"(10) This section also has effect in relation to members of the Northern Ireland Assembly but as if—
(a) references to the House of Commons were to the Assembly and references to the Speaker were to the Presiding Officer; and
(b) in subsection (7), for "provided by Parliament" there were substituted "appropriated by Act of the Assembly"."

*Insolvency Act 1986 (c. 45)*

6  In section 427 of the Insolvency Act 1986 (members of the House of Commons who are adjudged bankrupt etc.), after subsection (6B) insert—

"(6C) Subsection (1), as applied to a member of the Northern Ireland Assembly by virtue of section 36(4) of the Northern Ireland Act 1998, has effect as if "or Northern Ireland" were omitted; and subsections (4) to (6) have effect in relation to such a member as if—

  (a) references to the House of Commons were to the Assembly and references to the Speaker were to the Presiding Officer; and

  (b) in subsection (4), for "under this section" there were substituted "under section 36(4) of the Northern Ireland Act 1998 by virtue of this section".""

*Audit (Northern Ireland) Order 1987 (S.I. 1987/460 (N.I.5))*

7   In Article 6(2) of the Audit (Northern Ireland) Order 1987 (expenses and accounts of Northern Ireland Audit Office)—

  (a) for "the Department", in the first place where it occurs, substitute "the committee established under section 66 of the Northern Ireland Act 1998"; and

  (b) for "the Department", in the second place where it occurs, substitute "that committee".

*Copyright, Designs and Patents Act 1988 (c. 48)*

8   (1) The Copyright, Designs and Patents Act 1988 shall be amended as follows.

  (2) In section 12(9) (duration of copyright in literary, dramatic, musical or artistic works), for "166A" substitute "166B".

  (3) In section 153(2) (qualification for copyright protection), for "166A" substitute "166B".

  (4) In section 163(6) (Crown copyright), for "166A" substitute "166B".

(5) In section 164(1) (Crown copyright in Acts of Parliament, etc.), after "Scottish Parliament" insert ", Act of the Northern Ireland Assembly".

(6) After section 166A insert—

**"166B Copyright in Bills of the Northern Ireland Assembly**

(1) Copyright in every Bill introduced into the Northern Ireland Assembly belongs to the Northern Ireland Assembly Commission.

(2) Copyright under this section subsists from the time when the text of the Bill is handed in to the Assembly for introduction—

(a) until the Bill receives Royal Assent, or

(b) if the Bill does not receive Royal Assent, until it is withdrawn or rejected or no further proceedings of the Assembly may be taken in respect of it.

(3) References in this Part to Parliamentary copyright (except in section 165) include copyright under this section; and, except as mentioned above, the provisions of this Part apply in relation to copyright under this section as to other Parliamentary copyright.

(4) No other copyright, or right in the nature of copyright, subsists in a Bill after copyright has once subsisted under this section; but without prejudice to the subsequent operation of this section in relation to a Bill which, not having received Royal Assent, is later reintroduced into the Assembly."

(7) In the definition of "parliamentary proceedings" in section 178 (definitions), the words ", of the New Northern Ireland Assembly" shall cease to have effect.

(8) In section 179 (index of defined expressions), in column 2 of the entry for "Parliamentary copyright", for "and 166A(3)" substitute "166A(3) and 166B(3)".

*Official Secrets Act 1989 (c. 6)*

9 (1) Section 12 of the Official Secrets Act 1989 (interpretation) shall be amended as follows.

(2) Subsection (1)(b) shall cease to have effect.

(3) After subsection (4) insert—

"(5) This Act shall apply to the following as it applies to persons falling within the definition of Crown servant—

(a) the First Minister and deputy First Minister in Northern Ireland; and

(b) Northern Ireland Ministers and junior Ministers."

*Fair Employment (Northern Ireland) Act 1989 (c. 32)*

10 (1) The Fair Employment (Northern Ireland) Act 1989 shall be amended as follows.

(2) The following shall be substituted for section 1—

**"1 The Equality Commission for Northern Ireland**
In this Act "the Commission" means the Equality Commission for Northern Ireland."

(3) In section 9(6) (approval of Code of Practice), for "section 27(2) of the Northern Ireland Constitution Act 1973" substitute "section 31(1) or (2) of the Northern Ireland Act 1998".

(4) In Schedule 2 (minor and consequential amendments), paragraphs 5 and 6 and 22 to 28 shall cease to have effect.

*Social Security Administration Act 1992 (c. 5)*

11 In section 189 of the Social Security Administration Act 1992 (regulations and orders: general)—

(a)   in subsection (9), for "175 and 178" substitute "and 175"; and
(b)   in subsection (11), for "any of sections 177 to 179" substitute
      "section 179".

*Social Security Administration (Northern Ireland) Act 1992 (c. 8)*

11 In section 165 of the Social Security Administration (Northern
   Ireland) Act 1992 (regulations and orders: general)—
   (a)   in subsection (10), for "152 and 154" substitute "and 152"; and
   (b)   in subsection (11), for "any of sections 153 to 155" substitute
         "section 155".

*Environment and Safety Information (Northern Ireland) Order 1993*
*(S.I. 1993/3159 (N.I.14))*

12 In the second column of Schedule 1 to the Environment and Safety
   Information (Northern Ireland) Order 1993 (enforcing authorities),
   for "section 43(2) of the Northern Ireland Constitution Act 1973"
   substitute "section 4(1) of the Northern Ireland Act 1998".

*Civil Service (Management Functions) (Northern Ireland) Order 1994*
*(S.I. 1994/1894 (N.I.9))*

13 In Article 3(1) of the Civil Service (Management Functions)
   (Northern Ireland) Order 1994, for paragraphs (a) and (b) substitute
   "which, by virtue of a prerogative order made under section 23(3) of
   the Northern Ireland Act 1998, is exercisable by the Department of
   Finance and Personnel".

*Olympic Symbol etc. Protection Act 1995 (c. 32)*

14 In section 4(16) of the Olympic Symbol etc. Protection Act 1995 (definitions), in the definition of "Royal Commission", for "by the Secretary of State in pursuance of the prerogative powers of Her Majesty delegated to him under section 7(2) of the Northern Ireland Constitution Act 1973" substitute "by a Minister, within the meaning of the Northern Ireland Act 1998, or Northern Ireland department in pursuance of the prerogative powers of Her Majesty exercisable by the Minister or department under section 23 of that Act".

*Disability Discrimination Act 1995 (c. 50)*

15 (1) The Disability Discrimination Act 1995 shall be amended as follows.

(2) In Schedule 8—

(a) for "the Council" and "the Northern Ireland Disability Council" substitute "the Equality Commission for Northern Ireland";

(b) for paragraph 33(1) substitute—

"33 (1) In sections 50 to 52, for "the Council" substitute, in each place, the "Equality Commission for Northern Ireland".

(1A) Section 50(1) shall have no effect."; and

(c) for paragraph 52 substitute—

"52 (1) Schedule 5, except paragraph 7(a) to (c), shall have no effect.

(2) In paragraph 7(a) to (c), for "Secretary of State" wherever it occurs substitute "Department of Health and Social Services"."

*Commissioner for Complaints (Northern Ireland) Order 1996 (S.I. 1996/
1297 (N.I.7))*

16  In Article 9(3) of the Commissioner for Complaints (Northern
Ireland) Order 1996 (matters not subject to investigation), for
"section 22 of the Northern Ireland Constitution Act 1973" substitute "section 78 of the Northern Ireland Act 1998".

*Ombudsman (Northern Ireland) Order 1996 (S.I. 1996/1298 (N.I.8))*

17  In Article 10(3) of the Ombudsman (Northern Ireland) Order
1996 (matters not subject to investigation), for "section 22 of the
Northern Ireland Constitution Act 1973" substitute "section 78 of
the Northern Ireland Act 1998".

*Race Relations (Northern Ireland) Order 1997 (S.I. 1997/869 (N.I.6))*

18  (1) The Race Relations (Northern Ireland) Order 1997 shall be
amended as follows.
(2) In Article 2(2) (interpretation), in the definition of "the
Commission" for "the Commission for Racial Equality for
Northern Ireland" substitute "the Equality Commission for
Northern Ireland".
(3) Article 42(1) and (3) to (5) and Schedule 1 (establishment of
Commission for Racial Equality for Northern Ireland) shall
cease to have effect.

*Northern Ireland (Elections) Act 1998 (c. 12)*

19  (1)  In Schedule 1 to the Northern Ireland (Elections) Act 1998 (the
Assembly), for paragraph 8 substitute—

"8 (1) For the purposes of the law of defamation, absolute privilege shall attach to—
  (a) the making of a statement in proceedings of the Assembly; and
  (b) the publication of a statement under the Assembly's authority.
(2) In this paragraph "statement" has the same meaning as in the Defamation Act 1996."

*Data Protection Act 1998 (c. 29)*

20 (1) In paragraph 4 of Schedule 7 to the Data Protection Act 1998 (miscellaneous exceptions), for "Northern Ireland department" substitute "Northern Ireland authority".
(2) Renumber that paragraph (as so amended) as sub-paragraph (1) and after that provision as so renumbered insert—
"(2) In this paragraph "Northern Ireland authority" means the First Minister, the deputy First Minister, a Northern Ireland Minister or a Northern Ireland department."

**SCHEDULE 14** Section 100(1)

TRANSITIONAL PROVISIONS AND SAVINGS

*Human rights*

1  In relation to any time before the Human Rights Act 1998 is fully in force, sections 6(2)(c), 24(1) and 71 and Schedule 10 shall have effect as if that Act were so in force.

*First Minister and deputy First Minister*


2  Any election of the First Minister and the deputy First Minister
   held before the appointed day shall on and after that day have effect as if it had been held under section 16.


*Ministerial offices*


3  Any determination of—
   (a) the number of Ministerial offices to be held by Northern
       Ireland Ministers; and
   (b) the functions to be exercisable by the holder of each such
       office,
   made and approved before the appointed day shall on and after
   that day have effect as if it had been made and approved under
   section 17.


*Northern Ireland Ministers*


4  Any nomination of a person to hold a Ministerial office made before the appointed day shall on and after that day have effect as if it
   had been made under section 18.


*Junior Ministers*


5  Any of the following made and approved before the appointed
   day—
   (a) a determination of the number of junior Ministers to be
       appointed;
   (b) a determination of the functions to be exercised by the holder
       of each junior Ministerial office; and
   (c) an appointment of a junior Minister,

shall have effect on and after that day as if it had been made and approved under section 19.

## Department of First Minister and deputy First Minister

6 Any Northern Ireland department established before the appointed day under the charge of the First Minister and deputy First Minister acting jointly shall be treated on and after that day as if it had been established by an Act of the Assembly under section 21.

## Prerogative orders

7 Any prerogative order made by the Secretary of State under the Letters Patent of Her Majesty dated 20th December 1973 before the appointed day shall on and after that day have effect as if it had been validly made under section 23(3) by the First Minister and the deputy First Minister acting jointly.

## Agency arrangements

8 Any arrangements made under section 11 of the Northern Ireland Constitution Act 1973 before the appointed day shall on and after that day have effect as if they had been made under section 28.

## Statutory committees

9 (1) Any committee of the Assembly established before the appointed day to advise and assist a Northern Ireland Minister in the formulation of policy with respect to his responsibilities as a Minister shall be treated on and after that day as if it had been established by standing orders under section 29.

(2) Any appointment of a member, or the chairman or deputy chairman, of such a committee made before the appointed day shall have effect on and after that day as if it had been made under section 29.

## Elections of members

10 Any order made under section 2(5) of the Northern Ireland (Elections) Act 1998 before the appointed day shall on and after that day have effect, with any necessary modifications, as if it had been made under section 34(4).

## Vacancies

11 Any order made under section 3 of the Northern Ireland (Elections) Act 1998 before the appointed day shall on and after that day have effect, with any necessary modifications, as if it had been made under section 35.

## Disqualification

12 A person elected on 25th June 1998 shall not be disqualified from membership of the Assembly by virtue of section 36 if he was not disqualified from such membership under section 4 of the Northern Ireland (Elections) Act 1998.

## Presiding Officer and deputy

13 Any person appointed or elected under paragraph 3 of the Schedule to the Northern Ireland (Elections) Act 1998 who holds office immediately before the appointed day shall on and after that day hold

office as Presiding Officer or, as the case may be, deputy Presiding Officer as if he had been elected by the Assembly under section 39.

## *Standing orders*

14  Any standing orders made by the Secretary of State under paragraph 10 to the Schedule to the Northern Ireland (Elections) Act 1998 before the appointed day shall on and after that day have effect as if they had been made by the Assembly under section 41.

## *Civic Forum*

15  Any such arrangements as are mentioned in subsection (1) of section 56 which are made and approved before the commencement of that section shall have effect, after that commencement, as if they had been made and approved under that section.

## *Comptroller and Auditor General for Northern Ireland*

16  Any appointment made by Her Majesty under section 36(1)(d) of the Northern Ireland Constitution Act 1973 before the appointed day shall on and after that day have effect as if it had been an appointment made by Her Majesty on the nomination of the Assembly under section 65.

## *Social security and child support*

17  Any regulations made under any enactment repealed by virtue of section 87 shall have effect, with any necessary modifications as if

they had been made under subsection (4) or, as the case may require, subsection (5) of that section.

*Certificates by Secretary of State*

18  Section 90 shall have effect—
   (a) in relation to any act done before the appointed day, as if the refer-ence to section 24 were a reference to section 19 of the Northern Ireland Constitution Act 1973 so far as relating to a member of the Northern Ireland Executive or other person appointed under section 8 of that Act or a Northern Ireland department;
   (b) in relation to any act done before the commencement of section 76, as if the reference to that section were a reference to section 19 of that Act so far as relating otherwise than as mentioned in sub-paragraph (a); and
   (c) in relation to any such act as is mentioned in sub-paragraph (a) or (b), as if—
       (i)  the reference in subsection (1)(b) to a certificate were a refer-ence to a certificate purporting to be signed by or on behalf of the Secretary of State and certifying that an act specified in the certificate was done for the purpose of safeguarding national security; and
       (ii) subsection (3)(b) were omitted.

*Devolution issues*

19  In relation to any time before the first appointment of the Advocate General for Scotland, paragraphs 22, 23, 33 and 34 of Schedule 10 shall have effect as if references to him were references to the Lord Advocate.

*Relations with Republic of Ireland*

20 The repeal effected by this Act of section 12 of the Northern Ireland Constitution Act 1973 shall not affect the operation of any agreement or arrangement made under that section.

*Discrimination in legislation*

21 The repeals effected by this Act shall not affect the operation of sections 17 and 18 of the Northern Ireland Constitution Act 1973 (read with section 23 of that Act) in relation to—

(a) Acts of the Parliament of Northern Ireland;

(b) Measures of the Northern Ireland Assembly established under section 1 of the Northern Ireland Assembly Act 1973;

(c) Orders in Council under Schedule 1 to the Northern Ireland Act 1974; and

(d) relevant subordinate instruments (within the meaning of section 17 of the Northern Ireland Constitution Act 1973) made before the appointed day.

*Discrimination by public bodies*

22 The repeals effected by this Act shall not affect the operation of section 19 of the Northern Ireland Constitution Act 1973 (read with section 23 of that Act)—

(a) so far as section 19 relates to a member of the Northern Ireland Executive or other person appointed under section 8 of that Act or a Northern Ireland department, in relation to any act done before the appointed day;

(b) so far as section 19 relates otherwise than as mentioned in sub-paragraph (a), in relation to any act done before the commencement of section 76.

*Members' Pensions*

23 The repeals effected by this Act shall not affect the operation of the Ministerial Offices Act Northern Ireland) 1952, the Ministerial Salaries and Members' Pensions Act Northern Ireland) 1965 or the Members' Pensions (Northern Ireland) Order 1976 in relation to service completed before the appointed day.

## SCHEDULE 15 Section 100(2)

## REPEALS

| Chapter or Number | Short title | Extent of repeal |
|---|---|---|
| 3 Edw 7 c.27. | Irish Land Act 1903 | Sections 27 to 42.<br>Section 47. |
| 10 & 11 Geo 5 c.67. | Government of Ireland Act 1920 | The whole Act. |
| 12 Geo 5 c.2 (N.I.). | Exchequer and Audit Act (Northern Ireland) 1921 | Section 5.<br>Section 28(1). |
| 14 & 15 Geo 5 c.11 (N.I.). | Ministers (Temporary Exercise of Powers) Act (Northern Ireland) 1924 | The whole Act. |
| 10 & 11 Geo 6 c.37. | Northern Ireland Act 1947 | Section 8.<br>Section 9(1) and (5). |
| 1 & 2 Eliz 2 c.3. | Public Works Loans Act 1952 | Section 6. |
| 1 & 2 Eliz 2 c.15 (N.I.). | Ministerial Offices Act (Northern Ireland) 1954 | The whole Act. |
| 1 & 2 Eliz 2 c.33 (N.I.). | Interpretation Act (Northern Ireland) 1954 | Section 13(2). |
| 1965 c.18. | Ministerial Salaries and Members Pensions Act 1965 | The whole Act. |

| Chapter or Number | Short title | Extent of repeal |
|---|---|---|
| 1969 c.7 (N.I.). | Superannuation (Miscellaneous Provisions) Act (Northern Ireland) 1969 | Section 4. |
| 1972 c.22. | Northern Ireland (Temporary Provisions) Act 1972 | The whole Act. |
| 1973 c.17. | Northern Ireland Assembly Act 1973 | The whole Act. |
| 1973 c.36. | Northern Ireland Constitution Act 1973 | Sections 1 to 9. Sections 11 to 32. Section 33(1). Section 36(1)(d). Section 37(1). Sections 38 to 40. Schedules 1 to 5 . |
| 1973 c.69. | Northern Ireland Constitution (Amendment) Act 1973 | The whole Act. |
| 1974 c.28. | Northern Ireland Act 1974 | The whole Act. |
| 1975 c.24. | House of Commons Disqualification Act 1975 | In Schedule 1, in Part II, the entries relating to the Commission for Racial Equality for Northern Ireland, the Equal Opportunities Commission for Northern Ireland, the Fair Employment Commission for Northern Ireland and the Northern Ireland Disability Council; in Part III, the entries relating to the Additional Commissioner of the Commission for Racial Equality in Northern Ireland and the Additional Commissioner of the Equal Opportunities. Commission for Northern Ireland. |

| Chapter or Number | Short title | Extent of repeal |
|---|---|---|
| 1975 c.25. | Northern Ireland Assembly Disqualification Act 1975 | Section 5(1). In Schedule 1, in Part II, the entries relating to the Commission for Racial Equality for Northern Ireland, the Equal Opportunities Commission for Northern Ireland, the Fair Employment Commission for Northern Ireland and the Northern Ireland Disability Council; in Part III, the entries relating to the Additional Commissioner of the Commission for Racial Equality in Northern Ireland and the Additional Commissioner of the Equal Opportunities Commission for Northern Ireland. Schedule 2. |
| 1976 c.25. | Fair Employment (Northern Ireland) Act 1976 | Section 1(2). Section 58(1). Schedule 1. Schedule 6. |
| S.I. 1976/426 (N.I.8). | Member's Pensions (Northern Ireland) Order 1976 | The whole Order. |
| S.I. 1976/1042 (N.I.15). | Sex Discrimination (Northern Ireland) Order 1976 | In Article 2(2), the definition of "the interim period". Article 54(2) to (4). Schedule 3. In Schedule 6, paragraph 2. |
| S.I. 1979/1573 (N.I.12). | Statutory Rules (Northern Ireland) Order 1979 | In Article 7(1), the words from "subject to" to "1974". Article 11(4). In Schedule 4, paragraph 14. |
| 1981 c,35. | Finance Act 1981 | Section 137(1) and (2) |

| Chapter or Number | Short title | Extent of repeal |
|---|---|---|
| S.I. 1982/713 (N.I.10). | Probation Board (Northern Ireland) Order 1982 | In Schedule 1, paragraph 1(2). |
| 1982 c.38. | Northern Ireland Act 1982 | The whole Act. |
| S.I. 1984/1821 (N.I.11). | Fire Services (Northern Ireland) Order 1984 | In Article 5(1)(f), the words "under section 12 of the Northern Ireland Constitution Act 1973". |
| 1987 c.22. | Social Security Act 1986 | In Schedule 9, paragraph 6. |
| 1986 c.53. | Building Societies Act 1986 | Section 122(2) |
| 1985 c.56. | Parliamentary Constituencies Act 1986 | In Schedule 3, paragraphs 1 and 2. |
| 1986 c.60. | Financial Services Act 1986 | Section 209(2). |
| S.I. 1986/595 (N.I.4). | Mental Health (Northern Ireland) Order 1986 | In Schedule 5, in Part II the amendment of the Ministerial Salaries and members' Pensions Act (Northern Ireland) 1965 |
| 1987 c.22. | Banking Act 1987 | Section 109(2). |
| 1987 c.43. | Consumer Protection Act 1987 | Section 49(2). |
| S.I. 1987/460 (N.I.5). | Audit (Northern Ireland) Order 1987 | In Article 2(2), the definition of "the interim period". Article 4(2), (6) and (7). Article 6(6). Article 11(2) and (3). In Schedule 1, paragraph 4(3). In Schedule 2, paragraph 4(3). |
| S.I. 1987/2203 (N.I.22). | Adoption (Northern Ireland) Order 1987 | In Schedule 4, paragraph 1. |
| 1989 c.6. | Official Secrets Act 1989 | Section 12(1)(b). |
| 1989 c.32. | Fair Employment (Northern Ireland) Act 1989 | In section 21(1), the definition of "the Commission". In Schedule 2, paragraphs 2, 5, 6 and 22 to 28. |
| 1989 c.40. | Companies Act 1989 | In section 213(7), the words from "Subject to any Order" to the end. |

| Chapter or Number | Short title | Extent of repeal |
|---|---|---|
| 1990 c.37. | Human Fertilisation and Embryology Act 1990 | Section 48(2). |
| 1990 c.42. | Broadcasting Act 1990 | In Schedule 20, paragraph 19. |
| 1990 c.43. | Environmental Protection Act 1990 | Section 3(8). Section 153(5). |
| 1991 c,48. | Child Support Act 1991 | Section 23(4) and (5). Section 56(2) and (4). In Schedule 5, paragraph 2. |
| S.I. 1991/2628 (N.I.23). | Child Support (Northern Ireland) Order 1991 | Article 49(2) and (3). |
| 1992 c.5. | Social Security Administration Act 1992 | Sections 177 and 178. Schedule 8. |
| 1992 c.8. | Social Security Administration (Northern Ireland) Act 1992 | Sections 153 and 154. In section 167(1), the definition of "Joint Authority". |
| 1992 c.40. | Friendly Societies Act 1992 | Section 124(2). |
| 1993 c.36. | Criminal Justice Act 1993 | Section 79(11). |
| 1993 c.39. | National Lottery etc Act 1993 | Section 63(2). |
| 1993 c.48. | Pension Schemes Act 1993 | In section 163(2), the words "section 177 (co-ordination with Northern Ireland". Section 187. |
| 1993 c.49. | Pension Schemes (Northern Ireland) Act 1993 | In section 163(2), the words "section 153 (co-ordination with Great Britain". |
| S.I. 1993/1252 (N.I.5). | Financial Provisions (Northern Ireland) Order 1993 | Article 8(6A). |
| 1994 c,26. | Trade Marks Act 1994 | In Schedule 4, the entry in paragraph 1(2) relating to the Northern Ireland Constitution Act 1973. |
| 1995 c.35. | Child Support Act 1995 | Section 29(2) to (4). |
| S.I. 1995/2702 (N.I.13). | Child Support (Northern Ireland) Order 1995 | Article 20. |
| 1996 c.11. | Northern Ireland (Entry to Negotiations etc.) Act 1996 | The whole Act. |

| Chapter or Number | Short title | Extent of repeal |
| --- | --- | --- |
| 1996 c.22. | Northern Ireland (Emergency Provisions) Act 1996 | In Schedule 6, paragraph 1. |
| S.I. 1996/1297 (N.I.7). | Commissioner for Complaints (Northern Ireland) Order 1996 | Article 23(1). In Schedule 2, the entries relating to the Equal Opportunities Commission for Northern Ireland, the Fair Employment Commission for Northern Ireland and the Commission for Racial Equality for Northern Ireland. |
| S.I. 1996/12987 (N.I.8). | Ombudsman (Northern Ireland) Order 1996 | Article 3(3). In Schedule 5, the amendments of sections 19 to 22 of the Northern Ireland Constitution Act 1973 and the Northern Ireland Act 1974. |
| S.I. 1997/869 (N.I.6). | Race Relations (Northern Ireland) Order 1996 | Article 42(1) and (3) to (5). Schedule 1. In Schedule 2, paragraphs 1 and 7. |
| 1998 c,12. | Northern Ireland (Elections) Act 1998 | The whole Act. |
| 1998 c,32. | Police (Northern Ireland) Act 1998 | Section 1(2). Section 18(4) |
| 1998 c.47. | Northern Ireland Act 1998 | In Schedule 13, paragraph 18. |
| 1998 c.48. | Registration of Political Parties Act 1998 | In section 2(2)(e) the word "New". |
| S.I. 1998/749 (N.I.4). | Financial Provisions (Northern Ireland) Order 1998 | Article 7. |

# BIBLIOGRAPHY AND INDEX

# SELECT BIBLIOGRAPHY

## Official documents

The National Archives Kiew
Records of the Prime Minister's office:
PREM 49/108; PREM 49/109: Correspondence relating to Northern Ireland
The Belfast Agreement/Good Friday Agreement 1998 – Gov. uk
Cm. 3883
Northern Ireland Act 1998 – legislation.gov.uk

## Secondary sources

Bew, Paul, *Ireland: The Politics of Enmity 1789–2006* (Oxford: Oxford University Press, 2007).

Blair, Tony, *New Britain: My Vision of a Young Country* (London: Fourth Estate Ltd., 1996).

Bogdanor, Vernon, *Devolution in the United Kingdom* (Oxford: Oxford University Press, 2001).

Deacon, Russell and Alan Sandy, *Devolution in the United Kingdom* (Edinburgh: Edinburgh University Press, 2007).

Mckittrick, Dvid, *Making Sense of the Troubles: The Story of the Conflict in Northern Ireland* (2018).

Mulholland, Marc, *The Longest War: Northern Ireland's Troubled History* (Oxford: Oxford University Press, 2002).

River, Charles, Editors: *The Partition of Ireland and the Troubles: The History of Northern Ireland from the Irish Civil War to the Good Friday Agreement* (2018)

Torrance, David, *Devolution in Northern Ireland*. House of Commons Library. Research Briefing, 7 June 2022.

Whysall, Alan, 'Post-election negotiations in Northern Ireland must set the Belfast Agreement on a firmer footing and re-establish constructive politics', *The Constitution Unit*, 20 May 2022. <https://constitution-unit.com/2022/05/20/post-election-negotiations-in-northern-ireland-must-set-the-belfast-agreement-on-a-firmer-footing-and-re-establish-constructive-politics/>

# INDEX OF NAMES

References are *to the documents* (not to page numbers). Posts indicated in brackets are those held in 1997.

# BY THE SAME AUTHOR

*Doris Lessing – A Life Behind the Scenes*
ISBN 978-1-800-791-83-1 / 160 pp. / 2021

*Heinrich von Kleist: Poems*
ISBN 978-1-800-790-43-8 / 96 pp. / 2020

*George "Dadie" Rylands: Shakespearean Scholar and Cambridge Legend*
ISBN 978-1-78997-639-9 / 462 pp. / 2020

*John Sparrow: Warden of All Souls College, Oxford: "I loathe all common things"*
ISBN 978-1-78707-506-1 /806 pp./ 2017

*The Seventh Earl Beauchamp: A Victim of His Times*
ISBN 978-1-906165-62-8 /521 pp./ 2016

*House of Lords Reform: A History*
*Volume 1. The Origins to 1911: Proposals Deferred*
  *Book One: The Origins to 1911*
  *Book Two: 1911–1937*
ISBN 978-3-0343-0749-9 /Book One: 632 pp., Book Two: 633pp./ 2011

*Volume 2. Hopes Rekindled: 1943–1958*
ISBN 978-3-0343-0954-7 / 886 pp. / 2013

*Volume 3. Reforms Attempted: 1960–1969*
ISBN 978-3-0343-1764-1 /956 pp./ 2014

*Volume 4. The Exclusion of Hereditary Peers: 1971–2014*
  *Book One: 1971–2001*
  *Book Two: 2001–2014*
ISBN 9783-3-0343-1856-3 / Book One: 632 pp., Book Two: 654 pp./ 2015

*A Daring Venture: Rudolf Hess and the Ill-Fated Peace Mission of 1941*
ISBN 978-3-0343-1776-4 /278 pp./ 2014

*A. V. Dicey: General Characteristics of English Constitutionalism: Six Unpublished Lectures* with a Foreword by Lord Plant of Highfield
ISBN 978-3-03911-955-4 /180 pp./ 2009

*Bishop George Bell: House of Lords Speeches and Correspondence with Rudolf Hess*
ISBN 978-3-03911-895-3 /241 pp./ 2009

To order, please visit <www.peterlang.com>

Printed by
CPI books GmbH, Leck